CBS
Reflections in a
Bloodshot Eye

CBS

Reflections in a
Bloodshot Eye
Robert Metz

Ꝙ⸱P

A PLAYBOY PRESS BOOK

PUBLISHED SIMULTANEOUSLY IN THE UNITED STATES AND CANADA BY
PLAYBOY PRESS, CHICAGO, ILLINOIS. PRINTED IN THE UNITED STATES OF
AMERICA. LIBRARY OF CONGRESS CATALOG CARD NUMBER: 74–33560.
ISBN 87223–407–X. FIRST EDITION.

To Liz

CONTENTS

PHOTO INSERTS

ACKNOWLEDGMENTS

The author wishes to thank the following individuals and organizations for their kind permission to reprint material in this book:

CBS for passages from *From Pearl Harbor into Tokyo*. Published by the Columbia Broadcasting System, 1945.

Alfred A. Knopf, Inc. for passages from *In Search of Light: The Broadcasts of Edward R. Murrow 1938–1961* edited by Edward Bliss, Jr. Copyright © 1967 by the Estate of Edward R. Murrow. Reprinted by permission of the publisher.

Saturday Review Press/E.P. Dutton & Co., Inc. for passages from *Maverick Inventor: My Turbulent Years At CBS* by Peter C. Goldmark with Lee Edson. Copyright © 1973 by Peter C. Goldmark and Lee Edson. Reprinted by permission.

Helen Thurber for passages from "Soapland" in *The Beast in Me* by James Thurber. Copyright © 1948 by James Thurber, published by Harcourt, Brace & Co. Originally printed in *The New Yorker*. Reprinted by permission.

PREFACE

IT IS SAID THAT AS SIR WALTER RALEIGH SAT IN A TOWER WRITING OF the ages, a battle raged below. Emissaries would climb the stairs from time to time to report on the conflict and each one gave a different version of what was happening. Finally, Sir Walter threw up his hands, saying that if he couldn't find out what was going on at his feet, how could he hope to write the history of the world?

As Walter Cronkite says, "That's, the way it is . . ." In writing the chapter called "Gentle Revolution"—the story of CBS's one significant technical success—three major figures at CBS told separate and distinct highly detailed stories of how RCA's David Sarnoff got the news of the CBS breakthrough. *Roshomon* revisited. As each filled in the details, the writer began asking himself fundamental questions like "What is truth?"

This kind of situation reflects, to a degree, cloudiness of memory. And memory tends to favor those elements of a story that play up the speaker's own role. For instance, the urbane Goddard Lieberson of CBS Records was told that the outcast Clive Davis, the man he preceded and then succeeded as president of the division, had claimed responsibility for some big marketing decisions in the division—decisions that Lieberson said would never even fall in Clive's area. Exasperated, he commented: "I don't know why everybody rushes to claim credit. However, I find myself doing it too."

This book is an amalgam of some 120 major interviews, as well as scores of shorter ones, and of course of "facts" gleaned from official sources when available. Is it accurate? I can only hope that when the balance is struck "they" will say that at least the story is supported by the facts available and that the general outline is sound.

If one man's facts weigh too heavily in the balance, then let me say that those who cooperate with a writer inevitably have the greatest influence, no matter how hard the writer struggles for balance. One can hardly write what isn't revealed.

Certainly the prize for the richest source goes to the late Victor Ratner who frequently sat smoking cigars offered by the author and told enough to cover 61 pages—typed, single spaced. Jap Gude, the agent, was the most helpful in suggesting "must" topics for the book. Mike Dann gave me much valuable information, many hours and just as many laughs. Ninety-five percent of the notes taken for this book were taken on the typewriter—the author's own idiosyncrasy.

When finally the publicity-shy Bill Paley was run to earth in his posh executive offices in Black Rock, the typewriter was put away and a more discreet ballpoint pen became my instrument. So also with Frank Stanton, Fred Friendly and Arthur Godfrey. The others will have to argue with Olivetti and IBM.

Here then are the major sources: Jim Abernathy, Goodman (Goody) Ace, Joseph Barbera, Edward L. Bernays, Ken Berry, Ted Bessel, Archie Bleyer, Les Brown, Carter Burden, Mike Burke, Arthur B. Church, Ralph Colin, Norman Corwin, Louis G. Cowan, Jack Cowden, Walter Cronkite, John Daly, Mike Dann, Clive Davis, Guy Della Cioppa, Sam Denoff, Lou Dorfsman, Dick Dorso, William Dozier, Lee Edson, Bob Evans, Freddy Fields, Irving Fine, Bill Fineschreiber, Mickey Frieberg, Fred Friendly, Emanuel (Manny) Gerard, Jackie Gleason, Arthur Godfrey, Peter Goldmark, Lester Gottlieb, Jack Gould, Mark Goodson, Merv Griffin, John G. (Jap) Gude, Spencer Harrison, Louis Hauseman, Dorothy Hart Hearst Paley Hirshon, Ann Hummert, Sal Ianucci, Merle Jones, Arthur Judson, Jack Kaplan, Harris Katleman, Sidney Kaye, Michael Keating, Doris Klauber, Paul Klein, Don Knotts, Robert Landry, Julius LaRosa, James Landauer, Norman Lear, Ernest Leiser, and Sheldon Leonard.

Also Isaac (Ike) Levy, Leon Levy, Goddard Lieberson, Dick Linke, William B. Lodge, Lawrence W. Lowman, Irving Mansfield, Mike Marmer, Ernie Martin, Howard S. Meighan, Sig Mickelson, John Minary, Bill Moyers, Adrian Murphy, Janet Murrow, Bob Newhart, William S. Paley, Joseph Papp, Arthur Perlis, Bernard Procktor, Martin Ransohoff, Victor Ratner, Joseph Ream, Carl Reiner, John Reynolds, Lee Rich, Bob Ritter, Hub Robinson, Andrew Rooney, Jim Rosenfield, Hughes Rudd, M. R. (Meff) Runyon, Richard Salant, Taft Schreiver, John A. Schneider, Marvin Sears, Herb Seigel, Charles Seipman, James R. Seward, Daniel Seymour, Fred Silverman, Helen Sioussat, Tommy Smothers, Benjamin Sonnenberg, Frank Stanton, Charles Steinberg, Peggy Stone, Ed Sullivan, David Susskind, Bob Sweeney, Bob and Sylvan Taplinger, Arthur R. Taylor, Davidson Taylor, Sandy Teller, Mike Wallace, Gerhardt Wiebe, and Robert D. Wood.

The following people were also interviewed or were otherwise helpful: Linda Amster, Clive Barnes, Bill Behanna, Hazel Bishop, Jerry Brody, Amanda Burden, Connie Chung, May Dowell, Senator John Glenn, Grace Glueck, Freeman Gosden, Robert Hendrickson, Howard Houseman, William Hyland, Paul Kagan, Bob Keeshan, John Kelly, Bill Leonard, Grace Lichtenstein, Larry Lowenstein, Tad Meyers, Leon Morse, Peter Model, Paul Porter, Quinton Proctor, William Rayburn, Harry Reasoner, Alan Riedel, John B. Rettaliata, Harry Schecter, Ken Schwartz, Stuart Schulberg, Mel Spiegel, Lesley Stahl, John Steinway, Robert Stolfi, Nancy Webb, Willis Winn.

Erik Barnouw's three-volume *History of Broadcasting*, the most comprehensive work in the field, was an invaluable source.

My thanks to Richard Warren Lewis who tracked the demise of CBS's *Smothers Brothers Comedy Hour* so exhaustively in *Playboy*— "St. Thomas & The Dragon" (August 1969).

I am similarly indebted to William Lambert and Richard Oulahan whose *Life* magazine piece in the issue of September 10, 1965 on James Aubrey was then and remains today the best on the subject.

My special gratitude to my friend and fellow reporter on *The New York Times*, Les Brown, whose book *Television: The Business Behind The Box* proved an invaluable source for me and, in my opinion, remains the best book about the business of television.

Finally, a different kind of acknowledgment—or admission. There is very little in this book—apart from random shrapnel from my Olivetti—about CBS crime shows. The reader is free to take this as a silent protest against bogus tough guys, car chases, assinine plots. The dramas —if they rate that description—star hot cars chasing each other's tails more often than hot stories. The scenarios do more violence to logic than the characters do to each other, if that's possible. I sometimes wonder how the actors manage to pant through such tedious twaddle. So far as I can tell, the women like Mannix; the fatties like Cannon; the sun-and-surf set like *Hawaii Five-O;* and Kojak likes himself. Kojak was occasionally diverting—he's a fast draw with a lollypop—but now he looks bored with half the scripts. As for the rest of criminal justice on CBS, call it, well, a necessary evil. But I couldn't watch it, even to write this book.

Amen, the "kidvids" as the industry labels the Saturday morning electronic playground; the plug-in babysitter. Bob Keeshan in his twentieth year as Captain Kangaroo rules his daily kindergarten with a gentle hand. So opposed is he to violence that even the commercials can only snap, crackle and pop. But if I never see another Flintstones cartoon, I'll thank my lucky hair shirt; and Bugs Bunny can take his updoc and can it. I suppose my three children will survive it—if the commercials don't get them first. All hail CBS, the mighty king of kiddieland—just don't ask me to watch.

INTRODUCTION

IN PIONEER DAYS, EACH LOG CABIN THAT DOTTED THE WILDERNESS WAS an isolated outpost in a disconnected world. The families that inhabited those drafty shelters lived and died knowing a world that measured only a few miles in each direction. A friend's visit was a major occasion. A stranger was someone to be feared. A storm was the only experience shared with neighbors beyond the distant hills.

The fireplace with its warmth and light offered a focus for the family —a place to huddle against the world; a place to be cozy; a place to dream and imagine as flames drew pictures and talked in snaps and pops.

Today there is another focus—warm, violent yet controlled like the fireplace of old, and talkative beyond the dreams of the loneliest pioneer. The television set that graces virtually every household in America speaks not in imagined tongues of flame but in many dialects, and it brings us the world's triumphs and ills minutes after they unfold.

A soldier on a battlefield in Southeast Asia dies for us in color, sighing as he bleeds to death within earshot of a microphone held by a newsman who must get his story to the people. Click . . . One turn of the knob away on the almighty box familiar faces make fools of themselves answering silly questions posed by an aggressively cheerful master of ceremonies. Click . . . We are immersed in the trials and tribulations of a supposedly typical American family.

Flash: A young president is shot and the nation mourns as one, sharing an experience some might not have learned about for weeks a hundred years earlier.

The televised world of shared experience draws together people in great cities and in distant mountain cabins, molding speech and thought patterns and setting styles of life. The ubiquitous TV antenna is the umbilical cord that binds us to our emotional food supply. We are all connected, tuned in, turned on. And all this is presented to us through the "courtesy" of manufacturers of soap, soup and sop. If the world debates its differences and walks to the brink during sponsored time, the family huddled before the magic box may have to wait for a station break to learn of its peril. Time marches on, to the tune of advertising jingles and ringing cash registers, operated and controlled by some of the most articulate, talented and assertive people alive. None, certainly, are more assertive than the people who have made CBS the dominant network in today's television.

When CBS was founded as a radio network in 1926, there seemed little chance it would become one of the nation's most powerful corporations in a few short decades—or even that it could successfully compete with the already established National Broadcasting Company which was backed by the Radio Corporation of America. Ironically, David Sarnoff, the irascible boss of bosses of the two NBC networks, was responsible for the creation of his competition when he abruptly turned down an artists' agent who was offering a package deal for the performers he represented. The rebuffed agent, Arthur Judson, proceeded to create his own network.

The infant rival to NBC quickly plunged deeply into the red, due to extravagant payments to its small system of station owners plus the difficulty the company had in finding sponsors for its network shows. The company's survival was often in doubt, and were it not for the shrewd ministrations of William S. Paley, a Philadelphia playboy who had grown bored with his father's cigar business and bought the network in 1928, CBS might have died even before the stock market crash of 1929.

In its early days CBS was not so much a company in the traditional sense as it was a concept being pushed by a small team of people in New York with virtually no physical assets. While other corporations could measure their wealth in manufacturing plants, real estate, forests and mines, CBS had only an idea that promised riches.

CBS's problem, shared with NBC, was to convince the world—and especially advertisers—that radio was not just a mystifying gadget but a useful article of trade as well; that it could draw dollars out of cookie jars and mattresses, strongboxes and banks, by the thousands, then millions; that it could play a unique role in feeding the insatiable maw of commerce. This role wasn't always clear to the public, either. "I certainly appreciate your wonderful entertainment," wrote a CBS listener from Milwaukee in 1928. "Why don't we have to pay for this? I can't believe that it's given to us."

CBS, blessed with brilliance in key posts, quickly established a leadership role in the new industry that belied the company's financial frailty. It was not NBC but CBS that people approached when they needed facts on broadcasting, thanks to an innovative promotion department. And it was CBS, early in the game, that established the standards for broadcast journalism.

There were heroes, villains and scapegoats just as there are in any great corporation. It was a company so tightly knit in the beginning that each member of the CBS team felt a sense of identity with it. They worked beyond weariness to thrust Columbia into the forefront, to conquer the NBC Goliath with the sling of brilliance and pebble of tenacity.

No single volume could tell it all. Don't look here for an historian's footnotes, then, but for color and hue—a portrait emerging from broad strokes. Mostly, the story is told in terms of the people and how they shaped CBS. Some are unimportant in the grand scheme, perhaps, but notable bits of the mosaic, nonetheless. Others have enjoyed national stature.

Walter Cronkite, the father figure who could in a rare moment of advocacy and in a few well-chosen words make the federal government rethink its involvement in the Vietnam war. And Frank Stanton, the plodding but awe-inspiring president who helped make CBS perhaps the most influential corporation in the United States. Stanton is gone now, victim of a policy he himself dictated—compulsory retirement at 65.

But Bill Paley stays on—nine years past the deadline. The CBS chairman, who jealously guards his privacy, has sat astride a colossus for more years than any other leading executive at work today.

Bill Paley: bon vivant; seeker after the richest personal experiences the world has to offer; sometime lover; husband to one of the world's most admired women; a gourmet who flies 3000 miles for a unique eating experience; a man who redecorates any of his several luxurious homes at the drop of a drape; a practical genius who knows whether you will watch for nothing tomorrow a star you paid to see yesterday.

Bill Paley, occasionally a ruthless man, tells those bigger-than-life entertainers when they are over the hill. A complex and enigmatic man, he more than anyone else in the brief history of broadcasting has decided which world the people huddled around the set shall know. A man of exquisite personal tastes, he has nevertheless set the tone for what Newton Minow of the FCC called a "vast wasteland." But he has also brought you much that is excellent. His influence has at times been so pervasive that he has more or less dictated even what the other networks would present.

But CBS is much bigger than Bill Paley. It is a restless 24-hour-a-day mover and shaker of the national consciousness, irritating and pleasing, enlightening and vulgarizing by turns. Its story is a story of our own history over the past several decades. It is a story of triumph and disaster, of vigor and weariness, all reflected in the corporate eye of CBS.

PART ONE
SALAD DAYS

CHRONOLOGY

IN 1927 WILLIAM S. PALEY, 26 YEARS OLD, COMES TO NEW YORK TO look into the operations of United Independent Broadcasters, a frail and financially strained network of 16 stations. Radio is still a curiosity, though there are already seven million sets in use in the United States. Paley, who has become fascinated with the prospects for radio after his father's cigar company sponsored an early radio variety show, decides to buy UIB.

. . .In 1928 Paley arrives in New York to complete the deal. There are 16 network employees ensconced in the company's surprisingly opulent headquarters in the Paramount Building in Times Square. Before 1928 ends, the network, renamed Columbia Broadcasting System, has 47 affiliates. It also owns WABC—later WCBS New York—its first company station.

. . .On September 18, 1929, just weeks before the stock market crash, CBS occupies newly completed headquarters at 485 Madison Avenue. There are now 60 stations in the chain.

. . .In 1930 Edward Klauber, former night city editor of *The New York*

Times, joins Paley's team and begins to impress his personality and journalistic instincts on radio. He decrees that radio must provide objective news reports regardless of the likes and dislikes of the sponsor.

. . .Through the Depression the promotion department, headed by a public relations genius named Paul Kesten, works and schemes to convey the impression that CBS is the broadcast industry's leader—though compared to the Radio Corporation of America and its two NBC networks, CBS is a gnat annoying an elephant.

. . .In 1931 CBS begins, on an experimental basis, the first regularly scheduled television broadcasting in the nation with New York Mayor Jimmy Walker, and a chubby girl named Kate Smith singing "When the Moon Comes Over the Mountain." The programs are cast into the void—to be seen by a few curious network advertising executives and electronics experimenters.

. . .In 1932 CBS begins its forays against an unbeatable NBC attraction, *Amos' n' Andy,* presenting a young singer named Bing Crosby in that time slot.

. . .By 1932 radio is enormously popular—even profitable despite the worst depression in modern history. CBS earns $1,623,451 on radio's surging strength.

. . .In 1933 newly inaugurated President Franklin Delano Roosevelt chooses radio to make direct appeals to the public, with four "fireside chats" broadcast on all radio networks. Using gentle language and mien, beginning with a consoling, "Mah friends . . . ," he exploits the intimacy of the medium. Newspapers testing reaction hear again and again that individual listeners feel FDR is speaking to each of them directly, sensing their individual problems.

. . .In 1934 economic pressures cause CBS to accept advertising for wine and beer—but not liquor. For four years now the New York Philharmonic Orchestra's Sunday afternoon broadcasts conducted by Arturo Toscanini have been the most popular serious-music program.

. . .In 1934 CBS's *School of the Air* is heard by six million children. The educational programs on geography, history, English, music and drama help keep broadcast regulators at bay (the Federal Communications Commission is created in 1934). As the time spot grows valuable, the show will prove expendable.

. . .In 1935 the *Lux Radio Theater* goes on the air and the initial offering features the "first lady of the stage," Helen Hayes.

. . .CBS has a banner 1935 and leads both NBC networks (the Red and the Blue) with 97 affiliates. More important, its net profits of $2,810,079 also surpass those of the other two networks. In 1935, Frank Stanton, a shy 27-year-old psychology instructor at Ohio State, is hired by CBS for $55 a week.

. . .In 1936 CBS makes its first raid into NBC territory to grab the best of the radio amateur hours, Major Bowes; his fatal gong—"I'm sorry, I'm sorry!"—in the middle of disastrous amateur performances has become a nationally known symbol of failure.

. . .The *Columbia Workshop* begins in 1936 with Archibald MacLeish's verse drama, *The Fall of The City,* starring Burgess Meredith and Orson Welles. Other distinguished authors later featured on the show include W.H. Auden, Stephen Vincent Benet, Maxwell Anderson and Edna St. Vincent Millay. Paley has the CBS advertising rate cards carry the line "withheld from sale" for this show, as a lofty noncommercial stance. Actually the dramas run opposite Jack Benny on the NBC Red Network and that period is regarded as unsalable on CBS.

. . .Nineteen thirty-six is also a year of comedy, with Burns and Allen, Eddie ("If you knew Susie like I know Susie . . .") Cantor, Ed Wynn and Joe ("Wanna buy a duck?") Penner on the CBS roster.

. . .In 1936 Peter Goldmark, a Hungarian inventor, joins CBS to work on the development of color television and on records that play slower and longer than the standard 78 rpm records.

. . .In 1937 Edward R. Murrow, a nonbroadcast functionary, goes to London as war clouds gather. In 1937, CBS stock is first listed on the New York Stock Exchange.

. . .In 1938 a nervous population is stunned as *War of the Worlds,* directed by Orson Welles, uses the news-bulletin format to interrupt dance music and inform listeners of the destruction being carried out by Martians who have landed in New Jersey. The broadcast causes panic though CBS has put the script through 38 changes before the broadcast to emphasize to the listeners that the whole exercise is drama, not fact.

. . .The late 1930s are the heydays of daytime soap operas. CBS has 20, including *Our Gal Sunday* ("The story of a girl, laid in Old Kentucky"); *Ma Perkins* ("Landsakes alive!"); *The Romance of Helen Trent* and *Life Can Be Beautiful*. *Joyce Jordon, Girl Intern* spends nine radio years completing her internship.

. . .On March 13, 1938, as German armies march into Vienna, CBS responds with a landmark broadcast. The first *World News Roundup* features live reaction from five European capitals, with Edward R. Murrow and William L. Shirer managing the complex operation for the network.

. . .In 1938, CBS rounds out an odyssey by purchasing Columbia Records, the company that gave CBS its name. In 1927 Columbia Records bought into the fledgling network but unloaded its interest a few troubled months later, leaving behind the name Columbia for the network.

. . .In 1939 Ed Klauber matches the American Society of Composers, Authors and Publishers insult for insult. ASCAP's Gene Buck doesn't show up at an August conference that brings the nation's far-flung broadcasters to New York to discuss a new royalty deal for ASCAP-controlled broadcast music. Then at a later meeting Buck doubles the organization's rates. With an imperious "Get me my hat!" Klauber leaves the hall. Broadcasters set up rival Broadcast Music, Inc. and prove listeners tune in to bandleaders and singers, not composers. ASCAP is freezed out and soon capitulates.

. . .By the time World War II begins with Hitler's invasion of Poland in 1939, radio has reached a certain maturity and television holds great promise for the future. Small though it remains, CBS is now a fixture, not just a shooting star in the corporate firmament.

. . .More than two decades later, Marshall McLuhan, in *Understanding Media*, interprets the basic appeal of radio. He calls the listener's experience an essentially "private" one and also sees an almost mystical dimension to it: "The subliminal depths of radio are charged with the resonating echoes of tribal horns and antique drums. This is inherent in the very nature of this medium, with its power to turn the psyche and society into a single echo chamber."

CHAPTER 1
Seas of Red Ink

IN THE 1920S, A FEW YEARS BEFORE CBS WAS FORMED, RADIO was regarded as remarkable. It pulled sound out of the air in some strange manner only a few understood. Radio was even more miraculous than the movies. The "magic lantern," whose glow beamed through acetate film onto a screen, was based on an observable phenomenon, the reflection of light. Radio was not.

Children, comfortable in a world of fantasy, could believe that Lilliputians inhabited the sturdy mahogany boxes, to be awakened by the twist of a knob. The dwarves then spoke forth in stentorian tones, or, accompanied by miniature instruments, burst into song.

There were no radio networks in the early 1920s, only local, independent stations. Perhaps typical of the kind of entrepreneurs who owned these stations was Isaac Levy, who bought Philadelphia's WCAU in 1922 from an engineer with little taste for the business that had grown up around radio. "Ike" Levy, a brash young lawyer who finished his law training in 1914, was a scrappy poker-playing wheeler-dealer who would play a major role in CBS's history. Almost as soon as he set up his law practice, Levy began to sense that his strong suit was an ability to do things, "Not good—but fast as hell," as he put it.

He once astonished a distinguished client from New York who approached him for help in an important, ticklish negotiation. Levy listened patiently, then promptly picked up the telephone and settled the matter in ten minutes. That was his style: He learned who to call and what to say for quick results. He also learned to tolerate with dignity the "hire yourself that little Jewish lawyer" recommendation passed along by insensitive but appreciative clients.

Ike said he had to "fight, kick and bite" to win. Once, he was challenged on a legal matter by the mighty William Randolph Hearst organization. He considered their challenge absurd, but he listened quietly to the Hearst position. He then told his adversaries, "I'm not even going to answer that, but if you do what you intend to do, we'll take it all the way to the high court and you know we'll win." Hearst and company threw in the towel.

When WCAU came his way, Levy had already become involved in a number of business deals, sometimes with partners. His poker-playing buddies included Irving Berlin, Harpo Marx and playboy Tommy Taylor. They listened to Ike Levy pitches more than once. Ike had developed a technique of telling a man enough about a deal in a single tantalizing sentence to get a nibble. At that point his prey usually asked the questions, growing more interested with each baited response, and finally begged to be let in.

Ike Levy figured he could handle the WCAU deal with a single associate—his law partner, skilled trial attorney Daniel Murphy. Ike conveyed the exciting and potentially profitable aspects of radio to Murphy and convinced him that the two ought to buy the Philadelphia station for $25,000. They put up some cash and financed $18,000 through a bank.

But Ike was strictly a deal man. He was not geared to the relatively routine chore of running a business. So he turned to his brother, Leon, a dentist with a thriving practice. Less abrasive than Ike, Leon was equally smart and more suited to the day-to-day routine. And though a couple of years younger than Ike, he was no stranger to business. Leon and Ike had already worked together, investing in the Atlantic City Race Track. To meet his new responsibilities to the station, Leon began scheduling all dental appointments for the morning hours. In those days, WCAU's broadcasts began at night.

Like his brother, Leon was an opportunist determined to live high on the hog. They had both known poverty at firsthand. Their mother had run a shop to put them through college and graduate school. Leon decided that the best way to become established was to marry well and he began looking for a suitable bride. When he learned that Peggy Mastbaum, whose father owned a chain of motion picture theaters, would sail with her family to Europe, he wasted no time.

He approached Sam Blitzstein, a private banker, for $1000 which Leon promptly blew on his passage and a costly but abortive shipboard courtship of Miss Mastbaum.

Undaunted, he tried a more direct approach. Seeking out a member of the wealthy Publicker Liquor family, Leon told him he wanted to marry his daughter, whose dowry would be ample. The outraged father, a big man given to direct action, promptly threw him out of the house.

In time Leon turned to Blanche Paley. A fretful girl, given to sieges of hypochondria, Blanche was the daughter of Sam Paley, who with his brother Jacob owned Philadelphia's Congress Cigar Company. Blanche and Leon were married on September 22, 1927, about the time Blanche's brother Bill was becoming involved in the radio broadcast business.

There would be a fascinating replay of all of this a generation later, which is detailed in a 1974 best-selling novel called *You and Me, Babe*. The novel is the thinly disguised autobiography of Chuck Barris, a dentist's son yet, who got the cold shoulder from Leon and Blanche Levy when he asked for their daughter Lynn's hand. Chuck married Lynn anyway, scratching for a living. By the time Barris became rich as producer of *The Newlywed Game*, the marriage had ended in divorce.

Leon apparently never lost his appreciation for feminine pulchritude. He hired a Miss Rasmussen to be a receptionist at WCAU, a girl endowed with a figure that drew considerable admiring comment. One day, Miss Rasmussen showed up at the station wearing "a big hunk of expensive jewelry" as one Philadelphian recalls. He also notes that receptionists were notoriously underpaid, then as now. The other girls at the station gathered around Miss Rasmussen and began oohing and aahing and wondering where she got the treasure. Finally, after persistent questioning, the flustered Miss Rasmussen blurted, "My uncle gave it to me!"

At that, one of the girls pointedly remarked, "Next time you see your uncle, tell him we could all use a raise."

Considering the fact that the Levy brothers and the Paleys all belonged to the Philmont, a Philadelphia country club, and thus knew each other fairly well, it is not surprising that the ambitious Leon married Blanche. Nor is it surprising that the Congress Cigar Company became an important early advertising account for WCAU. Leon was to become a pivotal figure in the evolution of CBS.

Bill Paley was not a native Philadelphian. His family had originally operated their cigar business in Chicago where Bill grew up. That it was strictly a family business was made clear by the name of the cigar they produced—La Palina, a variation on the family name—and the fact the cigar bands bore a picture of Bill's mother, Goldie. Bill attended Western Military Academy in Alton, Illinois, graduating in 1918. Then he entered the University of Chicago. After his first year there, his family decided to move their cigar business to Philadelphia to escape some labor problems. Bill transferred to the Wharton School of Finance in Philadelphia.

His years at college, though cushioned by his father's wealth, weren't particularly happy ones. At Wharton, he learned about discrimination. Charming though he was in his quiet way, Bill's background was held against him. Not only was he discriminated against by gentiles for being a Jew, but he was also discriminated against by prideful German Jews for his Russian ancestry. He settled for a Jewish fraternity described by a former dean as "Class B."

Bill Paley seems never to have forgotten his unhappiness at Wharton. Despite his many charities, he has never made a major gift to his alma mater. He also has harbored ambivalent feelings about his Russian-Jewish origins, which he does not advertise and which did not stand in the way of his two brilliant marriages to Christians.

Restless and quickly bored by detail, he was an indifferent student. At Wharton he would frequently become excited by an enthusiasm of the moment, whether for a corned beef sandwich he found exceptionally good (he loved food) or a costly Hispano-Suiza car his father bought him. His sensational idea of the morning was often as not forgotten by nightfall. This butterfly trait caused some thoughtful people to label him shallow. Yet this apparent failing stemmed from a zest for living —an eagerness to enjoy to the fullest all that life could offer—that would play a role in his success.

He also possessed a shrewdness and a talent for managing money. As

Wharton crew manager, he turned in record-low expense accounts, a suggestion that his father's money hadn't affected his common sense.

Few believed, however, that this playful ladies' man and heir to millions would find a direction of his own; likely he would remain in the comfortable niche his father had prepared for him in the cigar business. Indeed, after graduating with a B. S. degree in 1922, he did enter the family business. He lived at home, drove expensive cars, enjoyed the girls and learned the business—from a high perch. He was probably well prepared to begin as production chief; his father, a business genius of sorts, had been schooling Bill in the cigar trade for years. Still, there was something slightly indecent about his quick promotion to advertising manager as well as vice-president and secretary of the company by 1925. His salary: $50,000 a year. Not bad for a boy three years out of college.

While the Levys were running WCAU and Bill Paley was learning the cigar business, the world of radio was turning attention to a new concept in which local stations would receive radio programs from a central source. Local stations had found phonograph records and local talent unsatisfactory. They longed for a means to present nationally recognized stars live. Networks were the obvious answer.

The nation's leading seller of radios, the almighty Radio Corporation of America, set about filling that need. RCA was an amalgam of wireless interests, set up and then made independent by some of the most powerful corporations in America—American Telephone & Telegraph and its affiliate, Western Electric; and set makers General Electric and Westinghouse.

Once it became clear that RCA was going into the network business, it was also clear the company would be a major force. For RCA was famous for fully marshaling its enormous power. Its methods of discouraging the scores of other radio makers through threats based on alleged patent infringement would have incurred the quick wrath of the federal government in this day and age.

Another man who would play a critical role in CBS history was Arthur Judson, a well-known impresario who managed both the Philadelphia and New York Philharmonic orchestras and such important artists as Heifetz, Horowitz and Ezio Pinza as well as conductors George Szell and Bruno Walter.

13

Judson was a tall powerfully built man with a forceful personality, and he was a realist. A couple of years ago at age 92 he told the author in a piping voice why he hadn't become a professional violinist. "Let me tell you a profound secret, young man . . . I simply wasn't good enough."

He was cultured though, conversant with serious music and an authority on Elizabethan literature—just the sort to represent artist to employer and to broadcaster if, as he expected, radio became an important entertainment medium.

Thus it was that in 1926 he approached RCA czar David Sarnoff proposing to organize a bureau to provide leading artists to the new network. In response to Sarnoff's request, Judson provided a plan. According to Judson, "Sarnoff read the plan with great interest and said that if it was within his power when he got his chain organized he would certainly put me in charge of the programs and of supplying the artists."

Sarnoff, like Bill Paley, was a Russian Jew, but apart from this and the fact that both men had talent and ambition, there were few similarities between the two. Paley was born to luxury. David Sarnoff was ushered into the world in the tight grasp of poverty.

Sarnoff had been a refugee from a wooden-hut village in southern Russia—one of thousands of Eastern Europeans who settled in the tenements of Manhattan's Lower East Side around the turn of the century. David arrived in 1900 at the age of nine in the company of his mother and two brothers to join his father in the New World. When the family was reunited they found that the father had worked himself to the point of collapse over the past six years, painting houses to raise the money for his family's passage. Thereafter, David's father took to his bed—an invalid until the day he died.

David became the head of the family at the age of ten, running a newsstand on Tenth Avenue and earning extra money by singing in a synagogue choir for $1.50 a week. When his voice changed at age 15, he wandered into the New York *Herald* building looking for a full-time job. The first desk he passed was the postal telegraph office. Fascinated by the wireless, David signed on as a messenger at $5 a week. He used his spare time to learn Morse Code and soon developed a great "fist." He landed a job as a telegrapher and progressed through a series of posts, including a stint on a sealing ship in the Arctic Ocean.

Eventually he was assigned to the wireless room that had been installed by Wanamaker's in its New York City department store so that there could be instant written communication between its New York and Philadelphia operations. David was just 21 on April 14, 1912, when he picked up a faint but terrifying signal from the North Atlantic: "S. S. *Titanic* ran into an iceberg. Sinking fast." For the next 72 hours, David Sarnoff was the sole communications link with what proved to be the worst disaster in commercial shipping history.

The *Titanic*'s passenger list was studded with the names of the rich and the near-rich. Soon David was in touch with the *Carpathia* which steamed to the scene to pick up the survivors. He worked around the clock relaying messages, some to members of New York's "400," including the Astors and the Strauses who crowded the wireless room listening in dread anticipation for news of relatives on board.

Three days passed. Finally, when the lists of the living and the dead were complete—1517 persons died when the ship slipped beneath the icy waters—David set aside his telegrapher's key, had a Turkish bath and went to bed—famous.

Sarnoff used his newfound fame as a start on his way up the executive ladder. Tough and irascible, he fought his way to the top of the Radio Corporation of America.

Though studious and uncommonly bright, he lacked social finesse and, more than that, showed a decided contempt for his underlings. The bantam-sized executive thrust himself into the limelight, drawing a curtain of obscurity around those who helped him reach the heights. He collected medals and awards like a boy collects baseball cards—a style remarkably different from that of his career rival, Bill Paley.

When Sarnoff created the National Broadcasting Company in 1926, he split it into two chains and signed up most of the important stations in the land for one net or the other.

RCA announced its networks and Arthur Judson was ready. He had organized the Judson Radio Program Corporation in September 1926 to serve the NBC stations. But he was in for a shock.

Alarmed when he heard nothing from Sarnoff, he approached the RCA chief again and asked him what he planned to do about the Judson proposals.

"Nothing" snapped Sarnoff, and Judson reeled in surprise. Regaining his composure, Judson announced, "Then we will organize our own chain!"

Sarnoff, fresh from interminable negotiations with American Telephone & Telegraph over long-line service to pipe broadcasts to affiliated stations, roared with laughter and said flatly, "You can't do it!" It had taken a full year and a commitment of $1 million to get AT&T service for NBC.

Judson left Sarnoff's office fuming.

In retrospect, Judson's plan to build a network to rival those of RCA seems foolhardy. He had little experience to qualify him for so massive an undertaking—one that would require the building of a national organization and raising and spending millions of dollars over the space of a few years. He was bound to make costly mistakes he could ill afford.

In fact, he had no money. His only hope of getting any was through sympathetic friends and acquaintances in the concert world. Some of them were rich, to be sure, but they hadn't built their fortunes by backing ventures as risky as the one Judson proposed.

Arthur was aware of all this, so it was with some reluctance that he approached an old friend, Betty Fleischmann Holmes, to ask for money to launch United Independent Broadcasters, Inc., a name chosen more as a protest against the RCA monopoly than anything else. Mrs. Holmes was a concert enthusiast and a member of the board of directors of the New York Philharmonic Orchestra. A Cincinnati girl who had long ago left Ohio to make her home in New York City, she was a philanthropist and heir to the Fleischmann Yeast fortune.

"We are losing our shirts," Judson admitted. But Mrs. Holmes, impressed that Judson planned to stress classical-music programing, said gaily, "I'm a good sport. I want to come in." She gave Judson $6000.

Meanwhile, Judson had taken on associates. One of them was George Arthur Coats, an ebullient salesman who once sold paving machinery. Mrs. Holmes's money sent him to the hustings where he hoped to sign up affiliates for the new network.

Coats's first stop in his quest for outlets was Philadelphia and WCAU. Leon Levy listened receptively to Coats's plan and offered to put Coats in touch with other station owners Leon had cultivated. He also counseled Coats on the kind of deal they would go for, terms he would be happy to agree to himself. Coats signed up Leon and traveled to other stations signing up one important outlet after another. His trip was a splendid personal success—and a giant headache for UIB.

For Coats, with Levy's prompting, had agreed that the new network

—which was hardly more than an idea at this point—would begin buying ten hours of air time a week from each station at a rate of $50 an hour. This sum—$500 a week per station—was enough in those days to buy a brand-new Chevrolet and too much of a commitment for a struggling outfit like UIB.

Twelve stations hastened to sign on the dotted line. Some station owners turned Coats down on the theory that he was either a fool or a con man from the big city. One wonders whether Judson or his other principal associate, Major J. Andrew White, realized the significance of what Coats had promised. Major White was a radio veteran and a sober enough man to have had apprehensions about UIB's future under those terms.

A distinguished-looking man who wore a pince-nez on a drooping black ribbon, Major White was dignified and proper. His stiff reporting style reflected his innate sense of decorum. During the 1924 Democratic National Convention at New York's original Madison Square Garden, Norman Brokenshire, a young radio newcomer with a zest for controversy, took over the mike while Major White went to lunch. Soon Brokenshire was in the thick of a battle between delegates in the aisles. He wrote: "I concentrated on the fight and let everything else go by. [It was] one of the finest donnybrooks I'd ever seen. Delegation signs were banged on opponents' heads, chairs and decorations were destroyed. I had a ringside seat. I was letting the audience in on the fracas when Major White walked in. His face turned pale; he grabbed the microphone from me and signaled the operator to take us off the air."

Seconds later Major White returned to the air with "elegant composure." Then, in an off-the-air reprimand, he explained to Brokenshire that the station had been granted rights to air the convention with distinct instructions that no disorders would be reported.

Major White had been a radio pioneer, first as editor of *Wireless Age* before he became an announcer. Now in charge of daily operations at UIB, he toted up the costs of Coats's generous contracts which eventually covered 16 stations. The $400,000-a-year figure seemed astronomic at a time when there was absolutely no assurance that the company could line up advertisers to sponsor the time—or even get the necessary telephone lines to pipe broadcasts to affiliates.

But on the latter score, Coats delivered. While Judson was negotiating with AT&T in New York, Coats left for Washington; he was armed with two checks—one for $1000, the other for $10,000. Judson authorized the checks but never said what they were for. However, before Coats left he told Judson he expected to stir up pressure at the agency that regulated telephone companies—the Interstate Commerce Commission. He alluded mysteriously to a man who he said could fix such things. Judson was nevertheless surprised to receive a telephone call from Coats shortly thereafter. Coats cheerfully reported from Washington that UIB had the AT&T lines. They would be ready in the fall of 1927.

So there was both good news and bad news for UIB. The new network had 16 eager stations plus rights to use the telephone lines to deliver their programs. But it also had enormous costs and no income from sponsors yet. Prospects, then, were for seas of red ink.

Meantime, WCAU's Leon Levy was not only wooing Blanche Paley, but also Blanche's father, Sam, and her uncle Jacob. Nationally, cigarette sales had been soaring, largely at the expense of cigars, and La Palina sales had suffered enormously. Leon and Ike convinced the Paleys to try radio advertising and negotiated a $50,000 contract. The company's advertising chief, William Paley, wasn't around to help negotiate it; Bill was in Europe enjoying himself. His father and uncle acted without consulting him in what was undoubtedly the most important advertising decision the company had ever made.

By the time Bill returned, miffed that he hadn't been consulted, his father had begun to think the advertising contract was a mistake. Bill, who was already something of a gambler, watched La Palina Cigar sales carefully, gauging the effect of this new advertising medium.

The company sponsored two shows. One was a quarter-hour program featuring the popular entertainer Harry Link. Link was billed as the "La Palina Boy." He played the piano and in a pleasant bathtub baritone sang popular songs, including his own hit, "I've Got a Feelin' I'm Fallin'." La Palinas also sponsored an early soap opera, *Rolla and Dad.*

Despite the fat La Palina contract, Ike Levy's law partner, Daniel Murphy, was finding radio a distraction from his law practice. During the La Palina campaigns on CAU, Dan Murphy told Ike Levy he wanted out. This sent the Levys scurrying for money, and what more obvious source of capital than a rich, satisfied customer? La Palina sales had begun responding to the radio exposure and thus the Paleys were receptive when Ike and Leon urged them to buy a one-third interest in CAU. The Levy brothers retained the remaining two-thirds of CAU in equal shares.

If business was catch-as-catch-can for a local station like WCAU, it was nip and tuck for a shoestring network like UIB. Saddled with the costly affiliated-station contracts and the heavy tariff they'd have to pay the telephone company for its long lines when they began operations, Judson and White were frantically looking for a major financial angel. Mrs. Holmes had helped again and again, but that was stopgap. UIB needed a rich partner.

The men looked far and wide. Atwater Kent, a radio-set maker, was approached to no avail. Paramount Pictures' Adolph Zukor seemed tempted, but made too many conditions. Finally, in the summer of 1927, UIB approached a company that was almost as apprehensive about the future as the network—but for a different reason. The company was the well-financed Columbia Phonograph.

Columbia was a leader in the record-pressing business, but its world was changing rapidly because of radio. Records sounded scratchy and tinny on the mechanical players in most homes and were no match for a good radio carrying live or even recorded music. Columbia officials were wringing their hands not only over the ever-more-popular entertainment novelty, but also over the prospect of even more strenuous future competition from their archrival, Victor Talking Machine Company, which was about to be gathered into David Sarnoff's protective arms and become a part of giant RCA.

Desperation thus served desperation. Major White nervously approached nervous officials of Columbia and persuaded them to buy the operating rights of UIB for $163,000. That figure was "probably arrived at" according to Judson "simply by the amount of money we then needed."

The new partners set up an operating company called Columbia Phonograph Broadcasting System and began planning a gala debut. Judson happily assumed the role he had always intended for himself. Columbia contracted with the Judson Radio Program Corporation to supply ten hours of programing a week for around $10,000 a week. The network was to resell the programing to sponsors and Judson's unit thus became the programing division. (Judson remained active in concert management until the age of 90. When he died in early 1975, he had one-third of a million CBS shares, a figure topped only by Bill Paley himself, and was a millionaire many times over.)

After the Columbia money came through, Judson went to conductor Howard Barlow, asking him to leave the New York Neighborhood Playhouse and come to the network to direct a 23-piece staff orchestra. Barlow was a fine but obscure conductor whose first musical recital came a few weeks after he found and taught himself to play a cracked cello which had been collecting dust in a church attic back home in Ohio. Nevertheless, he told Judson he couldn't afford to join him for less than $15,000 a year. Judson answered—perhaps more magnanimously than he should have—he wouldn't want Barlow if he wasn't worth $15,000 a year. Barlow was to conduct on the night of Columbia's first major broadcast to its 16 network affiliates.

Columbia planned a spectacular debut. Metropolitan Opera artists under Barlow's direction would present *The King's Henchmen,* a work by composer Deems Taylor and the distinguished poet, Edna St. Vincent Millay. The appointed hour arrived on September 18, 1927. Switches were thrown in New York while personnel from flagship station WOR monitored from the station's men's room—the only soundproof space ready at the new WOR offices at broadcast time.

Everything went according to plan—except that west of the Alleghenies nothing came through. The debut of Columbia was marked by nearly 15 minutes of dead air. A thunderstorm had broken the wires. Finally, the wires repaired or bypassed, the Voice of Columbia came through faintly, punctuated by terrific static.

Still, the show went on—and on. It ran a full hour and a quarter past schedule. Thousands of listeners in the areas around 16 cities where affiliates were located, from Boston to St. Louis, heard their first opera. Regardless of downed wires and static, Columbia was launched as a broadcast network.

Columbia Phonograph had been aboard less than three months when that first broadcast put the network on the map, and the company's $163,000 was already spent. Successive Fridays arrived and passed with no paychecks for the talent and staff.

Columbia had quickly discovered that it was not particularly hard to sell advertisers on the idea of radio—just impossible to land them for the home team. Once an advertiser was sold by Columbia, he marched over to RCA and sponsored time on one of the NBC networks. Columbia officials were completely disenchanted and wanted out. The same month *The King's Henchmen* was broadcast, they sold the operating company back to UIB for $10,000 in cash and 30 hours of free broadcasting. In a decision that seems curious at this point, they allowed UIB to keep the Columbia name.

Frantically short of cash once again, Major White and Arthur Judson hardly knew where to turn. White, a Christian Scientist, called his practitioner for advice. In a more practical mood, Judson sent a wireless message to Betty Fleischmann Holmes, aboard a ship in mid-Atlantic, saying that he needed between "forty and forty-five thousand dollars." The good lady responded as before sending a wireless to her office instructing them to send a check to Judson for $45,000. The money paid AT&T the $40,000 it was owed for long-lines service but covered little else. Mrs. Holmes's "gifts" repaid her handsomely. Years later she sold her CBS stock for $3 million.

Down in Philadelphia, Ike and Leon Levy had been watching these events closely. Fascinated by the possibilities—and anxious for the network to succeed—they were receptive when Arthur Judson confided his financial problems. They turned to a friend, Jerome H. Louchheim, another member of their club world. Louchheim was a subway and bridge builder, a sportsman and a lover of the arts. More important from Judson's point of view, he was both wealthy and interested in radio.

The Levy brothers were interested in having a financial stake in the business as well. They respected their mother's judgment, so Ike approached her and asked how she would feel if he and Leon got involved in an enterprise involving hundreds of thousands of dollars.

Mrs. Levy urged Ike to delay his decision for a few days: "I never want to hear you say later that you wish you had thought of this or that."

A few days later, Ike, then in his mid-thirties, went back to his mother to say he believed he had thought of everything. Her advice: "Then shoot crap now—not when you're fifty."

With Ike's and Leon's participation, Jerome Louchheim agreed to buy a controlling interest. As Louchheim prepared to put his name on the contract, his attorney, Ralph Colin, issued a dour warning that was ironic in terms of Colin's later affiliation with CBS; he said that the network could be a bottomless pit: $100,000 now, a quarter of a million later. It might go on and on. That was true, Louchheim agreed, "but after all, it is my money." He then scratched his name on the contract and made an initial payment with the Levys of $135,000. On November 1, 1927, Columbia's new owners sent American Telephone a check for $100,000 to avoid cancellation of the network's long-line service.

But immediate surgery was needed to stanch the flow of blood. Either the affiliates gave up their $500-a-week network guarantees or the network could not survive. So Major White and Leon Levy hit the road with new contracts in their pockets. This time, Leon's sympathies were clearly with the network. Rather than a guarantee, the two men offered payment only for sponsored network shows actually broadcast by the affiliate.

The two men evidently presented their case well, for each of the 16 affiliates agreed to the new terms. With that, the network's balance sheet tipped to a less precarious angle. But it was still a marginal enterprise. Advertisers were skeptical and the network found it difficult to land important sponsors. Losses continued to pile up at the rate of $20,000 a week. This went on for many months.

One day in August 1928, Ike Levy and Jerome Louchheim were walking together on the boardwalk in Atlantic City. Louchheim had been infusing more cash and after 5 A.M. breakfasts of frogs' legs at Louchheim's the two men would sally forth to Columbia headquarters in New York two or three times a week. But Louchheim felt the need for a stronger hand by the Philadelphia group. Leon, who loved Philadelphia, refused Louchheim's urgings to go to New York and become president. It was grim. Ike recalls: "We were down about one million dollars and no big sponsors were in sight. . . . Louchheim asked, 'Ike, how long do you think we ought to keep it going?' and I said, 'Let's give it another ten days.'"

Meanwhile, Major White had been negotiating a major deal. Seven days after Ike Levy and Jerome Louchheim took their walk a contract arrived in the mail from Vitaphone, a subsidiary of Warner Brothers, for $750,000 worth of advertising.

"Had that contract arrived three days later," says Ike Levy, "there would have been a sheriff's notice on the door."

CBS—the name already shortened to Columbia Broadcasting System—was in the black for the first time.

La Palina sales were percolating nicely in the WCAU area in apparent response to the warmth of "La Palina Boy" and *Rolla and Dad*. Obviously impressed, Bill Paley signed a $6500-a-week contract with Columbia to air a network show, *The La Palina Smoker*, that was to pioneer a technique that made an advantage of radio's primary disadvantage—the lack of a picture.

Unable to see what was going on in the studio, the listener was forced to use his imagination. A clever script writer could play to the listener's imagination to build a "theater of the mind" by providing the listener with enough clues so he could form his own mental picture. In *The La Palina Smoker*, the listener was given a scenario: a smoking room in which several men were gathered around La Palina—the one woman present—bandying wisecracks.

The show worked and became a hit. Even more important, it was a brilliant commercial success. Twenty-six weeks into *The La Palina Smoker* run, La Palina Cigar sales jumped from 400,000 to a million a day. It was a spectacular achievement for radio and a stunning revelation for William S. Paley.

Although he had a secure future in the cigar business, it was hardly a career for a man as innovative, restless and ambitious as Bill Paley. Radio seemed to offer possibilities. His brother-in-law Leon Levy introduced him to an ailing Jerome Louchheim and Paley expressed interest when the builder offered to sell out.

Bill Paley is said to have had a million dollars to play with. It is also said that Sam Paley had once before given his son a million dollars and that Bill had blown it in an unsuccessful attempt to enter cigarette manufacturing. *This* million dollars, Sam now stressed, was to be Bill's last million.

At any rate, Bill didn't put all the money into CBS—at least not right away. Nobody except Bill Paley himself and perhaps members of the family seem to know what that initial investment was. Robert Landry, a veteran *Variety* writer who worked for CBS in radio days, believes the investment was just $275,000. He adds, "I made a definite effort to find out."

Fortune magazine reports that subsequent investments raised Bill

Paley's original stake to about $1.5 million. Whatever the figure, Paley bought the bulk of Louchheim's holdings, and the Levys and other Paleys also invested.

On September 26, 1928, William Paley was elected president of the parent company, a little more than a year after its operating arm, Columbia, aired that first fragmented nationwide broadcast.

Major White stayed on as president of the operating company. Paley had expected to spend perhaps two days a week in New York, but was quickly drawn full-time into the network's churning affairs. He saw that if the 22-station network was to succeed it would have to grow fast. The long-line telephone wires over which the frail network was broadcasting 16 hours a day were to cost $1.1 million, an astronomical figure in 1929. This was a sum that even the wealthy Bill Paley must have found alarming.

He soon decided to relocate in New York City to personally direct the network and its 16 employees. His mother, Goldie, gave him advice that was somewhat out of place in the rough-and-tumble world of a failing corporation. She warned him that he should never do anything for himself that someone else could do better, and, to emphasize the point, gave him a manservant. His father's advice was along the same lines but more practical: "Hire smart people," he cautioned, "then have the good sense to listen to them."

Youthful as Bill Paley was, he looked even younger. When he arrived at the network offices in 1928 to complete arrangements to buy it, the office boy refused to let him in, saying Major White was conducting an important meeting and wasn't to be disturbed. If an office boy could ignore him Paley knew how his age and looks could affect older established businessmen. So he hired a tailor to make him dozens of high-collared shirts and to fashion conservative suits that would project an older image. According to one source, this stratagem partially backfired: The many suits he wore to the office were identical and this caused employees to think he owned only one. Actually he lived lavishly. At times his opulent living style came across as gauche. Once he visited a wealthy and unpretentious investment-banking family, the War-burgs, and arrived for the weekend accompanied by his manservant who was totally out of place in the Warburgs' relatively modest suburban home.

At CBS he was all business. Studying the telephone company's rates, he reasoned that CBS could do four times as much business on the same long lines for an additional half million dollars annually, a total of $1.6 million. The situation called for a dramatic idea that would make local stations eager to join the CBS group rather than the prestigious Red and Blue networks of NBC.

An analysis of the NBC affiliation contract showed that the affiliates could preempt the network; that is, if an NBC affiliate wanted to run its own program during a time when one of NBC's clients wanted a national hookup, then NBC could not deliver its full network. The NBC contract also stressed "sustaining programs"—charging local stations for unsponsored attractions to fill gaps when neither affiliate nor network had sponsored broadcasts to air.

To Paley, the emphasis in the NBC contract was clearly in the wrong place. Why not give affiliates sustaining shows for nothing? In exchange, Paley would insist that the local stations allow CBS to preempt local time during hours when national sponsors were most anxious to reach the entire nation, some of that valuable time without payment. But for preempted hours in excess of a stated number, CBS would pay local stations and do so on an attractive sliding-scale basis. "The more they took, the more money they got from us," as Bill Paley expressed it.

Soon after Bill Paley arrived in New York City, he and Major White wired invitations to the leading unaffiliated station owners east of the Mississippi River to come to the Ambassador Hotel on Park Avenue in New York City and listen to the Paley plan.

Paley touched a responsive chord. The cost of talent for unsponsored local shows was slight in terms of network outlays, but constituted a heavy expense for the independent station. Every first-class station broadcast 16 hours a day—from 8:00 A.M. until midnight—and it wasn't always easy to sell enough time to commercial advertisers for profitable operation. In fact, independents—even those in major areas —struggled to sell three hours of sponsored time a day. And that left the station with 13 hours to fill—a total of 4745 hours a year. The station could skimp on talent, hiring artists by the week, having them participate in several programs a day, using a lot of free talent and some recorded material. Under those circumstances a major Cleveland independent spent $35 an hour on unsponsored shows which worked out to $170,000 a year.

Under the Paley contract, the $35 an hour the Cleveland station paid for local talent could be more or less eliminated if the station affiliated and gave up some of the best evening hours to CBS. For this the station would be paid something less than $100 an hour by the network—on a sliding scale.

As a network affiliate, the local station would be piping the music and entertainment of national stars who received $2000 to $3000 from the network for a 15-minute performance. The local station's prestige would soar. A Price Waterhouse survey would later suggest that the average independent station seldom had more than one-tenth the number of listeners its competitive network station had—even in areas in which the smaller stations offered a satisfactory signal.

The local station owners clearly realized the value of affiliation with a financially viable network. To a degree, Paley had to finesse the financial side of the story. His personal magnetism helped and there were credible rumors that he came from a family of substantial assets. (His father ultimately left an estate of some $30 million.)

Paley was an excited young man at the Ambassador as one station owner after the other signed the contract. Those heady hours at the Ambassador, when CBS grew from 22 stations to 47, convinced Bill Paley that he had chosen the right field for his talents.

He was certainly confident of CBS's future, if the deal he made with Adolph Zukor, the shrewd chief of Paramount Pictures alive today at 100, is any guide. CBS operations were then housed in the Paramount Building in Times Square and Zukor was watching the network's progress with interest. He was concerned that radio was potential competition for motion pictures. Moving to protect his flank, Zukor offered to buy a half interest in CBS from Paley and his associates—directly. Paley accepted for his group in the fall of 1929, trading 50 percent of the CBS stock owned by him and his friends for 58,823 shares of Paramount Public Corporation. More interesting than the bare bones of that contract was its curious clause that may have appeared to be frivolous on Paramount's side and to be overreaching by Paley.

The two sides agreed that Paramount would buy back Paley's Paramount shares—then worth $3.8 million—for $5 million or $85 a share by March 1, 1932, *provided* that CBS earned $2 million in the ensuing two years.

CBS was a tottering infant company in September 1929 when the handshakes were exchanged, and the CBS earnings clause offered an apparently insurmountable obstacle to the repurchase of Paley's Paramount stock. A month later even Paley wondered whether he had a fighting chance as the stock market crashed, changing million-dollar dreams into nightmares.

A couple of years later, however, when the day of reckoning arrived, CBS had chalked up $3 million in profits, not just two. At this time Paramount's stock had been clobbered in the crash and was trading at 9. Yet the motion picture company was obligated to buy back at almost ten times that price. Not surprisingly, Paramount found itself short of cash. So Paley and his friends offered to buy back Paramount's CBS shares for $5.2 million. The purchase would provide Paramount with the necessary wherewithall to buy back the 48,000 Paramount shares which the Paley group still held. The tariff for Paramount: $4 million.

Paley's group raised the necessary $1.2 million, got back the CBS shares and let Paramount off the hook. Thus everyone concerned made a profit, in one way or another.

Bill Paley might have made a fool of himself—the deal might even have lost him control of the company. But at this stage of the game, anyway, his luck was holding. Or perhaps he saw the future more clearly than did others.

CHAPTER 2
485 Madison

JIM LANDAUER, A SUAVE YOUNG REAL ESTATE MAN, WAS MAKING THE rounds one day in 1928 and looked in on the struggling CBS network in the Paramount Building. CBS was a live prospect that year, and Landauer wanted to sew up the business for himself. He chatted with Major White for a bit, and during the conversation White mentioned the company's new president, a man named Bill Paley.

"Bill Paley from Philadelphia?" Landauer asked, remembering a young man he had met at a party during his undergraduate days at Dartmouth. Landauer asked to see him and discovered his old acquaintance seated behind a desk in an enormous, beautifully paneled room. The room is said to have cost the original owners of the network half of their initial $80,000 capital. It embarrassed Paley who told an early associate that he was the third "sucker" to buy the network since so much money had been spent for show at a time so little capital was available.

The two young men spoke about the old days and then turned their attention to business. Paley explained that he was anxious to find space where CBS could grow. One major need was for soundproof studios, which required unobstructed space equivalent to two floors in a normal building. Most of the CBS programs at the time were broadcast from the penthouse at Steinway Hall on Fifty-seventh Street off Sixth Avenue; CBS concerts were broadcast from the Steinway Concert Hall downstairs. (The symbiosis between CBS and Steinway has run full circle. CBS acquired the piano-making company several years ago.)

No existing building could accommodate CBS's studio needs. Ballrooms had been adapted as radio studios, but they were less than ideal. Paley and Landauer decided to look for a building presently under construction that could be altered before it was completed. Landauer took a walk, trying to recall just where he had noticed a building under construction in the Fifties on Madison Avenue. He discovered it at 485 Madison Avenue. Landauer asked the owner-architect, John H. Carpenter, if he would be interested in the network as a tenant with the proviso that the upper stories be altered to accommodate radio studios.

Bill Paley was enthusiastic about the location because even then Madison Avenue was the symbol of advertising, and Paley knew advertising was the future for radio. While Landauer recalls Carpenter's concern about the financing behind CBS, Bill Paley remembers, "The owner never asked for credit references. . . . We were doing pretty well, but were wobbly then. . . . I was amazed we got the building."

Perhaps Bill Paley's enthusiasm and intelligence disarmed the owner-architect. More likely, the terms of the lease pleased Carpenter. Here was an ebullient young man, running an exciting new business, who was willing to commit himself and his company to a $1.5-million long-term lease for ten floors in a building not yet completed. On September 18, 1929, CBS moved to its new quarters. Miss Radio of 1929 cut the ribbon at the door while Bill Paley, looking stiffly formal in high collar, stood next to her. Paley brought in all of the expensive paneling from the Paramount Building and installed it in his corner office, a big, airy room with pilasters, fireplace and a decorative grille that concealed a radio. Outside that office Paley installed a severe-looking male secretary named Frank Kizis, clothed in black suit, black tie and stiff collar.

One of Paley's early concerns was the fact that CBS was so underrepresented in the Far West that it could hardly call itself a national network. His emissaries there had been working on the CBS equivalent of the Louisiana Purchase, but without success. Their Napoleon was

Don Lee, a personable and crafty businessman who owned radio stations in Los Angeles and San Francisco and had affiliation contracts with others in Washington and Oregon.

After Lee "refused to have anything to do with a couple of my people," Paley recalls, he picked up the telephone himself and called Lee on the Coast. As Paley attempted to outline a proposition, Lee interrupted. He did not discuss important matters by telephone, Lee said. Paley would have to come to the Coast. The last thing this young executive needed was a long train ride and hours of possibly fruitless negotiation with the West Coast entrepreneur. But it was travel to the Coast or forget the deal.

When he arrived, there was still another surprise. Lee announced that he was about to leave for a cruise and Bill would just have to join him on his yacht. Though he protested, Paley found Lee immovable once again. Bill looked tired, Lee said, the trip would do him good.

Paley finally shrugged in resignation and joined the cruise. He returned to Don Lee's office several days later, confident of a contract —the two men had gotten on famously. But there was yet another surprise for Paley. The artful executive introduced Bill to his secretary and announced that Paley would dictate a contract for Lee's signature. "Oh, no," said an apprehensive Bill Paley. "You know I'll lean over backwards to make this contract *more* than fair to you. I'll go further on your side than if we negotiate."

Lee was cordial, and, as usual, immovable. They would either do it his way or not at all. Bill Paley, realizing then that he was licked, dictated a contract which was as fair as he could make it to both sides.

He showed it to Don Lee, who, says Paley, "signed without changing a word." CBS was now a bona fide coast-to-coast network.

The housewarming Bill Paley gave the press at his new apartment in January of 1930 was a notable event—and there was certainly cause for celebration. In little over a year at the helm of CBS, Paley had embarked on ambitious expansion plans. At the end of 1929 sales had reached $4 million.

The six-room apartment at 480 Park Avenue was lavishly furnished at a cost of $10,000 per room, an astronomical figure for the era. Radios in each room were completely concealed in the walls. In his bedroom the young executive could lie in bed and tune a hidden radio by remote control, without so much as raising his head. He could turn on various combinations of lights and reach for any of several hundred books in the shelves behind him. There were racks for 100 shirts and neckties. One room contained a piano concealed in the wall with only the keyboard protruding into the room. An aluminum staircase in a central room led to a silver-painted balcony. And there was, of course, a bar. This was a crowd of worldly newspaper men who expected to be served drinks even during Prohibition. Everyone was transgressing the law. The awestruck reporters, who were probably paid under $50 a week, drank their fill, then proceeded to file their stories.

Paley's newly appointed public relations counsel, Edward L. Bernays, was sleeping soundly when the telephone woke him in the early hours of the morning following the party. It was a worried Bill Paley calling to say: "I've just heard from Chicago that the *Tribune* is publishing a story that I am a bootlegger. That will ruin CBS."

Says Bernays: "I called the *Tribune* and didn't ask anybody to do anything. I just asked for the City Desk and said that this young man was just starting his corporate life and would be ruined if they said he was serving liquor at his new home."

The paper pulled the story and "Bill Paley was saved for posterity," adds Bernays with characteristic modesty.

After allowing the press this one near-fatal peek through the keyhole, Paley became one of the most relentlessly private individuals in the world, rarely sharing his personal life with any except his closest non-business friends. Curiosity about him as a person and a rising young business executive kept growing, however. *Fortune* magazine reported that Paley was sometimes vague—apparently by design—but people who expected "clever, devious answers" were baffled by his simplicity and the rapidity with which he comes to the point. "Once his mind is made up—usually in a flash—he acts with unique authority and there is no question who is boss. Withal, he is hardly ever spectacular; though tense and fast in his thinking, he works quietly . . . there is never the shouting and desk pounding that is supposed to be characteristic of dynamic American leaders."

Bernays, a nephew of Sigmund Freud, attempted to make an analysis and wound up expressing both admiration and envy: "After a year's experience with him, I never knew how his decisions were arrived at —whether he communed with nature, whether earthly advisors directed him, whether he flipped a coin, or whether he possessed an innate wisdom and intuitive judgment.

"Whatever his methods they led to success. His closer colleagues confided to me that they never felt he exerted authority in their presence. . . ."

With a touch of snobbery, perhaps, Bernays added: "I felt that native shrewdness made up for a lack of intellectual grasp of the realities he was dealing with." Bernays felt that "practical considerations played a more important role than ideological ones."

There is little doubt that the executive offices at 485 Madison Avenue—universally called The Twentieth Floor—became the scene of an unusual and exhilarating adventure. Here Bill Paley and a crew of equally young associates were innovating each day in a major and entirely new field, one unbounded by tradition, unhampered by bureaucracy.

When an important matter came up, Paley and his "management presidium," as one veteran called it, would gather in the warmly paneled Paley offices or in the company dining room and flail away. A few wise decisions right off the bat—the Madison Avenue lease, his popular new affiliates contract—made Paley bold. Unlike many young men who were born with money, he developed the confidence that came from his personal success. He was clearly the boss in these meetings and several early associates recall that he had an uncanny knack for asking the one question they weren't prepared to answer. The open exchange of ideas proved productive since Bill had followed his father's advice: He hired smart men and listened to what they had to say.

He seemed to have little ego involvement in ideas. He would seize upon a good idea with an almost childlike eagerness even when it wasn't his own. He had no fear of being outshined by associates.

The management group was so small, and the circumstances under which they worked so intimate, that it resembled a close-knit college fraternity with fierce loyalties. Chief among the group was the cantankerous Ed Klauber, elder statesman among the Paley men, an ex–*New York Times* reporter and editor, who warmed to the chore of managing the day-to-day business details with the flair of a born executive. There was the brilliant and charming Paul Kesten who played a critical role in promotion. Soon Victor Ratner joined the CBS team, working under Kesten. Canny, critical, erratic and engaging, Ratner had been a copywriter. There was Sam Pickard, a handsome, courtly southerner formerly with the Federal Radio Commission, who, between drinking bouts, could get things done in Washington.

In fond recollection of those days of delicious uncertainty and fervor, Bill Paley comments: "It was much more fun then. We would make a decision and it would be implemented quickly."

The operation was easily controlled from the top then, and Bill Paley could personally act in mid-broadcast if necessary—as he did once in taking an intoxicated announcer off the air. In a recent interview he recalled the incident but refused to divulge the name of the announcer, except to say that it was definitely not Ted Husing.

Those days of lightning decisions were to change as the years passed. But for the time being, Bill Paley was having the time of his life.

Paley's sense of esthetics was clearly a matter of instinct, not training; he had the kind of knack that is unsettling to those who have had years of instruction but little intuition. It has been said that if Paley entered a museum filled with unfamiliar paintings he would naturally gravitate toward the best paintings there. He soon applied that instinct to radio programing, but not until after he'd been running CBS for several months.

An early associate describes a critical event in Paley's career while he was still finding his role in radio: "People at a dinner party he attended began asking questions about how a network operated and someone asked about a particular CBS program. Paley is supposed to have said something like this: 'Yeah, I know about that program, but I've never listened to it.' At that point another man said bluntly, 'My God, you just told us a little about the broadcasting business. I can't believe that you aren't familiar with your own product—entertainment.'

"That gave Bill pause. He suddenly realized that he was not aware enough of the very essence of the broadcasting business—programing."

After that, programing became his first order of priority. He was thinking about it one day while sailing for a European vacation. "I was on a ship and out walking around the deck. The son of a friend of mine was playing a portable phonograph—the same record over and over again. Finally, I stopped and looked at the record label. I sent a wireless to the head of our artist bureau saying, 'Heard vocalist called Bing Crosby. Please sign.'"

When Paley returned he asked about Crosby and was told that someone had gone to the West Coast to meet the easygoing song stylist, decided the vocalist was an unpredictable fellow and that as a result the idea of signing him was dropped.

Paley retorted: "We're not buying his reliability. We're buying his talent."

Crosby was hired, dropped into the 7:00–7:15 P.M. slot five nights a week—the spot CBS used to introduce new vocalists—and that was that. There were few ratings then and Paley didn't know how well Crosby was doing until one day he saw a front-page story saying that after a nightclub appearance Crosby had been mobbed by youngsters who yelled and kicked and screamed and tore at his clothing.

About the time that Paley discovered Crosby, he also discovered a beautiful, graceful girl with large brown eyes. The former Dorothy Hart, socialite daughter of a Los Angeles insurance broker, happened at the time to be married to John Randolph Hearst, a friend of Paley's.

Recently, Dorothy said she met Bill at "a small place sort of lost in the woods" on Long Island. Bill was 30 at the time, she said, which means that it was 1931. The occasion was "a small Sunday lunch with mutual friends."

Asked where that "small place" was, Dorothy responded with the kind of riposte she loves, "Not very many people know."

Dorothy Hart always had a knack for drawing men into conversations about themselves, and when she had the opportunity, would bone up on subjects she knew were of interest to her husbands' friends. (She has had three husbands to date.) She found out a lot about radio at some point.

In any event, she left John Randolph Hearst and married Bill Paley in Kingman, Arizona, in 1932. The Hearsts were mightily displeased. Some people regard it as more than a coincidence that columnists for the right-wing Hearst newspapers would paint CBS with a pink brush from time to time as the years went by.

Dorothy had a flair for decorating, as Bill soon discovered, and she very likely influenced him with her tastes which ran to warm colors and traditional styling. Bill delighted in giving Dorothy decorating assignments, and in time she did a blue studio for The Twentieth Floor. Guests in those early days of radio generally faced the mike in a stark setting. But Dorothy's studio was like a living room and was so warm, so relaxing, that it made CBS guests forget their mike fright and chat away.

(Few people relaxed in Dorothy's studio as thoroughly as did tenor Morton Downey one evening. Downey, a popular CBS entertainer, was a notorious practical joker. A CBS sportscaster had just begun reading his script when he was joined by Downey. The tenor reached down, untied his shoes and removed them. They were followed by his socks. He then took off his coat and trousers and then his underwear while the sportscaster, the victim of his employment contract, continued to do his broadcast under these trying circumstances.)

Bill's relationship with Dorothy was outwardly smooth. Says a companion of the period, "He was always very sweet and gentle and would give way to her. He had a great sense of humor and she didn't seem to have any. She would get on a subject, speak with apparent erudition and would refuse to get off it.

"Regardless of who was talking he was always an interested listener. She didn't want to listen at all. She wanted to talk. But they were always nice to each other."

Bill and Dorothy had their unpleasant moments in private—like any other couple. In an interview, Dorothy was told that several of Bill's business associates said he never raised his voice. She responded archly, "Oh? . . . He never raised his voice?"

Whether Bill Paley spoke quietly or with feeling at home, his marriage to Dorothy ended in July 1947.

For good reason, Paley gave special attention to the 7:00–7:15 P.M. time slot, where he placed Crosby. At that time CBS faced the most formidable competition in radio. Two ex-vaudevillians using a simplistic racial theme had put together a show about Negroes that was the talk of the nation. However degrading to the American black it might seem today, the National Broadcasting Company's *Amos 'n' Andy* greatly appealed to listeners then and represented blackface minstrel humor at its best. Their fame epitomized NBC's superiority.

Freeman Fisher Gosden was Amos, and Charles J. Correll, Andy. Gosden was born in Richmond, Virginia, in 1899 and went north to take a job as a tobacco salesman. Soon he joined the Joe Bren Company, a road-show group, where his Negro dialect stories and banjo playing were a hit. Correll joined the company later as a piano player and soft-shoe dancer. The two began working up a blackface act and wound up in Chicago where they got a bid to do radio and were destined, among other things, to become a thorn in Bill Paley's side.

In the show they created, Amos was trusting, simple and unsophisticated. Andy was domineering and lazy. The two came from Atlanta to the big city to make their fame and fortune. After a year in Chicago they owned the Fresh Air Taxi Company of America, Incorpulated, which consisted of one desk and one swivel chair for the president to rest in and think. The action often took place in a South Side rooming house and the two men were frequently found attending meetings of the Mystic Knights of the Sea, chaired by a fellow called the Kingfish. All of the characters including Kingfish were played by one or the other of the two men in the early years of the show.

Amos 'n' Andy shows, sandwiched between commercials, lasted ten minutes and required from 1500 to 2000 words—all of them written by Gosden and Correll. The language was a pseudodialect calling for phrases like "Recordin' to the figgers in de book . . ." and "Wait a minute, heah! Whut is you doin? Is you mulsiflyin' or revidin'?" and "Splain dat to me."

Calvin Coolidge reportedly did not like to be disturbed at the White House when the show was on the air. Sanitary engineers finally figured out why the sewer pipes barely carried a flow between 7:00 and 7:15 P.M., then erupted with a roar immediately thereafter. No one in the audience, estimated at 40 million, wanted to miss a minute of *Amos 'n' Andy.*

Says an early Paley aide, "I listened to *Amos 'n' Andy* even when I was at CBS." That was the problem—everybody listened to them, even those who shouldn't have.

For Paley it was maddening. He had to make a dent in the 7 P.M. time slot because that marked the beginning of the radio evening. The network that controlled that time period usually controlled the next time period as well. Listeners had a tendency to stay with a radio station, especially with the static involved in switching stations in those days. Different stations came in at markedly different sound levels, depending upon distance of transmission and power. That, too, made the tuning process difficult.

If the show that followed *Amos 'n' Andy* was even mildly arresting, there was little dial spinning. The problem faced Bill Paley from the beginning. *Amos 'n' Andy* had been an NBC fixture since March 19, 1928.

Paley's sorties against *Amos 'n' Andy* wound up launching several important new careers and served as a profitable farm system for CBS. Though Paley never really succeeded in overpowering the NBC feature, ultimately he lured it away. Bing Crosby was an early entry in the sweepstakes. In those days he affected a mustache and looked like a well-bred mafioso. Bing was something entirely new in the pop singing field—a relaxed "crooner" who bent his notes and added little ba-ba-ba-boos to the ends of phrases. Says the CBS publicity aide who was secretly devoted to the opposition: "Bing was a member of bandleader Paul Whiteman's Rhythm Boys Trio. Bill simply reached out for him, signed him up and shoved him into the seven-to-seven-fifteen slot against *Amos 'n' Andy.* We really loosed a publicity buildup and Bing made a dent."

Later Bing broke house records for 20 consecutive weeks at the Paramount Theater in New York City. Soon he was very much in demand, but no sponsor would take him on CBS so long as he was placed opposite *Amos 'n' Andy.* Crosby and those who followed him proved that, in radio at least, you could run second and still win. Even if you didn't dominate your time slot, you could pick up your chips, move to a new time period, lead the ratings there and become a big star.

Paley established a pattern with Crosby, and began using the time slot in the same way over and over. When the head of the CBS artists bureau called to ask him to hear four black fellows who had just bummed their way into New York from Cincinnati, Bill was too busy. Prevailed upon to delay his lunch date and hear just one song, he delighted in the Mills Brothers and missed his lunch entirely. So Paley tried four honest-to-goodness blacks against a couple of whites in blackface. The Mills Brothers became famous but the time slot remained in the enemy's hands.

Then there was Kate Smith. Paley signed her immediately. "She was so good." Kate was an overweight girl with a big pleasant but untrained voice that appalled classicist Howard Barlow, director of CBS's serious-music musicians. She was not well educated and was sensitive about her English and enunciation. Because she had some difficulty reading, the spellings in her scripts were specially geared for her, "ya," for instance, for "you." Yet this fat but charming girl struck a responsive note. She captured the heart of America with a rendition of "God Bless America" that became so popular during World War II there was spontaneous movement to substitute the number for "The Star Spangled Banner." Ironically, when Irving Berlin wrote the song in 1918, he regarded it as "too sticky" and threw it in his trunk. Twenty years later he reluctantly got it out and let Kate use it on the air.

With each success Paley grew more confident of his ability to read the American taste. Soon he would be ready for a full-scale talent war with NBC, a war in which *Amos 'n' Andy* would once again be an early target.

CHAPTER 3
The Father of
Broadcast Journalism

IN AUGUST 1930, A CAREFULLY DRESSED, STERN-VISAGED MAN IN HIS mid-forties walked into Bill Paley's office on The Twentieth Floor to discuss prospects for a job. Bill Paley, who was almost 15 years younger, was a bit nonplussed. As he put it later, "I wasn't sure he was the man I needed. Actually I wanted someone to handle my mail and so forth; to work as my assistant."

Ed Klauber was not a mail clerk. The man who would quickly rise to become No. 2 at CBS had once been night city editor of *The New York Times* and was a stiffly formal individual, quite unlike the aggressively informal men populating the world of journalism in that era.

Klauber had come to New York from Louisville after abandoning the study of medicine to enter the "romantic" world of journalism—first at the New York *World* and then at the *Times* where his uncle had been a drama critic. Associates remember him as a German Jew who denied his Jewish ancestry.

He was so egotistical about his own writing that he would tell a reporter whose copy didn't please him to look at an Edward Klauber–bylined piece as a model of reporting. He played favorites as an editor, but was so personally unpleasant most of the time that he was often merely tolerated by the very ones he favored. He was not only stuffy —given to impeccable shirt-tie-and-jacket attire in the shirt-sleeve informality of the newsroom—but could also be cruel, taking personal delight, for instance, in selecting for a particular assignment the reporter who would be most inconvenienced by it.

Strangely enough, though, he was capable of unexpected kindnesses. When a young news assistant at the *Times* was caught swiping the expensive Ramseses cigarettes Klauber smoked at the time, Klauber asked the shaken youngster, "Why don't you ask me for them?" and from then on would offer them to the fellow.

He was also a devoted and compassionate husband. He left his night job at the *Times,* an important post, in order to spend his evenings with his wife. Years later when she was dying of cancer he cared for her lovingly, shielding her from the knowledge that her disease was fatal.

Klauber's pride in his own reporting was justified, for it was top-drawer. He labored over his assignments, nailing down elusive facts and then writing as carefully as any man could. His story on the famous Wall Street explosion at the J. P. Morgan & Co. Building—which was blamed on anarchists and killed 30 people and injured 100 more—was regarded as one of the best pieces of newspaper work of that era.

Before Klauber married his first wife, he had courted publicist Edward L. Bernays's sister-in-law. Knowing that Klauber was unhappy at the *Times* and wanted to spend more time with his wife, Bernays set about finding him a more satisfactory position. First he helped Klauber get a job as public relations director of Lennen & Mitchell, Inc., an advertising agency. But within a year Klauber tired of the work, and Bernays brought the jut-jawed Klauber into his own office. Klauber proved to be a difficult man in Bernays's small organization, so he went to his new client, Bill Paley. "I told him the truth" about Klauber, but stressed the man's exceptional executive ability and urged Paley to hire him for CBS. Klauber's reputation as a curmudgeon had preceded him. Paley had already refused to work with him at Lennen & Mitchell. But he allowed himself to be persuaded that Klauber's executive skills would make up for his prickly personality, and hired the man.

At 43, Klauber became the old man of the organization. Paley and his other top assistants were still in their twenties and early thirties. As late as 1934, when Paley worked with Jimmy Roosevelt to set up a CBS pension plan, the average age of all CBS employees was 26.

Within months, Klauber became the top assistant to CBS's young president. Paley sensed that Klauber could be an important man to him, one who could handle the daily details of administration that Bill never enjoyed.

Says Paley: "Klauber had an almost fatherly attitude toward me. He made up for some immaturity that I had. I had had little administrative experience and so had he, but he caught on very quickly. He had very good judgment and was a man of wonderful character, an excellent sense of right and wrong."

More important than his "sense of right and wrong" was the fact that Klauber had the steel to do the job. Bernays got a call from Klauber asking him to have lunch. After they met at the Berkshire, Klauber told Bernays that the CBS budget could not carry two public relations advisers—Bernays and Klauber himself, part of whose job was public relations, admittedly an odd part for such a crusty character.

Bernays was understandably upset to learn that Klauber did not intend to renew. He told Klauber that he should never have accepted the job with Paley if this was the way Klauber felt. Klauber said, "Conditions are what they are. It is unjust to saddle two public relations expenses on Columbia."

Soon after the lunch, Klauber turned around and brought in a new public relations man, T.J. Ross of the Ivy Lee firm, Bernays's chief competitor.

In those days, Bernays, a Jew, could hardly help break the ice in the WASP society of New York. Ivy Lee was well oriented to that society and represented, among others, Rockefeller interests. New York industrialists then were predominantly gentile.

Some time later, Frederick Birchall, acting managing editor of the *Times*, told Bernays: "Why didn't you call me before you had Paley hire him? I could have told you about him. Klauber used to send men on the *Times* to cover a fire on Staten Island when he knew they were about to go on their honeymoons, or to the Bronx on Christmas Eve when they had planned to decorate a Christmas tree."

From 1930 until 1943, whenever economic conditions or policy forced the network to cut back, Klauber was Paley's hatchet man. Someone in authority had to do the firing; it was just that some felt Klauber *enjoyed* it too much. On the other hand, Helen Sioussat (who was a talks director at CBS) believes Klauber was, though a "very strict disciplinarian," nevertheless quite fair. "You always knew where you stood with Klauber—always. If he found he was wrong he would apologize." And Meff Runyon, a CPA who came to CBS from Price Waterhouse as treasurer, agrees even though others remember that Klauber would often browbeat Runyon after calling in others to observe. During 1930, as the economy worsened, everyone at CBS had to take a 15 percent cut in salary, but Klauber told Runyon, "If this means the difference between eating and not eating for someone, I want to know about it." A couple of such cases referred to Klauber received interest-free loans to tide them over.

Klauber once called in young Bill Lodge, a CBS engineer he had heard was to be married soon. At the *Times* this would have had ominous overtones. But Klauber couldn't have been nicer to Lodge, giving him a "long and fatherly talk" on the care and feeding of young brides, and urging him to make an effort to understand a woman's point of view.

Yet women in business were anathema to him. He insisted that he and Paley both have male secretaries. He was "absolutely wild" when his talks director, a young executive named Edward R. Murrow, hired the fetching Helen Sioussat, who later succeeded Murrow at the job. Klauber was "rude and cross" with her until he saw her in action, telephoning cabinet members, interviewing them quietly and efficiently following the Japanese attack on Pearl Harbor.

Thereafter Klauber was solidly behind her—even when there was an outcry over a Sioussat decision from the powerful National Association of Manufacturers whose members sponsored the bulk of CBS's shows. When a NAM delegation came to Klauber's office to complain that the organization was not getting enough broadcast time on Helen's talk shows, Klauber refused to discuss the matter until he could summon Helen to the room. She came with her records arguing that the NAM demands for time were excessive. Klauber nodded, then told the delegation that it was Helen's responsibility to decide such things and the decision would stand.

Klauber loved children though he had none. Nonplussed in their presence, he tried awkwardly to show his goodwill. He once showed Meff Runyon's young son a $20 bill, asking if the lad had ever seen one before. When the boy said no, he thrust it into the boy's hand saying, "This one is yours!"

Yet Klauber's furies were monumental and could be directed against anyone, particularly a staff member who failed to measure up, even a new recruit—as Bill Fineschreiber will never forget.

Fineschreiber had applied for a job at CBS when he left Princeton in 1931. Despite the Depression, the 22-year-old had reason to feel confident. He was a summa cum laude graduate, had been on the staff of the campus newspaper, wrote for the Princeton literary magazine and still found time to excel in tennis, boxing and wrestling. In addition, Bill's father had been Paley's rabbi in Philadelphia and was a top figure in the Jewish Reform Movement. Fineschreiber understood when Paley sent him to personnel without recommendation: Paley wanted to avoid any hint of cronyism at CBS. Fineschreiber didn't need it anyway. Sent to apply for a job in the publicity department, someone gave him a release to write and he performed quickly and well. He was hired on the spot and told he would be making $45 a week, so long as he was approved by the company's No. 2 man, Edward Klauber.

Bill Fineschreiber describes what happened when he met Klauber: "He took one look at me and one at the record and bawled the bejesus out of me. 'You must think you are something—Phi Beta Kappa, BMOC, etc. As far as I am concerned you have nothing. Your one attribute is the fact that you don't know anything. You don't have anything to unlearn. Around here you will *not* be a big man on campus, but a cog in a wheel. And with your record, if you put your mind to it you may do okay.'

"With a sour expression on his face he then shook my hand and said, 'You're hired.' I left hating his guts."

His next encounter some months later with the executive vice-president of CBS was to be quite different. Philco decided to sponsor a "fascinating new musical idea." The fiery Leopold Stokowski would conduct a single movement of a symphony with the Philadelphia Orchestra on a 15-minute show in prime time. The Philco deal was "news" and Bill Fineschreiber was assigned to publicize it. He recalls: "I got Stokowski to write a statement to go into the initial release. It was written in the most amazing pidgin English. He was a great showman, but it didn't occur to me that he was doing it on purpose. I foolishly edited it.

"I went down to the Academy of Music for the final rehearsal and press conference before the opening of the show. There were all of the most important radio writers for newspapers and wire services waiting to get this big story. We were in Stokowski's dressing room. After I talked about it a bit, the maestro began to make a speech in the pidgin English he affects. I handed out the release with the edited version of his statement.

"Stokowski quietly asked, 'May I have a copy?'

"He came to the first sentence and went right through the roof. 'This is a lie. This is false. This is untrue. This is a disgrace. I will have nothing to do with this program. I will have nothing to do with CBS . . . etc.' He said he would resign from a program that would treat his stuff this way. I was twenty-two. You can imagine how I wanted to sink through the floor. I went back to my father's home on Rittenhouse Square in Philadelphia—about five blocks away. From there I immediately phoned Ed Klauber and told him I had lost a multimillion-dollar contract for CBS."

Bill was hardly ready for what followed.

"Klauber was completely understanding. He assured me that Stokowski would not run out on the contract and that this was a publicity stunt. He asked me to get a good night's sleep and to see him in the morning in New York City and not to worry.

"The next morning when I got back to the office I went up to see him. Again he was very friendly. He told me that things would come out all right. . . . A lot of executives would have fired me."

It was inevitable that there would be a confrontation sooner or later between the newspapers and radio. Even before Klauber arrived, CBS had occasionally scooped newspapers with bulletins concerning events of major importance. And in the elections of 1928, announcer Ted Husing, staying on the air from 8 P.M. to 6 A.M. and doing all compiling himself, had given the public the results well in advance of the newspapers. Even more dramatic was an event in 1930 that illustrated just how effective radio could be in giving listeners a sense of immediacy about a particular event.

It began undramatically on Monday, April 21, 1930, in the overcrowded Ohio State Penitentiary in Columbus. At 5:30 P.M. prisoners set a seemingly trifling blaze to register their discontent. Suddenly the flames were out of control, raging through four cellblocks and killing

335 convicts within an hour. Through the worst of it, a black convict known only as the Deacon (he had become deeply religious after being sent to prison for hacking his wife and mother-in-law to death) broadcast a graphic account of the holocaust from the prison's Protestant chapel which was wired into Columbus's station WARU to permit broadcasts of the prison band. WARU was affiliated with CBS and a telephone call led to a nationwide hookup and one of the most dramatic broadcasts in the short history of radio.

Listeners were transported to the prison itself, with the sound of falling timbers, sirens and shouts ringing in their ears. Through it all ran the Deacon's solemn account of the courage of his fellow prisoners, men he was proud to call his brothers.

The next day *The New York Times* carried six columns of news beginning on page one. Sandwiched into the reports farther back was a four-paragraph item on the Deacon's broadcast. The *Times* and other newspapers certainly realized that such broadcasts were potentially devastating competition.

Ed Klauber was hired four months after the Deacon's stunning broadcast. He also knew the news potential of radio, impressed it on Paley, and began assembling a staff with journalism backgrounds. As his No. 1 assistant he hired an ex–wire-service star, Paul White, a newsman down to his toes. White had a bulldog face and was as scrappy as his looks suggested. He hated getting scooped and was a good choice to carry the banner for CBS in the brewing war between press and radio.

The stock market crash of 1929 triggered the war of the media. It wasn't until that cataclysmic event that advertisers slashed their budgets and publishers became aware of just how much of the national advertising dollar was being poured into radio. Until then the conduct between the print and broadcast media had been, as described in Paul White's book *News on the Air*, "Like that of two nicely-brought-up sisters trying to attract the same man." Many newspapers in metropolitan areas issued weekly radio sections that carried advertising by set makers and "extravagantly detailed schedules." If it was a music show, for example, the tunes to be played were listed.

But after the crash, publishers adopted resolutions urging newspapers to quit listing radio schedules altogether—or, failing that, to reduce them to a level that gave barest information. White explained that a rundown of the NBC "powerhouse" of Sunday evening 1946/47 would have been listed under the bare-facts rule as follows:

> 7:00 Comedy
> 7:30 Music and Comedy
> 8:00 Comedy
> 8:30 Comedy

It would be up to the radio listener to remember that the newspaper was referring to Jack Benny, Phil Harris and Alice Faye, Charlie McCarthy and Fred Allen in that order.

The New York City Publishers Association put this bare-facts policy into effect, but competition broke the solid front. Scripps-Howard's *World Telegram* decided it could boost circulation with more informative program listings, plus a column of radio news and gossip. The public responded by buying more *World Telegrams* and the rest of the New York papers reluctantly followed the *World Telegram*'s example. But that was only one local victory for radio in the larger war between the media. The major battles were fought over news. Before broadcasting came of age, newspapers always carried the first word of important events. If the story was big enough, the papers rushed extra editions to the street. The newsboys would roam the streets shouting, "Extra! Extra! Archduke Ferdinand Shot! Europe at war! Read all about it!"

The battle was joined in earnest shortly before the 1932 presidential election. For this contest between Franklin D. Roosevelt and Herbert Hoover, Paul White and CBS were prepared to go all out, devoting the entire election evening to nothing but the results as they came in. CBS approached the United Press and obtained a contract whereby UP would supply its news service for the nominal sum of $1000. But a few days before the election, White got a call from UP President Karl A. Bickel, who said UP would have to abrogate the contract. Paul White yelled into the telephone, "I'll be right over!"

At UP headquarters in the *Daily News* Building, White argued at the top of his lungs. He threatened to sue, but Bickel called his bluff asking how White could prove any damages. White changed his tone and pleaded for mercy. But Bickel still refused. According to White, "Bickel pointed out his organization's income was derived almost wholly from newspapers and that the present temper of publishers was such that the UP would lose thousands of dollars if he permitted CBS to use the service." White left the UP offices defeated.

But then Kent Cooper, general manager of the Associated Press, not knowing that the UP-CBS contract had been canceled, offered the AP election service to both NBC and CBS for nothing, fearing that UP would get the upper hand. That broke the dam and on election night the broadcasters had all three leading services, one way or the other—UP, AP and International News Service.

But the aftermath was complete withdrawal of all the services by late spring of 1933, under heavy pressure by the newspapers. Then followed a period in which Paul White and his opposite number at NBC, A.A. Schechter, Jr., showed how the telephone, the pastepot and ingenuity —not to mention a liberal sampling of the leading newspapers—could provide broadcasters with surprisingly thorough coverage of the day's leading news stories. The telephone was the key to the effort—and still is, as any office-bound reporter will tell you even today.

The name of the game was "verification." Get a line on a story— from a ham radio operator or even from a short item in a newspaper —and use the telephone to verify it. Then, whenever possible, get a more impressive yarn. Beat the newspapers on their own stories. A call from CBS saying, "This is the office of H.V.Kaltenborn" or at NBC, "This is Lowell Thomas's office calling," and a reluctant but flattered official would open up.

Disastrous floods in Peru? The newspapers had reported that, but they had no details. Who's on the scene with radio equipment? Pan Am. A call to Pan Am's publicity director put New York in touch with the Lima airport by shortwave radio relayed through Texas. Result: a scoop for radio with full details. Lowell Thomas did it that time, but CBS would the next. Paul White gritted his teeth and tried harder.

But this was a makeshift effort. Thus when General Mills came to CBS in the summer of 1933, wanting to know if CBS could organize a radio news service of its own, the food company found the network enthusiastic. If the costs of the service were $3000 or less a week, General Mills would pay half and become the sponsor.

Klauber and White responded quickly. Within a month the Columbia News Service was organized on a remarkably complete basis, and the end of the war begun by the publishers was in sight.

What the publishers had overlooked was a simple economic fact. If there is a demand for a product in a competitive society, that demand, barring monopoly, will be met. And there was no monopoly on the news. CBS turned to the offbeat news sources and was able to get comprehensive coverage. It purchased the Dow-Jones ticker service, which gave much Washington news in addition to financial news. CBS also bought the reports of Exchange Telegraph, a British news agency that had worldwide coverage. CBS opened bureaus in New York, Washington, Chicago and Los Angeles, and managers of these bureaus soon lined up correspondents in every United States city with more than 20,000 population.

CBS commentators H.V.Kaltenborn and Boake Carter were well supplied by the new CBS news-gathering organization. News shows were broadcast each weekday. Sometimes the news agencies would beat CBS by several hours. And on occasion CBS beat the agencies. The New York newspapers turned their backs on a major forest fire in the Pacific Northwest. CBS covered it night after night until it finally became front-page news in the East.

Perhaps the greatest flattery came from low-budget newspapers that were straining to pay for the leading wire services; at least three newspapers asked CBS to sell its service to them. CBS refused this opportunity and thus avoided war on a new front. However, the American Newspaper Publishers Association campaigned with some success to get major newspapers to drop program listings of local CBS affiliates. This hurt the network's advertising efforts vis-à-vis NBC which, by and large, managed to keep its listings.

Before the situation became more serious, Frank Mason, a former Hearst executive and then a vice-president of NBC, arranged a series of radio-press peace conferences. Paul White explains the temper of the meetings that followed: "You could tell from the start that these were peace conferences—because of the warlike attitude of all the participants."

But the war was recognized as futile on all sides. Pacts were signed limiting radio news reports and providing for detailed program information in the newspapers. But the demand for full radio news and program information brought ultimate victory to radio.

Ed Klauber set about to develop a newspaper mentality in the studio —refusing to allow advertisers to direct which items were news and how they should be covered. In World War II, CBS would have one of the most comprehensive news services in the world. It would feature such world-famed correspondents as Edward R. Murrow and Eric Sevareid. And the impetus for this growth and prominence was due largely to a strong-willed newsman named Edward Klauber.

CHAPTER 4
Elegant Puffery

THERE WAS A CURIOUS DUALITY AT CBS IN THE EARLY YEARS. ON THE one hand it was necessary to appear earnest and settled. This small team of young men had to convince older men running long-established companies that radio advertising was a sound business investment. On the other hand they also needed youthful dynamism and brashness to compete with the much richer and far more powerful NBC networks. Often the brashness got the upper hand, and stunts were pulled that would have won the admiration of P. T. Barnum.

It was New Year's Day, 1930, and King George V was to speak at the opening of the London Five-Power Naval Disarmament Conference. CBS and other broadcasters in the United States had pooled resources to bring Americans a history-making live broadcast from across the Atlantic. Aired in England in the late morning, the king's remarks would be heard in America at 5 A.M. New York time via trans-Atlantic cable.

A CBS promotion man, Robert Taplinger, remembers traveling to 485 Madison Avenue in the predawn darkness and seeing light after light flicker on as New Yorkers rose to hear the broadcast. The question Taplinger had been mulling was how to get publicity for CBS when NBC was airing the exact same broadcast. The answer came in the form of an unexplained three-second gap in the king's speech.

An enterprising reporter for the New York *Telegram*, sensing there might be a story in the brief dead air time, asked CBS for an explanation. Taplinger had no idea of the true answer but he wasn't about to argue with the reporter's news instinct.

CBS had just moved to Madison Avenue and the studio control boards were a mass of temporarily installed wires. So the promotion man showed the reporter the tangled wires and explained that a cable had parted. A CBS engineer saw it happen, Taplinger explained, and realized a heroic act was called for to bring in the king, so he grasped the hot cable in his hand and the broadcast resumed. Who was that self-sacrificing engineer? Taplinger quickly reviewed the engineer roster in his mind to pick the one whose courage would be most appreciated. Why, it was Vivian Ruth, a Canadian and loyal subject of the king, he decided. The next morning, the *Telegram* had an exclusive page-one story, and the rest of the papers played it big in catch-up accounts.

The CBS "hero" lived in Woodside, Queens. Before the reporters could track him down, Taplinger sent a doctor to get a bandage on Ruth's hand. Ruth, a simple, honest man, was aghast. He kept saying he hadn't done anything, but the reporters naturally took this for modesty.

The story grew bigger. Children in Canada began collecting dimes to help pay medical bills for the injured engineer. The bewildered Ruth grew more and more distressed. Finally, he disappeared, never to return to CBS.

Meanwhile, the story had crossed the Atlantic and was carried in the British press. The king read about it and wanted to show his appreciation, but Vivian Ruth was unavailable so he chose to honor the president of this young and enterprising new radio network.

Three months later, Taplinger recalls, an apprehensive William Paley took a train to Washington, D.C., to receive an award from the British ambassador. It was an engraved gold watch. Paley may have been embarrassed, but he accepted it.

Joining CBS a few months later to head its promotion department was a young man who picked up the network's brash spirit and added to it a surpassing touch of elegance. Paul Kesten had an extraordinary intelligence, superior intuition and a zest for life. He was a writer with a shrewd, practical turn of mind and his mastery of words, figures and promotional schemes soon gave CBS a stature that belied its frailty.

Kesten was from Milwaukee, of Welsh and German ancestry. Though confident of his intellect, he occasionally felt self-conscious about not having finished college. He was brought to CBS by Ed Klauber who had been impressed with the younger man during a brief tenure in an ad agency where Kesten was a hot copywriter.

With bulging, slightly froglike eyes, Kesten bore a resemblance to Socrates. He was not handsome, but he was a striking man. Physically sensitive, he could not bear the smell of a cigarette smoldering in an ashtray. A fastidious dresser, he cared about the right tie, the proper billow to his pocket handkerchief, to the point of eccentricity. A visitor to his office might be surprised to see his reflection in the soles of Kesten's shoes, if the executive put his feet on the desk as he sometimes did. For Kesten kept a special pair of shoes for office use only, and the soles were as highly polished as the tops.

At CBS Kesten blended his writing facility with a grasp of statistics. Only a poet with an understanding of math could write a phrase like "The pale stare of decimals."

Before the end of 1930 Kesten hired an assistant who became a faithful protégé, a coconspirator in outrageous promotion schemes and interoffice politics, and eventually, Kesten's successor as promotion chief. Victor Ratner, brilliant but undisciplined, seemed the antithesis of his boss. Ratner had rough edges. He was anything but a clothes horse; he dressed carelessly, was even unkempt. For years he affected a long cigar and Groucho Marx mustache, consciously modeling his appearance after the comedian. Like Groucho, Victor was given to cutting remarks: "The whine of sour grapes" and "Marriage is seeing a bit too much of somebody you enjoy seeing a great deal," a sentiment that didn't endear him to his then wife.

Ratner worshiped Kesten and would "gladly have cut off" his right arm for him. He was, nevertheless, objective about him as he was about everything. Speaking of Kesten's gift for writing promotional copy, Ratner remarked, "Kesten had a gift for making shit sound classy." And describing Kesten's particular style of originality, he said: "There are two kinds of brilliance—Einstein's, the kind that resulted in ideas nobody else could have thought of; and Kesten's. Kesten would come up with ideas that nobody had ever thought of before but were nevertheless so evident, once expressed, that others would say the ideas were obvious."

Ratner shared with Kesten a cynicism for the manipulative arts of advertising and promotion. In late 1973, a year before he died of a heart attack, Ratner expressed his attitude in an interview in which he described an encounter he had with a dyed-in-the-wool advertising man late in his career.

I had recently joined Benton & Bowles as a fifty-thousand-dollar-a-year V.P. and was alone in an office with Bill Baker, a principal of the ad agency. He insisted on reading something aloud to me from a newly published study of the advertising business, *Madison Avenue, U.S.A.* by Martin Mayer. Its opening pages quote some verbatim (but anonymous) autobiographical reports by successful practitioners, each telling how he found his way, when young, into the art of selling other people's products. Bill was so indignant about one of these he felt impelled to share it with someone. He read it to me:

I came from a professional family; at the age of five I was told I was going to be a surgeon. . . . At the age of fourteen I rebelled; I ran away to sea. . . .
[Later] I went to college but couldn't finish and in my family not finishing college was worse than having a venereal disease. (My father was a doctor, as my three brothers were to become.)
In my twenties I had what I guess was a nervous breakdown. I worked as a shipping clerk, and was the worst shipping clerk in New York. At twenty-four I suddenly thought—I don't know why—I'll go into advertising. Advertising can use my virtues (I had always been verbal) and tolerate my vices.
Only a few years ago I realized that what I had done was to run away (again) to something I did not think was significant. What advertising meant to me was simply that I was not being a doctor. I could work at it because I couldn't respect it. . . .

As Bill sourly read on, I could only hope my best poker face hadn't cracked, particularly when he came to the end and looked up at me to add: "Isn't it awful, Vic, to have people like that in advertising?" Not for one instant did he suspect that it was *my* story.

Kesten and Ratner had become associates almost by accident. Ratner had been out of work for four months in late 1930. Kesten had been looking for an assistant and had run an ad in *Printers' Ink* that brought in hundreds of letters from promotion men idled by the Depression.

Ratner reasoned that he hardly stood a chance with an orthodox approach in the midst of so much competition. He decided that the easiest way to make an impression would be to do something different rather than try to be the best. He later told the story:

"I walked in and saw this dapper kind of elegant man somewhat older than I. I was about twenty-eight, he about thirty-one. I had determined to take a chance. Earlier, I had written a poem for my sister-in-law's obscenity party in San Francisco. She was going to have douche bags and condoms hanging all around the place and she wanted me to write something appropriately obscene to read at the party."

Victor's poem, *Rhapsodia Sexualis,* began with an Invocation, "O holy Muse of Hole and Cock . . ."

The poem read, in part: "The lovely day, four hours before/ Had slid away, soft as a villain's smile. . . . / Sleek whores clayed their faces. . . . / Maisy, the regularly menstruating/ Nothing-to-worry about virgin. . . . / John, multiplicable, humped beneath the blanket/ Arches his back into a sickly curve, rubs and rubs/ The dull projecting stick. . . . / Maisy's unknown breasts and restless skin/ Comes to him like a gauzy dream. . . . / A jingling of loose nerves, a thick spitting, and John sleeps./ In John's room the ancient smell of goats hangs drearily, and fades."

Ratner showed Kesten the poem as a sample of his work, taking a wild chance that Kesten wasn't a prude. Ratner later learned that Kesten never used coarse language himself, and was always extremely courteous. (Once he took three months trying to relocate his secretary within CBS; he couldn't stand her, but he was incapable of firing her.) Kesten, however, wasn't offended by the vulgar poem.

"This odd man evidently saw something in the writing that he liked," Ratner recalled. "I was hired at seventy-five dollars a week and we started out our relationship on something larger than a strictly business basis."

Ratner found Kesten very hard to please, though he had a "marvelous" way of concealing his negative reactions. Unlike Ed Klauber, Kesten was so sensitive to other people's feelings that Ratner thought him a "concealed neurotic." Ratner explained Kesten's style:

"People would come to Kesten with copy or a layout. He would never say what he thought of it. He would say, 'Hmmm. Interesting . . . How

53

about doing this?' One of our artists came in one day with a layout and Kesten began his 'How about this? How about that?' routine and finally wound up redoing the entire layout without the guy ever feeling it.

"After the artist left the office, Kesten said to me, 'Wasn't that layout terrible?' My heart sank because I realized he had done it to me on occasion. I used to go away from similar encounters thinking that I had come close.

"On the other hand, even after Kesten moved up and I was named head of promotion, I would come in and he'd redo so much of my work that I would walk out with my tail between my legs.

"But this is how you learn: apprenticed to a master. After a while I began to catch on. He taught me the rhythm of a sentence. He would spend two hours to get the right word. He got a genuine inner joy out of excellence, about something being right. He loved it. It took me four years to begin to please Kesten. Then one day, he finally said, 'Gee, Vic, that stinks.' At that moment I had a wonderful sense of being accepted; a great sense of euphoria."

The two men operated on the old advertising theory that things are not so much what they are in fact, but rather what they seem to be. And they succeeded in creating an image for CBS that won the network advertising rates 10 to 15 percent higher than it deserved in terms of its ability to deliver listeners.

In comparing statistical listener studies between CBS and NBC, Kesten would use every conceivable device to aid the cause. When he ran two-page magazine ads showing how CBS compared with the competition, NBC's best figures had a way of ending up in the hard-to-read "gutter" between pages.

Another approach was taken in an early double-page ad in *Fortune* magazine. It showed actor Leslie Howard as Hamlet, standing on a stone step, with the area around him and most of the rest of the two pages solid black. There was a quote from Hamlet: "The air bites shrewdly." The copy told how radio brought the world together, making one community of the nation. Signed: Columbia Broadcasting System.

Another Kesten effort was a promotion piece titled, "The Added Increment." It was typical in its graceful use of language conveying a message that captured the essence of radio as a sales medium.

A man wakes, restless, in the dark. Instinctively, he reaches toward the table at the side of his bed—his fingers, without faltering, lift the lid of a square box, remove a cigarette, carry it to his lips. The dark is briefly broken as he lights it.

He has done it before—soothed his nerves this way in the night. That box of cigarettes is always on that table. Its place is habitual. His reaching toward it is a habit. Remove that box from the table, and the habit is broken—the smoker must grope and search. . . .

Your secretary writes the letter you have dictated. Her eyes follow her notes—her fingers spell the words without a glance at the keys.

She has done that before—over and over again. Her fingers have learned habits—because each key is always in the same *place.*

Change the *place* of one key—and you will get misspelled letters for a week. . . .

PLACE

—is a powerful factor in people's lives—in their habits.

There is another powerful factor in their lives and habits, a still more powerful factor—the factor of:

TIME

Time makes one man hungry at 12 o'clock, and another man hungry at 1:00. Time wakes one man at 6:30 in the morning, and lets another sleep until 8:00—because each has made a habit for years of rising at a certain hour. . . .

Time makes people catch trains, punch clocks, meet friends—because time, in this country more than any other, dominates the daily, personal habits of 130,000,000 people.

Most advertising, printed or painted, exists in:

SPACE

Only radio advertising exists in:

TIME

On this one basic distinction hinges another and still more important distinction . . . self evident as soon as it is stated.

Space advertising, by its very nature, whether magazine or newspaper, cannot exploit, except feebly, the

TIME HABITS
of the public

You can buy a preferred position on the back cover of every magazine in the country, and get *some* extra attention. But that position
becomes only a place-habit for yourselves—it becomes no part of the
habits of the public. You cannot make it comparable to the box of
cigarettes on the table in the dark, or the fixed keys of a typewriter.
. . . Nor can you make people *look* for your printed advertisements,
eagerly, personally, regularly. Their contact with your advertising is,
at best, accidental.

But you can buy a certain time on the air and make your radio
program a vital, personal habit—animate and intimate—in the lives
of millions of listeners. You can make it a habit almost as regular as
the habit of hunger, the habit of waking, the habit of clock-punching
and train-catching. More than that, you can make your radio program a conscious habit, a pleasure-habit, in their lives. When you
have done this, you have completed the contrast between time and
space advertising. You have made people turn to your advertising
voluntarily. You have made their contact with it regular instead of
spasmodic. You have made it a *habit* instead of an accident. . . .

And when a radio program has been on the air long enough, and
successfully enough, to have become a daily, personal listening-habit
among millions of families, we submit that it is then a two-fold, or
five-fold, or ten-fold better investment for its sponsor than it was
when it started. . . .

The advertiser's franchise upon a given period, on a certain night
or nights, then becomes, in reality, a franchise on a segment of the
lives of millions of consumers—a franchise on their attention and
their interest in the intimacy of their own homes. . . .

Kesten and Ratner knew, however, that they couldn't rely on pretty
prose to persuade advertisers. They decided early on that statistics were
the most convincing kind of material. The two promotion men were
constantly making the case for CBS in terms of tabulated listener
responses—whenever they could get them. Statistics were little understood then, and lent themselves to chicanery. It was almost inevitable
that these two men who shared an amused view of the world's foibles
would eventually experiment as "creatively" with statistics as they did
with words.

One of the earliest statistical surveys of radio and advertising was
originated by Robert Elder, a professor of marketing at MIT. Elder had
his students poll Boston citizens by postcard to find out what products
they purchased. He then correlated product use with radio commercials

the people surveyed listened to and found that people with radios used more products advertised on radio. He sent his findings to Kesten who was, of course, delighted with the Boston results. He commissioned Elder to do a similar study in ten cities.

But Kesten and Ratner were also wary. Suppose it turned out that radio didn't pull in the other cities the way it did in Boston? As Elder sent his cards out to the ten cities, Ratner and a secretary spent an evening marking identical survey cards as though they were responding, adding brand names of products they learned of through radio—especially products advertised on CBS. The bogus cards were carried to the ten cities so that they would bear appropriate postmarks. The two men did it, says Ratner, with no sense of guilt at all. "It was fun and games. We felt confident we were going to get the right result, but we wanted to be sure."

The survey completed, Kesten traveled to Boston to meet with Elder. He walked into the office and faced a stern-faced professor with two stacks of cards. Elder had carefully separated the valid responses from the faked ones.

Ratner and the secretary were sure they had done their job carefully. Neither Ratner nor Kesten could guess how Elder had been able to pick out every single faked card, and they never did find out. But Kesten was on the spot. He would have to account for the discrepancy and at the same time protect CBS from the threat of exposure.

Thinking quickly, Kesten professed to be as indignant as Elder, telling the professor that the bogus cards had to be the work of a moonlighter. The company, he said, had hired the man to work nights because—it was important that Elder not check with the head of research—this moonlighter was to replace the head of research, who hadn't yet been told he was through. Kesten added that the moonlighter had a tubercular sister and, apparently, in his zeal to curry favor and clinch the new job he must have done this utterly immoral and senseless thing—jeopardizing CBS's reputation in the process.

He asked to use Elder's telephone, got Ratner on the line and told him in icy fury about the moonlighter's obvious perfidy. The bewildered Ratner began to catch on as Kesten fed him the clues. Then the CBS promotion chief demanded that Ratner obtain a detailed, notarized confession from the culprit, explaining why he did it.

Kesten hung up and looked at the cards with regret. "We've got to throw the whole thing out, of course," he said. "CBS wouldn't touch it."

Elder, who had his own stake in the study, sensibly said, "No, we don't have to throw it all out," picking up the bogus cards, "only these."

Kesten allowed himself to be persuaded—he knew from Elder that the valid cards proved the point they had set out to make.

Meanwhile, back in New York, Ratner in his role of nonexistent moonlighter wrote the story of a man with a sister who was on her deathbed. The confession accounted for the fact that his immediate superior didn't know about him. Ratner put it in affidavit form and headed for the Waldorf Astoria to have it notarized. After the notary had put his seal on the document, Ratner reached into his pocket and found he didn't have money to pay the man.

Would the notary accept a check? Of course—Ratner looked honest. He wrote out the check. Then, just before signing it, he realized he would have to pen "Victor Ratner" on the bottom line. Embarrassed, he excused himself, went back to 485 Madison Avenue and got the money for the notary.

Years after the Elder episode, the research man, John Karol, who was supposedly being undercut by the nonexistent moonlighter, ran into Professor Elder and got into a long conversation. Later, he said to Ratner, "What is this strange story Elder mentioned to me—something about a man who worked for us at night years ago?"

Ratner hesitated before answering, then decided there was just no way. "I never heard it."

Kesten and Ratner never again attempted outright fabrication of a listener survey, but that was mainly because they had marvelous statistical stories to tell that were mostly true. This was even more the case after they hired a young professor named Frank Stanton and taught him how to transform his pure research into a sales weapon.

If Frank Stanton, a vain but shy Ohio State University industrial psychologist, had realistically weighed his chances in the commercial world in 1935, he might never have left academe and pointed his Model A Ford toward New York City. He headed for CBS where his

Ph.D. dissertation—"A Critique of Present Methods and a New Plan for Studying Radio Listening Behavior"—had come to the attention of Paul Kesten who had sent him a very flattering telegram: "I don't know of any other organization where your background and experience would count so heavily in your favor or where your talents would find so enthusiastic a reception. . . ." Stanton accepted a $55-a-week offer from the network.

Like any sensible young man during the Depression, Stanton wasn't looking for fancy accommodations that first night in New York. The blond, blue-eyed son of a Muskegon, Michigan, manual-training instructor located a Y.M.C.A., parked the Model A and checked in.

Stanton, though gifted, was a somewhat colorless man of plodding habits and dogged tenacity. A thoroughgoing pedagogue, with what amounted to a reverence for the sanctity of pure research, he could hardly have been prepared for the two cynical molders of public opinion who welcomed him to his new job.

At the time Stanton joined them, Kesten and Ratner were still busy inventing schemes to help CBS project a leadership image over its towering competition, NBC. They quickly pressed Stanton into service. Almost nobody in network radio apart from Kesten and Ratner cared anything about who was listening to what and why. Thus Stanton was a find—a man who could provide quality grist for the propaganda mill. If he only would.

Frank was flabbergasted to learn that his new associates—who seemed like nice people—weren't the slightest bit interested in the truth with a capital T.

Ratner explained what happened:

Like any advocates, we weren't looking for the facts as such, but for the facts that would make the best case for CBS. We were perfectly willing to tell a whopping lie if we could get away with it.

In time, an interesting thing happened to Frank psychologically. He began looking for data that could be used by salesmen. It was quite a different thing from looking for data showing the facts as they really were.

Frank said a year or two later that he could never go back to honest research again. He had been corrupted like us. He had been an academic, he said, and we had turned him into a salesman.

In time, Stanton would urge those who worked for him, "Don't buy it, sell it." By that he meant, don't write a presentation that you yourself believe in, but a presentation that will sell the customer.

Stanton, once converted, may have been the hardest-working "salesman" in CBS history. From the outset he put in 12 to 14 hours a day at CBS. He neglected his wife, Ruth, who had been his high school sweetheart, as many broadcast executives working so hard inevitably do. Though divorce plagues the higher echelons of the industry, Stanton and his wife remained loyal to each other.

Some speculated that Frank Stanton put all his energies into the job because he was both ambitious and unsure of himself intellectually: "He couldn't count on being brilliant," an early associate said. This assessment would surprise many who knew him well at the height of his career and regarded him as one of the most secure of human beings —something of a renaissance man with the broadest possible interests and an intellectual capacity to match.

But Victor Ratner believed Frank Stanton was a "frightened man" who couldn't bear to have brilliant people around him. Ratner insisted that Stanton was frightened because he recognized himself as incapable of leadership, and saw himself rather as the ideal No. 2 man, sort of a "Swiss hotel clerk" who carried out the decisions of the sage hotel owner. Ratner said: "Stanton knows all the literature and all the facts in the field, but he cannot think innovatively. The woods are full of guys like that. Some called him brilliant because he knew so many facts. Frank can follow a formula as well as anyone, but when someone departs from the formula it scares the hell out of him."

By contrast, said Ratner, Bill Paley in the early days was a bon vivant who played as much as possible and never invested much visible effort, even in decisions involving millions of dollars and great risks. (Curiously, in later years, Bill Paley would find it necessary to keep longer hours—whenever Frank Stanton was in town.)

While Frank Stanton toiled, Ratner continued, Bill Paley did not have to. Quick decisions seemed to rule with him; everything came easy to Paley. In contrast to Stanton, Paley reveled in the brilliance of others.

Paley would get guys like Stanton to do the administrative detail work. And he was courageous where Stanton was meek. Paley dared to make mistakes. He was so successful overall that his mistakes were smothered in profits.

Don't be misled, though, Paley could be tough. He always got very hard-nosed when profits fell off—though he left it to Frank to do the firing when that became necessary.

Stanton's life represents the fruits of enormous effort. Paley's, the luck of the draw. He happened to get into broadcasting where his tastes as a lay person were of great value. Stanton cared little about entertainers. Paley was enormously sensitive to creative talent—whether entertainers or people within the organization. Paley's decisions were fast and perceptive. The earth-bound Stanton, meanwhile, worked far into the night and worried about the future.

Stanton eventually learned how to blend public relations with statesmanship in representing the broadcast industry. Paley had that sense from the beginning. On May 13, 1935, for instance, Paley announced, in response to heavy attacks on CBS for its many laxative commercials, that henceforth laxatives and other products involving "questions of good taste" would be banned. The policy would take effect as quickly as "present commitments" to clients expired. CBS was widely praised —even by the FCC which congratulated Paley on his "wise leadership." But there were believed to be relatively few radio listeners in the summer months and as a consequence many sponsors left the air. The laxative makers saw that by exercising renewal options in their contracts —by staying on the air in the summer and helping CBS stem the exodus of summer sponsors—they could continue to advertise on CBS indefinitely. Thus Paley and CBS not only drew considerable praise for statesmanship but also had one of the best laxative years in history. Eventually, the laxative ban was simply forgotten.

Whether Ratner's assessment of Stanton as a Swiss hotel clerk was right or wrong, Stanton was initially apprehensive about his prospects. At a time when Stanton was feeling particularly inadequate, he assumed that a meeting scheduled with Kesten had been set to announce his dismissal. Instead, Kesten offered him the promotion that sent him on his way toward the top.

Stanton made an impression on Paley shortly after he was named head of research. In a rare conversation with his underling, Paley asked

61

what Stanton was doing in research. Says Gerhart Wiebe, once a Stanton aide, "Stanton pulled out a pack of five-by-eight cards, each one with a project neatly outlined on it. He then started reviewing the projects for Paley. It was a kind of ho-hum question by Paley and he was bowled over by the answer. Stanton didn't have to shoot from the hip because he was always ready. Paley must have been impressed with him from that moment."

Some say "Little Annie" epitomized Frank Stanton. Little Annie is the program-analysis system developed by Frank Stanton in 1937 with Dr. Paul Lazarsfeld of Columbia University. It has had as big an influence on the daily lives of Americans as instant coffee. And both have played a role in watering down our culture. Frank Stanton dismisses Little Annie with a touch of embarrassment as of no importance to his career.

Little Annie arose out of the need to gauge the probable appeal of radio shows and is now used for TV. It is supposed to answer the question: "How big an audience will this show be likely to draw and will it therefore be commercial—salable to a sponsor?"

Stanton's "analyzer" calls for a small screening room with about a dozen seats spaced evenly before a long table. Each location has a pair of push buttons, which are wired to a central recording device. CBS pulls in people from tourist centers in Los Angeles and New York and flatters them by asking if they would like to help pick the shows the nations' viewers will watch on CBS. The participants sit at the table, their left hands on the red buttons, their right hands on the green. They watch pilot shows on the screen and are asked to give their push-button reactions. Anything the viewer deplores gets the red button, anything he particularly likes gets the green button. The responses are graphed on the control-room board where a network observer watches.

The mechanical exercise is followed up with a questionnaire asking whether the viewers liked or disliked the show, its major episodes, characters, etc. Then the network man conducts a seminar, probing in greater depth the sample viewers' likes and dislikes. For each of its pilots, CBS collects the opinions of about 80 panelists, and the monitor summarizes the findings in a report running about a dozen pages.

Not so long ago Robert Goldfarb, a young man affecting a corncob pipe and long black hair, wrote the reports. He explains:

My boss, Jay Eliasberg, has likened this job to selecting an animal for the zoo, an animal you know people will want to see. The zoo keepers tell me that they've already got an animal with legs like tree trunks and a skinny tail and a nose that picks up fruit, and people come to see that animal. They want more animals like that. I can't see the new animals; I must rely on other people's vision. So I ask the other people about some new animal, and they tell me it's got rough skin and it's skinny like a snake and it's gray and it's like a wall, and I say, "Hey, that's an elephant!" and I go to the program department and I say, "You've got a winner. . . ."

[Little Annie] defies a hundred marketing rules. . . . It's lousy research. The sample stinks, it's not representative of any group. It's not large enough. People view in an unnatural situation. The way they register their opinions is unnatural. You can go on and on and show why it shouldn't work. But it works—our batting average is 85 percent.

It works, Goldfarb and Eliasberg believe, because of the men who run it. But still, it's Frank Stanton's Little Annie that rules.

In the 1930s, while the country was in the Depression, CBS was piling up record profits. The company was still young and growing, free of the kind of internecine struggle that so often characterizes corporate life. A sense of adventure and a unity of purpose permeated the offices at 485 Madison.

Typical was the kind of effort Victor Ratner, the promotion whiz, and Frank Stanton, the superb researcher, put forth on joint projects. Toward the end of 1937 Ratner and Stanton were working every day including holidays doing sales presentations with crisis deadline schedules. As Ratner remembered it,

Frank would put together this marvelous research and I would sell the shit out of it. . . . At the time, Liggett & Myers had four half-hours on CBS—all their radio advertising. They were talking about moving some of that to NBC. Paley and Kesten went down to convince them not to do it. Paley is a great salesman and so is Kesten. At the last minute, to keep L&M from making the decision that Friday afternoon before Labor Day weekend, Kesten asked them to allow us to make a presentation in their offices at eight A.M. Tuesday morning. It was a sheer delaying tactic.

Coming back in the cab, Kesten said to Paley, "You know, Vic and Frank have been going awfully hard. They'll have to work over the holiday weekend."

Paley said, "Okay, let's forget it, then. We don't want to kill them." It was a wonderful gesture by Paley—"Forget it"—but he must have known Kesten would tell me about it. Of course, when Paul told me the story, I said, "Hell, we'll do it." Frank and I had to figure everything out and prepare the charts, etc. We were at it all through the weekend. We finished at seven A.M. Tuesday morning after working all through the night. I delivered the presentation to Kesten at seven-thirty A.M. For the life of me I can't think what the hell the arguments were that we thought up. But Paul and Bill took it to L&M and they saved the time, all of it.

Some personal jealousies were bound to emerge. The main one at CBS in the 1930s was between Kesten and Ed Klauber. An occasional shaft was launched from the promotion department at the office of the executive vice-president, but not so much as part of a power struggle as an impish exercise in deflating pomposity. For Kesten and his No. 1 ally, Ratner, were so full of energy they couldn't leave the sober-sided Klauber alone.

As the old man of the shop and a victim of his own personality, Klauber harbored insecurities. He bowed to the hypocrisies of his trade despite his stiff demeanor. Though CBS served all the major cigarette makers—Camels, Philip Morris, Lucky Strike and Chesterfield—Klauber at that time smoked only Camels. Each morning his secretary would get out a new package of each brand of cigarettes, remove the contents and put Camels in all of them. Klauber could then offer sponsor-visitors the appropriate brand from a packet on the table and then haul out the same package for himself and smoke the Camels inside.

Frank Stanton says that Klauber cried over the fact that Paley, though he respected Klauber, would not accept him socially. Klauber compensated by placing a high premium on the perks of power—including his right to put down aides. According to Ratner, "Klauber was full of tricks to emphasize how important he was. Everyone else was young and didn't give a shit about things like that."

Once Kesten wanted to give Ratner a $25-a-week raise. In those early days every raise was subject to Klauber's approval. Klauber did not okay the raise, though Ratner was clearly underpaid, working nights and weekends.

Klauber wanted to use the occasion to show Kesten how to handle such situations. Klauber would get Ratner to "volunteer" to forgo the raise for the good of the organization in those troubled times. But Ratner—with Kesten's connivance—was determined not to be manipulated. He hadn't asked for the raise, but that wasn't the point. He wasn't going to let Klauber accomplish his goal.

I had taken my cue from *The Gadfly*, a romantic book about the illegitimate son of a priest and [about] Italian politics in the nineteenth century. The gadfly is a gadfly against the church, a skillful, hard-hitting journalist during the fight for Italy's independence. He is captured and tied down in prison. His father, an archbishop, comes to see him. The archbishop is torn between saving his son, getting him free, and the damage that will do to the church if he admits a bastard. He says to the son, "What shall I do?" and the gadfly says, "This is your decision, don't ask me to make it for you."

Klauber called me in, the general summoning the corporal. We talked for an hour on this thing. I'm being stubborn and having fun. Finally he said, "What do you think?" I said, "Mr. Klauber, I can't make that decision for you. I can't guarantee what this will do to my morale." He said, "Okay," gave me the raise and sent me out of the office.

This was only the first of several encounters with Klauber over money. Ratner continued:

By 1936 when CBS was booming and I was working my ass off doing sales presentations, I woke up to the fact that I was the second man in the department and only making six thousand dollars a year. Kesten was getting twenty-two. I thought I was being underpaid and so did Kesten.

Everything I did at CBS was a game that I—and Kesten—played against everybody else. We thought they were so stupid. We spent hours gossiping about the others.

I decided to write a memo to Klauber—not to Kesten. I have never lost a memo battle in my life. I really work on them—like advertising copy. I did this memo with Kesten's connivance. He had probably said, "Klauber will have to okay this, I can't."

So I wrote this memo saying how long I had been there and how hard I had worked and how successful CBS was. I surrounded it with cotton batting, but I indicated I was being exploited by CBS. When Klauber read it, he was absolutely furious. He considered the affront important enough to take to Paley. Paley read the memo and said, "I guess Vic's right."

Klauber called me in and gave me a dressing down for writing this type of memo—how indiscreet, how bad. He gave me the lecture even though he couldn't stop the raise.

The funny thing that happened was that at just about that point, Kesten moved up and they made me the head of the promotion department and raised me to ten thousand. But I was conscious of the fact that Kesten had been getting twenty-two thousand in that job. Kesten said to do some work and then raise the issue. I had argued for ten thousand as second man in the department and I wanted at least twelve as department head.

Everybody was surprised—and that includes me—as to how much I had learned from Kesten. Kesten had been doing most of the print stuff and I did the sales presentations. I couldn't begin to compete with Kesten on print. My soul backed up at the thought. But I managed. . . . Kesten had been training me for five years.

At some point, I wrote Klauber a memo and said I wanted fifteen thousand dollars. Then we had another Klauber meeting. He gives me another dressing down saying he's not going to have a pistol put to his head by anybody. He conceded that an outsider would have to be paid thirty-five thousand—because the job was worth that when well done.

He was trying to harness me—I was a colt. He told me how much they appreciated me. I said, "Mr. Klauber, the only way a corporation can show love is money." He said, "We are going to give you what we have decided to give you and I won't tell you what it is."

I got my check the first of the year and it turned out that they had given me the fifteen thousand dollars I had asked for. But Klauber wouldn't give me the satisfaction of telling me at the meeting. He was more concerned with putting me down. He was making something like eighty thousand dollars at the time.

Ratner had still another encounter with Klauber over money, but this time he was arguing for a man whose attitude in the early years was quite different from his own. Frank Stanton never asked for a raise but waited for it to be awarded to him. It was 1940 and Stanton was director of research, reporting to Ratner as promotion chief. The radio business was increasing geometrically, and Ratner's department had gone from 20 to 80 people in five years. Anytime a new advertiser came along, Ratner and Stanton would work up a new presentation to persuade the advertiser to come to CBS rather than NBC. Ratner remembers that he and Stanton worked every holiday—Christmas, New Year's, Fourth of July, until, he says,

I decided to leave, though I had no other job. I was fed up with tension. In the summer of 1940, Kesten was away for a month's vacation and I had to work directly with Klauber. I came home to my wife and said, "I'm thinking about leaving CBS." She said, "Why not?"

I had the green light, then, but I didn't want anybody to think there was anything funny about my leaving—I wanted them to know that it had been my decision. I spent a month writing my 165-page letter of resignation. I told why I was leaving, what was wrong with CBS and what was right about the promotion department.

Frank Stanton would sit and help me write it. That same month, Frank was offered a job at A.C. Nielsen. They offered him a five-year contract at forty-five thousand dollars a year in 1940 to come there and develop a whole rating system. . . . He was making fifteen thousand and I was getting twenty-one.

Stanton loved CBS and never thought he'd consider leaving his job for money alone. But, still, forty-five thousand dollars . . .

I was in a quandary, being his friend and also feeling some obligation to hold Frank for CBS. So he and I kept talking about it . . . whether to go or not. I was giving him all the freedom he wanted. He was very tempted, especially because I was going—we were very close then. I decided that the only way CBS could hold Stanton was to give him five thousand more a year without strings. A hell of a jump in those days.

I said, "I think I can get you a five-thousand-dollar increase." He said, "You're crazy." I went to see Klauber and explained the situation saying CBS might lose Frank over the weekend and that I wanted the authority to give him the five-thousand increase if I felt I needed to do so to hold him.

Klauber liked Frank very much. Frank had an immaculate technique for handling people around him. In any case, Klauber thought very highly of him. He asked me if I would mind Frank making twenty thousand when I was only making twenty-one. The thought had never occurred to me. I said, "Of course not." He authorized me to use it if I had to.

It was a kind of game. I was playing it with their chips. I came down and said, "Frank, you've got a five-thousand-dollar raise." He turned green. That's what kept him. It was a five-year contract with Nielsen . . . I was going, but that raise kept him there.

Ratner eventually decided he was having too much fun at CBS and never handed in his 165-page letter of resignation. He went to Washington during the war—in 1941—and returned in 1947 to be vice-president of promotion for two years. Then Macy's lured him away with a $60,000 salary to be director of advertising. "That impressed the hell out of me; sixty thousand dollars was a hell of a lot of money in 1949."

In an interview shortly before his death in 1974, Ratner said he had half a mind to call Frank Stanton and ask for that $5000 he got for Stanton years before. "He's got millions and I'm broke—but happily so."

It was all a game for Victor Ratner, up to the very end.

CHAPTER 5

Peggy Stone—"Today She'd Be a Vice-President"

AT CBS AS ELSEWHERE IN THE 1930S, THERE WERE FEW WOMEN IN jobs other than that of secretary. It took a highly motivated and capable woman to leap the chasm separating the men and their executive responsibilities from the women and their typewriters. Peggy Stone was one who made the jump.

In the bleak year of 1930, Peggy decided to trade the relative security of a teller's window at the Manufacturers Trust Company in Manhattan for the uncertainties of early network radio. The pert widow applied for a secretary's position at CBS.

A few minutes after her interview began with Sam Pickard, the executive in charge of station relations, they were swapping stories about radio, for Peggy had spent six months at a failing Dubuque station. When it folded she was given carfare to return to her native New York City.

Peggy could talk network and wavelength like a veteran and this was intriguing to Sam. Few men knew a kilocycle from a condenser in 1930 so to find a secretary who wouldn't waste his time sorting out such matters was a definite plus.

Peggy Stone could type, though her shorthand wasn't worth mentioning—and, hard-pressed to earn enough to support her two-year-old son, she didn't mention it. After Pickard hired her at premium secretary's wages of $45 a week and discovered that gap in her secretarial skills, he was mildly irritated.

But Peggy was quick. When Sam looked over that first batch of letters translated into Peggy's own literate style, he pronounced them "the finest letters I never wrote" and signed with satisfaction. From then on, he simply left Peggy notes telling her the ideas he wanted to convey and she did the rest.

Sam was too busy building a network—and a personal empire. And the affiliated owners seemed to like it that way. Peggy quickly became a CBS resident expert in clearing time—persuading affiliates in such important markets as Detroit and Cincinnati to accept network shows in time slots the affiliates were entitled to keep for local shows. She clicked, for example, for Campbell Soups and Popeye, securing the 7:00–7:15 P.M. slot in several markets where others at CBS had failed.

Soon affiliate owners addressed their correspondence directly to the feisty little Irishwoman who got them theater tickets and helped entertain them when they were in New York City. Peggy liked her job and worked well with Sam Pickard; she became so close to her boss and his wife that she would do his personal bookkeeping and baby-sit on weekends when the Pickards went out of town. She would take her son, Tom, along to the CBS executive's home to play with the two Pickard boys.

Even the worst thing that happened to Peggy in the early part of her CBS tenure turned out to be a lucky break. Peggy was accustomed to going out with station men and on one such date went with a station owner to a big party. Champagne flowed and Peggy had her share— at least. When she hopped into a taxi and slammed the door on her fingers, she was so anesthetized she barely noticed. But the next morning she awoke with two broken fingers.

When she showed the battered hand in a cast at CBS that day, a bullpen secretary was assigned to do her typing. Now that she had a secretary of her own, she began functioning like an executive. She served ex-officio as CBS vice-president for station relations a good part of the time, carrying on for the peripatetic Sam Pickard who held that title. When Sam wasn't away persuading prospective affiliates that he could turn a local station's backyard whisper into a thunderous regional voice, he was in Washington using old ties to deliver on these promises by juicing up the power allotment for the newly signed affiliates.

Even when Pickard was in New York, Peggy often stood the watch. Sam had a drinking problem so severe that the network sometimes hid him in a closet rather than expose station owners to his diluted charms.

Peggy was thriving—until Sam's other big failing drew the spotlight. Sam wasn't content to climb the ladder to success one rung at a time. He bounded upward, powered by the rewards of side deals. He convinced his former associates at the FCC to give additional kilowatt power to prospective affiliates and thus persuade them to join the network; he was then able to help the affiliates reorganize their corporate structure to serve the new realities. One of those realities was a silent and hidden partner—Sam Pickard. He once boasted that he would be a millionaire in five years. He probably pulled this off, though the extent of his perfidy, characteristically for CBS, has never been revealed.

To protect himself on the home front, Pickard enlisted and enriched one of Paley's school chums, who was occupying an executive position at CBS. But when they found Sam out, Paley's buddy couldn't help him. Pickard was canned in June 1936. (Paley's ingenuous friend kept his post but was separated from his backdoor booty.)

Despite being fired, Sam Pickard came out of the mess smelling like a rose. First, he was able to keep his station interests. Second, his prestige in Washington was such that CBS felt it politic to keep Sam on the payroll for years. Perhaps it was also gratitude on CBS's part. Sam had played a key role in the emergence of the network in the early days; without the supercharged affiliates he brought in, CBS might never have grown to big-time status.

But for Peggy Stone, unlike her boss, it was almost the end of the road. Executive vice-president Ed Klauber's assistant, Meff Runyon, was chosen to tell her she was fired. But she knew what was coming and interrupted him: "Before we settle anything, I'd like to take my vacation. I have three weeks coming. I'll be back to see you when it's over."

Peggy couldn't afford to get fired. Along with the rest of the staff she had taken a 15-percent salary cut in 1932, and later another 10 percent, again due to the Depression. (Sam Pickard kept the affiliates in the network through this difficult period, getting them without exception to accept a 15-percent cut in payments from the network for using CBS shows.) Only shortly before Pickard was caught, Peggy had climbed back up to her original salary of $45 a week. She needed that kind of money to raise her child. Where would a secretary without shorthand—one fired in disgrace—duplicate that in hard times?

Determined to survive the scandal, she made a pilgrimage to radioland, taking a boat to her first stop, New Orleans, where she visited Father Hines, the priest who ran the CBS affiliate at Loyola College. She spent a day or two there chatting and being helpful. When Father Hines asked if there was anything he could do for Peggy, she allowed as how there was. If he had found her help worthwhile, she would be grateful if he would write CBS and say so. She visited about a dozen affiliates in all, and each promised to send a mash note to headquarters in New York.

When she got back, she walked in and stated her case to Meff Runyon, saying, "I'd like a ten-dollar-a-week raise." The astonished executive said, "But you've been fired!" She said she didn't think that it was such a good idea to let her go, and doubted he would think so either after he had mulled it over. She pointed out that she was popular with the affiliates, as her fan mail showed; and as for her role in the Pickard affair, she hadn't taken a dime. Runyon could go over her checking account if he didn't believe her.

Runyon asked whether Peggy had known what Sam had going on the side. She said she had "suspected it, anyway," but told him, "Sam was *your* vice-president. It was your responsibility to catch him if he was cheating the company. As his secretary it was my job to serve him loyally." It wasn't for her to spy on her boss, she argued, and added, "I doubt if you would want it any other way."

Peggy not only kept her job, she got her raise. Things were never the same for her though. She missed Sam Pickard, a "charming, charming man," and her new boss was anything but that.

A dour engineer and a male chauvinist, Herbert Ackerberg wasn't happy about Peggy's clout and obvious closeness to the affiliate owners. Before he was promoted as Pickard's successor, Ackerberg had relatively little contact with affiliate owners; he had pored over massive books of maps showing the direction of radio beams, to seek locations for new stations. But now he was moving into an executive spot and he wanted all the frills that went with it. After all, *he* was vice-president for station relations, not Peggy. Why, then, did the affiliates insist on addressing letters to Peggy Stone and not to Herb Ackerberg?

Peggy was no fool. She dutifully opened the letters and placed them on Ackerberg's desk, though it galled him the more since they invariably began, "Dear Peggy."

In 1938, some time after Ackerberg came on the scene, Elliot Roosevelt (FDR's son) offered Peggy a job at Hearst Broadcasting. The Hearst job was to pay a whopping $150 a week—an unheard-of sum for all but the best-paid people then, few of whom were women. (In 1938, one could rent an attractive one-bedroom penthouse apartment for $150 a month.) Not only was Peggy to get the money, she was to have the title to go with it—vice-president for station relations at the five-station network.

But Peggy's loyalties were with CBS, and besides she suspected the new job might last only six months—Hearst was famous for short-lived careers. If she could get a raise, say to $75 a week from CBS, she might be better off.

She was quietly confident when Ed Klauber called her in. The austere executive vice-president was sitting behind his massive desk, and Herb Ackerberg was standing by, chain-smoking as usual.

Klauber said, "Miss Stone, I hear you are thinking of leaving us. After all these years, we would hate to lose you. . . . What would it take for you to stay?"

Says Peggy: "I explained that the Hearst job was a real executive position, but I said to Mr. Klauber that even though I had been offered a hundred and fifty dollars a week, I really did like CBS. I said that I had found it very nice to call myself 'Peggy Stone of CBS.' So I told him I would stay for seventy-five dollars a week."

She continues: "Mr. Klauber turned to Mr. Ackerberg and said, 'Well, Herb, don't you think Peggy is worth seventy-five dollars a week?' I was astonished and so was Mr. Klauber when Mr. Ackerberg said, 'No!'"

In a fury, Peggy turned to Klauber, making it clear that she was addressing herself to him and not to Ackerberg. She said, "Mr. Klauber, Mr. Ackerberg is your vice-president in charge of station relations. It seems to me that the job calls for the utmost tact and diplomacy. Had I been Mr. Ackerberg, I would have answered your question by saying, 'Miss Stone is worth a hundred and fifty dollars a week, but we can't justify paying her the seventy-five dollars she seeks in her job here.' Anyway, it doesn't really matter because I am leaving as of now."

Obviously upset and embarrassed by his executive's conduct, Klauber later called Peggy at her office and told her he had instructed Ackerberg to give a farewell party at Peggy's convenience. But, she notes, "Mr. Ackerberg never brought it up and I walked out of CBS quite alone."

The $150 a week helped relieve the pain of leaving what had been her home for nearly nine years. But within six months Elliot Roosevelt was fired and, as she had foreseen, Peggy too was notified that she was finished.

This however didn't stop her. She produced a contract for a full year that Elliot had signed as president of Hearst Broadcasting. For the remaining six months, in characteristic Hearst fashion for unwanted employees with contracts, Peggy was required to report for work at 9 A.M. every morning, but was given nothing to do. She spent the time lining up business for a radio-time-buying company she was organizing. Then she became chairman of the board of H-R Representatives, a similar company, and today she owns her own company and substantial pieces of two radio stations—WUNI in Mobile, Alabama, and WINR in Binghamton, New York.

She might not have done nearly as well if she had stayed at CBS. Most of her contemporaries who still work for the company are in relatively minor positions—like May Dowell who also started in the Depression. As talented as many a man at CBS who rose to high position, May is head librarian at CBS special projects, a post that carries no influence and not much salary.

Peggy still looks back fondly to the CBS years but doesn't know any woman there who can equal her stature in the business.

Others disagree, remembering Peggy Stone as something special. "Today she'd be a vice-president," one of her former colleagues insists.

CHAPTER 6
The World of the Soaps

CBS MAY HAVE IGNORED WOMEN WHEN IT CAME TO FILLING EXECU-
tive positions, but it didn't when it came to programing. The daytime
audience was mostly women, and their needs—or supposed needs—
had to be met. During the Depression, CBS and NBC provided housewives with daytime serials that featured families under stress who
survived through grit and high moral purpose. Named for their usual
sponsors, soap operas became immensely popular, added immeasurably
to the medium's success and certainly had a profound impact on CBS's
profits.

Drama critics were appalled by the soaps. If they bothered to review
them at all, they would ridicule and complain about plots that sometimes had the substance of a bubble and the speed of an inchworm.
James Thurber devoted several months to a study of "Soapland," as it
was called in a *New Yorker* magazine series. He clocked an early
favorite, *Just Plain Bill,* with a calendar and found that it took Bill four
days to give a man a shave in one of his infrequent labors over a hot
towel. The basin water, hot on Monday when the shave began, was still
finger-tingling on Thursday after the final stroke of the blade. When,
in another sequence, Bill said, "It doesn't seem possible to me that

Ralph Wilde arrived here only yesterday," Thurber commented, "It didn't seem possible to me, either, since Ralph Wilde had arrived, as mortal time goes, thirteen days before."

While critics just scoffed, sociologists and psychologists occasionally made serious complaints: Soap operas had a detrimental effect on the nation's mental health. They were concerned about the tendency of habitual listeners to identify with heroines of their favorite shows. In the late 1940s CBS commissioned a study of audience identification by Professor W. Lloyd Warner and his research associate, William E. Henry, at the University of Chicago. They chose listeners to *Big Sister* and selected women mostly of the lower middle class as subjects.

Almost all of them, the researchers found, were identifiers, in whom *Big Sister* aroused "normal and adaptive anxiety." They added:

The *Big Sister* program directly and indirectly condemns neurotic and nonadaptive anxiety and thereby functions to curb such feelings in its audience. This program provides moral beliefs, values, and techniques for solving emotional and interpersonal problems for its audience and makes them feel they are learning while they listen (thus: "I find the program educational"). It directs the private reveries and fantasies of the listeners into socially approved channels of action. The *Big Sister* program increases the women's sense of security in a world they feel is often threatening, by reaffirming the basic security of the marriage ties (John's and Ruth's); by accentuating the basic security of the position of the husband (Dr. John Wayne is a successful physician); by "demonstrating" that those who behave properly and stay away from wrongdoing exercise moral control over those who do not; and by showing that wrong behavior is punished.

The *Big Sister* program, in dramatizing the significance of the wife's role in basic human affairs, increases the woman's feeling of importance by showing that the family is of the highest importance and that she has control over the vicissitudes of family life. It thereby decreases their feeling of futility and makes them feel essential and wanted. The women aspire to, and measure themselves by, identification with Ruth, the heroine; however, the identification is not with Ruth alone, but with the whole program and the other characters in the plot. This permits sublimated impulse satisfaction by the listeners', first, unconsciously identifying with the bad woman and, later, consciously punishing her through the action of the plot. Unregulated impulse life is condemned, since it is always connected with characters who are condemned and never related to those who are approved.

Big Sister was one of the most popular of all serials. The only good that one critic would concede was that it "probably kept the housewives off the streets." More likely, it kept them from dying of boredom. But psychologically good or bad, literate or not, the networks liked soaps because they filled the time and the cash register.

Almost never did a soap opera depart from the "moral and uplifting" format, but one exception was recorded by Thurber: An old Shakespearean actor was struck dumb in an unexplained case of mike fright and rendered incapable of saying the line, "I am Sioux. I make no peace with Chippewa." Whereupon another actor, frantic at the possible loss of his livelihood in troubled times, yelled, "You're Sioux, you big goddamn ham, you make no peace with goddamn Chippewa!" This display of blasphemy was rewarded with an instantaneous flood of organ music.

Things got even worse for any dumb-struck actor in television. On CBS's soap opera *Search for Tomorrow,* Don Knotts played a catatonic, as he recalls: "I could talk to my 'sister' on the show but was to dummy-up with everybody else. We didn't use cue cards or Tele-Prompter—the whole show was rehearsed and memorized. My part was easy, of course, but this guy who was on with me froze. I couldn't possibly help without blowing the characterization once and for all. Finally, he looked at the floor manager and the manager started whispering. The actor cocked his head to hear the line and finally in exasperation yelled 'Line!' All of a sudden I began to have this eerie feeling we were rehearsing. The manager finally said the guy's line loud enough so that he could hear it and mercifully the show went on."

One wonders if anyone out there in the wasteland ever noticed.

Despite the complaints, the soaps would reign supreme on all radio networks during the Depression years and on through the 1940s and 1950s. Though daytime radio was less profitable than nighttime, it was still profitable: "After all," says a former CBS daytime-radio executive, "there were twice as many daytime hours as nighttime and having a lineup of soap operas on the air many hours of the day, year in, year out, was like having your own bank."

By the late 1940s, the average soap cost the sponsor about $18,000 a week. Of that sum, $3000 was paid for talent—writers, actors and directors. The remainder, less the standard 15-percent advertising-agency commission, went to the network. CBS then laid out 20 to 30 percent to affiliated stations in payment for each 15-minute time window and kept as much as $10,000 per show each week. When you figure that there were generally five hours of soaps a day, four shows per hour, it's clear that profits mounted at 485 Madison Avenue.

Urbane Frank Hummert and his prim wife, Anne, dominated the world of soap operas as completely as Shakespeare dominated Elizabethan drama. They brought the world its first bona fide soap opera, *Just Plain Bill* (Thurber's favorite, an NBC show), and for years afterward produced the cream of the soaps for both CBS and NBC.

Hummert was one of the great successes of the advertising world of the 1920s. At the agency where he worked, Lord & Thomas in Chicago, he had been billed by chief executive Albert Lasker as the world's highest-paid writer. And Lord & Thomas owed its enormous success to a stable of superbly gifted, richly rewarded copywriters. But in Frank's case, the agency had carried beneficence beyond utility. Frank was so well off by the late 1920s that he retired in splendor at the age of 41—and discovered boredom before he fairly molded his sitzmark in an easy chair. He responded to an offer from Blackett & Sample and went back to work.

In the late Twenties Anne Ashenhurst was strapped. After working her way through Goucher College writing for the Baltimore *Sun* at three cents a line, she sailed for Paris in 1926 to write about Americans abroad for the New York *Herald*. A short-lived marriage in Paris left her with an infant to support at age 23. At the going rates, newspaper work wouldn't keep her in baby food. Friends suggested she try her hand at advertising. She wrote a letter asking for an interview at Blackett & Sample.

Because Frank Hummert was an aloof sort of man, he never saw clients of his firm. It was agreed when he went with Blackett & Sample that the agency would deliver his work, not his body. A second problem was that, although Frank could explain anything in just a few words, he spoke so softly that agency employees often missed much of what he said. Too cowed by his importance to ask him to repeat, they left his office bewildered.

The solution was to find him an assistant—one cultured enough to get along with this man and sharp of hearing and memory.

Agency partner Glen Sample had been impressed with Anne's letter and asked her to come for an interview. But Frank had told Sample: "I don't want any women. They get into trouble and then they weep." But, he added, if Sample would deliver Anne by 1:10 P.M. that very day, he would see her. Understandably, the young woman wasn't put at ease by Sample's prologue. She recalls:

"I needed a job badly, but imagined the man to be a monster. Sample pushed me in. I saw a very gracious man who arose from behind a beautiful antique English kneehole desk and said, 'Won't you sit down?'"

She quickly told him that she knew absolutely nothing about advertising. He said, "That's great, because most things that people do know are no good."

Anne said she didn't care how many hours she had to work, but, she added, "If I do the work of a man, I expect to be paid like a man." Frank didn't see that that would be a problem.

The interview was a success, Anne got the job and, in addition to her responsibilities as an aide, she began writing—and rewriting—advertising copy. The two formed a highly efficient team, and Frank was soon depending on Anne for everything. He did, however, have trouble remembering her name, Ashenhurst. Anne recalls:

"He'd say to someone who came to him for assistance, 'Mrs. . . . Mrs. . . . ahhh . . . She'll do it for you. She'll explain it.' And I did and got on very well with the men. If they hadn't heard or didn't remember what he said, I told them. I had an excellent memory."

Anne began the job in 1929. Daytime radio—what there was of it at a time when most broadcasting was done at night—was sophomoric, featuring such entertainment as "how-to" recipe shows.

One day, Frank Hummert called Anne into his office and said, "I don't know if you are old enough to remember the nickelodeon." Anne, though 17 years Frank's junior, did remember. It was a movie-viewing machine. For five cents you saw a short drama which was continued the next week. The same idea in the form of movie serials was used in the regular movie theaters. *The Perils of Pauline* was one of the early favorites of this genre. Pauline was literally a cliff hanger—when she wasn't being tied to railroad tracks.

Frank thought the serial idea might just work on radio, but the stories would have to relate to some aspect of the American condition.

It was Frank who suggested as a possible series the story of an ordinary man, a barber in the Midwest—*Just Plain Bill.*

Later Frank created *The Romance of Helen Trent* for CBS. Helen was quite a departure in an era when people married by age 25 and gave up all romantic ideas thereafter. For millions of miserable housewives, the idea that romance could exist in a woman's life after age 35 was a refreshing and hopeful thought. For Helen's marriage had come to an end and she was seeking new romance. She found it many times in the next 27 years.

Frank Hummert had little trouble selling his program ideas. In radio's early years stations and networks regularly turned to ad agencies for help in programing. As a result, ad agencies became the dominant force in programing. They held this position until television came of age, costing so much that a single advertiser seldom could afford to finance an entire show.

Frank was happily married when he met Anne and remained so until his wife of 25 years died. Then, some seven years after they began their association, Frank asked Anne to be his wife. He told friends and associates that he married her because he simply could not remember her name. Frank was 47. Anne was 30.

Meanwhile, soap operas had become big business, perplexing the critics and then annoying the sociologists. Says Anne: "Nobody can understand the phenomenal success of the soaps without knowing when they were born. It was during the Depression. There was no Social Security, no welfare, nothing. The housewife was at home worrying about everything. Would her husband lose his job? Where was the family's next meal to come from? They found escape in the lives of the people on the soaps." Listeners often wrote letters addressed to the characters by name—warning against others in the story, suggesting solutions to problems.

Were they literature? Certainly not, says one of their severest critics —Anne Hummert. Stylish and confident still, and looking 15 years younger than her age, Anne Hummert remains impatient with critics who persist in evaluating soap opera in literary terms.

"This is nonsense. You can't continue for 25 years and have literature too. Compare the serials with the successful Campbell's Soup jingle: 'Mmm Mmm good. Mmm Mmm good. That's what Campbell's Soups are, Mmm Mmm good!' Is that opera?"

As their soap operas proliferated, the Hummerts formed a separate unit to produce serials and moved to New York. One commentator compared their methods to those of the elder Alexandre Dumas, who supposedly hired dozens of anonymous writers to form a literary factory. Each Hummert serial was defined in a detailed memorandum with follow-up synopses of sequences. Writers under contract filled in the dialogue, receiving a standard $25 per script—$125 per week for a five-a-week series. The writers were anonymous; they seldom, if ever, met their elusive employers. They got their instructions in writing or through six editors who checked each writer's work.

Broadcast historian Erik Barnouw was once hired by the Hummerts to pass on the suitability of children's scripts. He reports that Anne Hummert once told a new writer, "I want you to put God on every page." When the writer asked dryly, "Who's going to play the part?" Anne Hummert, who Barnouw describes as "high-strung," promptly fired her.

Though perhaps high-strung, Anne was by no means insensitive to the feelings of those who worked for her. More than a midwife to Frank's creative processes—he liked to invent plots then go on to the next one—Anne was both the editor-in-chief and casting director.

Speaking of the latter task in a cultured accent that sounds almost British, at a sedate lunch at the Regency Hotel in New York, she recalled: "I cast everybody," adding with assurance after a studied pause, "I have a dramatic feel. I gathered all the actors together and selected the ones I wanted. I hated to turn the others down."

Still, she lacked a sense of her own power. At one practice session she overheard a woman say, "Oh, careful, Mrs. Hummert is here and she's very severe."

"I could have shot myself," Anne says, "but I did feel an enormous sense of responsibility about spending someone else's money."

There were apparently few complaints at network headquarters about the way the Hummerts handled things. In 1938 a listener study showed that the average serial listener tuned in 6.6 serials. Most said they had never been bored and almost a third of the listeners questioned said they planned their day around them. This particular study found that 61 percent of the women interviewed used merchandise advertised on the serials they followed.

This is the important point for Anne Hummert and the one that brought her out of seclusion to talk to the author.

"I am a democratic liberal by leaning. Anything that provided jobs and escape from a terrible reality, I believed in—so long as it was not destructive. This daytime-serial business succeeded and became a terrific economic force. People wanted more and more of them. One industrial company after another wanted soaps because they made business improve. The soap operas provided jobs—certainly to actors and writers—in a terrible period in American history. This seemed to me important."

Anne and Frank enjoyed 31 years of very happy marriage before Frank died of emphysema in 1966. Anne Ashenhurst, who traveled from Paris to Chicago penniless and with a baby, had obviously found her ideal in her rich and elegant husband, and in the life of wit and good taste they shared. One is reminded of *Our Gal Sunday*, whose story intro asked the question each day: "Can a girl from a little mining town in the West find happiness as the wife of a wealthy and titled Englishman?"

"Who wrote that, Mrs. Hummert?"

"I wrote that," she said.

PART TWO
THE WAR AND POSTWAR YEARS

CHRONOLOGY

ON A SUNDAY AFTERNOON IN DECEMBER 1941, A CBS NEWSMAN breaks into a network broadcast to announce that the Japanese have attacked Pearl Harbor.

. . .The war quickly becomes the staple of broadcasting. Between December 7, 1941, and September 2, 1945, the day the Japanese formally surrender, CBS will broadcast some 35,700 war programs, both news and entertainment—nine solid months of war programing.

. . .A week after the Japanese attack, Norman Corwin, broadcasting's most prolific dramatist, prepares a program commemorating the 150th anniversary of the ratification of the Bill of Rights. While the New York Philharmonic plays the national anthem, President Franklin Roosevelt does the epilogue:
". . . We will not, under any threat, or in the face of any danger, surrender the guarantees of liberty our forefathers framed for us in our Bill of Rights. No power . . . shall shake our hold upon them."

. . .By 1942, 457 CBS employees are in military service. Elmer Davis, who has become the most respected journalist on radio since beginning his five-minute news report for CBS in 1940, is called to Washington to head up the Office of War Information.

. . .When Bill Paley departs for London as deputy chief of the Office of Psychological Warfare under General Dwight D. Eisenhower, Paul Kesten is named executive vice-president and wartime manager. Dr. Frank Stanton serves as vice-president and general executive. Ed Klauber is sidetracked at CBS and leaves, goes to Washington to become Elmer Davis's No. 2 man at OWI.

. . .CBS continues to broadcast a few radio entertainment favorites— *The Hit Parade, Suspense, Inner Sanctum, Lux Radio Theater* and *Molly Goldberg,* but foreign correspondents are the stars of the era, their broadcasts carried live or recorded. Even before the United States enters the war, Edward R. Murrow becomes a hero through his rooftop broadcasts during the London blitz.

. . .On Sundays CBS and the BBC strive for Anglo-American understanding with a program called *Trans-Atlantic Call.* In a typical broadcast, Americans explain the Tennessee Valley Authority to the British, then British workers describe conditions in a war plant in the midst of enemy bombings.

. . .At home, the government raises money through war bonds and CBS's Kate Smith sells $108 million worth in the last day of a four-day effort.

. . .In 1944 CBS's Charles Collingwood crosses the English Channel in an LST and reports D-Day from the beaches at Normandy.

. . .On May 8, 1945, the Nazi empire is finally brought to ruin and the European war ends. In August a terrible white mushroom cloud rolls over Hiroshima, and soon afterward the Japanese sign surrender documents in the stern presence of General MacArthur aboard the battleship U.S.S. *Missouri.*

. . .In September 1945, Paul Kesten's protégé, Frank Stanton, becomes president of CBS. Bill Paley moves up to chairman of the board.

. . .In 1945 there are 56 million radio sets serving the nation's 140,-468,000 people. There are also 16,500 massive and awkward-looking boxes with a small glass eye that lights up and flickers uncertainly.

...Unheralded, Dr. Peter Goldmark, CBS research director, struggles to usher in the television age with the full drama of color, at the same time working on what is to be his biggest triumph—the long-playing record.

...The stakes in the new contests with RCA—over television viewers, TV sets and the record business—will make the rich rewards of radio seem paltry by comparison.

CHAPTER 7

8:55: "Elmer Davis and the News"

IN THE DAYS LEADING UP TO WORLD WAR II, AND AFTER THE WAR BROKE out in the fall of 1939, CBS expanded its news staff in Europe to report on the momentous events. Early in 1940, CBS scheduled a five-minute news broadcast back home for 8:55 to 9:00 P.M., a peak radio-listening period. It carved the time out of one of the most valuable commercial hours, demanding that its most important advertisers relinquish these five minutes. The move was a shrewd one, since it drew mid-evening attention to CBS while making the network appear statesmanlike.

For this evening news roundup CBS could have chosen a newscaster with a golden throat to "rip and read" reports direct from the wire services. It could have given a commentator, such as CBS's own H. V. Kaltenborn, the nod and let him express his own opinions. But CBS decided to give the spot to a solid newsman who would fashion his copy personally but objectively, giving an analysis of the news and providing depth of understanding, but not personal opinion. The man CBS wanted for the assignment was Elmer Davis, who had only recently been persuaded to leave print journalism for broadcast journalism.

It is one thing to be a successful newspaper reporter and write accurate and occasionally brilliant stories; it is yet another to sparkle in electronic journalism. There are few reporters who do both well.

Davis was certainly no candidate for King Lear. Helen Sioussat, CBS's talks director who first put him on the air, knew that Davis's Indiana voice was nasal and grating. But she liked it because it lacked the pomposity of so many radio voices of the time. It was a voice with down-home authority.

The day Davis made his first broadcast, he left the studio and Helen Sioussat in a fluster, mumbling an embarrassed, "I'm sorry!" Davis had flunked his broadcast test in the eyes of his severest critic—himself—and vowed never to try again. But in the days that followed, Helen received numerous telephone calls about that man with the unusual midwestern voice. So, her instincts confirmed, she persisted in her attempts to get Elmer to return and wouldn't take no for an answer.

Davis returned, but still convinced he was awful, he refused to accept any money. Finally after three broadcasts and growing notice, Helen Sioussat added up the total due and made Elmer Davis accept his paycheck. The audience was pleased, Helen was pleased and Elmer's former colleague on *The New York Times*, Ed Klauber, was pleased. Davis, like H. V. Kaltenborn, had become a member of the distinguished news team nurtured by the irascible Ed Klauber, with the help of Paul White. Klauber put him in the new 8:55 time slot. He began on May 10, 1940, by which time he had found his direction. Organlike tones he had not, but he did have effective, authoritative delivery.

The show was an immediate success and helped make radio a vital war medium. Elmer Davis was so good, people would stay home in order not to miss his reports. John "Jap" Gude (so tagged because a case of jaundice in his teens made his skin yellow for months), a publicity man for CBS at the time and later Davis's agent, recalls that "Elmer had a marvelous knack of getting everything that was really important into that five-minute period." Actually, Davis spoke for just three and a half minutes of the five, and managed to sum up as many as 30 stories in that brief period. "He didn't rattle off a string of newspaper headlines," Gude explains. "He blended his news items with terse, sharp commentary. He would give a bulletin from Washington and immediately follow it with a one-sentence commentary on the item's significance."

Elmer Davis quickly became a nationally known news personality, whose talents came to the attention of Franklin Delano Roosevelt. Shortly after the Japanese attacked Pearl Harbor in 1941, the president called Davis to Washington to head up the Office of War Information.

The diffident commentator left the airwaves as abruptly as he had come, giving up the most eagerly-tuned-in news broadcast in radio for the relative obscurity of Washington, because the president convinced him that was where he could help the most.

For reasons that have never been fully explained, Bill Paley decided that Paul Kesten should be the one to take over CBS while Paley was doing his part for the war effort in London. This meant passing over Ed Klauber, his able No. 1 assistant and executive vice-president. It was a bitter pill for Klauber, though he said little. He resigned and allowed the word to spread that he had quit due to ill health. Klauber did have emphysema and he actually collected disability benefits for a time. He never mentioned to associates at CBS another source of despair; his first wife was dying of cancer just when he was shunted aside by the broadcasting company. (Years later, during the delirium of his final illness, his second wife, Doris Larson Klauber, remembers him mentioning something in bitterness about his CBS severance.)

And yet there remained a final role for Ed Klauber.

In Washington, Elmer Davis's inexperience as an executive was driving him nearly frantic. As he told Bill Paley when he asked to leave for the government post, "The most people I have ever run is half a secretary." Reporters generally do not have secretaries and even a man as important as Elmer Davis had shared one at CBS.

Davis put in a call to Klauber and said, "For goodness sake, save me!" It was something of a lifesaver for Klauber who was more than eager to accept, but explained that he needed the income he was receiving in disability payments. Davis got in touch with Paley, and Paley exercised one of the prerogatives of top executives. He picked up the telephone and personally called the president of the insurance company that was providing Klauber's benefits. He explained the situation and the contribution Klauber would be making to the war effort. Paley got the insurance company to waive its right to cut off Klauber's benefits.

Klauber was happy in his new job and thereafter refered to himself as "the nation's number-one No. 2 man." He did brilliant work by all accounts, handling the administrative chores for the agency with his customary élan, thus freeing Davis for executive decision-making.

But the Klauber appointment, motivated by need and, perhaps, to a degree by sentiment on Davis's part, was not universally appreciated back at CBS. Kesten in particular was not pleased that Davis had given his old rival a new lease on life.

CHAPTER 8

"This—Is London"

"THIS—IS LONDON." THAT'S THE WAY HIS COLLEGE DRAMA COACH AD-
vised him to say it when the bombs began to drop.

When Egbert Roscoe Murrow was still an infant, his family moved
from a farm in Polecat Creek, North Carolina, to the town of Blanchard in Washington State's lumber country. A picture taken there in
about 1913 showed a pudgy-faced boy in cap, knickers, black hose and
over-the-ankle shoes, posing in front of a clapboard house with his two
brothers, who were two and four years older. The older boys were ready
to leave for school when caught by the camera. Egbert, though studi-
ous-looking with book in hand, was indulging a fantasy since he was too
young for school.

To his brothers, Egbert at age five was "Eber Blowhard"—or just
plain "Blow"—because of the rows he made when they left him behind
to go to school and, later, because of the hollering he did so his mother,
bent on whipping him, would change her mind. ("Egbert, hush! What
will the neighbors think?")

Egbert and his family were Scots, with a half-Cherokee great-grand-
mother who added a touch of romance. The three brothers were all
outdoorsmen and good shots. They worked hard doing their duck and

rabbit hunting on the way to a regular round of part-time jobs pitching hay, weeding beets, milking cows and mowing lawns.

Their mother, tiny next to her tall, taciturn, 200-pound husband, was a bundle of nervous energy. She was also a woman of great moral strength and the biggest influence in the boys' lives. A Quaker who dressed and lived simply, she adopted Methodism when she came to Washington and instilled that religion's principles of restraint in her boys. There wasn't a big enough Quaker population in Blanchard for Sunday meetings.

As was common in certain pockets of the Appalachian Mountains, her English was the kind spoken in Elizabethan times. She intoned such Spenserian phrases as "It pleasures me" and "I'd not" and "This I believe." The boys picked it up, carrying the picturesque usage all their lives.

Egbert exhibited a competitive determination that led him to occasional foolhardiness. Once, on a brother's dare, he put his right forefinger between the descending surface of a cider press and the lower plate. Failing to withdraw it in time, he carried a twisted finger into adulthood. For failing to prove he was quicker in ducking than a neighbor boy was in shooting his new BB gun, Egbert caught a pellet between the eyes; he carried that mark through life too. Once, he allowed his brothers to tie him to a seatless, pedalless bicycle rescued from a junk heap. Launched with a shove, he rode helplessly into a drainage ditch. Another forehead scar.

Egbert also had a hot temper, but while it flared quickly, he usually managed to get it under control in minutes. Occasionally he showed a shyness, and was more at ease with the rough lumberjacks who were his companions in summer jobs in logging camps than with his peers. He drank some and smoked constantly. When an undergraduate studying speech at Washington State College, Egbert changed his name to Edward and shortened his middle name to the initial "R." Later he would make a name for himself professionally as well as legally. Much of the country would do as the CBS announcer suggested, "Listen to Murrow tomorrow."

There was a fair body of opinion at CBS News that Edward R. Murrow was a stuffed shirt. One ex-CBS news editor thought so. In the 1940s, this editor and his team of eleven overnight newswriters attacked their typewriters from midnight to 9 A.M., "beating their brains out" doing 16 to 18 newscasts ending with the 8 A.M. world news roundup which went to the whole CBS radio network. He remembers:

> One morning Murrow came in around nine A.M. His office was at the end of a corridor perhaps a hundred feet away from Paul White's office where these eleven characters and I were sitting around . . . all beat up—that shift was a killer.
>
> We noticed Murrow had taken his coat off and was pacing up and down the corridor snapping those famous red suspenders of his, and at the end of one pace he stepped into Paul's office and confronted us with, "Gentlemen, what do you think is the most important problem facing the world today?" Well, this bunch of exhausted newsmen just looked at him in astonishment.
>
> Nobody knew what to say. Our minds were too tired to respond.

It was that kind of thing that got Murrow his reputation, among some of his associates, as a somewhat pompous man whose celebrity was based as much on theatrics as reporting. At times it seemed that he was preoccupied with dramatic effects. And, in fact, Ed Murrow might well have become an actor. His drama coach at Washington State, Ida Lou Anderson, crippled from the age of nine by infantile paralysis, was a fine actress and a superb teacher. Murrow played the leads in several college plays and was Ida Lou's favorite pupil. When broadcasting during the London blitz, it was Ida Lou who urged him to pause for dramatic effect in beginning his broadcasts. Rather than hurrying the standard opening words, she had him say: "This—is London." It became his identification tag.

Understated but highly personalized, Murrow's style of reporting carried a subtle editorial slant. The style would be copied widely in the broadcast medium—rather than the more restrained style of his superior and later rival Paul White.

If Ed Klauber was the father of broadcast journalism, the talented, hard-drinking, gout-ridden and uncompromising newsman Paul White was its midwife. Paul was brought up in the tough environment of wire-service reporting. At United Press—number two in the industry and a mite compared with the large and well-financed Associated Press —he was one of the most competitive reporters. He sometimes found himself pitted against as many as eight Associated Press reporters, and beating them. He was ingenious, imaginative and an indefatigable worker.

Though Murrow often gets credit for it, Paul White was the man who built the CBS news team in Europe: William L. Shirer, Eric Sevareid, Larry LeSueur, Bob Trout, Charles Collingwood, John Daly, Cecil Brown and Murrow himself. The team dazzled the nation in World War II, often scooping the newspapers with reports from the scene of major breaking stories. Half of them went on to individual fame as writers and commentators.

Associates remember the ebullient White at his "piano" in his big office next to studio nine, where the CBS news director delightedly (and fully conscious of his audience) punched the buttons of a telephone console hookup that put him in touch with his far-flung correspondents and put them in touch with each other.

Paul White realized that people had to come into the news business with preconceptions; every human being had them. But he insisted that his reporters try to be objective, knowing that they wouldn't succeed completely. Paul White felt that broadcasters were "stewards" of the airwaves which belonged to the public and were franchised to the stations. In White's view, the opinions of newscasters were irrelevant. And he drew a fine line between analysis and editorializing. Those who crossed that line did so at their peril.

One evening during World War II, after Paul had left the studios, a news editor spotted a story on the wires that some major oil companies had been indicted. The upcoming 11 P.M. news was sponsored by an oil company. The editor left the story out of the news in an apparent effort to avoid embarrassing the sponsor.

A reporter who saw White the next day says:

I never saw a guy so furious in my life. He didn't fire the editor, but he sidetracked his career. The only time I saw Paul when he was more angry was when Cecil Brown came back from Europe in 1945 —a returning war correspondent and something of a celebrity.

Cecil was assigned to the eleven P.M. news, which was five minutes of news and five minutes of analysis. Paul's view of analysis was to give the background of a story—how it happened, why it happened, period. And it was *labeled* analysis.

Cecil was outspoken enough before and during the war to have gotten banned by the Germans in the Balkans and the British in Singapore, and this talented but difficult man had had a run-in with White before for editorializing. Anyway, after the war, he went on a kind of celebrity tour, visiting thirteen cities over a period of several weeks. He came back to New York and did a big double-dome think piece leading off with the phrase, "The American people think . . ."

Paul was livid and fired him the next day. He said, "You've been in thirteen cities and you spoke mostly to people in radio stations. You don't know *what* the American people think."

The famous commentator H. V. Kaltenborn had departed under similiar circumstances. He had gained considerable respect for his opinions concerning the events leading up to World War II and was a fixture at CBS for many years. He left in 1939 for NBC after a long battle with Paul White and Ed Klauber, both of whom deplored his editorializing.

It is understandable then that relations between Paul White and Ed Murrow, who could influence his listeners without appearing to show strong bias, were sometimes less than ideal.

Ed Murrow had never worked for a newspaper as had so many of his broadcasting contemporaries. He was an early and zealous advocate of American involvement in World War II to help save Great Britain and democracy. Whatever his flaws, Murrow was magnificent during the Battle of Britain, especially the London blitz, 12 days in September 1940, when Hermann Goering sent as many as a thousand planes a day to bomb the beleaguered city. Murrow put aside personal safety to live on a few hours of sleep and raw nerve in order to report the blitz on the scene. His broadcasts were called "metallic poetry" by a commentator of the day. He became the chief interpreter of the British to the Americans. His report on the dearth of news about Britain's weather at a time when weather news would have been valuable to the enemy illustrates his understanding of the British and also his wry humor.

Englishmen love to talk about their weather. Continentals have claimed that the Englishman's real home is in his barometer, that he is unable to forget it even during romantic unlit intervals. In prewar days Britain seemed to be a small island located halfway between a deep depression over Iceland and a high-pressure ridge near the Azores. Any Englishman could talk about his weather for fifteen minutes without repeating himself. But all that is changed. The weather is now dismissed with a few curt, but not always courteous, phrases. The weather prophets prepare their prognostications for the fighting forces, and the layman takes what comes. If it should rain soup the poor man would have no spoon, because he would have had no warning.

Early in the war Murrow reported on the sense of unreality the bombings held for him—a feeling shared by nearly all in those early days of the blitz. Murrow said:

[The bombs] don't seem to make as much noise as they should. . . . The sense of danger, death and disaster comes only when the familiar incidents occur, the things that one has associated with tragedy since childhood. The sight of half a dozen ambulances weighted down with an unseen cargo of human wreckage has jarred me more than the war of dive bombers or the sound of bombs. Another thing that has meaning is fire. Again, that's something we can understand.

Last night as I stood on London Bridge with Vincent Sheean and watched that red glow in the sky, it was possible to understand that that's fire, as the result of an act of war. But the act itself, even the sound of the bomb that started the fire, was still unreal. What had happened was that three or four high school boys with some special training had been flying about over London in about one hundred thousand dollars worth of machinery. One of them had pressed a button, and the fire and a number of casualties was the result.

We could see the fire and hear the clanging of the fire-engine bells, but we hadn't seen the bomber, had barely heard him. Maybe the children who are now growing up will in future wars be able to associate the sound of bombs, the drone of engines, and the carrying sound of machine guns overhead, with human tragedy and disaster. But for me the ambulance and the red flare of fire in the night sky are the outward signs of death and destruction.

Perhaps it was this unreality that helped Murrow remain calm in moments of danger. He insisted on riding about in an open roadster during blackouts and bombings, and became famous for his rooftop broadcasts that provided a stunning sound track of booming guns and falling bombs as a background for his understated delivery.

"I'm standing on a rooftop looking out over London. At the moment everything is quiet. For reasons of national as well as personal security, I'm unable to tell you the exact location from which I'm speaking. Off to my left, far away in the distance, I can see just the faint angry snap of antiaircraft bursts against the steel-blue sky, but the guns are so far away that it's impossible to hear them from this location."

But if there was an unreal quality in those dark hours of the night, the cold reality of the blitz was clear at daybreak. After a particularly destructive night, Murrow described downtown London looking as if "an angry giant had gone through it with an eggbeater."

Through the magic of his word pictures Americans could identify with the events 3000 miles away. In a broadcast the day after the first heavy raids on London, Murrow told Americans what he and two other American correspondents had seen from their position at the mouth of the Thames estuary:

We went back to a haystack near the airdrome. The fires up the river had turned the moon blood-red. The smoke had drifted down till it formed a canopy over the Thames. The guns were working all around us, the bursts looking like fireflies on a southern summer night.

The Germans were sending in two or three planes at a time, sometimes only one, in relays. They would pass overhead. The guns and lights would follow them, and in about five minutes we could hear the hollow grunt of the bombs. Huge pear-shaped bursts of flame would rise up into the smoke and disappear. The world was upside down. Vincent Sheean lay on one side of me and cursed in five languages; he'd talk about the war in Spain. Ben Robertson lay on the other side and kept saying over and over in that slow South Carolina drawl, "London is burning, London is burning. . . ."

It was like a shuttle service, the way the German planes came up the Thames, the fires acting as a flare path. Often they were above the smoke. The searchlights bored into that black roof but couldn't penetrate it. They looked like long pillars supporting a black canopy. Suddenly all the lights dashed off and a blackness fell right to the ground. It grew cold. We covered ourselves with hay. The shrapnel clicked as it hit the concrete road nearby. And still the German bombers came.

Such reporting brought fame to Murrow, not only in the United States but in England, too; in time, he began to broadcast to the British people explaining American ways. Murrow's fame became universal— or nearly so. Once he made a quick trip back to 485 Madison Avenue where he displaced Gene Autry, CBS cowboy star, as guest of honor. He enthralled the CBS executives with tales of his exploits dominating the conversation. As he was leaving, Autry walked over to the newscaster and said, "I certainly enjoyed what you had to say, Mr. Murray."

Murrow reported spontaneously what he saw and felt. But even his prepared broadcasts weren't written; he dictated directly to his secretary, Kay Campbell, so that the broadcasts would be more informal and immediate than journalistic writing. Kay Campbell, like Murrow, was a chain smoker. After a session of dictating and typing, it was sometimes difficult to see in the room where they worked, the smoke was so thick.

Murrow was a familiar figure in London and was eagerly sought out by members of Parliament, ministers of state, and leaders of exiled governments, some of whom he and his wife Janet entertained in their modest London apartment. Often, however, in the worst days of the blitz, he worked day and night, surviving on coffee and cigarettes.

When Bill Paley arrived in London in 1943 to join General Eisenhower's staff as deputy chief of the Office of Psychological Warfare, Murrow and Paley developed a close relationship. Paley enjoyed himself immensely in the company of Ed Murrow, and also Charles Collingwood whose fine sense of humor appealed to Paley.

One broadcast gossip says they were three of the handsomest men in London, and were "much admired by women." In any event, they were familiar figures in London war society, the magnetic Murrow introducing Paley to Allied chiefs and members of governments-in-exile; some say Bill Paley would have been too shy to meet such men on his own.

Paley and friends were amused when RCA's David Sarnoff arrived at the Claridge. The General was pleased with his accommodations until the next morning when a chambermaid delivered Colonel Paley's laundry and Sarnoff found out that his rooms had just been vacated by Paley for even more sumptuous quarters in the fine hotel. On the other hand, some say Paley, who reached the rank of full colonel, was jealous that his archrival became a brigadier general.

Even after London was safe from German bombers, and Murrow was enjoying his renown in London society, he still insisted on exposing himself to danger. Once he flew over Berlin with an American bomber crew, causing associates to again wonder if he had a death wish. He reported: "I began to breathe and to reflect again that all men would be brave if only they could leave their stomachs at home. . . . I looked on the port beam at the target area. There was a red, sullen, obscene glare. The fires seem to have found each other. . . . Berlin was a kind of orchestrated hell. A terrible symphony of light and flame."

Danger always seemed to stimulate Murrow to his best efforts. During the war it was the bombs. Later it would be the junior senator from Wisconsin.

CHAPTER 9

News from the Pacific Theater

IT WAS A QUIET WINTER SUNDAY IN NEW YORK CITY IN 1941. PAUL White, CBS director of news broadcasts, was at the office at 485 Madison Avenue clearing a few things off his desk and mulling over international affairs. The Japanese navy was maneuvering in the Pacific off Thailand, and there was some nervousness in Washington over this.

White picked up a telephone and called Fox Case who was attached to CBS radio station KNX in Los Angeles. Concerned that CBS was undermanned in San Francisco—sure to be a hot spot were the United States to go to war with Japan—he told Case to shoot over to San Francisco and get a news bureau going. Minutes later, the no-nonsense Case was packing his bag.

Suddenly—at 2:25 P.M.—the CBS newsroom in New York received a bulletin from Washington: "Flash—White House announces Japanese have attacked Pearl Harbor." John Daly of the CBS news staff, later famed as moderator of *What's My Line?*, ripped this and additional yellow UP copy from the teletype machine and, emotions churning, interrupted a network broadcast to announce: "The Japanese have attacked Pearl Harbor, Hawaii, by air, President Roosevelt has just announced. The attack was also made on naval and military activities on the principal island of Oahu. . . ."

Later Daly assessed the military situation. He reminded listeners that Britain had a formidable Far Eastern fleet with the 35,000-ton battleship *Prince of Wales* as flagship. Bob Trout of the CBS staff, he said, was standing by in London.

At 2:41 P.M. Trout reported that it was still too early for any official British reaction, but commented, "As you know, the British government made plain what would happen if America became involved in war with Japan."

At 3:01 Elmer Davis went on the air:

> . . . a week ago yesterday the Japanese said they wanted two weeks more for negotiation. It was obvious that they were allowing themselves the limit. . . . We just have a bulletin from London that President Roosevelt's announcement of Japanese air attacks on United States Pacific bases staggered London, which awaited fulfillment of Prime Minister Churchill's promise to declare war on Japan within an hour if she attacked the United States. . . .
>
> Here's more detail direct from the front, from Honolulu. The smoke of antiaircraft guns rose over the Pearl Harbor Navy Yard. Heavy smoke also drifted up from Hickam Field. . . . Witnesses said fires broke out on Ford Island . . . the navy air base . . . it's apparent that the Japanese . . . were trying to head off reprisals from the army and navy bombers which might possibly come back at the carriers from which the Japanese planes set off. . . .
>
> The argument when General Tojo came into power was that now at last we had one of the ruling clique in control of the government, and an agreement made with him was something that would stick. But it appears that this particular ruling clique has no idea of making any agreement at all, that the sole purpose of their negotiations at Washington was to gain time and to endeavor to throw American military and naval forces off guard, an endeavor which we hope has not been successful, so that they might make their attacks. . . .

William L. Shirer, the distinguished CBS correspondent who reported from Berlin until Hitler kicked him out of Germany, gave this analysis of the impact on the world military situation:

> We didn't want war with Japan, but now it's been forced on us and our people will learn one more lesson of these tragic times: that you

cannot stay out of war merely because you wish to. . . . Thus ends for the country twenty-three years and one month, the space of time which separates us from November 11, 1918, when peace came over the battlefields of France.

[At 5:51 Shirer tried to call in Honolulu by shortwave. No answer. He tried Manila. Ominous silence. He resumed:]

. . . a bulletin just in from London: The Japanese have bombed British bases in the Pacific. Just those laconic words. . . . Japan is an ally of Germany . . . she has irrevocably staked her whole future on Hitler's victory . . . as a matter of fact the future of all of us is staked on that man's victory or defeat. In the beginning, the Japanese attack on us today will benefit Hitler somewhat . . . for a while we can send less tanks and planes to Britain and Russia. It will mean —and I have often heard the German General Staff officers discuss this aspect—that we will have to concentrate most of our naval power now in the Pacific. These things will benefit Hitler . . . but only for a short time, for now there certainly can be no doubt of it: this country will be unified in the hour of its danger. And its temper, hitherto so sluggish, will rise and crystallize. . . . Vast new production, and the power behind the unity that will be the country's, henceforth will be used to bring down Hitler's allies, and then himself.

On December 9, at 10 P.M. EST, President Roosevelt sat before his hearth wearing a double-breasted pinstripe suit with a black band around his right arm. In a grim broadcast to the nation, he said: "So far the news has been all bad. . . ." The casualty lists, when compiled, would show "huge losses." He called for sacrifice and spoke of Americans as "builders" not destroyers. While it would be a "long war . . . and a hard war . . . we are going to win the war. . . . We . . . know that the vast majority of the members of the human race are on our side. . . ."

At 5 A.M. December 11, CBS reported a Tokyo broadcast claiming that the British battleship *Prince of Wales* and heavy cruiser *Repulse* had been sunk. Cecil Brown, CBS's correspondent in Singapore, had been aboard the *Repulse*. The next morning Brown's cable came through, to be broadcast at 5 A.M. and three more times during the day:

Here's the eyewitness story of how the *Prince of Wales* and the *Repulse* ended their careers in the South China Sea, fifty miles from the Malaya coast and a hundred and fifty miles north of Singapore.

I was aboard the *Repulse* and with hundreds of others escaped. Then, swimming in thick oil, I saw the *Prince of Wales* lay over on her side like a tired war horse and slide beneath the waters. I kept a diary from the time the first Japanese high level bombing started at 11:15 until 12:31 when Captain William Tennant, skipper of the *Repulse* . . . shouted through the ship's communications system, "All hands on deck, prepare to abandon ship. May God be with you."

I jumped twenty feet to the water from the up end of the side of the *Repulse* and smashed my stopwatch at thirty-five and a half minutes after twelve. The sinking of the *Repulse* and the *Prince of Wales* was carried out by a combination of high level bombing and torpedo attacks with consummate skill and the greatest daring. I was standing on the flag deck slightly forward amidships when nine Jap bombers approached at ten thousand feet strung in a line, clearly visible in the brilliant sunlit sky. They flew directly over our ship and our antiaircraft guns were screaming constantly.

Just when the planes were passing over, one bomb hit the water beside where I was standing, so close to the ship that we were drenched from the water spout. Simultaneously another struck the *Repulse* on the catapult deck, penetrating the ship and exploding below the marine's mess and hangar. . . . At 11:27 fire is raging below, and most strenuous efforts are under way to control it. All gun crews are replenishing their ammunition and are very cool and cracking jokes. There are a couple of jagged holes in the funnel near where I am standing.

It's obvious the Japs flew over the length of the ship, each dropping three bombs so that twenty-seven bombs fell around us at first in their attack. Brilliant red flashes are spouting from our guns' wells. *Prince of Wales* is half a mile away. Destroyers are at various distances throwing everything they have into the air. At 11:40 the *Prince of Wales* seems to be hit. She's reduced speed. Now they're coming to attack us. The communications system shouts "Stand by for barrage." All our guns are going. We are twisting and snaking violently to avoid torpedoes. The Japs are coming in low, one by one in single waves. They're easy to spot. Amid the roar from the guns aboard the *Repulse* and the pompoms of antiaircraft fire, we are signalled, "We've a man overboard."

Two Jap aircraft are approaching us. I see more of them coming with the naked eye. I again count nine. They're torpedo bombers and are circling us about a mile and a half or two miles away. 11:45— now there seems to me more bombers but they are circling like vultures at about one thousand feet altitude. The guns are deafening. The smell of cordite is almost suffocating and explosions are ear-shattering and the flashes blinding. The officer beside me yells, "Here comes a tin fish."

A Jap torpedo bomber is heading directly for us, two hundred yards above the water. At 11:48 he's less than five hundred distant, plowing onward. A torpedo drops and he banks sharply and his whole side is exposed to our guns but instead of diving away he is making a graceful dive toward the water. He hits and immediately bursts into flame in a gigantic splash of orange against the deep blue sky and the robin's egg blue water. Other planes are coming sweeping low in an amazing suicide effort to sink the *Repulse.*

Their daring is astonishing, coming so close you can make out the pilot's outline. One coming in . . . to our starboard just dropped a torpedo. A moment later I hear shouts of joy indicating that he was brought down but I didn't see that.

At 12:01 another wave of torpedo bombers is approaching. They are being met with everything we've got except our fourteen inchers. . . . 12:03: We've just shot down another torpedo bomber who is about four hundred yards away and we shot it out. All of its motors are afire and disintegrating pieces of the fuselage are flying about. Now it disappears over the surface of the water into scrap. The brilliant orange from the fire against this blue sky is so close it's startling. All the men are cheering the sight. . . . At 12:15 the *Wales* seems to be stopped definitely. I've been too busy to watch the attacks against her but she seems in utmost difficulty. Her guns are firing constantly and we are both twisting. One moment the *Wales* is at our starboard, the next it's at our port. I'm not watching the destroyers but they have not been subjected to air attacks. The Japs are throwing everything recklessly against the two capital ships. . . . The calmness of the crews is amazing. . . . Even when they are handing up shells for the service guns, each shell is handed over with a joke. I never saw such happiness on men's faces. This is the first time these gun crews have been in action in this war and they are having the time of their lives. . . . One plane is circling around, it's now at three or four hundred yards approaching us from the port side. It's coming closer, head on, and I see a torpedo drop.

It's streaking for us. A watcher shouts, "Stand by for torpedo," and the tin fish is streaking directly for us. Someone says, "This one's got us." The torpedo struck the side on which I was standing about twenty yards astern of my position. It felt like the ship had crashed into a well-rooted dock. It threw me four feet across the deck but I did not fall and I did not feel any explosion. Just a great jar. Almost immediately it seemed we began to list and less than a minute later there was another jar of the same kind and the same force, except that it was almost precisely the same spot on the starboard side. . . .

It was most difficult to realize I must leave the ship. It seemed too incredible that the *Repulse* could or should go down. But the *Repulse* was fast heeling over. . . . I was forced to clamber and scramble in order to reach the side. . . . Men were lying dead around the guns. . . . I am reluctant to leave my new portable typewriter down in my cabin and unwilling to discard my shoes which I had made just a week before. As I go over the side, the *Prince of Wales* half a mile away seems to be afire but her guns are still firing. . . .

That night Paul White, uncertain about British income-tax regulations and thus anxious to obscure his message, cabled Cecil Brown: "Have notified your bank you did one grand job." Brown received the message in Singapore and exclaimed to a companion, "My God! A thousand-dollar bonus!"

Nine months later, on August 14, 1942, Paul White received stunning news. A plane carrying Eric Sevareid on an observation flight over the Burma Road was missing. Twenty-six days elapsed before CBS learned that Sevareid and his fellow passengers had been forced to bail out over heavy jungle. Sevareid later told the CBS audience of his experiences. A motor had failed, Sevareid explained, and he heard the order to jettison baggage, then to jump:

There was a jam at the doorway. Everyone hesitated. Then John Davies [second secretary of the U.S. Embassy in Chungking], with a curious grin on his face, hopped out and was whisked away. I said to myself, "Good-bye John." I never expected to see him again. . . . John had broken the ice. A few more went over. Then I jumped, like the others for the first time in my life. . . . I can't tell you what

I was thinking because I wasn't thinking anything in particular. The plane had started to turn over on its side, the door side down, obviously going into a spin, so I just went, headfirst. . . . I closed my eyes. There was a terrific rush of wind over my body.

I seemed to know what I was doing and waited a second before pulling the ring, with both hands. I was jerked upright with a terrible jerk, and I said aloud with great surprise, "My God, I'm going to live." I opened my eyes and everything was silent. I saw a river and a native village. Almost directly below me a terrifying geyser of orange flame was spurting out from the mountainside where the plane had crashed. I could see three chutes, boys who had jumped later than I, and one was floating rapidly toward the flames. I looked away and said a short, concise prayer. . . .

I was drifting toward the wreck, blowing backwards, and I struggled to turn myself around. I had to avoid landing in those flames. I tugged frantically. But it wouldn't work and I was rushing headlong at the earth. I was tense now, waiting for the smash . . . hoping that when I hit I could somehow run . . . somehow escape the flames.

And then I was rolling over and over through a thick tangle of brush. When I came to a stop I almost laughed with the realization that I was quite unhurt. But that feeling didn't last very long.

I jumped to my feet and struggled desperately to get out of my parachute harness. There was, of course, no hurry, but panic was quickly possessing me. I could see no more than ten feet ahead in the incredibly thick underbrush. I was already soaking wet and felt the buzzing and stabbing of jungle insects. In my panic I began crashing through the brush in the direction of the wreck, trying to shout to the others between the pulses of retching. Those were the worst moments of my thirty years. I had no idea of my whereabouts, whether India, China or Burma.

[Sevareid heard voices and was joined by four of the plane's crew, two of them injured badly. They searched for the plane and found it a "smoking mess." A moment later they heard the motors of a DC-3 rescue plane.]

They parachuted two packets to us in the brush. One was an emergency pack with two Springfield rifles, jungle knives, blankets and food. The other chute didn't quite open. But from its yellow color we knew it contained radio equipment. We were hunting for it when we heard natives yelling behind us.

They came over the rise, carrying spears and knives, and were dressed only in a wide leather belt and kind of G-string. They were middle-sized muscular men with tattooed arms and chin. The handles of their knives were notched—one notch for each head taken. These natives were head hunters. I took a firmer grip on my jungle knife and waited, whispering to [Harry] Neveu [the injured pilot] not to reach for his gun nor show any sign of hostility or fear. For some strange reason, the visitors stuck their spears in the ground and came up smiling and offering us food and drink. By signs I got a dozen of them to hunt for the missing chute bag, which they quickly found. . . .

We are no longer lost. But we still had the job of getting everyone to the village a mile away and a lot of our group were still sweating up the hill. By late afternoon we had reached the outskirts of the native huts. A few of our group were already there. And when they saw us coming they ran up the hill to meet us.

Some minutes later we saw our rescue plane coming over again and most of us were running over the hillside retrieving bales of food and trying to keep the natives from running off with the parachute cloth, for which they fought one another with everything except, fortunately, their knives. Then for some reason, the plane circled and was coming back. I watched three bales come out and three chutes open.

I was too tired to move until the bales grew legs and turned into men. I couldn't have been more astonished. It was incredible that men would, of their own free will, come to us so far out in the wilderness. They were floating down the hillside, and I ran blindly after them—blindly. I know because for the first time during the whole catastrophe there were tears in my eyes. I came panting and sliding up to the first man who was calmly unwrapping protective bandage from his knees. He smiled and put out his hand. . . .

[The stranger identified himself as Col. Flickinger, a doctor.]

It was just unbelievable. My throat was stuck and I could scarcely get out a word, but only blinked. Flickinger and his aides had not received orders to jump. . . . But these men who could have been back at an airbase that night sleeping in bunks, eating well-cooked food and playing a hand of poker had jumped down to us anyway. And at that moment they didn't know whether they'd ever get out or not. Gallant is a precious word, but gallant is the word for what they did. . . .

CHAPTER 10
When Paley Came Marching Home

V. E. DAY, MAY 8, 1945. EDWARD R. MURROW, WHO HAD BEEN RE-porting on the Allied forces mop-up in Germany, returned to London for the celebration as the chimes of Big Ben tolled and Churchill stated, "The evildoers now lie prostrate before us."

Murrow observed the surging crowds of relieved Britons and re-marked in a broadcast:

There are no words, just a sort of rumbling roar. London is celebrat-ing today in a city which became a symbol. The scars of war are all about. There is no lack of serious, solemn faces. Their thoughts are all their own. Some people appear not to be part of the celebration. Their minds must be filled with memories of friends who died from Burma to the Elbe. There are a few men on crutches, as though to remind all that there is much human wreckage left at the end. Six years is a long time. I have observed today that people have very little to say. There are no words. . . .

In a broadcast later that day he spoke of his own personal memories that went, in part:

The war that was seems more real than the peace that has come. You feel a depression in the wooden paving blocks, and remember that an incendiary burned itself out there. Your best friend was killed on the next corner. You pass a water-tank and recall, almost with a start, that there used to be a pub, hit with a two-thousand-pounder one night, thirty people killed.

It was time to go home. Bill Paley helped set up the American occupation's communications empire in Germany, then returned to 485 Madison Avenue as chairman of the CBS board and named Frank Stanton president. Paley had asked Paul Kesten to stay on, but Kesten "almost cried," saying he had been quite ill for some time and hadn't wanted Paley to know. Paley said: "Kesten struggled along for years seeking a cure. When we get desperate, we turn to quackery. . . . There was a guy in Mexico who injected gold into him." Paul Kesten died "after a long illness," in Great Barrington, Massachusetts, on December 4, 1956.

Paley had postwar plans for Edward R. Murrow, by now the nation's foremost broadcaster: vice-president, news and public affairs. Paul White would have given his eye teeth for the job, but he was passed over, and small wonder. During the London years, Murrow's friendship with Paley had, as one observer put it, "cooked Paul's goose right there."

White couldn't overcome Murrow's lead nor could he overcome an even more formidable enemy—himself. Though he desperately wanted the vice-presidency, he was too uncompromising to get it. There was, for example, a period before Paley left for the war, when the Chairman called frequent meetings of department heads. White was a department head but an associate of those days says he "hated meetings more than anything in the whole world. I remember that he sent a note to Paley on The Twentieth Floor of 485 Madison Avenue:

'Dear Mr. Paley:
  I am very sorry, but my little boy, Paul, cannot be at your meeting today as he is down very bad with his syphillis.
                                                             Mrs. White.'"

While Paley respected Paul for his talent, his independence and for the great staff he had brought together, he wasn't predisposed toward this kind of brash insubordination, impish and appealing though it might seem to some.

Murrow didn't want the job of vice-president, protesting in vain that he had no taste for administration and wanted to continue as a broadcaster. But Paley was convinced that Murrow's popularity as a broadcaster would end with the war. He wanted Murrow to develop new programs and leave the broadcasting to the strong staff he had helped create.

Murrow would never be completely comfortable as an executive, or as a member of the board of directors. Ike Levy remembers him sitting at board meetings without making a comment. "I told him he was getting a hundred dollars for attending meetings and that he ought to make a contribution." Thereafter, Murrow would say a few things. Each time he did, Ike would write on a piece of paper, "$15" or "$5" or "$35"—evaluating the "contribution."

Nor was Murrow happy with the commercialism of American radio, having become accustomed to the BBC. But he did admire the strengths of American radio, expressing his feelings as follows:

There is something unique about the American system. . . . I believe that what comes out of the loudspeaker is the most honest and accurate reflection of what goes on in a nation. Radio reflects the social, economic and cultural climate in which it lives and grows.

Compare broadcasting and you are comparing countries. Our system is fast, experimental, technically slick. It is highly competitive and commercial. Often it is loud, occasionally vulgar, generally optimistic, and not always right. But the man who is wrong has his chance to be heard. There is much controversy and debate, and some special pleading, but frequently the phonies are found out.

That last sentence was curiously prophetic but no more so than one that followed. "A loud voice which reaches from coast to coast is not necessarily uttering truths more profound than those that may be heard in the classroom, bar or country store."

By all logic, Elmer Davis would have been expected to return to CBS after the war. One person who had good reason to expect this was his agent, "Jap" Gude.

Gude—diplomatic, bright and refined—was an ideal sort of man to become an agent for important talent. During the war he had left his publicity job at CBS, and in 1944 he wrote Elmer Davis to say that he hoped that when the war was over Elmer would decide to go back to broadcasting. If Elmer did, Jap and his partner Tom Stix wanted to represent him. (Stix was a "character" in his own right. A roly-poly, hard-drinking prankster, he once collected an anthology of crooked sports stories called *Say it Ain't So, Joe.*)

Davis wrote back to say that he would be happy to have the two men represent him, though he hadn't decided whether to go back to broadcasting or freelance writing. He had been a successful freelancer before he went into broadcasting.

After the war, Gude and Stix took turns traveling to Washington to convince Davis that he ought to return to radio. Davis, still modest, had to be convinced that he was a hot property.

Jap Gude told Davis: "I feel that you really belong at CBS. That's where you started. But I don't think you should just walk into CBS, hat in hand, and say, 'What kind of a deal can you make me?' You ought to see other networks too."

Davis thought that CBS should have priority but agreed to listen to all offers. Jap released an item to the newspapers saying that Davis was leaving Washington and that no career arrangements had been made. Every major network nibbled at the bait—every network but CBS. This though Jap had taken the precaution of writing a personal letter to Bill Paley whom he knew well from the early days at CBS. The letter simply told Bill that Elmer was coming back to broadcasting and that Elmer would like to give CBS first refusal.

There was no reply. Jap followed through and learned that Paley had quietly slipped off to the American desert to give himself a month to get readjusted after the "ravages of war," as one envious CBS man put it, noting Paley's plush foxhole in London's Claridge Hotel.

Meanwhile, Gude recalls, the other networks were "on Elmer's neck." Both NBC and ABC (the old NBC Red network that RCA had been forced to spin off in an antitrust action) wanted to talk with Elmer, and so did Mutual which was "a damn good network in those days." But still no word from CBS. Jap tried to call CBS news chief Paul White but learned that White was in South America. Edmund Chester, a White assistant, was also in South America. Jap called Davis and explained that Paley was incommunicado and he was hesitant about trying to break through to him, figuring Paley wouldn't like it. But, Jap said, there was always Kesten.

Davis sensed a deliberate roadblock and said: "No, if they are not interested, forget it. It seems to me that we have done everything reasonable to give them a chance."

Jap persisted and finally got Davis to let him call Kesten. Jap Gude was at CBS even before Kesten. Still he had trouble getting CBS's acting chief executive on the telephone and when he did, "he was brusque," says Gude. "I told him that I had written Paley and that maybe Paley hadn't received the letter. He said, 'Talk to Paul White.' I felt like saying, 'You really ought to know that Paul White is in South America!' I did say, 'Paul, this can't wait!' He said, 'It will have to.' I said, 'Well, Paul, it can't!' So he said he would have somebody call me."

It was at the next step in the charade that Gude really started to get angry: Kesten had Zack Becker call back. It was almost a joke—at Davis's expense. Though Gude considered Becker "an awfully nice guy," he was a talent coordinator—not a newsman. Offering Becker was in marked contrast to the kind of treatment promised Davis at the other networks which were proffering their top executives to negotiate.

"Becker and a lawyer started negotiating with Tom Stix and me as though Elmer was a piece of comic talent. I said, 'Look, gentlemen, you know me and you know Tom Stix. If you are interested in Davis on a long-term-contract basis, we would like to discuss with you a man who is possibly the most distinguished journalist in the United States.' I was pretty hot. They might have been engaging a singer.

"I cooled off after we got out and said, 'CBS is still where Elmer ought to be.' Tom agreed, but said we better call Elmer and put it up to him."

This time Davis was adamant. He said: "I'm not going to wait any longer. I don't want to go back to CBS. I don't want you to make any further advances. Forget them. You've done everything that anybody could ask for."

The other networks all made their offers now. As good as the Mutual and NBC offers were, the offer from ABC was "fabulous." What's more, Elmer liked ABC's Bob Kintner, once of Alsop and Kintner, columnists (who would later go to NBC), and he liked Mark Woods who was in charge of news and public affairs.

The top people showed up to negotiate at each network, and at ABC even the chairman of the board was there. This was the kind of attention Jap felt Davis deserved everywhere—and especially at CBS where he had spent so many years.

Years later Jap Gude met Ed Murrow for lunch and, in the course of a conversation, Jap said, "I'd better give Bill Paley a call." Murrow said, quietly, that he would make that call:

"He's never forgiven you for taking Elmer Davis away from CBS. It still rankles."

Guy Della Cioppa, Bill Paley's meticulous and deferential aide in London and Europe, remembers that Paley was quite moody for months when he returned to the States after the war. The cause of his distress: He and Dorothy were ending their marriage. The strains between Dorothy and Bill Paley that led to divorce might have begun even before the war.

On March 8, 1940, in Detroit, Michigan, a 28-year-old woman clad in a costly gray ensemble and a new silver fox cape, leapt to her death from a 17th-floor suite of the Book-Cadillac Hotel. When the Detroit newspapermen arrived at the scene they reportedly found that the woman, registered under her assumed name of Mrs. J. Stoddard of New York City, had taken oil paint and a brush and written the names of a number of prominent Detroit automobile executives on the mirror. Also on the list: William S. Paley. At the bottom the woman, an aspiring but unsuccessful actress, wrote the show business line, "Exit laughing."

Strewn about the hotel room were a number of expensive gowns, hats and underthings which a Detroit newspaper later described as "of a design popularly known as exotic." A floral gift card in the room bore the message "You're still lovely." There were $700 in cash and a solitaire game over which she had placed the ace of spades; police said that card was once called "death's card." She also left several love messages, poems and letters.

Reporters found two Burns detectives looking through Mrs. Stoddard's personal effects. The detectives would not identify their employer for the newsmen. At some point, the prominent names were discreetly removed from the mirror. But some letters—including one addressed to Bill Paley—were copied by reporters and taken back to the newsrooms.

Johanna Stoddard had begun life as Geraldine Kenyon in Battle Creek, Michigan. Some seven years before her leap she had deserted her husband, Dan Bourque, a Pontiac, Michigan, auto worker, and an infant daughter to seek a glamorous life in New York, where she met Bill Paley and many other men. Her husband said he hadn't seen her since the day she left him.

The letter to Paley, addressed but not stamped, and dated December 8, read as follows:

Dearest Bill,

I just wanted to thank you for your kindness. You know how things were with me. I may have said things in desperation that I didn't mean. I hope you do not hate me, and, I mean, I'm sorry. I know you will understand and forgive me. I'm not well. My lungs are in a precarious state, where I have to be so careful.

I still love you, but I guess you were right. I only fought so hard because my heart hurt so. You've been very white about everything. I can only hope to emulate you and try to do something good with my life. I am very tired.

Goodbye darling.

Johanna.

The story at CBS was that Dorothy was asked to put out a statement to the press. But the statement ultimately came from Bill Paley himself. It said:

I met Miss Stoddard about a year ago in a restaurant with a group of people. Although I had seen her only that once, she wrote letters to me six months later asking help on the ground that she had tuberculosis. She told me she was an entertainer, but she had no talent and, so far as I could find out, no experience that would justify putting her on the air.

Mrs. Paley and I both talked to her several times, trying to straighten her out, but she became more mentally disturbed all the time. Finally she began to write letters to me, declaring that she had developed an emotional attachment for me.

She had spoken of some relatives in Michigan, and through my lawyers we tried to locate those relatives in the hope that they could take care of her and induce her to come home. No relatives could be found, and meanwhile she kept writing and telephoning me that her health was getting worse and that she wanted to go out to Arizona. She refused to accept medical attention here and all my efforts to convince her that an association with her was impossible were in vain.

A few days ago I was informed that she was going to Michigan and then to Arizona. That was the last I heard from her.

In late July 1947 the divorce between Bill and Dorothy Paley made headlines. The New York *Daily News,* reporting from Reno, stated:

This rough and ready divorce capital gasped tonight when it learned that William S. Paley, president [sic] of the Columbia Broadcasting System, had given his wife a check for $1,500,000 as a settlement in the divorce she obtained today. Verification of the payment, largest ever made in this Mecca for parting couples, came from those who saw photostatic copies of the check. . . .

Mrs. Paley, so far as is known, has no future matrimonial plans, but the CBS president is reported planning to marry Mrs. Barbara (Babe) Mortimer, willowy socialite eyeful from Boston.

Barbara, chosen by the New York Dress Institute in 1945 as the best-dressed woman in the world, is the youngest daughter of the late surgeon, Dr. Harvey Cushing. She is the sister of Mrs. Vincent Astor and Mrs. John Hay Whitney. Barbara also got a Nevada divorce when she parted company with Stanley G. Mortimer, Jr.

The gossip had it right for a change. The wedding took place five days later—on July 28, 1947.

Helen Sioussat remembers that Bill and his new bride were very devoted: "At first he looked on her as a child. She was a lot younger than he. She'd sit on his lap and he would treat her just as a little girl. She and her two sisters were beautifully brought up and *very* attractive. They all had lots of charm and knew how to please a man. Babe was a little shyer—quieter than the other two. . . . Bill was very proud of Babe and she was crazy about him."

Before the wedding, Paley had gone to Frank Stanton to borrow some of the CBS president's movie cameras. Stanton was an avid photographer, and Paley had been a camera buff before the war. Frank was happy to lend Paley the movie equipment for the wedding. Paley then said he hoped Stanton wouldn't feel slighted by not being invited to the wedding since it was a family affair and no one from CBS was being invited.

Stanton understood, and he and another Paley associate from the old days, outside counsel Ralph Colin, met on the wedding day in Stanton's office to toast the bridal couple with champagne. Both men knew that Paley made it a strict practice not to mix business and social contacts.

Later, Paley returned Stanton's equipment with several rolls of film. He asked if Stanton would mind editing the movies of the wedding. Frank was happy to do so. His pleasure at doing his boss a favor was dispelled, however, when the film revealed a famous CBS vice-president, Edward R. Murrow.

CHAPTER 11
The Day Young Ernie Martin Made the Big Time

"GET IN ON THE GROUND FLOOR" HAS LONG BEEN STANDARD ADVICE TO the ambitious young. CBS, as a new and rapidly growing company, provided this opportunity to many a talented young man in the 1930s and 1940s. Being in a new and glamorous field, the network was able to attract some of the brightest talent of the day, and made an effort to move them along as fast as they could go. But while rapid advancement is often possible in the lower echelons of a company, politics sometimes prevents this policy from being carried out at higher levels. This happened to Ernie Martin who went on to become, with Cy Feuer, one of the most successful Broadway producers of our time.

In 1941, Ernie Martin was president of his senior class at UCLA. He was also tour guide, usher, then all-night switchboard operator at CBS's radio studios on Sunset Boulevard. Classified 4-F due to a respiratory disorder, Ernie was one of the few young men who continued working at CBS after Pearl Harbor.

After graduation the dark, lean, tall, 22-year-old Ernie Martin—a thin cigar protruding from his foxy face, his erect posture reflecting his innate cockiness—began his march up the CBS staircase. He became assistant to the chief censor. This job quickly brought the young man in contact with the stars. George Burns would put a double entendre in a script, and Ernie would try to talk him out of it. Hedda Hopper was always reporting that some young starlet or well-known personality was dancing with someone. The someone was usually married to someone else, and Ernie had to blue-pencil the reference before it aired and got CBS sued.

This was the era in which advertising agencies produced radio shows. CBS simply sold them the time. Benton & Bowles, Young & Rubicam and the other leading agencies had offices in Hollywood. Martin became "contact producer"—the network man who held a stopwatch and interrupted the agencies' locally produced shows to drop in the network's national spot announcements. He was moving up the ladder fast. His success brought him the assignment as national network representative in Hollywood. If a sponsor came to the West Coast studios, Ernie would be there in a blue suit with his best PR manner to meet him.

Suddenly Ernie, who had never been east of the Rockies, was handling all kinds of national correspondence, building relationships with people in New York. He was not involved in sales, the usual track to the upper echelons, but he was learning the ropes on the production side.

His education accelerated after he met CBS vice-president Paul Hollister. Hollister came west to suggest that Ernie start producing a 30-second promotional tease, using stars of CBS shows to urge listeners to be sure and hear so-and-so this evening. This assignment led to the big one.

In 1945, with the war still on, it was CBS's turn to plan the entertainment for the White House Correspondents' Dinner. Since Martin knew the stars he was asked to put on the two-hour show for the president of the United States, cabinet members and a hundred other notables. Ernie eagerly accepted.

Soon he was planning acts, making travel arrangements for the stars and handling the myriad details involved in a vast production. He worked with Fanny Brice and Hanley Stafford, who played Daddy to Fanny's Baby Snooks. Then there was the mailman on Fanny's show —Danny Thomas. Ernie created a special act for him. George Burns and Gracie Allen were lined up, and so was Danny Kaye, who was already a big movie star. Ernie asked Jimmy Durante to come, and to bring his old nightclub partners Clayton and Jackson.

When the 24-year-old kid from L. A. arrived in Washington and walked through the Statler Hotel ballroom, he read the place cards in disbelief. Just about every senator was to be there, and on the dais FDR's entire cabinet was represented—except for Secretary of Labor Frances Perkins. At the Correspondents' Dinner in that unenlightened age, ladies were only welcome as performers. The joint chiefs of staff were coming, including General George Marshall and the commandant of the marine corps. All the wheels from CBS were coming too, except Bill Paley who was still in London.

For once cocky Ernie Martin was taken aback. As the chairs began to fill, Ernie stood outside the ballroom with Danny Kaye, peeking in. Finally every chair was occupied except one, and the Marine Band struck up "Hail to the Chief." Ernie remembers: "All of a sudden this god rolled in in a wheelchair, biting on that long cigarette holder."

Secret Service men were standing around, their eyes shifting this way and that, as FDR was brought to his seat. Other Secret Service men were downstairs in the kitchen, tasting the food. Danny Kaye, who had been a big FDR supporter, told a Secret Service man that he and Ernie would like to go over to say hello to President Roosevelt. "You can do it," the man answered, "but if you take three steps in his direction, there'll be one less act tonight."

The show began. Baby Snooks asked who that man was with the cigarette holder. Daddy said he was the president and didn't Baby Snooks know who the president was. "George Washington?" Anyway, the president had been making peace at Yalta. "I want a piece of Yalta!"

Jimmy Durante did his "If Washington calls me I'll answer the call, but they better not call me collect" number. When he finished, some of the distinguished audience began yelling, "Wood, Wood!" This baffled Ernie Martin until he found out that it referred to a standard Durante routine, in which the comedian would break up practically every piece of wood in sight.

They did the routine and for the final thrust, Jackson, Clayton and Durante got behind the Steinway grand piano and pushed. It rolled off the stage with a tremendous crash and broke into pieces—strings and ivory flying everywhere. The evening was a smashing success.

And it was Ernie's night. He was well launched. Soon CBS vice-president Doug Coulter visited him on the Coast to convey Paley's decision to put CBS in the production business. Paley was convinced that the advertising agencies wouldn't be capable of producing the coming television shows. (Eventually he was proved right, but it wasn't until the mid-Fifties that television shows became too expensive for the advertisers to produce, and the networks took over the main production function.) Paley wanted CBS to go into the business of producing its own radio shows to get production experience and to prepare shows that could make the transition to television.

CBS had already done the Orson Welles *Mercury Theater of the Air* and the *Columbia Workshop* dramas. These were "high-class people doing high-class shows." Paley wanted Ernie to produce commercial shows—salable productions that could be put on the air on a sustaining basis (that is, unsponsored) and then sold to sponsors.

Paley was not only gambling about $1 million, as Martin recalls, but he was gambling on his young West Coast impresario, still in his early twenties, rather than "bringing in some guy from Young & Rubicam."

Martin hired a few key people, including writers, and went to work. Meanwhile, in New York, CBS created a program board to meet once a month to discuss production ideas and shows that were under way. Davidson Taylor, the entertainment-programing chief, and Ed Murrow, news-programing chief, were on it, and so were Paley, Stanton and Bill Gittinger, sales vice-president. Ernie Martin was on the board, of course, and each month he would fly to the East Coast.

His first sponsored program was the mystery drama *Suspense,* which was sent out from New York. On his own, Ernie helped develop *My Friend Irma, Life with Luigi* and a show featuring Abe Burrows. All of these would be quickly adapted to TV a few years later, providing CBS with the hoped-for lead-in to the new medium. There were failures as well. These included what may have been the first adult western—*Hawk Larabee,* which later became *Hawk Durango.* It ran on Saturday afternoon on a sustaining basis and was almost—but not quite—sold to Wrigley's Gum. The show, however, did pave the way for another adult western by the same young author, John Meston, who Ernie had hired "off the street." That second show was *Gunsmoke.*

Ernie Martin lived in a world of his own—and it was growing bigger and more important all the time. He was his own boss and got little second-guessing, except for constructive help at the monthly program meetings in New York. Busy and happy on the West Coast, he wasn't interested in office politics.

Perhaps that's why Frank Stanton called Martin one evening at the office CBS provided him at 485 Madison Avenue when he was in New York. Stanton was worried and apparently wanted to get something off his chest. Martin figures Stanton must have felt he would be a good listener who wouldn't gossip about what was said. The conversation gave Martin an insight into the insecurities that plagued one of the communication industry's most influential citizens all his life. And if Stanton's fears had any foundation, they also provided an insight into the mercurial personality of Bill Paley. Stanton complained that Paley hadn't relinquished much authority when he made Stanton president just a couple of months earlier.

Martin was astonished. "Gee," he said, "you've got a terrific job making fifty thousand dollars a year. That's a lot of money!" Stanton said, "Yes, but suppose Bill comes in one day with a stomach ache and decides he doesn't like my face? He could fire me. How many jobs are there for a network president? After all, I've got no stock."

Martin asked, "What's stock?" He claims today that he really didn't know.

Looking back on it now, Martin remembers: "I suddenly realized that men in high places had special terrors that were different from mine."

Martin now thinks that Bill Paley may believe he left CBS at age 26 because an executive realignment put a new man over him. Paley had explained to Martin that he was too young to sell to the board of directors as a vice-president. But Martin didn't really mind. He even helped Paley pick the new vice-president—Hubbell Robinson, an advertising man—and was happy to take Hub by the hand and show him the West Coast operation. Soon, however, he became annoyed at Robinson's disdain for some of the commercial shows Martin was turning out. He wired Paley: "Would you please keep your temporary vice-presidents from interfering with my permanent shows?"

It was an impertinent telegram and Paley and Stanton decided that they had to do something about it. Knowing that Ernie and a Hollywood bandleader were working on a musical version of *Charley's Aunt,* they decided to issue an ultimatum: Spend full time on CBS activities and give up the *Charley's Aunt* project—or go. Martin argued that *Charley's Aunt* would teach him much that could be applied to television. They wouldn't back down. So Ernie Martin got his hat and said goodbye.

Victor Ratner, who felt Ernie was one of the best young talents in the company, went to Frank Stanton, arguing that CBS couldn't afford to lose him. "Don't ask Ernie to be mature. We've got to be mature. Ernie's just a kid!"

Stanton said, "Well, their show will flop on Broadway and he'll be back."

Stanton was wrong, of course. CBS had helped Martin learn the producer business well. With his bandleader friend and partner, Cy Feuer, Martin produced the show, renamed *Where's Charley?*, with the incomparable Ray Bolger. It was a hit, as were four succeeding shows: *Guys and Dolls; Can Can; Silk Stockings;* and *How to Succeed in Business Without Really Trying. Cabaret,* the team's first movie, was an artistic success and grossed over $18 million, making the all-time top 50.

These days, the kid from the West Coast sits in his offices on Park Avenue, drinking directly from a quart bottle of mineral water—one of his few apparent eccentricities. Near his desk is a Steinway piano big enough to serve as the *pièce de résistance* in a performance of Jimmy Durante's "Wood."

While he still speaks with a jaunty confidence, it is clear that Ernie Martin has mellowed; the brash kid has melted into the past. A few years ago he ran into Frank Stanton on the street and they agreed to dine together. Martin got a copy of the CBS annual report to look up an item of information for their forthcoming meeting.

For by this time Martin knew what stock was. At dinner Martin told Stanton that, according to his estimate, Frank was worth close to $10 million in CBS stock—and Stanton was still president of CBS, however anxious he might still be about Paley's moods.

Martin hadn't done badly either. He too counted his chips in seven figures. And, thanks to a decision Stanton and Paley must have later regretted, Ernie Martin was his own boss.

CHAPTER 12
How CBS Almost Bought a Millstone

ALTHOUGH TELEVISION DIDN'T REALLY BECOME PART OF THE PUBLIC consciousness until after World War II, experiments had been going on for years in every part of the world. In 1923, while working for Westinghouse Electric, Vladimir Zworykin, who began his career as a communications specialist in the czarist army, obtained a patent on the iconoscope, the earliest practical pickup tube, and television was on its way.

CBS began spending on television in the 1930s and, according to Frank Stanton, laid out $50 million "before we saw anything back." But it all came out of radio profits, Stanton says, so the lucrative network didn't have to borrow a dime for the development of the wondrous device.

By the mid-1940s, CBS was in ferment over the new medium. The network realized that television would require an enormous volume of entertainment material even if, as then expected, telecasts filled only a few hours of prime evening time. Bill Paley was anxious to see what his company could learn from the medium that most closely paralleled TV—motion pictures. He turned to Howard Meighan, who joined CBS in 1934 and whose later career at CBS and elsewhere was either "brilliant" or "disastrous," depending upon who tells the story.

Three generations of Meighans had studied law, and Howard, in his turn, earned his degree at the Columbia School of Law before joining CBS only six years after Paley arrived. Meighan rose quickly to become a member of the top executive team, sharing with several others the title of vice-president and general executive. Though Meighan had a talent for bluster, his scholastic background gave his work substance. Thus, while there are those who distrust Meighan's flow of gab (Victor Ratner insisted that Howard was responsible for several major mistakes but talked his way out of them), he was certainly a central figure through much of CBS's history. A big man with a craggy face and longish white hair, he bears a striking resemblance to the eagle on the United States seal.

In addition to his executive responsibilities, Meighan worked hard to serve Paley's love of luxury, though his please-the-boss ploys didn't always succeed. Once, when Meighan was running things on the West Coast, he learned that Paley was headed to Los Angeles on business. Meighan browbeat a limousine service into providing its newest car and best chauffeur, even though that driver was already assigned elsewhere. Six months later when Paley returned to the Coast, Meighan once again demanded the limo company's newest car and the same driver, who this time was firmly committed to another VIP. It took some talking, but when Paley arrived he was guided to the limousine by a triumphant Meighan. His triumph, however, was short-lived. Glancing at the driver as he sank into the soft glove-leather seats, Paley whispered to Meighan, "Just my luck. The worst driver in the West and I get him twice in a row."

Meighan's position on the West Coast, where he was originally sent to seek a television–motion-picture alliance, resulted from a series of luncheon meetings at 485 Madison Avenue in the late 1940s. There was the unmistakable stamp of kingship to these occasions. The other top executives sat in their offices wrapping up details of one sort or another, or talking on the telephone, or glancing through *Variety*, or just fidgeting—while they waited. When Paley was ready, his secretary made phone calls to the chieftains and they all trooped to lunch.

One afternoon after the executives had eaten one of Paley's cherished stews (his favorite entree), the Chairman waxed enthusiastic about a proposal from MGM. "I've got a darned interesting offer," he began, and went on to tell his executive team that if CBS would add up the money spent by the network to that date, MGM would put up an equal sum as "seed capital" for a joint venture into TV. Each company would retain a half interest.

This offer came at a time when just about the only sure thing about television was that it was terribly expensive. Whereas you could do radio broadcasts from a glorified telephone booth, television was an entirely different proposition. It was already becoming clear that the public would soon demand production qualities rivaling those of the movies. Paley didn't like Hollywood's nepotism and loose spending, but the movie men had already mastered the art of putting pictures on a screen, and CBS would have to learn from them.

At a subsequent lunch, however, Paley announced that he had changed his mind about the MGM offer. He had a better idea: Rather than take on a partner, why not just pick the brains of somebody in the movie world so that CBS could strike out alone?

Paley's first instinct was to have someone meet with his friend, David O. Selznick, one of the few men in the world who knew Paley intimately. Selznick was also one of the great movie producers, the man who brought *Gone With the Wind* to the screen in 1939. Clearly, Selznick had the know-how, but Paley, knowing his friend too well, foresaw conflict. He told the lunch cadre the following week that after consideration, he had concluded that Selznick would want $4 million, would then use it to make a movie and that would be that.

Next Paley mentioned Cecil B. DeMille. Known primarily for his great film spectacles, DeMille had also created the highly popular *Lux Radio Theater* for CBS, converting major movies into three-act radio plays, a most difficult task which worked in the master's hands. DeMille was wealthy, hence independent enough to do anything he wanted and unlikely to seek CBS money to fund his own movie project. He was thoughtful, level-headed, and regarded as a decent man by the CBS officer corps.

Howard Meighan flew to the Coast to see DeMille. The visit was unsuccessful for CBS, though Meighan and DeMille became fast friends. The problem: DeMille was $2 million into the filming of the Barnum & Bailey Circus story, *The Greatest Show on Earth*, for Paramount.

Graciously rebuffed by DeMille, Meighan returned to New York and another luncheon meeting, where Paley presented still another idea. "I think what we ought to do is take somebody who knows broadcasting and send him to Hollywood to learn whatever we need to learn about the movies."

Meighan, who had just bought a home in Larchmont, New York, and had yet to move his family into it, was astonished when Paley gave him the assignment. Frank Stanton was told to see that Meighan's new home was sold.

Meighan hadn't been in Hollywood long when he realized that one thing television would have to borrow from the movies was the idea of horizontal movement. You couldn't move large props and heavy sets from floor to floor in a high-rise building. He thus became interested in the old Goldwyn-Pickford lot on Melrose Avenue in Los Angeles. He discussed the idea with Paley in 1949, and Paley told him to make a deal.

Meighan remembers the subsequent encounters well. "Goldwyn had a typical movie tycoon's office, a real eye-bugger. It must have been a third as big as a basketball court, filled with memorabilia of Goldwyn's films."

According to Benjamin Sonnenberg, Goldwyn's former press agent and later one of the nation's most powerful PR consultants: "Sam Goldwyn created a caricature of himself and then wore it as a disguise." Part of the caricature was his unique use of the language. It was Goldwyn who said, "I'll tell you in two words—Im possible." To a man who said he was from Iowa: "Out here we pronounce it Ohio." Also: "A man who goes to a psychiatrist needs his head examined." His form of malapropisms became famous enough to be known as Goldwynisms.

Goldwyn shared ownership of the studios with America's Sweetheart, Mary Pickford, who early in her phenomenally successful career had perfected a way of getting ever more money by affecting helpless femininity while arguing only for "what I am worth."

Though Mary owned 41/80 and Goldwyn just 39/80 when Meighan came along, each was entitled to use any part of the premises. And they were both ready to sell. The problem Meighan faced was that they had become deadly enemies—each determined to best the other in any deal to buy them both out.

As Meighan met with Goldwyn, the producer's property manager, Marvin Ozell, sat in. Goldwyn would make, as Meighan says, "one outrageous statement after another" and demand of his sycophant, "Isn't that right, Marvin?"

"Yes, sir."

The Ozell-seconded statements went on at lunch as Goldwyn spoke of the parallel careers he and Bill Paley had forged in new entertainment industries, each of them rising to the top.

"You're a lucky man to work with Bill Paley," Goldwyn said. "Isn't that right, Marvin?"

"Yes, sir!"

"Even though he was born with a silver spoon in his mouth and I had to work my way up, isn't that right, Marvin?"

"Yes, sir!"

Then Meighan spoke up, though he doesn't now recall why he was so ungracious at that point. "As a matter of fact, Bill Paley is a wonderful fellow. He loves an argument, though, so there's one thing he never has around him and that's a 'yes' man."

Goldwyn: "That's the secret to my success, too. Isn't that right, Marvin?"

"Yes, sir!"

When they got down to business, it was clear that Goldwyn was willing to sell, and they soon worked out an agreement. They shook on it and Meighan said, "I'll send you a memo," but Goldwyn said no, that a handshake from Goldwyn was like having a treasury gold bond.

Meighan had told Goldwyn he would not tell Pickford the sum agreed upon. Neither would know what CBS was paying the other. Goldwyn had agreed to it and Meighan insisted that Mary agree to it also.

Most of the time Mary Pickford remained in seclusion at Pickfair, her palatial estate. But she decided to come to New York to sell her share of the studios. There, when Meighan refused to tell her what Goldwyn was getting for his share, she said she would agree to sell if Meighan would tell her lawyers the figure. Meighan refused. Then she said, "I'll do it if you will tell Louis Pfau, my real estate man." Meighan refused again. Finally, Mary agreed and signed. Meighan flew to the Coast and met with Goldwyn and Marvin Ozell again. Goldwyn said, "Let me see Mary's contract."

Meighan reminded Goldwyn of their understanding that neither seller was to see the other's contract.

"I've got to be guaranteed . . ." Goldwyn began, but Meighan said quietly, "Mr. Goldwyn, we have a deal, remember? The handshake, Mr. Goldwyn? Isn't that right, Marvin? . . . Marvin!"

Meighan went back to the office empty-handed, cursing himself for having failed to send Goldwyn a memo. It would have been worth more than a gold treasury bill.

He fretted until he fell into a troubled sleep. But his subconscious was evidently at work because he awoke with a start at 5 A.M.— wondering why in hell he was negotiating to buy an old-fashioned, run-down manufacturing plant when CBS was embarking on a new business with unique problems. He remembered some figures he had worked out earlier with Arthur Unger, editor of *Daily Variety.* Under the best of circumstances, movie makers averaged just 1 3/4 minutes of finished, usable film per day of shooting. Thus it took nearly 60 days shooting time to complete a 96-minute film, and the cost worked out to $10,000 a minute.

By contrast, half-hour TV segments cost $1000 a minute, and even this was regarded as astronomically high, partly because the expectations of broadcasters had been molded by the relatively inexpensive medium of radio.

Howard recalled, "I said to myself, Christ, we can't manufacture for TV at anything like ten thousand dollars a minute. The unions alone would kill us." (In movie production, the union man who paints scenery off-set can't come on the set to touch them up because that is some other union man's job.)

Meighan flew back to New York and, after telling Bill Paley of his debacle with Goldwyn, suggested they were going down the wrong path in seeking a movie studio. CBS ought to be building its own studio —specifically tailored to the needs of TV.

No expert on architecture or the needs of television studios, Paley was an eager listener and ready to be convinced by intelligent argument. Meighan got the chairman's okay and approached Bill Pereira, a West Coast architect known for his ingenuity. Pereira was also on the faculty of the School of Architecture at the University of Southern California where he suggested that the students in advanced classes take up the CBS project. It would be called Television City and become the school's most famous one-semester design project.

Meanwhile, James Landauer, the real estate man who had located 485 Madison Avenue for Paley years earlier, began negotiations with Earl Gilmore, an enterprising Los Angeles sportsman who owned the Farmer's Market in L.A. and an adjoining property. This lot contained bicycle and motorcycle tracks, facilities for minor league baseball and

Gilmore's home. Gilmore was an ardent horseman, and Landauer remembers working out final details to buy the lot (excluding the Gilmore residence) while horseback riding with the master of the estate.

Pereira and Meighan explained to the students some of the unique properties a television studio should have—insofar as they understood them themselves. For example, how was CBS to deal with studio audiences while moving new sets in and old sets out during a busy broadcast day? There were no studio audiences on the movie set, and visitors could be scheduled at the studio's convenience. But TV audiences were coming to watch a particular show at a particular time.

With Frank Stanton checking details back in New York, a careful amalgam of 53 separate student offerings evolved. Not surprisingly, some features were regarded as unorthodox. One plan-ahead idea must have struck the builders as whimsical, at least. The pilings extended far beyond the building and on through the parking lot, a farsighted idea to allow for future expansion without broadcast-interrupting pile-driving.

But the outstanding design feature was the method chosen to keep scenery moving in a steady flow without interrupting the comings and goings of actors, directors, technicians, studio executives and audiences. Pereira and his design class decided it would be disastrous to try to move people and sets through the same corridors. Thus, ramps were designed to ring the exterior of the building and miniature trains would haul scenery from shop to set, through giant doors leading from the ramps to the four studios within the complex.

One day, when construction was well under way, a World War II general drove up in a limousine just as Howard Meighan was leaving the lot. Meighan made a quick U-turn, pulled up next to the limousine and welcomed an inquisitive but deeply embarrassed David Sarnoff to Television City.

Years later the archaic Goldwyn-Pickford studios on Melrose Avenue were still for sale. America's Sweetheart and that Goldwyn boy were still trying to outwit each other.

CHAPTER 13

Going to the Boss

ASK ALMOST ANY BROADCAST EXECUTIVE ABOUT ONE OF HIS NETWORK'S successful shows, and it's likely he'll tell you how *he* championed the program from its inception. In fact, many of the most successful programs almost got killed by those executives supposedly best able to recognize winning ideas. Fortunately for CBS, Bill Paley took a personal interest in programing and saved more than one program idea his executives would have vetoed.

When an idea for a radio show to be called *CBS Was There* first came along, you might think the network's program people fell all over themselves to grab the credit, the concept was so original and imaginative. The program would recreate a famous historical event, such as the French Revolution, as if it were just happening and being reported as news. There would be John Daly interviewing Louis XVI in Versailles, while other newsmen followed the mob that was storming the Bastille.

Certainly anyone in the business could predict that such a show would win critical acclaim as public-service programing, and, at the same time, make lots of money, which few public-service shows do. But, in fact, the idea was nearly lost to radio (and TV as *You Are There*) due to a policy which so frequently leads to disaster in corporate life:

a high executive shielding the boss from an idea he is sure the boss won't like.

Curiously, the distinguished Davidson Taylor was the shield in this story. Taylor in his earlier days at CBS had helped mold taste as the network's musical supervisor. Then, with the renowned radio writer Norman Corwin, he pioneered convincing radio sound effects to help dramatize Corwin's imaginative stories—*The Plot To Overthrow Christmas* and *Words Without Music* among them. Later, when Bill Paley was deputy head of America's World War II psychological warfare division, Taylor served as a set of sensitive eyes and ears for the boss.

It was Taylor who spotted a gaffe in a recorded message to Resistance fighters by General Dwight D. Eisenhower to be broadcast as the Allied forces stormed the beaches at Normandy on D Day. The general had recorded, "Do not needlessly endanger your lives until I give you the signal. . . ."

Taylor played the passage for Paley, and Paley then persuaded Ike, busy as the general was, that this seemingly callous disregard for lives had to be eliminated. The offending passage was rerecorded as "Do not needlessly endanger your lives. Wait until I give you the signal to rise and . . ."

Taylor's ability to polish a presentation to the nth degree helped him up the corporate ladder. But his inclination to think for the boss led to trouble for the creator of *CBS Was There*. For when the idea was broached at the network, Taylor, back from the war as a vice-president of programing, gave it a pocket veto. Unlike Mike Dann, a successor who kept the programing post longer than anyone else by learning to sense Paley's probable reaction even to a show idea mentioned in passing, Taylor was inclined to take too much on himself. It isn't clear why he wasn't enthusiastic about *CBS Was There*, but he became the biggest stumbling block.

The idea came from one of the most distinguished writers in broadcasting, Goodman Ace, a man best known for the droll radio show *Easy Aces*. The show starred "Goody" and his wife Jane, who played a delightful flutter-brained housewife any homemaking contemporary could laugh at, love—and feel superior to.

The *Easy Aces* script was built around what Goody Ace maintained was Jane's natural aptitude for malapropisms. She delighted listeners with such expressions as "a ragged individualist . . . a thumbnose description . . . words of one cylinder . . . we're insufferable friends . . . Congress is still in season." Other "Jane-isms," often written by her clever husband: "the fly in the oatmeal . . . up at the crank of dawn . . . the Ten Amendments . . . home wasn't built in a day . . . you could have knocked me down with a fender."

Ace was under contract to CBS so he couldn't sell his new idea elsewhere. And Taylor was not his only problem. Ace had approached Robert Lewis Shayon, his friend and a fellow employee. Ace found this writer-director-producer receptive, but Shayon reported back that the studio writers simply weren't excited enough by the idea to do anything with it.

So Ace and Shayon tried a sample script called "Abe Lincoln Attends Ford's Theatre." It was written and submitted to CBS for production. Nothing happened. Ace then said to Shayon, "You're a producer, why don't you produce it. All we need is a studio."

In those days of rational costs, it was a feasible suggestion. The two men assembled a cast, recorded the show on a disc and sent the side to Davidson Taylor. Again, nothing.

Ace then sought advice from Edward R. Murrow, who seemed mainly concerned with the title. Murrow said he didn't know whether it should be "CBS Was There" or "CBS Is There." Ace commented dryly in recollection, "I was desperate by then so I said I didn't care."

Then CBS people argued that the roles of the newsmen should be played by actors, not the actual news staff. Ace felt the show would lose punch if that were done. Time wore on, and Ace's patience wore out. So he asked a man of considerable influence, a man he did not know personally at the time, to come to CBS and listen to the recording.

The man, John Crosby, was a distinguished broadcasting critic for what was then the nation's most brightly edited serious newspaper, the New York *Herald Tribune,* which put its final edition to bed on April 24, 1966. Crosby came, listened and wrote two laudatory columns about *CBS Was There.* You might think that two prominently displayed features in a great newspaper would move mountains. It didn't wiggle molehills at CBS. Presumably, the original disc of the show continued to gather dust on Davidson Taylor's desk.

Thus, when Goodman Ace was scheduled to confer with Paley about a summer-replacement show he was writing, he decided to use the occasion to pitch *CBS Was There*. He knew that he would not be allowed to approach Bill Paley without an escort, and that escort would be Davidson Taylor, vice-president of programing. When the two men met in the corridor before the conference, Ace asked the meticulously dressed Taylor if it would be okay to discuss *CBS Was There*. Taylor said no. Ace was convinced that Paley would like the idea—"He has the best taste of any man I know."

Ace simply wasn't going to give up—even if it meant going over Taylor's head. After the summer-replacement show was discussed, Ace quietly but firmly began sketching out his idea for Paley. Obviously impressed, Paley looked at Taylor and asked, "Why aren't we doing that?"

Taylor, by no means stupid, said, "Oh, we're going to. . . ."

Somewhat later, CBS was faced with the embarrassing business of beginning negotiations for a property that was already scheduled to go on the air. Goodman Ace remembers being called into an executive's office to discuss the price. At the time George Burns was a big hit on CBS radio, and when the CBS executive asked how much he wanted for the show, Ace countered with "How much is George Burns getting?" The CBS man said $6500 a show. Ace said, "Shayon and I will take that."

At that, the executive began "ranting and raving" and Ace interrupted saying, "Wait a minute. Do you belong to Actors Equity?" The executive, taken aback, asked "Why?" Ace said, "Because if you don't you're not allowed to perform like that!"

As Ace had predicted, the show was a hit as soon as it was aired. The irony of his position grew with the show's success: He got a call from a CBS lawyer who said the network was being sued by several people who claimed CBS had stolen their idea. The lawyer asked Ace for details concerning his inspiration and Ace told him the whole story, including the fact that he'd first gotten the idea at a party at his home in Deal, New Jersey.

The lawyer seemed much relieved, until Ace added: "Don't expect me to say that in court."

"Why not?" the lawyer wanted to know. Still unpaid for the idea, Ace said that if the lawyer would "send fifty thousand dollars to Shayon and fifty thousand dollars to me, I'll be an excellent witness."

Eventually Goodman Ace got paid. *CBS Was There* was a fixture on radio for years and then it came to television as *You Are There.* Of course, the network executive who was most prominently involved got the credit. Erik Barnouw wrote in his definitive *History of Broadcasting:* "Under [Davidson] Taylor other challenging projects took shape, including the series, *CBS Was There. . . .*"

Goodman Ace was not the only CBS veteran at the time who bumped heads with executives intent on protecting the boss. Gertrude Berg had 20 years of radio under her abundant belt—14 of them on CBS—and a brand-new Broadway hit, *Me and Molly,* on the boards. But she was frustrated in 1948 when she set about to audition *The Goldbergs* for television.

A Jewish girl from the Upper East Side of Manhattan—then a tenement area—Gertrude Berg became a rainy-day entertainer in the Catskills after her father bought a million-dollar mansion there for $500 and his word of honor and turned it into a hotel. A born dramatist with a warm, funny manner, she mixed the characteristics of her relatives and guests at the hotel to compose members of a make-believe family, the Goldbergs. Though the flavor was distinctly Jewish, the show was poignant, funny and had universal appeal. Molly Goldberg became Gertrude Berg's alter ego, and Jake was her fictional husband:

JAKE: Molly, your soup is feet for a kink.
MOLLY: You mean a president. Ve're in Amerike, not in Europe.
JAKE: Oy, Molly, Molly, soon ve'll be eating from gold plates.
MOLLY: Jake, d'you tink it'll taste better?
JAKE: Soch a question?

Molly's radio family was so believable that Americans wrote thousands of fan letters to the characters as if they were old friends. But after 20 years on radio, some broadcasters felt that *The Goldbergs* simply would not "translate" to television. The late Gertrude Berg told the story in her own inimitable style in the book *Molly and Me:*

My agent would call me one day to say that NBC didn't think *The Goldbergs* could be a television show. Well, that was *their* opinion. I knew different. So I told my agent to get to work on CBS. He did and he called back a few days later to say an audition was all arranged.

Good! I started to think about a script. Then I got another call from my agent—the audition was off. They also thought the show wasn't for TV.

I got annoyed. I was also worried. If you're turned down by NBC and CBS then you're out of business, and that was something I decided I wasn't. That night I couldn't sleep. I tossed and I turned and I burned. About three in the morning I tried to wake up Lew and tell him about a decision I had made, but he was already awake listening to me fuming. I said I couldn't and I wouldn't take this lying down, that was my decision. Lew said I should relax, it was three in the morning, there wasn't anything that could be done. I couldn't even call my agent at that hour. So I tried to relax until daylight. At nine-thirty I picked up the phone. I had decided I wasn't going to talk to "executives," I was going to talk to their boss. A Boss is a Boss and if you're a boss it's not by accident. William S. Paley was the boss so I called and asked for an appointment. I was told that Mr. Paley was leaving to go on a cruise and he didn't have much time.

I said I didn't need much time. The secretary said would ten or fifteen minutes be sufficient and I said three minutes would be plenty.

I went to see Mr. Paley. I had never met him before and the only thing I knew about him was his reputation and the fact that he had a very beautiful wife. I knew his time was short so I said hello and got down to business. I told him that the show might be a flop on TV—or it might be great. I had been on radio for twenty years, fourteen of them on CBS, and I said I thought I deserved an audition.

That took two minutes. The third minute was Mr. Paley's. He got up from behind his desk, came over to where I was sitting, put a hand on my shoulder and told me that I would have my audition. That was that and I left.

By the time I got back home the phone began to ring. There were apologies from various quarters at CBS and an audition was planned. Believe me, there's nothing like three minutes with the boss.

As on radio, *The Goldbergs* gained immediate acceptance on TV. General Foods bought it, the show became a fixture on Monday nights at 9 P.M. and *The Goldbergs* were on television for almost ten years.

CHAPTER 14
The Great Talent Raids

BILL PALEY BELIEVED THAT THE WAY TO ESTABLISH CBS AS THE EQUAL of NBC was to build a formidable in-house talent roster and, whenever possible, do it at his competitor's expense.

When he finally did pull off his great talent raids, his network fully came of age. No longer would a president ask, as FDR had, "What do the letters 'CBS' stand for?" It was now the No. 2 company that was aggressively struggling to become No. 1.

Paley grabbed many important talents in his NBC raids, but none was so important, so characteristic of the Paley technique, so pivotal as Jack Benny. True, *Amos 'n' Andy* was even bigger in its heyday, but Benny's Sunday-night NBC spot had more long-term strengths. It had the familiar characters: Eddie "Rochester" Anderson, the black, sassy butler; Mary Livingston, Benny's "girl friend"; bandleader Phil Harris; announcer Don Wilson; plus Benny's old Maxwell which broke down each Sunday night with a "phat-phat-bang." It had Benny's portrayal of the listeners' own distant stingy uncle. It had the confidence of big-money advertisers. In short, Jack Benny was radio's undisputed king.

In June 1935, CBS was profiled in *Fortune* magazine—a glowing tribute to a company that had increased sales from $5 million in 1929 to $19 million in 1934 while quadrupling net profits during the Great Depression. But 20 pages back in the magazine was a full-page ad featuring a 39-ish Jack Benny, cigar in hand, speaking from a script into an NBC mike. The text: "Jack Benny's JELL-O program commands the largest listening audience of any program on the air."

Small wonder Bill Paley had his eye on Benny all those years. And if Benny went, so might some of the other NBC blue-chip stars. How to get them?

Taxes eventually provided the key. In the aftermath of World War II, patriotism was never more widespread, and under its banner Congress was able to "soak the rich" by thrusting the progressive-income-tax rates into the stratosphere. Those who earned in excess of $70,000 annually could keep only nine cents of each dollar above that figure. It was difficult for those whose talents were worth big money to keep more than $40,000 a year no matter how much they earned.

(Ironically, the vigorous, ambitious members of society who worked the hardest would find themselves on a tax treadmill while those who had money through inheritance could ride around in their limousines relatively unscathed.)

Many schemes were devised to deal with this problem. Comedian Red Skelton, for example, in a form of performer-versus-network blackmail, once refused to entertain the affiliate station owners unless CBS would parquet the floor of Red's Palm Springs home—over a weekend when Red was planning to be out of town. CBS triple-timed it, finishing the job in time to get Red back in without a single missed entrance. One man familiar with the episode thinks it may have cost CBS as much as $10,000. But Skelton knew how much more it would have cost him to do the job with after-tax dollars. And he knew how much it would have cost CBS to hire outside talent to entertain the affiliate owners.

"Uncle Deductible," as Red's famous tax lawyer, Bo Christian Boose, was called, thought about these things frequently. Once Skelton's wife Georgia visited Bonwit Teller and purchased some $500 worth of towels and linens. Bo happened to pull up at the Skelton place at the moment the Bonwit delivery man was unloading the packages. Bo demanded that the man take the packages back to the store, explaining to Georgia that the $500 worth of merchandise would cost Red the equivalent of $5000—since he kept less than ten cents of every dollar the network was paying him. Georgia still wanted the towels and linens, so Bo reordered them—after finding an apparently legal way to deduct the cost of the linens from Red's office account as a business expense.

In such an oppressive tax climate, what more powerful appeal to the show business personality than to offer a big chunk of "keeping money"? The idea, as it finally evolved, was to convert future earnings into present capital gains, since capital gains were taxed at a fraction of the rate that applied to earned income. It worked like this: CBS would buy a "property" owned by the show business personality for cash. If, say, the property brought the personality $1 million and cost him nothing, his capital gain would be the full million dollars, which under the law of the period would be taxed at rates ranging up to 25 percent. Thus the seller would keep a tidy $750,000, twice the keeping money were the million "earned" over five years.

Tax lawyers had been doing such deals for businessmen for years. CBS was the first to apply the gambit to show business in a big way.

The inspiration for this appears to have arisen out of a chance encounter. As CBS's Howard Meighan tells it, he ran into slop-jar philosopher Fletcher Wiley in an L.A. bar. Fletcher (his real name was Amiel de Poncier) was a CBS radio personality who was enormously successful entertaining the housewives, reading from, say, the encyclopedia about diamond mining in Brazil. He even organized the Housewife's Protective League to add the spice of conspiracy to his show.

His first name was taken from Fletcher's Castoria, (a laxative) and the surname from Dr. Alexander Wiley, a popular WOR radio personality. Fletcher's radio popularity was such that he had organized similar programs for CBS elsewhere—including *Galen Drake* in New York. Each received reams of material from Fletcher to be used in the individual performer's own way. Then local material was used to flesh out the broadcasts. The formula should have been making Fletcher very, very rich.

Fletcher and Howard drank a lot that evening and soon the entertainer was complaining about how little he kept of the $400,000 CBS paid him each year. Hung over during a noisy prop-driven flight to New York, Howard suddenly had the idea that CBS might buy the copyright names—Fletcher Wiley, Galen Drake, et al. Then Wiley could keep the proceeds less capital-gains taxes. So he asked CBS taxman Arthur Padgett back at 485 Madison Avenue about it and "Padge" was sure it could be done.

Meighan adds: "Frank Stanton and I used to have a joke that no memo should cover more than one page—but this was complicated. I dictated a memo on one page, written from edge to edge, top to bottom, suggesting that we buy Fletcher's names for up to $750,000. Padge had initialed it. It came back the same day with an 'Okay FS.'"

Fletcher né Amiel was a man of great simplicity. When Meighan asked, "How'd you like it if we put $375,000 in your pocket—net after taxes?" Fletcher didn't bicker over price. While this represented a pretax offer of $500,000, substantially less than Meighan was prepared to pay, Fletcher quickly said he'd like that fine.

News pulses quickly over the Hollywood grapevine—especially when money is involved. MCA, which was the leading talent agency, never let a good idea go unnoticed. They quickly approached CBS and asked how the network would like to buy *Amos 'n' Andy* for $1 million to each of its creators and actors, Gosden and Correll. CBS said that would be fine, negotiated and wrapped it up. Amos and Andy were very important names—so important that there was clearly no problem in establishing the fact that the two names were "properties" suitable for sale.

But when it came to negotiating for Jack Benny, in 1948, the question was, how to change a name into a property. Jack Benny's legal name was Jack Benny. He played himself. There was no name to sell. And even if CBS could find a way to apply the capital-gains scheme, Benny had many very powerful reasons to stay at NBC. Not only was NBC tops in radio, the network's lineup of talent for Sunday night— the biggest night in radio—was spectacular.

In addition to Benny, in the No. 1 spot, there were Phil Harris and Alice Faye; Fred Allen; Edgar Bergen and Charlie McCarthy. Bandleader Horace Heidt followed Bergen and his wooden alter ego. The momentum helped Heidt pile up big ratings at a late hour for Sunday-night radio. There was just no need to turn the dial.

Today everybody knows the play's the thing, not the theater. But back in the 1940s there was no precedent for moving to apparent obscurity from the Big Spotlight. With the prospect of a network switch, Benny's powerful current sponsor, the American Tobacco Company, began to rock like a canoe in choppy water. All American

THE NEWS

Ted Husing explains the 1928 election.

Elmer Davis explains the world.

Richard S. Salant, president of CBS News.

Edward Klauber—the ''father of broadcast journalism.''

UPI

Dan Rather nursing a sore gut after a fracas at the 1968 Democratic convention. Rabbit ears courtesy CBS News. ▷

Roger Mudd from Capitol Hill. ▽

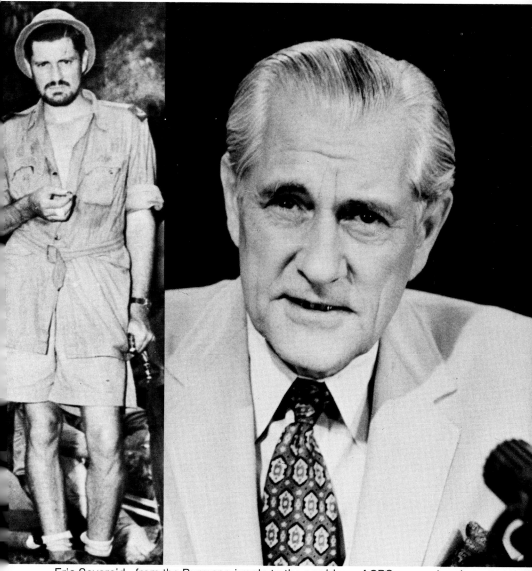

Eric Sevareid—from the Burmese jungle to the corridors of CBS, upward and onward to wisdom and white hair.

◁ Ed Murrow, between wartime bombs in London.

Wallace and Haldeman—the interview that cost CBS a bundle.

Wallace in Chicago—tossed out of the Democratic convention, 1968.

Uncle Walter—how could you doubt him?   CBS

CBS

Ed and Joe—the famous 1954 confrontation.

CBS

Tobacco knew was that NBC was drawing the biggest rating in radio for Lucky Strike at the most important hour on the airwaves.

In view of all that NBC clout, CBS had to offer irresistible attractions in a bid for the top comedian. Obviously, the tax break would mean the most—but human considerations would play a role as well.

There's a story about a little boy who tasted his first ice-cream soda and called it "Just a lot of sweet air." The comment fits General David Sarnoff's apparent view of entertainers—frothy and not worth much bother. He saw talent almost as a necessary evil, a means of keeping radio alive so that listeners would buy RCA radios. When Sarnoff did pay attention to programing, he took most pride in NBC's success in live coverage of major events—Joe Louis fights, Winston Churchill speeches. He was blissfully unaware of talent, and especially of Jack Benny's particular needs. In fact, as astonishing as it may seem in view of Benny's preeminence, Sarnoff had never met his Sunday-night star. Thus, had he looked for ways to insult Benny, he couldn't have been much more successful. And it would take a lot of insults and insensitivity for Benny to make the switch, for he was an intensely loyal person.

Ironically, once the two men did meet years later, they became good friends. Irving Fine, who was Benny's manager, says that if Sarnoff and Benny had met before the negotiations, the comedian would never have considered making the switch.

At any rate, NBC showed very little willingness to negotiate for the purchase of Amusement Enterprises, the "property" that was the focal point in the discussions. Not surprisingly, Benny owned most of the stock of Amusement which in turn owned *The Jack Benny Show*, some opera films and a summer replacement show for Benny starring an obscure comic by the name of Jack Paar.

But there was another factor that may have weighed in the situation: In 1939, an acquaintance of Benny's, a self-styled South American diplomat who was actually a con man of considerable charm, caught up with the vacationing comedian at the train station in Cannes, France. The man, Albert N. Chaperau, offered to take some jewels Benny had purchased for his wife, actress Mary Livingston, back to the States in his "diplomatic pouch." It was pointless to pay the duty, Chaperau said. Benny resisted, but Chaperau was insistent, so Benny shrugged and gave in. The jewels cost $1452.

Chaperau was later exposed, and as a consequence Benny was indicted for smuggling. So was his good friend, George Burns, who had also bought jewelry abroad for his wife. Benny pleaded guilty and, like Burns, received a suspended sentence.

Benny had to appear before a judge in New York who was obviously rankled that a man who earned $12,000 a week wasn't clever enough to avoid the clutches of unscrupulous people. He treated Jack like a criminal, shouting at him to "stand up" when he noticed the comedian slouching over a chair as the facts were read into the record.

The judge was right, of course. It was a sleazy thing for the highly paid entertainer to do—especially one so revered as Benny. And it was quite out of character. Despite his radio character as a skinflint, Benny was actually thoughtful and generous. More typical of Benny was his attitude toward young talent. He would help show business hopefuls in any way he could with gifts of both money and script material.

United States Attorney John T. Cahill prosecuted the government's case against Jack Benny. When Benny was negotiating with CBS over a possible switch to Columbia, the lawyer Sarnoff hired to handle negotiations for NBC was—John T. Cahill, now in private practice.

That was the big insult. But it wasn't the only one. The official NBC attitude seemed to be "Why should we buy something we already have?" Which in retrospect may have been one of the most short-sighted attitudes ever taken in show business.

NBC's indifference to stars and their egos even filtered down to parking privileges. During the negotiating period, Jack cracked, "I wonder if they have free parking at CBS?" In those days, everybody paid a quarter to park in the lot behind the NBC studios.

NBC's indifference was in sharp contrast with Bill Paley's solicitude.

The negotiations had been under way for some time with neither Paley nor Benny giving the go-ahead. One day, Bill Paley went home with the Benny deal very much on his mind. Itchy all during dinner, he called for his car as soon as he finished and returned to the office. It was late in the evening. He sat in his swivel chair wondering whether the $3.2 million CBS was offering was a sound investment.

As he pondered the Benny idea, he looked at the beautiful paneling of his office, the extravagance of which had so appalled him at the Paramount Building that he brought it along when he moved CBS to 485 Madison Avenue—as a reminder. Was it ego—this desire to land the nation's biggest radio star at a very considerable figure—or a sound business judgment?

Paley picked up the telephone and called Jack Benny's home on the West Coast. It was three hours earlier there, about dinnertime, and he was told that Benny was dining at a friend's home. Paley called the friend's house, got Benny on the telephone, chatted for a while and then got down to business. He remarked that while his people and Benny's—lawyers, accountants, agents—had talked about the deal again and again, Benny and Paley hadn't talked about it. Paley wondered what interested Benny about CBS and Benny wondered why Paley was so anxious to have him. Paley sketched his broadcasting philosophy for Benny: Broadcasting wasn't kilowatts and stations—it was talent; listeners tune in performers, not stations. He went on to say that he admired Benny as a great talent with a wonderful wit and as a man who never used offensive stories. "I'd be proud to have you," he concluded. But, he said, adding Benny to the CBS roster was going to be a terribly expensive proposition.

Benny said he was glad to hear that Paley thought talent was radio's most precious asset; that he, in all modesty, shared that opinion. This attitude was so pleasing to him that in view of it and all the rest involved, he would be happy to work for Paley. He even suggested he would help bring some of the other NBC stars to CBS.

The agreement was made during that telephone call.

Paley did a lot of soul-searching over the Benny deal because the acquisition could have been prohibitively expensive. The only way the American Tobacco Company would go along with the switch was if Paley guaranteed them $3000 for every point that Jack Benny fell below his Hooper rating at NBC—$3000 per point per week. At the time, Benny's Hooper rating was a formidable 24-plus. The move could cost CBS a fortune if Paley's theory about listeners was wrong—if they in fact tuned in stations not performers. But it was the kind of gamble that Paley understood and was willing to take. His was a high-stakes business and he played it that way.

The network launched a major advertising campaign announcing the switch which was to take place on January 2, 1949, right in the middle of the radio season. Meanwhile, NBC, stunned by its loss and anxious to prove its pulling power, decided to put Horace Heidt into the Benny spot and ballyhooed his forthcoming move to "The Number-One Spot in Radio." The shows were aired and two sides tensely awaited the rating decision. The result: Jack Benny pulled a 27-plus—a full three points above his rating on NBC.

Benny was a big hero; Paley was a big hero. True to his word, Benny helped persuade his friends to make the switch. Burns and Allen came over, so did Edgar Bergen; and then Red Skelton. Bing Crosby, discovered by CBS before he switched to NBC, was coaxed into returning.

Finally alarmed by the wholesale defections, Sarnoff made a big-money deal to keep Fred Allen and another one to hold Phil Harris and Alice Faye. It was an interesting turnaround for NBC. When Benny defected, the network issued a stiff statement saying it would "continue to refuse to purchase stock in so-called production corporations where the artists who control such corporations are performing on the NBC network.

"Such arrangements are bound to lead to charges of discrimination between artists who are paying income taxes at the higher regular rates and those who are paying at the lower rates of only 25 percent on so-called capital gains."

CBS defended itself and twitted its rival in response when it said all such deals—if and when made—would be submitted to the Treasury Department for approval or disapproval. "Therefore, how, by any stretch of the imagination, can there be any question as to the propriety of such transactions? Mr. [Niles] Trammell's [president of NBC] statement is unwarranted and reflects unfairly on many creative artists who have done no more than abide by our tax laws like any businessman or corporation."

Even in official statements, then, Bill Paley's shrewd solicitude for performers—both those under contract and those he wanted to sign—showed through.

As a matter of fact, Jack Benny was challenged when he claimed the sale of Amusement Enterprises as a capital gain. But the government's charge that Benny's organization was a personal holding company, a kind of business vehicle that wasn't qualified for capital-gains consideration, failed. Benny fought all the way to the Supreme Court and won. Benny had his keeping money and Bill Paley had his star. One more thing: Paley made sure Jack Benny would never pay a dime to park his car in the CBS studio lot.

After Benny's Supreme Court victory, other "creative artists" formed their own companies. But such corporations are not very useful anymore. The artist runs the risk of having his corporation declared a personal holding company, to be taxed at punitive rates. And it's a time bomb as the late author Robert Ruark discovered. He got the bad news from Uncle Sam years after he began enjoying the fruits of incorporation. Besides, tax rates are much reduced today. The top tax on earned income is 50 percent, a far cry from the 91 percent ceiling that prompted Benny to incorporate. Add "income averaging" which permits the artist to spread a bonanza over a number of tax years, and the system becomes fair enough to discourage all but the most intrepid.

CHAPTER 15

Gentle Revolution

IN THE MOVIE VERSION OF THE LIFE OF THOMAS EDISON, A TINKERER employed in the Edison labs in the 1890s was shown playing with a makeshift device consisting of a rotating piece of metal with a pointed piece of metal scratching its surface. The device was full of sound and fury—and signified a great deal. Edison seized upon the idea and labored to construct a better device. Eventually he was seen speaking into a metal diaphragm whose vibrations in turn wiggled a needle pressed against a rotating cyclinder of wax. And thus, supposedly through idle play, came the first permanent "record" of ephemeral sound. By any measure, it was an invention of genius.

Public relations people at CBS claim that resident genius Peter Goldmark invented the long-playing record. Goddard Lieberson, who heads Columbia Records, puts it differently. He says that Edison invented recorded sound; that all subsequent developments of the medium—including the 33 1/3-rpm long-playing record—sprang from Edison's invention and thus were merely refinements. He notes that a full decade before Goldmark developed the LP in 1948, a standard-size record that played nearly three times as long as the normal 78-rpm record of the time was presented to CBS when it acquired Columbia Records.

But Goldmark did more than just extend the playing time of a record, enough so that full symphonies could be put on a single disc. He also improved record fidelity from the raspy, scratchy sound familiar to exasperated generations of music lovers to glowing reproduction that captured the full, rich tones of the concert hall. And his discovery didn't come as a sudden insightful "Aha!" but through a less dramatic, plodding approach. Through painstaking investigation of each element of the sound-reproduction system and their complex interrelationships, Goldmark and his team brought forth the long-playing record that revolutionized the music business.

Working at CBS, owner of a major record company, and being a serious amateur musician as well as an inventor, Peter Goldmark quite naturally was drawn to the problem of trying to improve recorded sound. Goldmark is a native of Hungary where his great-uncle, Karl, was considered the nation's greatest composer since Franz Liszt. Music was the dominant theme in his home—so much so that one evening, during civil disturbances in Budapest in the wake of World War I, Peter's mother once ignored an order from the street to "turn out the light" when she and her family were playing a Mozart string quartet. When a warning bullet tore into the ceiling of the fourth-floor apartment, 12-year-old Peter, on the cello, panicked, but his totally absorbed mother, on the violin, would not turn from the score until the last notes were played. She then rose calmly, closed the window and pulled down the blinds.

Shortly after World War II, Peter Goldmark spent a musical evening that was marred by a different kind of interruption. With friends at their home in Westport, Connecticut, he was listening to a recording of Brahms's Second Piano Concerto played by Vladimir Horowitz and conducted by Arturo Toscanini. Peter remembers that though the recording was on new 78-rpm records, there were eight sound defects scattered through the 12 sides, intrusions as jarring to his ear as "having the phone ring at intervals while you are making love." In addition there were the periodic interruptions of the records being changed.

He asked his friends to play the records again; and while they did so, he sat gritting his teeth and racking his brain. Finally, he produced a ruler and started calculating, counting 80 grooves to the inch, and he began pondering the principle of the phonograph—how sound was captured on a record and held there and how it might be done with greater fidelity to the original sound.

He concluded that he could get more mileage by slowing the turntable speed while crowding significantly more grooves onto a disc. Later he chose a 33 1/3-rpm speed to match the radio transcription discs then used in recorded broadcasts.

Changing speed and grooves-per-inch weren't his major problems. The more important challenge was to get higher fidelity; RCA in earlier attempts had slowed the turntable speed, but got worse results, not better.

As a first step, Goldmark was inclined to discard the standard record material, shellac, for Vinylite. This new material cost twice as much but was light and unbreakable, and it would end up being cheaper if an entire symphony could be put on one record.

Next, after discovering that 90 percent of all symphonic works could be played in 45 minutes, he settled on 12-inch discs, also practical because turntables were already designed for that size.

All he needed now was a go-ahead, and he went to Edward Wallerstein, who ran Columbia Records, to get it. Wallerstein had worked for RCA, but Bill Paley hired him away on the strength of Wallerstein's reputation as the best phonograph salesman of his day. Wallerstein listened to Goldmark for "exactly three minutes" before saying he didn't like the idea. Peter recalls that "he put an arm around my shoulders, and suggested in a fatherly manner that I drop the entire project and do something in the television line instead." Wallerstein also told Goldmark that RCA had tried and failed with a 33 1/3-rpm record for the consumer; and that clearly if RCA with its superior resources had failed, CBS efforts were doomed as well. Fortunately for CBS, this was a totally inappropriate approach to take with Peter Goldmark. The thin, nearsighted Ph.D. and inventor, who had gotten an Austrian patent on an early television device in 1930, had always been driven to more strenuous efforts by skepticism.

This first confrontation between Wallerstein and Goldmark, both men of high standards and keen musical ears, marked the beginning of a long struggle. Goldmark went to Paul Kesten who was still running the company. He listened attentively and said that if Peter thought he could do it to go ahead and he would back him with $100,000 of CBS money. Kesten didn't seem to think Wallerstein's "no" was important. Though Wallerstein proved to be a stumbling block all along the road, this negative challenge seems to have provided the impetus that brought better results in the end.

Again and again, as Goldmark and a carefully assembled team made some progress, Wallerstein would find fault. When Goldmark and company cut the grooves finer and finer until they were able to get 15 minutes to a side compared with 4 minutes on a standard 12-inch disc spinning at 78 revolutions per minute, Wallerstein promptly reminded him that a Berlioz movement would take 20 minutes. Peter labored again and stretched the side to 22 1/2 minutes, then to a full 25 minutes, but, predictably enough, the sound went sour. If it had been that easy, RCA would have solved the problems years earlier. Peter noted that the violins sounded like flutes, while small cutting variations changed the pitch of the instruments.

Wallerstein had ears "like a bat" and each unsuccessful cutting brought an "I told you so." The Goldmark team worked harder, cutting on vinyl, hoping to produce an orchestral recording with accurate pitch. At last they thought they were successful. They played the recording with anticipation, only to have Wallerstein shake his head and ask, "Where is the fuzz on the bow? I don't hear it. When you get the fuzz, then come back." Peter argued to no avail that the "fuzz" was the noise of the shellac on the old records. Not so, said Wallerstein—it was the scrape of the resin from the violinist's bow.

The Goldmark team had just about reached the point of absolute frustration. But Peter's Belgian-born recording engineer, René Snep-vangers, who had been in charge of NBC transcriptions before Peter lured him away, suggested a new approach: Fire pistols, record the sound and see what resulted. Such a sharp report would certainly be a critical test of delicate equipment. They tried it. The crack of the pistol came across on the recording like the sound of a "baked potato falling on the floor."

Component after component was tested as Peter dashed back and forth between his laboratory and the studio next door where the sound was recorded. Everything checked out fine—until they got to the microphone. Was it possible, as a German research study had suggested, that the ribbon microphone was causing "phase distortion"?

When speaking into a ribbon mike, the standard microphone of the day, the sounds traveling along the ribbon failed to arrive at the end of the ribbon in the same sequence as they left the source. Thus, in theory at least, certain sounds reproduced unnaturally.

Condenser microphones, a new design specifically created to elimi-nate this distortion, were just beginning to come off the assembly line in a German factory. Goldmark obtained one—and the distortion vanished! Excited, Goldmark and two fellow employees sneaked up to a special secret studio. An engineer had his violin, a secretary sat at the piano and Peter set up his cello. They cut a Bach number on vinyl and called in Wallerstein. *Voilà!* The results were brilliant, though Goldmark says they left something to be desired musically. This time even Wallerstein showed enthusiasm.

But there was far more to do if this "invention" was to become part of the CBS product line. Wallerstein pointed out that Goldmark would have to find a way to transfer the existing CBS record library, universally recorded on four-minute master discs, onto long-playing records —a tricky but necessary step for Columbia to avoid competing with its own 78-rpm records. The task was to join the four-minute segments so neatly that the listener would not be aware that there was a shift from one turntable to the other. Goldmark had to develop a "musical computer" capable of timing records electronically to hundredths of a second. A timer was used to start the second turntable, then the third. Sometimes the orchestra had recorded four-minute segments on different days so that the pitch of the instruments was slightly different, due primarily to their weather sensitivity. The sound on the different platters had to be blended so well that the listener wouldn't be able to detect it.

The musical computer was perfect—or so Peter thought. It was tested at Columbia Records with Goldmark and Wallerstein standing by. The first turntable on the first cutting finished and the second was cued in when a yell came from Wallerstein: "Hold it! You lost a bar."

"The man was inhuman," Goldmark recalls. "I permitted myself a minor artistic luxury. I swore politely under my breath in Hungarian."

In time, though, the cuing system was perfected and Paley was called in along with Frank Stanton. Paley was interested but he had to rely on Wallerstein's ears, since in Goldmark's words, he had "no sense of pitch." Paley's chief concern was that if the new records were used only for classical recordings, the audience would be small, the profits perhaps nonexistent, yet the new product could touch off a major battle with RCA which he wasn't eager to finance. While Paley was confident the LP was better than anything the General could come up with, Paley was unwilling to announce the development until he knew the probable RCA response.

Goldmark says Paley pondered the question and decided that the thing to do was to invite RCA to join forces with CBS in putting out the 33 1/3. Goldmark thought the idea ingenious, and Philco, which had already agreed to manufacture the record players, agreed to go along. Paley, according to Goldmark, telephoned Sarnoff and invited him to a demonstration of CBS's new record. The call from CBS must have jarred the General, in terms of his smug attitude toward CBS as a technically inferior company. But Sarnoff agreed to listen to the CBS records. He arrived at the CBS boardroom with a retinue of eight engineers to be greeted by Paley, the cool Frank Stanton, Wallerstein, Goldmark and Peter's boss, Adrian Murphy. Goldmark tells the story:

Paley stepped forward and smoothly explained that I would first be playing an ordinary seventy-eight and then I would follow it with the CBS invention. I could see Sarnoff stiffen and become attentive. I played the seventy-eight for about fifteen seconds and then switched over to the new record.

With the first few bars Sarnoff was out of his chair. I played it for ten seconds and then switched back to the seventy-eight. The effect was electrifying, as we knew it would be. I never saw eight engineers look so much like carbon copies of tight-lipped gloom. Turning to Paley, Sarnoff said loudly and with some emotion: "I want to congratulate you and your people, Bill. It is very good."

Paley offered to delay the announcement of our long-playing record if RCA would join CBS in a simultaneous move so that both companies could benefit from the growth of the business. Paley offered know-how and a franchise.

Sarnoff said it was a generous offer that he would discuss with his staff. With that statement, Sarnoff and his entourage rose and left the boardroom.

I later learned what happened after the group returned to RCA headquarters. Sarnoff, who had been so affable and congratulatory, had gone into what could only be described as an executive tantrum. How could little CBS, with a two-by-four laboratory, beat RCA? he demanded. . . . A few days later, Sarnoff phoned Paley to say that he had decided not to come in with us on the record.

Howard Meighan has a different memory of the event: On the eve of a press conference to be held at the Waldorf to announce the LP,

RCA was still in the dark. He called the preparations which involved Philco's production of record players—half to carry the CBS name, half Philco's—"a remarkable job of secrecy."

In Meighan's version, Paley had been sitting with his top staff in the executive offices of CBS on the twentieth floor of 485 Madison Avenue. He asked his staff: "Don't you think as a courtesy I should call Sarnoff and tell him we are going to do it?" After a lively debate, Paley made up his mind and called Sarnoff.

According to Meighan, Sarnoff's reaction to the CBS development was that there was "really nothing new to the idea," since he already had seven different long-playing records. Paley said rather skeptically that he'd like to see those seven records, and Sarnoff replied, belligerently, "How early in the morning?" Paley threw back an "Eight A.M." and Sarnoff told him to come on out to the RCA labs in Princeton, New Jersey. Paley left the next morning, Meighan says, while his senior staff waited anxiously in New York.

Later, Paley walked into the CBS executive offices and told his staff that RCA did indeed have seven different versions and added that they must have worked all night getting them ready to demonstrate. But, Sarnoff supposedly told Paley, the two companies had a big investment in the 78, and the public was satisfied with it, so what would be the use of introducing something different and getting into that kind of competitive struggle? Says Meighan: "Paley explained this so persuasively to the four or five of us that Frank Stanton turned to him and asked apprehensively, 'Do we go at two P.M., then?' [He was referring to the press conference.] Paley said, 'I thought about that all the way back. The answer is yes.'"

Frank Stanton volunteered still another version in an interview a year after he left CBS. Stanton explained that he had a "good, warm relationship" with Sarnoff though the two had "fought like tigers" in representing their respective networks in Washington. "I asked him to come over to my office for lunch and had an RCA speaker in the office, which he saw immediately. He said, 'What's that over there?' I put the needle down on the record and let it play."

And the record played and played and, says Stanton, Sarnoff kept "looking and looking. I said, 'Don't worry, it is going to run for thirty minutes.' I had given him a cigar and I thought he was going to bite the end off it. . . . His reaction was, 'How could it be that the Great Victor Talking Machine Company didn't know about this?'"

It was appropriate that CBS would one day be a giant in the record business. Columbia got its name from a brief association in 1927 with Columbia Phonograph. It was a kind of bailout for the struggling network that didn't work.

By 1938 Columbia Records itself needed bailing out. By chance, as Ike Levy tells it, the record company was offered to him. The old deal maker, who had played a pivotal role in CBS's early years and had remained on its board, was approached by Raymond Rosen at a poker game at Ike's New York City hangout, the Manhattan Club. Rosen said he had an option to buy Columbia Records from Republic Pictures for $800,000.

Ike says: "I was in a big game with Harry Sinclair; Joe Brooks, son-in-law of Patterson of the *Daily News;* Tommy Taylor, a playboy; Joe Skenk; Irving Berlin; and Harpo Marx. Also a man named Guinzburg, owner of Viking Press. I asked them if they wanted to join me [as buyers] and they all said yes. The next day I happened to tell Bill Paley. He begged me to turn it over to CBS. Bill always had a way of getting what he wanted out of me. So I asked my poker-playing friends to release me from the deal and they did."

Ralph Colin, the caustic ex–CBS counsel, says there is more to the story than that. He remembers that Ike and Leon Levy didn't sell all their Columbia Record shares to CBS, but kept from 10 to 20 percent for themselves. Since it has been widely reported that CBS "bought" Columbia Records for $700,000 and Ike said the price tag was $800,-000, it may be that the Levy brothers' interest was $100,000 worth, or 12.5 percent. In any event, other shareholders of CBS found out about the residual interest and complained that the Levys' position was inconsistent with their obligation as directors; they should have turned over all the Columbia Records shares to CBS. Paley found this argument persuasive and made the Levy brothers sell their remaining shares to CBS, Colin says.

Ten years later, in 1948, CBS was serious competition for RCA in the record business. Therefore General Sarnoff was foolish to refuse Paley's offer of a license. When Sarnoff decided to fight against Columbia's superior system he was guilty—and not for the first time—of allowing pride to triumph over good sense. Paley believes that Sarnoff refused the offer because he was angry with CBS for having just landed Jack Benny.

RCA, as it turned out, had been ready to go with a seven-inch version of the 78, spinning at 45 rpm, which Goldmark says RCA called "Madame X." Madame X had been kept on the shelf—presumably in case of some unexpected emergency. Several weeks after CBS introduced the LP at the Waldorf—to relatively little fanfare in the press that failed to comprehend the importance of the development—RCA announced that it was coming out with the four-minute 45. RCA claimed virtually "instantaneous" and inaudible changes from one record to the next. But the 45 had a hole in the center bigger than a quarter, requiring a disclike plug that caused confusion and no little annoyance. RCA was compelled to offer new record changers at a loss in order to get Madame X under way, while CBS was busy developing a changer that would play 78s, 45s and 33 1/3s.

Peter Goldmark says it was Arturo Toscanini who finally persuaded Sarnoff, a number of years later, to see the light and enter the long-play market. Toscanini had listened to Bruno Walter conducting on a Columbia LP and was infuriated that Walter's performance was uninterrupted, while his own renditions were constantly interrupted by record changes. Through his pressure, Sarnoff finally relented, but not before the record business was cluttered with the 45 that, while useful for pop singles, has always been a stepchild in a world that spins at 33 1/3. As for the 78, it has been relegated to collectors' files.

CHAPTER 16
The Great Color TV Disaster

IN 1946, ACCORDING TO PETER GOLDMARK'S RECOLLECTION, A 19-YEAR-old blonde beauty named Patty Painter was televised in color from CBS in Manhattan to the Tappan Zee Inn in Nyack, New York, where the four members of the Federal Communications Commission sat before a television screen.

At the time, fewer than twenty-five thousand television sets had been sold, and these brought the viewer a drab picture in black and white. Yet here was CBS transmitting brilliant color that clearly highlighted Patty Painter's glowing pink flesh and blue eyes. The commissioners could hardly believe it. Charles Denny, the commission's new chairman, a austere bureaucrat, was especially impressed.

The only problem with the CBS color system was that color broadcasts could not be picked up by the existing black-and-white sets. Nevertheless, seeing how impressed the commissioners were at the Tappan Zee Inn, CBS was confident that the FCC would quickly approve CBS's petition to begin color telecasts—even if such approval meant that black-and-white television would be doomed before it fairly got off the ground. So convinced were Bill Paley and his management presidium of FCC endorsement that they backed away from plans to buy—at bargain prices—four key television stations. For the stations were on the very-high-frequency (VHF) band, and CBS planned to colorcast on the ultrahigh-frequency (UHF) band, as yet unexploited.

But optimism turned to anxiety at 485 Madison Avenue when, despite the enthusiasm over Patty Painter in color, word got around that the FCC was backing off. When the commission finally decided the question on January 30, 1947, chairman Denny himself called the CBS system "premature." He and his colleagues turned it down.

No one can say for sure why the FCC took this position. But what stuck in the craw at CBS was Denny's departure from the commission within six months—to become a vice-president of RCA's National Broadcasting Company.

There was understandable panic at CBS. The company was left with only one VHF outlet—CBS-TV in New York—and now had to scramble to pick up VHF stations at swollen prices. But CBS didn't give up the fight for its color system. Peter Goldmark, CBS's resident inventor, modified his color system for the established VHF band and refined it to improve reception.

Meanwhile, feverish efforts were under way at the RCA labs to perfect that company's electronic color system. Although lagging behind CBS in color development, RCA did have one advantage—it was developing a "compatible" system, that is, black-and-white sets would be able to pick up its colorcasts (in black and white, of course).

In September 1950, CBS and RCA presented their color systems to the FCC, competing for approval. The CBS system worked beautifully, while the three color guns in the RCA tube scattered color like a "crazed Van Gogh," as *Newsweek* put it. The FCC gave the CBS system its stamp of approval.

Yet RCA managed to salvage victory when the issue was finally resolved—after several years, $150 million in development and a brilliant selling job in Washington. First, RCA tied the issue up in court. CBS was stalled like a fly in molasses while black-and-white television sets were mass-marketed by the millions. Then RCA began a public relations campaign, devoted in large part to confusing the public about CBS's color system.

Basically simple though it was, the system would prove difficult for CBS to explain in the midst of a barrage of enemy propaganda. It depended on a spinning color wheel that hostile press agents, and even some astute reporters, suggested was a primitive device in an age of electronic marvels. Actually the wheel dovetailed nicely with underlying electronics, and later on could be eliminated entirely from CBS sets, but its alleged shortcomings were skillfully impressed on the public as an integral part of the CBS package. The truth was, while RCA engineers struggled to get a coherent color picture, the CBS color wheel whirred away quietly, bringing forth excellent results. Some at CBS claim that the CBS system is still the best, though others disagree.

The color wheel worked like this: The basic colors out of which all others are formed in TV transmission—red, blue and green (not red, yellow and blue as in painting)—were used in filters that comprised the segments of a disc. One such disc was spun at an identical rate as the lens of a television camera and the camera's image-pickup device. In time this color wheel in the camera would be no more than a couple of inches in diameter. The light "observed" by the camera was passed through the color disc and "seen" in the retina of the camera. The reds in the field of vision passed through the red filter, the blues through the blue filter and the greens through the green. Intermediate colors —blue-green, for example—sent some light through the blue filter and some through the green.

Since the individual color values are expressed in the "picture" sent over the airwaves, they must be blended together again at the TV set to reappear in their original hue. That was the function of the second color wheel—within the TV set. It was synchronized with the one in the television camera so that the various colors would pass through the filters on both ends at the same time.

The problem for CBS was that black-and-white television transmission operated according to RCA scanning standards. Had the FCC given its okay to CBS in 1947, conversion units would have solved the problem for owners of the RCA-type sets. Peter Goldmark estimated that converters—electronic "black boxes" that would unscramble CBS's signal for black-and-white reception on RCA sets—would have cost less than $100. And a color wheel could have been included at not much more expense to permit these old sets to pick up CBS color. Likely being among the wealthier, these early TV owners could probably have afforded the conversion units, while subsequent buyers could have chosen models with the color wheel.

But it was a complicated matter. Technically, this is what was involved:

In transmitting a television picture over the airwaves, the image is scanned horizontally by "lines." The scanning is done electronically, a line at a time, and at a rapid rate of speed. The even lines are scanned and then the odd lines, so that each set—even and odd—is scanned 30 times a second for a total of 60 passes or "fields." One complete scanning of both even and odd lines—two fields—is the equivalent of a "frame." Just like in the movies, the viewer sees so many frames a second—30 in telecasts—that the picture emerges without flicker. The eye retains an image for a fleeting moment after that image has disappeared, thus creating the illusion of continuity.

The CBS color picture was sent over the airwaves "sequentially." That is, the red values viewed by the camera were scanned line for line on odd lines, followed by a scanning of blue values on the even lines, then green on the odd lines. Then the three colors were scanned sequentially on the lines not previously scanned in each color. Once again, scanning was done so rapidly—at a rate of 60 fields per second —that a continuous picture emerged to be passed through the viewer's color wheel for blending.

By contrast, RCA's relatively primitive colorcasts were obtained through a system many believed was potentially superior, if the nation was to pass through an extended era of black-and-white television before moving to color.

The essential difference in the two systems was that the RCA method required just two scannings compared to the six scannings required by CBS color. RCA black-and-white telecasts also required only two scannings and so its color system was "compatible" with black and white. The six scannings called for by the CBS system required different circuitry at both the transmitter and the receiver. It was thus said to be "incompatible."

Set makers who opposed CBS feared delays and the costs of retooling. They were also skeptical of CBS's technology and the feasibility of using it to bring in the age of television in full color, leap-frogging the black-and-white era.

CBS was anxious to win final approval quickly—before black-and-white sets using the RCA system flooded the market. Programs transmitted in CBS color lost the entire black-and-white audience. So the CBS strategy had to be: Win quickly, commit the nation to color immediately.

Still another drawback to the CBS system was that the color wheel had to be twice the diameter of the picture tube. And since the public was bound to demand big pictures in time, the CBS set would have to be much larger than the RCA type. Even a 12-inch-picture set would have to be as large as one of today's 24-inch models.

These were major problems to be sure, but the lengths to which CBS opponents went to describe these shortcomings bordered on the absurd. The color wheel was made to sound as cumbersome as a Conestoga wagon wheel and as nonsensical as a Rube Goldberg device. CBS's rivals also tried to convince the public that the color wheel at the set was vital to the CBS approach. This was not true, for once a color tube was perfected—whether by RCA, CBS or someone else—it would pick up CBS signals so long as they were transmitted in the appropriate manner.

DuMont, which manufactured black-and-white TVs, made one of the more outlandish presentations in an effort to discredit the color wheel. At an FCC hearing, they brought forth a color wheel that was at least six feet across, implying that such a wheel would be required for the viewer to watch color television on a large screen. DuMont asked the commissioners to imagine the armor plating that would be required in the family room to prevent a neighborhood catastrophe if a wheel such as the one it displayed, spinning at the necessary high speeds, were to explode into pieces.

Actually, wheel dynamics were perfectly understood—which is a lot more than one could say for electronics. The vacuum tube, for example, was the workhorse of every electronic device, and tubes—like light bulbs—were relatively unreliable.

But none of that mattered when, in 1951, RCA's appeal of the FCC decision finally reached the Supreme Court. The nine justices sat in their black robes looming like great birds high above the courtroom floor—high enough on their elevated platform to give the impression they were getting guidance from a Higher Authority.

The lawyers opposing CBS went through the standard arguments: the monstrosity of a giant disc spinning to beat hell in private homes; the prospect of an American public pock-marked with color-wheel shrapnel. RCA did its job well, organizing and orchestrating the cabal of those who had something to lose if the CBS system went through. The clock was ticking away the last months of RCA's 17-year patents on black-and-white television tubes. Without a victory in the color television fight, the company's licensing arrangements and patent fees would skid precipitously.

General Sarnoff was also worrying about the ignominy of a loss to "that tobacco fellow," as he called Bill Paley. It was okay to lose a programing battle, but a technical battle—never.

Pity the poor justices, who probably had about as much interest in color tubes and spinning wheels as they had in the breeding habits of the tsetse fly. But they listened with a gravity befitting their station— and they were clearly impressed with the reputation, background and years-in-the-business of RCA and confreres.

Finally, the time came for CBS to present its case. The late Sam Rosenman got to his feet. An eminent judge himself once, he had been a confidant and adviser to the late Franklin D. Roosevelt. Several of the justices owed their high position to FDR—and just possibly to Sam Rosenman. Accustomed as he was to hobnobbing with potentates and kings, presidents and cabinet members, Rosenman was hardly cowed by his surroundings. He realized the nine justices by now had gigantic color wheels etched in their minds, so in his characteristically bland manner he opened by saying, in essence: Now, gentlemen, having heard what you just heard, I wouldn't blame you if you thought that the Federal Communications Commission and everyone else who favors the CBS system are totally and absolutely out of their minds to attempt to foist this system on the public.

Rosenman then went on calmly to rebut the specific arguments offered by RCA and the others, while trying to make clear to the Court the technological advantages of the CBS system and the wisdom of the FCC's position.

In view of the high-powered campaign RCA and its allies waged, the decision of the Supreme Court may be regarded as a surprise. On May 28, 1951, the Court ruled that the FCC had acted within its mandate, and its decision favoring CBS was allowed to stand.

But the victory was only temporary. RCA continued its campaign. And in 1953, the FCC reversed its own ruling favoring CBS and approved a modified and improved RCA system.

While the FCC's decision favoring RCA in 1947 was a questionable one, its 1953 decision was probably best for the country at large. As early as the second FCC ruling in 1950, there were 2.5 million RCA-adjusted sets sold, and the number reached 7.5 million by the time of the Supreme Court decision in 1951. A year later, there were 9 million sets, and in 1953, when the FCC reversed itself, 12 million.

True, CBS had proven its system was practical. But while converting relatively few sets to a system superior to the early technology of RCA was one thing, converting even 2.5 million sets at a time of rapidly improving electronic technology would have been too much. RCA had caused the delay and RCA had benefited by this tactic.

Jack Gould, however, gives a different interpretation to the color television fight. Gould says that the CBS color system had its technical drawbacks but Sarnoff worried plenty about it. However, had CBS won, there would have been serious problems. According to Gould, "There was something called 'color break-up' in the CBS system. When you turned your face away from the screen you could still see a figure or scene in red, blue and green. The problem cropped up again when the CBS color-wheel camera was used to send relays from the moon to the home screen." What Paul Kesten was really trying to do when he was pushing CBS's color system with the FCC after the war was to delay all televison. Why? CBS didn't have enough stations. So, in effect, Kesten said, "Don't go for black and white now; color is just around the corner."

In the wake of the Supreme Court ruling endorsing the FCC's choice of the CBS color system in 1951, Bill Paley made a decision that haunted him for the next decade and even caused, in the opinion of many who know him well, a fundamental change in his executive personality. The purchase of Hytron Radio and Electronics for what would prove to be an extortionate price was a mistake, but an understandable one. Paley had been at the crest of a wave of victories over NBC in the talent field which was the talk of the entertainment world, each coup bringing a golden jackpot to the CBS profit statement. Flush with success, Paley tried to top himself in an area in which he was much less well equipped. Perhaps his boyish enthusiasm for once interfered with better judgment when he looked to best Sarnoff in the General's own preserve—manufacturing.

The telegrapher-turned-tycoon dominated the world of electronic manufacturing with an irascible genius and more than a touch of tyranny, as everyone knew. In his book, *Plain Speaking*, Merle Miller tells how Harry Truman got on an elevator occupied by the General whose leg was in a cast. Truman said, "Well, General, I guess now for a while you'll have to kick people in the ass with the other leg, won't you?"

The General was not only wily and capable of fighting a brilliant battle on the technological front, but a man who clearly would stop at nothing to short-circuit Paley and CBS. That shrewd Philadelphia lawyer, Ike Levy, who was a confidant of both Paley and the General and often served as their intermediary, warned Paley that Sarnoff would "knock his brains out" if he took CBS into manufacturing. But Ike couldn't sway the ebullient Paley at the pinnacle of his success.

The trouble with being Paley's kind of executive—a gambler with sure instincts—is that sooner or later gamblers stray off the home table and play for high stakes in someone else's game. When this happens, the risk-to-reward ratio, as they say in Wall Street, becomes intolerable.

Devastating mistakes in high-profile businesses are usually discovered in public, so to speak, and then the spotlight's glare is merciless; there is no place to hide. But one reason Bill Paley's ill-fated take-over of Hytron Radio and Electronics is so fascinating is that he got away with it. Though Hytron ultimately represented a corporate disaster every bit as expensive as Ford's abortive introduction of the Edsel, as far as the public was concerned it came off looking like a coup. This was because it was lost in the extraordinary profitability of broadcasting, particularly television.

At the time CBS bagged Hytron, even the price seemed to be in line. To understand this, it is important to realize that CBS, important broadcaster though it was, was not really a very big fish in the corporate pond. It was more of a minnow compared to such giant tuna as, say, Eastman Kodak, Westinghouse Electric and . . . RCA. And even these companies were small in comparison to the whales of industry—companies such as General Motors and American Telephone.

CBS was certainly well known, however. The CBS logo was constantly on the air. The listening and later the viewing public *knew* CBS. But in 1946 CBS was a radio broadcaster and little else. In a world of billion-dollar corporations, CBS had sales of $68 million. Then the color battle erupted in the press to put CBS in the same class, at least in the public mind, with RCA. Also, television had its enormous impact on the company's sales and launched CBS on the road to billions. By 1951, a mere five years later, sales had soared more than two and a half times, to $176 million, largely as a result of the snowballing television revenues.

When Hytron came along in 1951, TV's explosive profitability hadn't been reflected in CBS stock to any marked degree. Thus, in terms of dollars, the shares CBS gave for Hytron—largely to the Coffin brothers, Bruce A. and Lloyd H.—were of modest value relative to the worth they would attain. CBS paid the equivalent of $17.7 million on June 15, 1951, when Hytron, maker of television sets, became CBS's poor relation.

If it is true, as many claim, that CBS turned down a deal to buy DuMont, a small but blue-chip maker of TV sets, for $10 million to $20 million in cash, the Hytron deal looms as an even bigger catastrophe. The DuMont deal was anathema to Frank Stanton, it is said, because it involved cash. If so, it was a case of penny (cash) wise and pound (stock) foolish.

For the stunning fact is that the $17.7 million represented almost exactly a quarter of the stock of CBS. Specifically the company gave 621,544 shares—310,772 of class A and 310,772 of class B, a distinction which would soon be eliminated—out of 2,530,496 shares outstanding.

The Coffin brothers, according to a CBS associate, "looked like a couple of Midwestern Kiwanis Club members." But that dowry in this marriage was like the cups of uncooked rice the bride throws in the boiling water. Of insignificant mass in the beginning, when cooked the rice pot runneth over. The Coffin brothers became superrich on puffed rice. By Columbia's 40th anniversary in 1967—only 16 years after the acquisition—the shares given for Hytron would be worth *over a quarter of a billion dollars.*

In 1951, the CBS welcome to Hytron was unreserved. The Coffin brothers and David H. Cogan, president of Air King, Hytron's set-making division, were named to the 15-member CBS board of directors. Cogan and Stanton at first became "inseparable" according to Peter Goldmark. (Stanton later became so wary of Cogan that he would ask CBS executives sent to oversee Hytron not to discuss business matters on office telephones but to call at the Stanton residence.)

In his autobiography, *Maverick Inventor,* Goldmark says:

Paley was hypnotized with Air King. So was Stanton. Both men personally traveled to [the] Brooklyn [plant] in chauffeur-driven limousines and became involved like goggle-eyed kids with the style and coloring of the sets and what knobs and ornaments to use. Long discussions ensued over the answers to such questions as should tuning be horizontal or vertical? I guess if you're in the entertainment business, you carry these small superficialities wherever you go. It seemed incredible to me that two of the leading communications figures in America should be spending so much time fiddling with dials and knobs.

It was soon apparent that CBS had not checked the marriage bed for lumps. Perhaps in addition to Paley's fervor for the new and exciting, Frank Stanton's passion for technology and all its inner workings contributed to the excessive initial enthusiasm for the deal. But the shoddiness of the Hytron investigation was certainly out of character for Stanton, whose meticulousness was legendary. A maintenance man at 485 Madison was once ordered to put bigger light bulbs in a men's room temporarily used by top executives, because, as he told a curious middle-management man, "that blond fellow" couldn't see himself in the mirror. Stanton would hand his secretaries typo-free letters to be redone because they weren't perfectly centered on the page. He also sent a massive study back to the Nielsen people saying, simply, that it was wrong. It took the viewer-samplers some time to learn what he meant: One column of figures in a table was off a couple of tenths and didn't add up to precisely 100 percent.

As so frequently happened when CBS got involved in fields outside of broadcasting, it sent the wrong people to check out Hytron–Air King. CBS inventor Peter Goldmark was one.

It was Goldmark's boss, Adrian Murphy, who asked the scientist to take a preacquisition look. Peter explains it this way:

I shot out to Brooklyn to see Air King's set manufacturing and then to Newburyport, Massachusetts, to look over the firm's tube plant, and I came away with the feeling that the company knew how to make excellent tubes and TV sets at low cost. It was in fact the fourth largest manufacturer of radio and television tubes in the country. But I pointed out in my report to Murphy that if we did go into manufacturing, we should not attempt to emulate Zenith, which was noted for high quality in engineering and manufacturing, without a base in research. Accordingly, I urged that we marry our own research organization with the expertise in manufacturing of Hytron and Air King by creating a central research division to serve the entire corporation, including the manufacturing arm. I suggested also that we retain Sears as a [Hytron] customer because it would force us to maintain the quality of manufacturing.

Despite Goldmark's advice CBS soon gave up the assured markets Hytron–Air King had with both Sears and Montgomery Ward and set off on a costly program of building its own distributor-dealer network to sell the "CBS Columbia" line of radio and TV sets. Pride was obviously a factor.

Despite Goldmark's kind words for the Air King line, the sets simply weren't in the same class with the other leading TV manufacturers, including RCA. It's possible that Sears and Montgomery Ward had only settled for Air King products because they couldn't get the majors to build for them. It was a time of enormous demand for television sets, and each builder was anxious to carve out a slice of the market under its own medallion.

But Goldmark was certainly right about the necessity for CBS-Columbia to upgrade the product, and also keep pace with the newly developed transistor. Hytron's reaction to the transistor seems ominous in retrospect. The Coffin brothers told Paley there was no need to finance research in transistors. In Goldmark's presence, Paley asked Hytron's chief engineer, Charles Stromeyer, for his opinion. He responded that "the transistor is a toy. . . . It will never beat the vacuum tube!"

On Stromeyer's behalf it should be said that he subsequently had a hand in perfecting a Marshall Wilder–Goldmark color tube with a shadow mask. RCA looked at the tube, dropped its own costly research and accepted a CBS license. The patented tube, still in use, has earned CBS $15 million.

But offsetting that one big plus were many minuses, among which loomed a huge inventory. CBS's auditors had dutifully trooped to Brooklyn and Newburyport and certified that Hytron had all the vacuum tubes it said it had, and that Air King had all the television sets it claimed were in the warehouses. What the auditors did not understand was that obsolescence, like a cloud, was settling over the Hytron–Air King inventory. Millions of vacuum tubes, many valued at "market prices" of several dollars each, were actually worth, perhaps, 25 cents each. At least, that's what the engineers ultimately concluded. And they were only worth 25 cents if they could in fact be sold; the world was getting more and more excited about the transistor, which would in time replace the vacuum tube. Further, one CBS engineer claims that "whole warehouses full" of Air King television sets were similarly overvalued.

Not long after the acquisition, CBS's Hytron inventory losses ran into the millions. By 1953 the Coffin brothers and David Cogan were removed from the CBS board and there were those at CBS who counseled bringing suit as soon as the inventory situation was understood. But CBS stock had risen as a result of the acquisition and the promise of a CBS color set. A suit might torpedo the stock, and Paley and Stanton would lose face—or worse. At this point, color production was out of the question in view of the turmoil at Hytron. Meanwhile the FCC was reconsidering the wisdom of its decision to give CBS the go-ahead. What to do?

There is a story that could be apocryphal, though people who usually know the facts swear that it is true.

Once the inventory problem was discovered, a dapper PR consultant was hustled off to Washington to show Eisenhower's director of defense mobilization, Charles E. Wilson (the same "Engine Charlie" of "What's good for General Motors . . ." fame), a list of materials that would be needed in color sets. With hostilities still under way in Korea, what did Mr. Wilson think about CBS making color sets that used so many vital materials? Wilson said he didn't like the idea and asked the PR man to use his good offices to get CBS to drop the idea. The timing was perfect. Bill Paley, patriot, was able to "volunteer" not to make color sets for the duration, and other set makers were then ordered to follow suit. It was the best of all possible results for CBS under the circumstances.

Exactly what led to the government order may be cloudy, but Engine Charlie did indeed request that CBS "suspend its plans for the manufacture of color television receivers in order to conserve critical materials until such time as these materials are in sufficient supply to warrant production." Thus reads the CBS 1951 annual report, quoting Mr. Wilson himself.

Thereafter CBS conducted a monumental effort, setting up a distributor-dealer network for its black-and-white sets, and at least had some success in building an organization. But losses in this division continued unabated and when people at CBS expressed misgivings, Paley told them that his hired help at Hytron had promised profits—this year. CBS continued to try to buy a place in the market.

Paley gave it the old college try. He sent a CBS design emissary to Air King to dispose of the division's shoddy sales literature and replace it with brochures bearing the unmistakable stamp of CBS quality. Paley called in Paul McCobb, a distinguished furniture designer, to create distinctive boxes to house the electronics. But it was slipping silk over the old sow's ear. CBS dealers continued to find the product less reliable than that of the majors.

Each year, the CBS annual report carried glowing copy about the prospects for a new product, a new plant, a new line of radio and television sets. On several occasions, the board of directors got a new face, as some Hytron manager showed promise of turning things around. But nothing really worked.

By this time Paley realized his mistake and was growing more depressed and pessimistic about Hytron all the time. Even the name Hytron was blotted out in 1959. The annual report for that year said CBS-Hytron would thereafter be known as CBS Electronics—"reflecting the planned expansion into broader and more diversified areas of electronic products," semiconductors among them.

Always something of a hypochondriac—he had chronic back trouble that seemed to flare up during bad times at CBS—Paley grew so concerned about his health in 1959 that he entered a hospital for exploratory surgery to make sure he didn't have cancer. Arthur Godfrey lost a lung to cancer that same year and he is convinced that Paley had this operation because he identified with Godfrey's condition. Others agree that the chest operation was totally unnecessary.

CBS's outside counsel Ralph Colin said of Paley during that period: "When [Hytron] proved to be a colossal judgmental error he was stunned, and from then on had the greatest difficulty making decisions and often reversed himself." According to Colin, Paley would frequently call special meetings for 5 P.M. on short notice, sometimes causing top officials including Frank Stanton to break engagements to attend. Then he would grow uninterested and leave. Or, if he stayed and came to a decision, he often changed his mind the next morning.

Colin claims that Paley blamed Peter Goldmark for Hytron. But, adds Colin: "I am sure that if Hytron made millions, Peter would never have gotten the credit. Paley was a big boy. His company found Hytron and presumably studied it, and the responsibility for the bad choice must remain with Paley and the board."

In 1961, Paley finally called it quits with Hytron. When the chairman swept out the residue, CBS had run up manufacturing and related losses of an estimated $50 million. And the Hytron-based CBS shares were still outstanding, still rising with the continuing optimism over the future of television and CBS.

The Coffin brothers sold most of their CBS shares sometime after they were forced to retire from the CBS board. They live quietly today in palatial splendor in Marblehead, Massachusetts. Marblehead is a rocky peninsula of the sort where—in the books we used to read as kids—pirates buried treasure. The Coffin brothers proved once again that the pen is more powerful than the sword—especially when that pen is wielded by an experienced bookkeeper.

PART THREE

THE AGE OF TELEVISION: GOLD AND DROSS

CHRONOLOGY

TELEVISION BEING A NEW FIELD IN THE LATE 1940S, CBS HAS TO BUILD its own cadre of competent broadcast personnel. The network raids its mailroom for bodies, sends them to the television studios it maintains in Grand Central Station and improvises shows to give them experience as cameramen, boom men and technicians.

. . .In 1948 folksy Arthur Godfrey makes his TV debut with *Talent Scouts,* closely followed by *Arthur Godfrey and his Friends.*

. . .That same year, CBS begins a variety show called *The Toast of the Town,* an amalgam of vaudeville features leavened with dance and classical piano, hosted by a stone-faced, ill-at-ease newspaper columnist named Ed Sullivan.

. . .In 1951 Frank Stanton taps J. L. Van Volkenburg as president of CBS's new television division. A former adman who had worked his way up in CBS through sales, Van Volkenburg is a tough, hard-drinking poker player with a tenacity that serves him and his employers well. In his four years as president, he lands a major share of newly licensed television stations as CBS affiliates.

. . .Lucille Ball speaks a universal language of wacky humor and warmth, and when *I Love Lucy* comes to television in 1951 it is an instant success.

. . .In 1951 Frank Stanton asks William Golden, creative director of advertising and sales promotion, to develop a new trademark for television. Golden designs an eye backed by floating clouds.

. . .CBS, celebrating its 25th anniversary in 1952, reaches a vast television audience through several big-city stations owned by the company and 74 television affiliates.

. . .In 1952 Television City is completed in Los Angeles. This new plant is used for *Playhouse 90,* a series that helps label the 1950s TV's "golden age." Among its original productions are *Requiem for a Heavyweight, Days of Wine and Roses* and *The Miracle Worker.*

. . .In 1953 *You Are There* begins dramatic re-creations of historical events, narrated by genial Walter Cronkite.

. . .One of Bill Paley's favorite radio shows, an "adult western" called *Gunsmoke,* comes to television in 1955. The show makes the top ten for 13 years and inspires a host of imitators.

. . .In 1955 on *See It Now,* Ed Murrow attacks Senator Joseph McCarthy, the demagogue who insists the government is riddled with communists.

. . .The first big television quiz show—*The $64,000 Question*—debuts in 1955.

. . .In 1956 Elvis Presley appears on the Ed Sullivan show, but only from the waist up.

. . .In 1957 Nikita Khrushchev is interviewed from Moscow on *Face the Nation,* stern and genial by turns.

. . .Columbia markets stereophonic records and phonographs for the first time in 1958.

. . .In 1959 broadcasting is hit by two scandals: Disc jockeys are playing records in exchange for "payola," and TV quiz shows are fixed.

. . .In December 1959, James Aubrey becomes president of CBS

Television. His shows feature rural settings, sexy women, innocuous plots. An unreal world of happy, healthy uncomplicated people sets the program tone. CBS ratings soar, earnings bound upward and the stock becomes a Wall Street favorite.

. . .In 1961 *CBS Reports* films "Biography of a Bookie Joint," using an 8-mm camera concealed in lunch pails, pocketbooks and transistor radios to show illegal gambling operations inside a Boston key-repair shop. The report leads to the resignation of the Boston police commissioner.

. . .In 1961 CBS's million-dollar prestige symbol leaves, in dismay, to head up the United States Information Agency. Edward R. Murrow had found that his instant access to Bill Paley had been cut off.

. . .In 1963 CBS has nine out of the top ten nighttime shows on television and all ten top daytime shows. For the tenth consecutive year, CBS-TV is the world's largest single advertising medium. Net income jumps to $41.8 million.

. . .In November 1963, President Kennedy is shot in Dallas. CBS (like the other networks) abandons all commercial broadcasting. Television news is on the air four straight days and nights.

. . .Mod Michael Burke, with his stylish gray hair, heads a new effort to broaden the CBS income base in the early Sixties by acquiring other companies. In 1964 CBS buys the champion New York Yankees, the best in baseball, paying $13.2 million for 90 percent of the action. The Yankees drop from first to last in two years.

. . .In February 1965, an era ends as Jim Aubrey is fired amidst growing dissatisfaction with his deals and persistent talk of Aubrey's involvement in a scandal.

. . .CBS expands its acquisition program in 1965, acquiring Fender, a leading maker of electric guitars and amplifiers. (Soon, however, musicians begin to sense that the product is changing in CBS hands. A 1973 issue of *Buy Lines* advertises a number of guitars as "Pre-CBS Fender Guitar.")

. . .In 1965 CBS moves its headquarters to "Black Rock" at 51 West

52nd Street, the only skyscraper designed by famed architect Eero Saarinen.

. . .In 1965 Fred Friendly, president of CBS News, resigns because CBS refuses to drop a Lucy rerun to give live coverage to Senate hearings on Vietnam.

. . .Nineteen sixty-six is a disappointing year for Frank Stanton. William Paley unexpectedly decides not to retire as chairman despite reaching the company's mandatory retirement age of 65.

. . .In 1966 CBS has 17,178 employees, earns $64.1 million and has net sales of $814,533,621.

. . .In 1967 CBS acquires publishing company Holt, Rinehart & Winston—and finds that "broadening its base" can be expensive. CBS's net sales for the year are $904 million. Television has made it a giant corporation in fact as well as image.

CHAPTER 17
Arthur Godfrey: Every Man's an S.O.B. to Someone

"HE'S THE DUMBEST GENIUS I EVER MET." THAT'S THE MIXED TRIBUTE Arthur Godfrey receives from the one writer he never fired, a man who experienced the frustration and pleasure of working for this strange man who became an American institution.

In 1930 Godfrey was an obscure disc jockey who specialized in informal patter in a stiffly formal broadcast world. At WJSV in Washington, D.C., a station then owned by CBS, Godfrey came to the attention of Arthur Hull Hayes, manager of CBS's New York City station. Hayes brought Godfrey to the Big Apple.

Years passed and Godfrey thrived. But he was restless for a network spot and began beseeching Hayes to get him a spot—*any* spot. "Give me your *worst* time period," he would say.

Hayes carried the appeal to Frank Stanton, and Stanton appealed to Paul Kesten. Finally, during the World War II years, Godfrey got his wish. *The American School of the Air*, a prestigious but low-rated educational program, got the axe and Godfrey moved into its morning time period five days a week.

He was phenomenally popular. His nasal baritone soon became almost as familiar as coffee at the breakfast table. His approach was folksy and appealing—like that of a benign door-to-door salesman selling a brush to a young married woman. He introduced his cast of singers and musicians with references to their personal lives that made them more appealing too. He read letters from admiring fans and commented humorously on the news.

By 1949 Godfrey was running a formidable duchy within CBS. In addition to his popular morning radio show, he had two hit evening presentations on TV—*Arthur Godfrey and His Friends,* an hour-long Wednesday production; and his half-hour Monday-night *Arthur Godfrey's Talent Scouts.*

In the early 1950s his three half-hours of evening TV consistently ranked in the top five half-hours of television prime time and it was claimed that he reached as many as 82 million people every week. In the later years, a substantial part of his weekly TV broadcast output was simulcast on CBS radio, thus adding to his legions of listeners.

So important was Godfrey to the CBS profit pump in those days that James Seward, an avuncular CBS vice-president, became more or less officially vice-president in charge of Arthur Godfrey. Seward, a cordial man with a voice and manner startlingly reminiscent of actor Jimmy Stewart, had other duties as well, of course. But his prime responsibility was to keep mercurial Arthur happy.

By 1954 Arthur Godfrey's combined broadcasts accounted for 12 percent of the network's total revenues. It was strange that a man so without talent—except as a ukelele plucker—should become a superstar. Musically, he was second-rate at best. While he worked with incredible application to master the rudiments of musical instruments, a charitable evaluation ranked him as a gifted amateur. He played passably and sang about as well.

In acting roles, which he occasionally attempted late in his career, he exhibited a school-play amateurism that pained professional and armchair critics alike. He attempted only comedy parts, mugging his way to embarrassment, but he might have been funnier in serious roles.

Apart from his superb instinct for patter, so limited were his performing skills that he refused to appear with the heavy talent that was so readily available to him. He once admitted to an associate who suggested that he have big stars on the show, "You know I stand in great awe of talent. I just can't work with big stars." Nor with strong support either, it would appear. At least that's how Archie Bleyer, Godfrey's musical director, saw it.

"One time we did a show," Bleyer says, "and I had worked very hard on all the numbers. I thought that everything we did was quite good, the way the songs were set up and so forth. He was dreadful that night —I thought because everything around him was high caliber. I also remember one time he came in at the last minute and tossed out our carefully rehearsed numbers and just had the kids walk on and do songs. He was great that night. It seems to me that he was at his best when things around him were not too good." Bleyer was later fired for disloyalty after he recorded a song with Godfrey's bush-league competitor, Don McNeill. Godfrey said Bleyer's perfidy left him feeling like a husband who came home to find a cigar in the ashtray.

It's a near miracle that Godfrey was even alive in the 1950s, much less a huge success. On a road near Washington, D.C., in 1931, a truck suddenly veered and collided head-on with Godfrey's car. The two men in the truck were thrown clear, landed in the brambles and collected a few scratches. The impact was so powerful that the truck engine wound up in the passenger seat of Godfrey's car. Godfrey was crushed to the edge of death. His pelvis was broken in 27 places. His right hip was smashed beyond repair, his left hip joint was permanently injured, both kneecaps were smashed and he had a collapsed lung—to mention just the most serious of his many injuries. He awoke to the whisper of a student nurse praying in his ear, pleading with him to fight for his life. When he was fully conscious the doctors said his walking days were over.

Godfrey had been on his way to fly a glider and he had no intention of giving up walking, or flying for that matter. Patched together by surgeons, he managed to do both, but he was even more ambitious than that. During World War II he wanted to fly for the United States Navy. Turned down repeatedly, he was finally helped by Eleanor Roosevelt. She had listened to Godfrey many mornings in the mid-1930s when he was still an obscure Washington radio emcee. When she learned that he wanted to join the navy but had been turned down by the Bureau of Medicine and Surgery, Mrs. Roosevelt told her husband of Godfrey's frustration. The president called in a navy officer who was in a position to reverse the bureau and asked why the navy was saying no to Godfrey. The man told FDR that the navy couldn't give Godfrey a commission because of his leg injuries.

According to Godfrey, FDR said, "Can he walk?" "Well, yes, he can *walk,"* the navy aide replied. "Give it to him, then," FDR said impatiently. "I can't walk and I'm the commander-in-chief!"

Even before his accident Godfrey had suffered hardships. His father might have given him everything. The elder Godfrey, born in Liverpool of an Irish mother and an English father, inherited a fortune upon reaching manhood and could have lived comfortably on the interest. Instead he chartered a yacht and embarked on a world cruise with friends. He sailed and sailed—until finally, six years later, the money ran out. Arthur's father spent the rest of his life as a near-penniless, somewhat bitter writer-lecturer. He was 48 when he married Arthur's auburn-haired mother, then a talented girl of 20.

Mrs. Godfrey sang, played the piano, and even composed, notably a number called "The Marine Boys' March," which became a favorite of André Kostelanetz. She was also a fine cook, according to her five children. Arthur, the eldest, was born in 1903 and grew up in Hasbrouck Heights, New Jersey.

He worked hard to help the family financially and learned how tough the world could be. At 13 he was a bank clerk, poorly paid and often hungry. Occasionally he would take five cents' worth of stamps out of the bank's drawer and buy a candy bar for lunch. He always replaced the stamps on payday, but despite his scrupulous restitutions he was reported. Though he owed nothing at the time, he was called before the full board of directors and turned out of his job.

After Arthur's father died, the family had to split up from time to time. Arthur went to live with and work for a baker while in high school. When the baker died in an influenza epidemic, Arthur kept the shop going, often skipping school. Chastised for missing class and told by the principal that he couldn't head the sophomore debate team, Arthur said to hell with it and headed for New York City.

He arrived during hard times and in 1919 slept between the rolls of newsprint at the old New York *Tribune*. A 30-year-old woman, an ancient to the teen-aged Godfrey, slid in beside him and befriended him, often buying him coffee and food. Her frequent departures during the night perplexed him, however, and he later learned he had shared his cozy nook with a streetwalker.

It is perhaps easy to understand then why years later Godfrey befriended a kid from Brooklyn named Julius LaRosa who had an unpolished singing talent. It was in the early 1950s and Godfrey was the world's foremost talent scout as a result of his Monday night show. He was still an avid flyer and had persuaded the navy to send him to Pensacola, Florida, so he could qualify for carrier landings. LaRosa was serving out a three-year enlistment as a navy electronics crewman and was known in a couple of local bars as "the kid from the U.S.S. *Wright* who sings."

When LaRosa's buddy from the galley slipped a note to Godfrey at the base officers' quarters, asking Godfrey to audition his friend Julie for *Talent Scouts*, Godfrey agreed. The "agent" was self-appointed and the first Julius knew about his buddy's note was when Godfrey wired him. LaRosa remembers the telegram practically word for word: "Be at the Sea-Air Enlisted Man's Club this evening and Godfrey will audition you as your shipmate requested."

Says LaRosa, "I thought, My God, I'm going to sing for Arthur Godfrey! But I didn't realize anything might come of it. The thought that I might some day be a successful singer had only been a fantasy. . . . Scared? I don't think I was smart enough to be scared. I just called up a girl I was dating and we went over together. That night there was a big mob at the club because everybody knew they would see Godfrey in person and that one of their buddies would sing for him."

LaRosa had worked with the club's trio before—"They knew my keys"—and Godfrey, never one to miss a human-interest story, had arranged to put the audition on film. Godfrey took the mike and cracked a few jokes, then LaRosa did two songs—"Don't Take Your Love From Me" and "The Song Is You."

Godfrey told LaRosa that he liked the numbers and said the film would be used on his TV show. Ingenuously LaRosa said, "I don't know if my mother is a fan of yours or not. If I give you her phone number, will you give her a call and make sure she watches?" Apparently, Godfrey was charmed by LaRosa's innocence and humility.

It was some months before anything happened—the film hadn't worked out. But Godfrey didn't forget, sensing that his audience would respond to LaRosa's unspoiled charm.

Then LaRosa was suddenly summoned to New York—"It was almost an order." Godfrey had arranged a special leave with the navy so Julie could sing on the Wednesday night show, *Arthur Godfrey and His Friends*.

Carefully rehearsed and primed for his debut, Julie waited in the wings for Arthur to call him forth so the two of them could do "Sam's Song" in duet. LaRosa wasn't aware of it, but Arthur had a policy of letting a good thing run—"bits of business," joshing with the performers and other unexpected diversions that were working. While LaRosa stood fidgeting in the wings, one good thing led to another and time ran out.

LaRosa was furious and recalls: "My *mother* was looking, goddamn it, and I had called all my friends."

He stomped off to confront Godfrey's producer, the late Larry Puck, and gave him his reaction in a few choice remarks. Had Julie met the boss and not the buffer, his career might have ended right there. But Puck spoke soothingly to the young man, urging LaRosa to wait until Puck talked to Godfrey.

In time LaRosa learned that those waits in the wings were sometimes intentional, a device employed by the boss to deflate performers with swelled heads. Sometimes Godfrey would let a performer wait so long his number had to be done in a breathless race with the clock. And when Godfrey was really miffed he let the clock run out, so that besides the agony of a fruitless wait, the performer drew no pay.

But nothing Machiavellian was intended in LaRosa's case. In a couple of days he got a call from Godfrey's office. An extension of his brief leave had been arranged and he would appear on the show the following Wednesday.

LaRosa was treated "marvelously" this time. His singing was well received by the audience, and while the show was still on the air Godfrey invited LaRosa to drop in next time he was home. Julie did just that, and, sure enough, Godfrey put him on his Christmas show. To LaRosa's great surprise, Godfrey told his obviously pleased studio audience that when "Julie gets out of the navy he'll come and see us." It was a firm job offer and LaRosa was back as soon as he was discharged.

Godfrey exploited Julie's good looks and the puppy-dog gratitude that LaRosa had projected from the beginning. For the audience, LaRosa seemed to represent that lucky break everyone hopes to get and the kind of unspoiled innocent everyone likes to see get it.

But in time LaRosa achieved stardom and grew more and more popular with the CBS listeners. With a childish paranoia, Godfrey began to feel that LaRosa was overshadowing him. When the letters flowing into the CBS offices for LaRosa exceeded Godfrey's fan mail, the trouble began.

Threats—real or imagined—brought out the worst in Godfrey, and at such times he was fully capable of destroying performers he had catapulted to fame. LaRosa remembers that at a cast meeting—called "prayer meetings" out of Godfrey's earshot—Godfrey once said, "Remember that many of you are here over the bodies of people I have personally slain. I have done it before and I can do it again."

When sure of himself, however, he was charitable and sympathetic. Once when a singing member of the cast was ill, Godfrey jokingly asked if a member of the studio audience would like to fill in. Sure enough, a hand went up. Taken aback, Godfrey said something like "Well, there's a lady out there. Too bad she doesn't have her music with her." The lady's other hand went up, her sheet music clasped between her fingers.

There was no way out—Godfrey invited her up. Godfrey's organist, Lee Irwin, played the number, a Christmas carol, and the woman began to sing—atrociously. Musical director Archie Bleyer remembers sitting there thinking black thoughts, wondering how the boss was going to get out of this one. When the woman had finished there was a pause, then Godfrey said, "That's America for you. Someone comes into your home and wants to sing and she sings." Then, turning to the lady directly he said, "You sang that with great sincerity and I thank you." Says Bleyer: "I felt like two cents."

Exhaustion from overwork and constant pain from his injuries may explain Godfrey's lapses into ugly behavior. But his celebrated arrogance no doubt also reflects the corrupting effects of too much power. His warmest fans were appalled when he buzzed the tower at Teterboro Airport in New Jersey. Godfrey excused the caper as common sense: "I flew over the top of it—sure I did—I had to. It was right smack ahead of me at the time. I could have turned away from it in either direction, but then I would have lost sight of it, and any experienced pilot will tell you you'll live longer if you keep obstructions in sight until you clear them."

But that explanation, given in the old *Saturday Evening Post*, didn't explain why Godfrey was aiming at the tower in the first place. Nor has he explained his past arrogance in telling flight controllers to "get those planes out of the way, I'm coming in on important business!"

In some ways, Godfrey displayed a more basic down-home honesty than many people in his business. He honored his responsibility to his audience; either he believed in a product, or he would not accept the sponsor. He knew that he could send listeners rushing to the store by casually mentioning anything from soup to soap.

In his prime, Godfrey was the best salesman any sponsor could hope for. Thus when Godfrey-writer Andrew Rooney took some of the better human-interest stories mailed to Godfrey to Simon and Schuster and suggested a book, the publisher was very interested. Realizing how profitable a book called *Stories I Like To Tell* by Arthur Godfrey could be—providing Godfrey mentioned it occasionally on the air—the publisher paid what was for that period a thumping $25,000 advance for the book. Godfrey got half the money and Rooney and another writer got the rest. The two writers then got out the pastepot and glued the stories to typewriter paper, adding a line or two of continuity along the way. Presto! Instant book. Changeo! Instant disaster.

The book came out, and all week the publishers waited in vain for Godfrey to mention it on the air—to send the folks running into the bookstores. Unfortunately, nobody had told Godfrey that he was expected to beat the publicity drum. Toward the end of the week, the frantic publisher beseeched Rooney to ask Godfrey "How come?" Godfrey's red-hot reactions to advertiser interference were legendary, and the diplomatic Rooney approached his boss with considerable reluctance. Godfrey was surprisingly pleasant with Rooney, but he was also adamant. He couldn't mention the book, he said, because he hadn't really told those stories—or even seen them. It would be dishonest to suggest to his listeners that he had.

The publisher had believed they were buying a million dollars' worth of free publicity for $25,000 and had given that message to the bookstores. Apologies went out, and the books came back. Most of the 15,000 hardcover copies were sold to Lipton Tea, Arthur's sponsor, for giveaways.

One product that Godfrey did plug on the air—the spoken-history album "Hear It Now"—didn't earn Godfrey a dime. In a New York bar in the late 1940s, agent Jap Gude was chatting with an obscure producer named Fred W. Friendly. Friendly had been experimenting with tape recorders and had become very excited over their potential. You could do anything with these machines, he told Gude—record live or from a disc, or a radio broadcast, then cut and splice with razor blade and Scotch Tape, swiftly and inexpensively creating a record of events that had taken place at widely disparate times and locations.

Friendly hoped to interest a publisher in turning out a record album featuring important speeches by Churchill, Roosevelt, even Stalin. Gude thought that sounded like *Only Yesterday*, a famous picture book with text by Frederick Lewis Allen. He got a copy for Friendly, who read it and became more excited than ever. The two men approached Frederick Lewis Allen who was too busy to do the narration but urged them to go ahead with the idea without him.

Friendly, disappointed that Allen couldn't do it, was wary about seeking a Hollywood personality instead. It would need not a Hollywood name but a newscaster. He hesitated, thought a bit, and said, "We need somebody like Ed Murrow."

Gude remembers saying, "Why not Ed Murrow? . . . I'm his agent." Murrow's voice was familiar to every American from his rooftop broadcasts during the London blitz. Fred Friendly was a nobody, but when the two got together they took to each other immediately. Murrow liked the album idea and said he would be happy to narrate it if others would do the work of putting the material together.

CBS's Goddard Lieberson, head of the Masterworks division, was happy to have the project since the musicians had struck the major recording studios, idling most projects. No such nonmusic record had been done before and Lieberson was eager to see if this kind of thing could succeed.

In assembling the material, the producers included an extended sequence of the Franklin Delano Roosevelt funeral services. They were surprised to recognize a familiar voice narrating a part of the Roosevelt funeral procession—Arthur Godfrey's. Godfrey, on the CBS payroll in 1945, had been asked to help cover the funeral because he had begun his career in Washington. Whoever arranged it probably didn't know how beholden Godfrey felt to the late president, the man who had made it possible for the disabled entertainer to fly for the navy. When Godfrey began to describe the solemn procession—the riderless horse, the caisson bearing FDR's casket—he went to pieces. He stayed with it, though, speaking through tears. It was a remarkable moment in a remarkable record.

Then came the question: Could they use this recording without paying Godfrey, or did it belong to Godfrey? The legal department at CBS—which now employs more than 50 lawyers—had detailed only one man to the records division. The lawyer was reasonably sure the material did not belong to Godfrey but the law on the point was not clear-cut.

Jap Gude had worked for CBS from 1930 through the early Forties, and he had known Arthur Godfrey for years. Gude felt he ought to take the rough-cut disc to Godfrey and play it for him, more as a matter of courtesy than in an effort to seek clearance.

The entertainer was at the peak of his career, a busy man hard to get an appointment with. Gude told Godfrey he wanted only two minutes of his time, he wanted him to listen to something. But he refused to tell the curious entertainer any more except to say, "It's not a sales pitch."

The next day Gude met Godfrey at the studio.

We went to the recording booth, and just to give Arthur some idea what the project was about, I played him about thirty seconds of Murrow's narration. Then I jumped the needle to the Godfrey section, marked with a crayon pencil. My whole attention was on the turntable and the disc. I wanted to be sure to get the needle in the groove at the right spot and to take it off when the segment was over.

Godfrey's voice came on, speaking from his perch somewhere overlooking Pennsylvania Avenue. We had cut it down to probably a minute at the outside. When it was finished, I lifted the needle and turned to find Arthur with the tears streaming down his face. "Just a minute," he said, wiping his eyes, and he went to the door of this little recording booth and yelled for his secretary down the hall. "Mug! Tell those guys I can't see them for lunch," he said and came back in and shut the door, saying, "I want to hear this whole thing."

Jap Gude says it hadn't even occurred to him that Godfrey might plug the record. "But he plugged it and plugged it and it became a runaway best seller. I would guess that Godfrey was responsible for at least half of the records sold." He wasn't paid a penny for the plugs or his part on the record.

At the time of the famous LaRosa incident, Godfrey had been away for three months recovering from an operation on his hip, while his show went on with substitute hosts. As Godfrey tells it, his "friends" (employees) had gotten big heads because they had learned they could make big money playing the nightclubs. Much more, in fact, than they could make on the Godfrey show.

Godfrey returned to chaos, according to his own account.

My producer, the late Larry Puck, said, "Come up and see this, you won't believe it." Instead of going in the back way at the Ed Sullivan Theater, I went in the front door on crutches and sat in the darkened theater, listening for half an hour while the performers refused to rehearse, etc. I finally spoke up and said, "You bastards. If I ever see this kind of thing again, I'll take a broom and sweep you all out." They weren't all doing it. LaRosa was the ringleader. . . .

A day later, I heard from LaRosa's lawyer who said, "In the future when you want to speak to my client see me first."

LaRosa remembers the circumstances differently. Though he agrees that he instructed his lawyer to write that letter, he denies being a ringleader of anything. In the summer of 1953 LaRosa had made a record with Archie Bleyer called "E Cumpari," which was a "gigantic hit." It was bigger than anything LaRosa had done before or would do thereafter. As he tells it: "I was getting six to seven thousand fan letters a week. I understand Godfrey was getting five thousand—something like that. That summer, I am sure that I was getting a little cocky. But I maintained a sense of respect for the man, even a kind of submissiveness to his authority which reflected my sense of appreciation for what that man had done for me.

"I was cocky though and you've got to remember that in the framework of those ballet lessons."

At the time, Godfrey was very conscious of a need for gracefulness on television and of his own stiffness caused by the hip injuries. He had decreed that every member of the cast would take skating and ballet lessons to develop grace of movement. Godfrey paid for the lessons, just as he paid for the agents he had representing his family of performers. Godfrey was concerned about his cast in his own paternalistic way.

LaRosa was at the first ballet class—the only man to attend. Like many men, he considered ballet effeminate and resented the lessons. Nevertheless, he planned to come to the second session.

Arthur wanted us there and you can bet your ass that I was going to be there. It was a Thursday. That morning I got to work and mother called to say there was a family problem. I went to the boss and told him that my mother wanted me home in Mount Vernon and that I would try to get back in time for the lesson. He gave me his permission.

Well, it turned out that I wasn't able to get to that class. Friday morning I found a note on the bulletin board addressed to me that said, "Since you felt your services were not required at ballet class yesterday, your services will not be required on the show this morning."

Furious, LaRosa ran to the Lexington Hotel where Godfrey lived and asked for his suite on the house phone. The operator said she would get Godfrey, but soon came back on the line and said in obvious embarrassment, "I'm sorry, he's not in." LaRosa noticed Godfrey's Rolls waiting outside to take him to the studio. At that point he went to his lawyer and said, "Tell him from now on that when he wants to talk to me to get in touch with you."

Godfrey had dinner with Paley and Stanton and says Paley told him he didn't have to put LaRosa on just because he was under contract. But Godfrey wanted complete victory. Thus he was more interested in Stanton's suggestion, which was, according to Godfrey: "You hired him on the air, why don't you fire him on the air?"

As Godfrey remembers it, he twitted LaRosa on the show that day before his number: "You're doing pretty good, aren't you? Getting big money in the nightclubs, and so forth. This show must be a pain in the neck to you." LaRosa protested to the contrary. Then came LaRosa's song in the dramatic spot just before the end of the show. LaRosa finished to applause and Godfrey said, "That was Julie's swan song," wished him "Godspeed" and signed off.

Julie was still just a kid. He didn't know that a "swan song" was the legendary last utterance of a dying swan. Someone had to tell him he'd been canned—on the air.

The two men met in Godfrey's office afterward, and Godfrey insists the meeting was cordial. Maybe so, but he still gets incensed when he recalls the episode today. He says LaRosa used the word "bewildered" to describe how he felt. "Somebody must have told him to say that," Godfrey says. "He wouldn't know the meaning of a word that big."

Godfrey claims that press agents then told LaRosa to bring romance into the picture. In any event, LaRosa and Dotty McGuire of the McGuire Sisters, regulars on the Godfrey show, showed up at the Stork Club, and the press was called in to be told that LaRosa was fired because Godfrey didn't approve of his love for Dotty McGuire. Godfrey says that this was ridiculous because Dotty was happily married, that the press realized this and dropped the story in two days.

LaRosa says otherwise: "I was in love with Dotty. She had a husband in Korea but that was over. We had been thinking about getting married. . . ." But Godfrey was to prevail. Much to LaRosa's chagrin, he put the pressure on Dotty to stay with her husband, playing heavily on the patriotic theme.

In winning the battle, though, Godfrey lost the war. At a press conference explaining the LaRosa firing, Godfrey was astonished that "some sixty-five to seventy reporters and photographers" showed up. "It knocked me over. They wanted the LaRosa story so I told it to them. They said, 'Why did you do it?' And here's where I made my mistake. I said, 'I don't know, I guess he lost his humility.'"

Several ex-associates of Godfrey argue that the firing of LaRosa—and of Archie Bleyer whom he fired the same week—was the beginning of the end. Godfrey was on television for another six years, but after the LaRosa episode the press, less friendly, began to look for more examples of the Godfrey arrogance. He says reporters hid in the rest rooms and attempted to bribe elevator boys, bellhops, waiters and "even the maids" at the Lexington Hotel.

Godfrey remembers speaking of the injustice of it all to Bernard Baruch in 1954. The great financier said, "What did they think about Baruch?" Godfrey mentioned statesman, advisor to presidents, park-bench philosopher, millionaire philanthropist. Baruch showed him scrapbooks filled with yellowed clippings. "Baruch: Wall Street Jew: Keeper of Concubines," said one that Godfrey remembers. There were pictures of Baruch with his reputed mistress, then pictures on the same page of his family "looking glum."

Baruch said to Godfrey: "Do you know where the sons-of-bitches are who wrote those stories? Dead, goddamn them, dead!"

Godfrey felt the strength of a resentment that had smoldered in Baruch for 50 years, but Baruch urged Godfrey to ignore the press. Still, Godfrey hopes that one day he will come out "smelling like a rose," as he puts it.

It wasn't until 1959 that Godfrey gave up his TV shows, and then only because of health. He did so in a tearful on-the-air farewell during his bout with lung cancer. He didn't want his viewers to watch him waste away. He continued to do his radio show and had the lung removed in a successful effort to confine the cancer.

His TV-comeback attempt began when he was asked by CBS to help Allen Funt get *Candid Camera* started. It ended a short time later when the famous Godfrey temper flared. Says Godfrey: "Funt came to my house and cried like a baby. 'Make something of me on the air,' he pleaded, and I did it in two weeks. In a rehearsal for the third week (as a master of ceremonies) I said, 'Here's a joke for you, Allen,' and he suddenly exploded, saying, 'I'm sick of this! Who the hell are you to tell me what to do?'"

Godfrey walked out, never to return to regular TV. He remembers "that little short shit Mike Dann" saying Godfrey, because he walked off the Funt show, would never return to TV for CBS as long as Dann was there. (Dann isn't there anymore but it hasn't improved things for Godfrey.)

Godfrey's visits to CBS after that were fruitless. His final lunch meeting with Paley in 1962 had sinister meaning in Godfrey's mind. Paley, says Godfrey, wanted $50,000 for the Paley Foundation. Godfrey said, "I'm sorry, but I just gave seventy-five thousand dollars to a hospital in Virginia. You'll have to wait a couple of years." Godfrey remembers Paley's reply as a noncommittal "Okay," and he adds, "There has never been a word since, except a card each year that says, 'Merry Christmas, Bill and Babe.'"

Stanton also seemed to grow remote. Godfrey said that previously Stanton had always closed his office doors and cut off the telephones when Godfrey visited.

In 1966, the last time I was there, the telephone rang and rang and the secretary was constantly in and out. I didn't see Stanton again until 1969 or 1970 when we both got a Peabody Award. We stood on the same platform and he kept his back to me.

He did write me a note that he would like me to come for cocktails. He would look for me in his office and mentioned a day and a date. I wrote back:

Dear Frank:
No I won't be available Tuesday because that is not the 18th. The 18th is a Saturday and I'll be someplace else. No I do not care to discuss my plans with you.

There it was again, that sudden Godfrey arrogance, assuming the worst motives or a put-down in what was at the very least a conciliatory note.

But perhaps Godfrey knew that there was no point in discussing his plans because his era was over. So much public exposure to slick TV entertainment was diminishing the market for Godfrey's cracker-barrel informality. Godfrey was at his best when the show was kept loose. Sophisticated television had been growing all around Godfrey, featuring slick choreography, big-name entertainers and carefully rehearsed numbers. Informality was for the late-hour talk shows; prime time was for skillful productions timed to the split second.

For a while you could see him on television, limping around an auto showroom, selling cars. Remnants of the old spontaneous charm can be seen in the commercial, but he was obviously mouthing words someone else had written. It was Chrysler's mistake. Not only did he lack believability, but he appealed only to the old folks.

But one thing is sure—Godfrey is and always has been his own man. And he can still be unpredictable. Two years ago he ran into Julius LaRosa on the street. Godfrey shook hands with LaRosa, clasping both of Julie's hands warmly in his. LaRosa, smiling and happy with the man he still credits with his success, cautioned that they had better watch it, or someone would "make an item of us." Godfrey released LaRosa's hands and said, with a twinkle, "Fuck 'em," and walked on.

CHAPTER 18

The Redhead, the Great One and the Marshall

WHEN TELEVISION CAME ALONG, HOLLYWOOD SNEERED. A TELEVISION show just wasn't a movie, and its performers were obviously second-rate compared with movie actors and actresses. Hollywood had its star system for decades before the upstart television began searching for performers, and richly rewarded, few of these big-money stars were tempted by TV offers.

But TV did have some things to offer in competing for talent. Even in the early 1950s a network show could offer a bigger audience than the average movie. And TV would offer the same kind of fabulous riches the movies promised. So it was inevitable that television would quickly establish its own star system. And three of the biggest were CBS's Lucille Ball, Jackie Gleason and James Arness.

If it were possible to stay awake for all the 495 Lucille Ball telecasts and view them without interruption—179 *I Love Lucys*, 156 *The Lucy Shows*, 144 *Here's Lucys* and 16 specials—this madness would consume 10 days and 15 1/2 hours. Which is not to say it would be over. Though Lucille Ball announced her retirement from weekly television and had no new show in 1974 for the first time in 23 years, reruns will continue. Her face has already been seen more often than the face of any human being who ever lived. A mad fan with insomnia, and some kind of yet-to-be-developed television receiver that can pull in any station on the air, could have his beloved Lucy on view almost 24 hours a day—if not in English then in Greek, Portuguese or Bantu.

The shows represent formula writing of a rather low order, but feature a comedy performer who is so good that she overcomes the material. Like Jack Benny who stayed with a vain, penny-pinching character and made it last a lifetime, Lucy has been smart enough to remain "Lucy." Says she: "Today's TV shows are constantly looking for ways to change. . . . I never changed. People could tune in and see what they expected to see. The only changes were of necessity—when Bill Frawley died, when I divorced Desi and when I sold the reruns and had to change the title. But my character always remained the same. I think that accounts for my longevity."

Lucille Ball, if you take a second look, is an uncommonly beautiful woman. Even at age 60 or thereabouts she displays legs that are the envy of women a third her age. She might even have become a sex symbol with her flaming red hair and dazzling good looks. But this gorgeous creature with a mouth as flexible as a rubber band used her face to stop custard pies and pizzas. She walked into walls, fell off ladders, dangled from tall buildings, made up as a clown and set her nose on fire. She did all this and more in an incredible range of bizarre and unflattering getups—including a suit of armor in which she was trapped with a lighted cigarette, the visor down. All in all, she was a lovable and hilarious klutz who denied her beauty in favor of slapstick humor.

In those pre–Gloria Steinem/Betty Friedan days, Lucy established her role as the harebrained housewife who schemed along with neighbor Ethel Mertz (Vivian Vance) to wheedle goodies from their breadwinning husbands (played by Lucy's then real-life husband Desi Arnaz and actor William Frawley). Her intricate attempts to aid her bandleader husband's career inevitably backfired. It was the reverse of the usual sitcom in which father knew nothing and mommie saved the day.

In a typical episode Lucy pretends to take up skydiving to persuade her children to give up their own dangerous pastimes. Inevitably she finds herself in an airplane, parachute on her back, terrified and desperately needing someone or something to rescue her from her foolishness. It was wonderful, entertaining nonsense.

It is hard to believe but during the red-baiting years Walter Winchell once wrote that Lucy was a communist. An executive of Philip Morris, Lucy's sponsor, made an urgent call to public relations consultant Ben Sonnenberg who asked cannily, "Is it your package or CBS's?" The answer was "CBS's." "Then let them handle it." But when it came right down to it, Lucy handled it.

Far from intimidated, Lucy confidently met the press, though it was in the early days of *I Love Lucy* when a scandal could have ended it all quickly. But she knew she wasn't a menace to America. It all started with her grandfather, she said, a lovable old gent—a furniture worker active in labor and politics. Once a reader of the *Daily Worker*, the communist newspaper, her harmless grandfather wanted her to join the party. So, she told the press with that famous wide-eyed innocence, she did. It wasn't a question of conviction—just a question of pleasing a zany old man.

And that was that. Back to the set and business. She saved herself and her show and ultimately kept the CBS network in *Lucys*—always a contender for top ratings—for 23 years.

As Dick Cavett says admiringly, she has a "hard-bitten showgirl quality . . . a quality that I happen to like very much."

When a show lasts a generation it is perhaps inevitable that a performer's personal life becomes folded into her professional life. Less than a year after *I Love Lucy* began its run in 1951, Lucille Ball became pregnant. By November 1952, the publicity mills began grinding out news of the impending event. There was such sensitivity to questionable language in those days that Lucy wasn't pregnant—not on the CBS network—she was *enceinte*.

Lucille delivered right on schedule and everyone sighed with relief when the child turned out to be a boy, Desi Jr. There's just so much waiting you can do in television. It was necessary to write scripts in advance and the sex couldn't be left indeterminate. Fortunately, the writers had decided on a boy.

News of the birth was carried on page one in many parts of the nation—along with a story about Dwight D. Eisenhower's inauguration as the nation's 34th president.

But, in time, the domestic problems of the Arnazes began to surface. Desi reportedly once spent the night sleeping in a chair in the lobby of the Beverly Hills Hotel because Lucy locked him out. The root of the problem: Desi's taste for the girls. A friend once suggested that

Desi would have fewer problems with Lucy if he were at least discreet enough to avoid well-known women. But the first nobody Desi took a fancy to rushed off to sell her story to a magazine.

When, inevitably, Lucy and Desi split, the pot of marital discord had been simmering for a long time. Lucille Ball had first filed for divorce way back in 1944. The final decree on the new action came on May 4, 1960.

The split entailed a splitting of the properties and this involved big money. The Arnazes had been highly successful apart from *I Love Lucy*, producing and packaging a number of other shows and running one of the most profitable studios in Hollywood. Some thought the complexities of the situation would ultimately end one of the more durable shows on the CBS network, or at least that Lucy wouldn't be capable of running things as well as Desi did. He had always done the negotiating and was both resourceful and tough. A CBS lawyer remembers that when Desi and Lucy were still together and wanted to make their first capital-gains deal, Desi had big ideas: The two would sell five years of *I Love Lucy* reruns to CBS and buy back a 25-percent interest in Desilu Productions, which they had sold to CBS. Says the lawyer:

This time Desi was asking $4 million-plus for the Lucy shows in the cans—and other less important properties—but he was unwilling to pay more than $1 million to buy back the 25-percent CBS interest in Desilu. He kept raising the price on the reruns and each time he did we escalated the price he would have to pay to buy back the 25 percent. He was determined to keep CBS from profiting on its Desilu investment. Paley wouldn't let him get away with it. But Desi was always in there plugging away and he generally got most of what he wanted.

When the divorce became final, Lucy remained in control of the show. She didn't have Desi to keep CBS at bay, but that didn't matter. As the same CBS lawyer says, "Lucy is no dope. Underneath that mop of carrot hair is one bright woman. She's been smart enough to find the right advice. As a businessman who had faced her as an adversary, I can tell you one thing for sure: She's no communist.

Almost anyone who knew Jackie Gleason in the 1940s would tell you The Fat Man would never make it. His pals at Toots Shor's and Lindy's watched him spend what money he made as freely as he soaked up the booze. He once hired an orchestra to keep him company for an afternoon at Toots's. The show-biz handicappers would follow the latest Gleason caper, shake their heads and mark him down as an "inside celebrity"—one destined to be a favorite of Broadway characters and nightclubbers but hardly one to make it with the general public.

They smiled knowingly when Gleason gave up a promising TV series, *The Life of Riley*, which William Bendix later succeeded in. But Gleason knew he could do bigger things. A series of film clips was assembled with Gleason in roles some thought imitative of Chaplin, Abbott and Costello, and Laurel and Hardy. It was many months before the idea was sold to the old DuMont television network for its *Big Parade of Comedy*.

He was a smash and was soon regarded as a contender for the Mr. Television title upon which NBC's "Uncle Miltie" Berle had fastened a viselike grip for many years. CBS signed him up in 1952 and put him on Saturday nights.

Every week the show opened with the June Taylor Dancers, then Jackie would come onstage, wearing a smoking jacket, and do a monologue, usually including a recap of some "late-late-late show" he'd seen "featuring the ever-popular May Bush" and interrupted by a commercial for "Mother Fletcher's Pastafazool." He'd then aim his obese body at the wings of the television theater, his hands thrust perpendicular to his blubber as he mugged, "And a-way we go!"

Gleason's characterizations ranged from understated silent comedy in The Poor Soul—a helpless individual who could come to grief at the Automat's coffee-vending machine—to the confident, loquacious Joe the Bartender, who had advice and an opinion for the unseen "Mr. Dunahy" on every topic that came up. There was also Reginald Van Gleason, a top-hatted millionaire who enjoyed the good life. ("Ummm, that's good booze!")

His most popular role was Ralph Cramden, a bus driver who was always coming up with plans to get rich quick, which his acid but loving wife Alice (Audrey Meadows) would endure or save him from. Alice's sarcasm is well illustrated in this episode from "The Honeymooners":

ALICE: Look, Ralph, maybe until you get something for yourself I could get a job and help out.

RALPH: Oh, no, you don't. When I married you I promised you'd never have to work again.

ALICE: But it won't be for long.

RALPH: I don't care, Alice, I've got my pride. Before I'd let you go to work, I'd rather see you starve. We'll just have to live on our savings.

ALICE: That'll carry us through the night, but what'll we do in the morning?

Art Carney offered a marvelous foil as upstairs neighbor Ed Norton, a sewer worker with a Brooklyn-Bronx accent. He often ad-libbed lines for his part during rehearsals including this one, which ended up in the script: "The first time I took the test for the sewer, I flunked. I couldn't even float."

The Jackie Gleason Show—and especially "The Honeymooners" segment—was an instant hit. And Gleason always knew how to parlay success into money. He managed to negotiate a contract with CBS that called for a $7-million commitment for two years of shows, plus a guarantee of $100,000 a year for 15 years even if CBS never put him on the air.

A CBS lawyer who specialized in contracts, and describes himself as "rather tired" after years in the wearing business, remembers one "terrible session" with a calm, cool Gleason in the dressing room one evening before a Gleason show.

"Gleason wasn't dressed and he wasn't going to go on unless he got his concessions. He outbluffed me. Thirty seconds before eight P.M. when the show was to start, we capitulated. By the time the overture was over, he was fully dressed and on stage. I firmly believe—or would like to believe—that he wouldn't have gone on if we hadn't given the concessions. I never even told Paley about that one."

Gleason was good at this sort of thing—even when he wasn't trying. During a luncheon negotiation with Bill Paley he fell asleep ("I had a terrible hangover"), prompting Paley to remark to aides, "If he's *that* disinterested, you better give him the money."

One of Gleason's talents was his ability to impress just about anyone he had to deal with—so long as he was personally in control. Once he designed and built a modern house—seen from above, it was shaped like a keyhole—in Peekskill, New York, and soon after moving in invited the local dignitaries to a lavish party. A Catholic, Jackie was separated but not divorced from his first wife at the time. A beautiful blonde with enormous gray eyes, whom I'll call Sally, his inamorata of several years, was there with her mother, the two acting as proper hostesses. Jackie was being "quite careful," according to a guest, a lawyer for CBS, because he needed concessions from the Peekskill officials; he still had problems with city ordinances in connection with his unusual house. As the lawyer tells it:

> The Blonde undertook to show us the house. The dining table popped out of the floor at the press of a button. There was a huge circular room downstairs with a grand piano, a bar and fifty speakers in the ceiling. The walls were of glass so that the house was totally open. The center area of the main room rose to a giant skylight. It was a one-bedroom house—$650,000 and one bedroom! The Blonde walked us up the stairs to that bedroom, which was behind a balcony. It was a big round room with a round bed, and, eager to show off another of Jackie's numerous gadgets, she pressed a button and a TV set dropped slowly out from the ceiling. Then this gorgeous girl remarked, innocently, "It's set at exactly the right angle so you can watch while lying in bed."
>
> She totally destroyed the impression of respectability Jackie had worked so hard to create. Did the visiting town fathers laugh? They smiled. They weren't a laughing group."

Jackie knew how to keep people laughing—even while they paid through the nose. When Jackie decided to do his show from Miami Beach and live in the Miami Country Club where he could play golf every day of the year, CBS officials swallowed hard and took the keyhole-shaped house off his hands. The network tried to sell it but wound up owning it for years.

In 1970 Gleason and CBS disagreed over the kind of show he should be doing. CBS wanted a full hour of *The Honeymooners*, which for a year in the mid-Fifties he had done as a separate half-hour show, but Jackie preferred a variety package including "The Honeymooners."

Gleason gave some thought to the CBS proposal, but it would have meant memorizing 55 minutes of script in four days—about as much dialogue as the lead part in a long one-act play. Jackie claimed, "I could have done it," as he sipped a giant J & B Scotch, "but I would have had to cut out everything else."

So Jackie politely said no to Bill Paley and retired to his new 14-room Glea Manor in Inverrary, Florida. Like a great ball club three-deep in every position, CBS officials reasoned that it pays to keep talent on the bench and thus out of the opposing club's lineup. Gleason's contract called for his being paid even if he wasn't used, and CBS kept writing $100,000-a-year checks while Jackie sat on his ample *derrière*.

Gleason is one of those performers who can take it or leave it. He is confident that he can make a show business comeback whenever he feels like it and thus doesn't particularly miss it. He obviously enjoys the pleasures of his home in Inverrary, a 1000-acre residential and recreational complex near Fort Lauderdale. The sumptuous playroom of this more practical Gleason design is the size of a two-bedroom house and features an elaborate pool table, an organ and a stuffed six-foot gorilla. Gesturing grandly, he quipped, "Not bad for a couple of Joe Miller jokes." Relaxed and expansive, he mixed drinks from a sunken bar that dominated one end of the playroom. The bar was rimmed with padded leather and was just high enough for elbow-bending from a standard chair. It must be one of the few places in the world where a tippler can look down on the bartender. But Gleason has—as he generally does—the upper elbow. He lives lavishly on the CBS largess. A modestly appointed golf cart parked in front of the house carries him to one of Inverrary's three golf courses every morning. His No. 1 golf cart, parked at the links, is fire-engine red and is replete with siren, AM-FM stereo radio and a bar.

Gleason is never very far from liquid refreshment; there is a bar in virtually every room and several of them pop up at the touch of a button, like bread from a toaster. He once gave David Susskind all the reasons why other people drink and concluded, "Me? I drink to get bagged."

As it turned out, Jackie didn't renew his contract with CBS when it finally wound down and those $100,000-a-year checks, which used to drop down the chimney as if from a mad Santa Claus on his roof, suddenly stopped. Anxious to get a deal more to his liking than an hour of *The Honeymooners,* he jumped ship and joined NBC where, at this writing, his career is in limbo.

It may be that Bill Paley was right about Gleason's variety format. Doing a special in the old format in those last months on CBS, Jackie was far from fighting trim and looked tired. But the anxious reader can be sure of one thing. Gleason isn't hurting for money and he is content being at Glea Manor with his third wife, June Taylor's sister. Speaking of his aversion to New York, where he once racked billiard balls in Brooklyn, he says, "I have no desire to go back. It's dirty, noisy and frightening."

With that he looked out a picture window at a wanton gray cloud in an otherwise perfect Florida sky, gave it a withering Reggie Van Gleason glance, took a long sip, and sighed with contentment.

When *Gunsmoke* was to make the switch from radio to television in 1955, there was never any question in CBS circles as to who should play Marshall Dillon. The part was written for and tailored to the dimensions of John Wayne. The Duke was everybody's idea of the heavyweight good guy who tamed Dodge City with country wisdom salted with brute strength and peppered with lead.

William Conrad, whose mellifluous radio voice and acting ability had defined the role of the marshall and helped make *Gunsmoke* important in the first place, wasn't even seriously considered. This audio star was just too heavy for the part on television—you could hardly mount Marshall Dillon on a plow horse. Like silent films' dashing John Gilbert whose squeaky voice drew snickers in early talkies, Conrad was made obsolete by a new medium—at least for the part of a lean marshall. Much later he found his lucrative spot on TV, as the fat and now famous detective, Cannon.

Apart from Conrad, there were few candidates for the job: The role didn't strike enough sparks to ignite a campfire. The major movie actors thought that being a TV marshall, like being a real marshall in the Old West, would be suicide. For despite the explosive public interest in the animated box, in 1955 Hollywood was still on history's greatest ego trip; the only stars worth hooting about were still playing at the Rialto, not in the living room.

Naturally, then, John Wayne wasn't interested. But when he turned it down, he did suggest a candidate—a big fellow named Arness who was under contract to Wayne's production company. At the time, James Arness was a candidate for actors anonymous. His diverse credits included a simplistic role in a John Wayne anti-red propaganda film; his biggest hit—the title role in *The Thing*—had required a virtuoso growling performance as a 250-pound vegetable from outer space. But he was well over six feet tall, great-looking in a ten-gallon hat, and, more important, projected an inner serenity that passed for wisdom. And he could remember his lines. He'd done westerns—or rather laid eggs in them—and was about to do another when John Wayne turned down Matt Dillon.

When Arness showed up for a test, excited studio executives thought the man just reeked of horse sweat and manly charm. He was, in short, Right for the Part.

Where writers had pictured a quiet man, executives who had gotten to know Arness say "stolid" would be a more appropriate adjective. He's not part Indian like Burt Reynolds, or a genuine cowboy like Tom Mix, or anything that might remotely suggest that he was molded out of western clay and prairie-dog tails. In fact, he's a Swede.

Arness does not grant interviews to the press, hasn't for years. Nope. His enemies say that's the smartest thing he does. Of course, signing to do *Gunsmoke* was pretty smart, but it almost never happened—for James Arness did not want the part. His agent, Kurt Frings, wasn't enthusiastic either. Perhaps Frings was indifferent to the broadcast medium because of the international acclaim the movies were bestowing on his client Liz Taylor. Frings knew little about TV and apparently cared less. Still, Arness was free and Frings committed him to do the part. Thus the production, its leading man under contract, began to roll.

On the night before Arness was to show up for wardrobe fittings, CBS was notified that he had changed his mind; he had decided against going into TV and was, in fact, already shooting a western for Republic Pictures. But the network had ordered sets, hired other actors and was already pouring thousands of dollars into the production. Tough luck, pard. You can forget that CBS contract. Arness had spoken.

He hadn't bargained, however, with William Dozier, then West Coast director of programing for the network. Dozier was a determined man and a veteran of the kind of live-and-let-die warfare that is played in Hollywood as casually as viewers switch channels on TV. A gaunt man with a worn-out face dominated by pale blue eyes, Dozier was used to having his way—even with a few of the world's more formidable women. Once married to Oscar-winning beauty Joan Fontaine, he is now the husband of onetime film ingenue Ann Rutherford. Dozier now picked up the telephone and bluntly told Arness: "You don't know me, but I want to tell you that you are about to do something very unprofessional."

Even an established star (which Arness wasn't) thinks twice about doing something regarded as "unprofessional" by an important entertainment-capital executive. Powerful people trade gossip at Hollywood parties, gossip that can end a career without the victim even knowing why his telephone has suddenly stopped ringing.

Something very unprofessional? "What's that?" asked Arness. Dozier told him, and Arness said he just didn't think he wanted to do the *Gunsmoke* project. Dozier didn't argue on the phone. He invited Arness to his house so that he could "Pump some sunshine up his ass," as he told others. At the meeting, Dozier and fellow executives explained the contract—why it was a good one for Arness and why he shouldn't break it.

Whether Arness was sufficiently impressed with Dozier's conversation or not, he could hardly have failed to appreciate the kind of wealth television showered on the chosen few, including this CBS executive. For the setting, Dozier's home, symbolized all that money can buy. Located far into Hollywood's elegant Beverly Hills, it could have served as Scarlett O'Hara's pad in *Gone with the Wind*. The house is a striking Georgian colonial manor with a spiral staircase off a central sitting room two stories high. In the rear, spacious windows frame a magnificent garden—a veritable jungle, though well ordered and carefully tended.

Whether Arness saw the light or simply felt the heat, he lived up to the terms of his contract—and discovered a gold mine. *Gunsmoke* more than lived up to Dozier's positive forecast. This endless western saga dominated the Saturday night scene at 10 P.M. for years, galloping along at or near the top of the ratings well into the mid-1960s. It was 12 years before NBC movies managed to gun it down, and by then Arness had become as familiar as the postman to millions of viewers the world over. In fact, his handsome open face was almost as well known as that of his mentor, Duke Wayne.

Gunsmoke's appeal stems, in part, from its nitty-gritty version of reality in the Old West. Matt Dillon as played by Arness is a plainspoken man in plain work clothes—none of that black hat/white hat stuff for Gunsmoke. A horse is a horse—to be ridden and fed—not loved. He carries a single gun on the unspoken premise that if you need two you're unqualified for the job. He's always *liked* saloonkeeper Kitty (Amanda Blake) and she obviously loves him and would like to marry him. But it was years before he fell in love, and then it was with

Michael Learned (who won an Emmy for her role as the mother on *The Waltons*). The romance was short-lived, only one show in the long-lived series.

It was a typical *Gunsmoke* episode. Matt was tracking a loner (Victor French) across the desert. The loner had killed a man who deserved to die, but Matt's job is to serve the law. The loner dry-gulches Matt and leaves him for dead. Along comes Miss Learned, a courageous widow, and she nurses him back to health at her ranch. Matt's wounds cause amnesia, he forgets about Dodge City and learns to love the widow. Meanwhile a local VIP hires the loner to butcher the widow so he can have her land. Matt comes around and does his duty and as memory returns the two reluctantly split. It sounds corny in the telling and I guess it is. But the acting is superior—though one tends to feel Arness is typecast to a fare-thee-well—and the writing is as good as you ever see in a western.

The language is suitably stylized and, though undoubtedly a travesty on that really used in the Old West, believable. It is as *New York Times* writer "Cyclops" put it, "a lingual compost of all our ideas about the West, knotty analogies, brutish poems, the inchoate cleverly tortured into expressions of feeling—that myth marched in and made itself at home." *Gunsmoke's* like that after two decades. It inspires awe.

However, Jack Gould's final word on *Gunsmoke:* "It's very professional, workmanlike, routine junk."

Arness became a millionaire several times over, and network minions were at his call to answer every whim in those golden years. No requests however unreasonable would be lightly denied. When Arness wanted to get out from under his ranch, the cowboy crooked a finger and CBS came forward with its seemingly bottomless purse, kissed the financial bruises and bandaged them with greenbacks. This kind of bailout kept the stars happy, and happy stars make for a happier, more prosperous network. So CBS parqueted Red Skelton's floor, took Jackie Gleason's glass house off his hands and solved James Arness's ranching problems.

Whether CBS would have been this attentive to Arness's financial needs in 1967 is more doubtful. Obviously, the longer a show lasts, the older its audience gets, and 12 years into its run *Gunsmoke* was suffering from hardening of the arteries—its own and its fans'. Advertisers want the big spenders in the "demographic" stream—the 18- to 49-year-olds; folks who are starting to raise families, buying houses, rising on the corporate ladder. Even if you keep a big chunk of this much-sought-after audience, you begin to lose advertiser appeal after years of success if you don't continue adding younger viewers.

ABC killed Lawrence Welk partly for this reason, even though the bandleader quickly syndicated his program and managed to top the ratings for all such shows as recently as early 1973. CBS axed Red Skelton on the same theory—that and the fact that the customary annual 8-percent raises the stars generally enjoyed priced the cantankerous comedian out of the market.

Most of the young people preferred NBC's movies, and thus *Gunsmoke* at long last was reluctantly canceled. James Arness was about to descend once again into the world of mortals. But then, the day after the farewell cast party, the impossible happened. Bill Paley, who had always loved *Gunsmoke* and who still had faith in its broad appeal, was brooding about its fate at his lush Bahamian retreat on Lyford Cay. He called dapper Tom Dawson, then CBS's vice-president of sales (later he briefly graced the network's austere presidential suite with sport-jacket informality while dark-suited rivals conspired to have him dismissed). Paley asked Dawson for "a read" on two new Monday night comedies that were placed back-to-back at 7:30 and 8 P.M., and Dawson confirmed Paley's impression that they weren't selling. Paley then said something like, "I don't know why you fellows don't put *Gunsmoke* in that slot"—a casual manner of speaking the curiously shy Paley uses when he gives a direct order.

The show was back in the schedule the next day—in prime time, no less—and it has remained there ever since.

It wasn't as though *Gunsmoke* suddenly acquired a significantly younger audience, though the viewers were undoubtedly of a somewhat different demographic makeup. According to Mike Dann, for years the network's senior v. p. for programing, *Gunsmoke*'s demographics were probably among the worst in television on the basis of the number of young people in the audience, but with an audience as large as *Gunsmoke* enjoyed, "Who cared whether they all wore dentures?"

It cost a pretty penny to resurrect the show. The cast—Amanda Blake as Kitty, Ken Curtis as Festus, Milburn Stone as Doc—were all well-off by this time and fully aware of Paley's interest. So they had to be approached and signed again.

James Arness signed, mounted up and rode back into Dodge City for another eight years, finally loping off into the sunset at the end of the Spring season in 1975. Bill Dozier guesses the man is worth perhaps $20 million today, and all because of a part he didn't want.

Dozier just had to pump a little sunshine into the right place.

CHAPTER 19
$64,000 Indigestion

IT WAS JUNE 7, 1955, AT SHORTLY BEFORE 10 P.M. A WORK-WEARY ED Murrow and his producer Fred Friendly were waiting to do the regular *See It Now* broadcast—a month after Alcoa had announced that it was ending a courageous four-year association with the controversial show.

Murrow, the most honored broadcaster in history, was puffing a cigarette, waiting to do part two of a report on smoking and lung cancer. While he waited, he watched fascinated and horrified as the new "lead-in" to his show—the show occupying the previous half-hour —enjoyed its debut. He turned to Fred Friendly and said, "Any bets on how long we'll keep this time period now?" The program was *The $64,000 Question*. Murrow knew that a hit show always makes the following time slot very appealing to advertisers, and *See It Now* wasn't a commercial enough program to cash in on the opportunities.

For many months Charles Revson, a wily show business buff and the president of Revlon, Incorporated, had been in a desperate search for a way to stimulate sales. Hazel Bishop lipsticks were "murdering" Revlon, having gained the advantage through television advertising, and Revson was convinced that television could also provide Revlon an

Charles Van Doren—"Don't prompt me, I'll get it!"

Red Skelton plays gin rummy.

Wide World

Photo World

Lucille Ball
and Danny Kaye—
a couple of muggers
in Television City.

CBS

The Beverly Hillbillies
on location.

Kate Smith, in 1932, was to become an even bigger star.

James Arness as
Marshal Dillon—
weatherbeaten
all the way
to the bank.

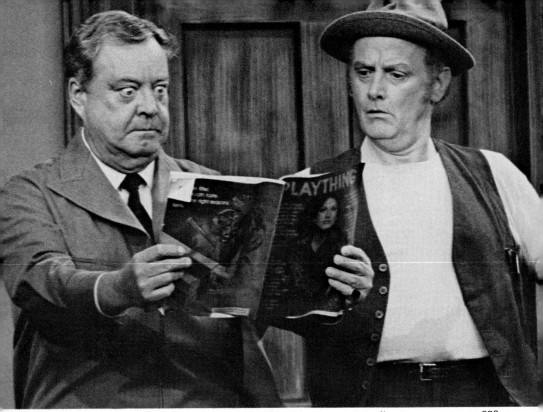

Gleason and Carney in "The Honeymooners."

When Archie talks, the dingbat listens.

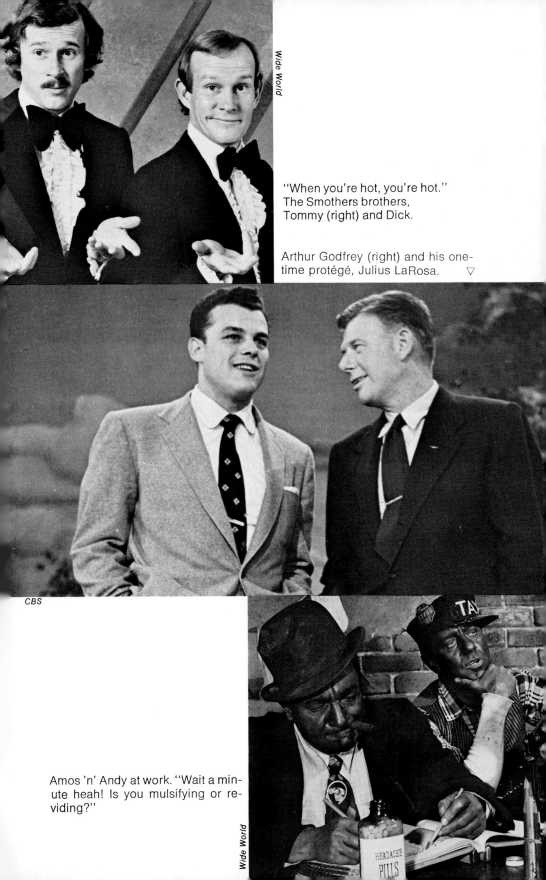

"When you're hot, you're hot."
The Smothers brothers,
Tommy (right) and Dick.

Arthur Godfrey (right) and his one-
time protégé, Julius LaRosa. ▽

Amos 'n' Andy at work. "Wait a minute heah! Is you mulsifying or re-
viding?"

Ed and Jackie—
characteristically
graceful.

Benny, Rochester and the Maxwell.

appropriate counterthrust. But he wanted to make a big impression, with something more arresting than just any run-of-the-mill show.

Every TV packager in the business was attempting to capitalize on Revson's need, and among these people was Walter Craig, an ex-vaudeville hoofer turned writer, then television producer. He was a partner in the newly formed ad agency of Norman, Craig & Hummel. When an emissary from Louis G. Cowan, an independent producer of television shows, told him about a concept for a show called *The $64,000 Question,* Craig's heart leaped.

A quiz show promising a fat ransom to the winner and given the full-blown television treatment just might rivet national attention. The idea itself was a variation on an old radio quiz show that awarded $64 to the ultimate winner. The show had been popular enough to make the expression "That's the sixty-four-dollar question" part of the language.

Besides upping the money a thousandfold, Cowan wanted to seek out contestants with strong audience appeal and to build suspense by putting them in a glass isolation booth—to prevent tips from the studio audience. Winners would be "continuing heroes" having to trek their way to the Big Question over a period of weeks; and solemn financial men from banks or accounting firms would sanctify the proceedings by handing the master of ceremonies the questions in sealed envelopes.

Craig outlined the idea to Revson, got a nibble and arranged the following morning to closet himself, Revson, their aides and CBS officials in an office. He locked the door and said dramatically that no one was to leave the room until a contract was signed. The meeting lasted through the lunch hour and food was sent in. Still the men talked, thrashing out details. The discussions dragged on until 4 A.M. the next day, when they ended as Craig had predicted—with signed contracts.

No one—not even Lou Cowan, a six-foot-three intellectual with a voice as soothing as a lullaby—could have guessed the degree to which *The $64,000 Question* would sweep the country. There was that big $64,000 prize to begin with and, as an added fillip, the consolation prize —a Cadillac—for the loser. No one could resist the game. Or was it the players?

Living Lipstick, the Revlon product pitched by chic Wendy Barrie, all but vanished from the nation's retail shelves, as viewers showed their gratitude and gullibility. Hal March, the master of ceremonies, had to plead with the nation's womankind to be patient. They were doubling, tripling production to meet demand. The audiences continued to build, eventually taking a record 84.8-percent share of the television watchers at that hour. When Richard S. McCutcheon, a marine captain, pitted his knowledge of cooking against all comers and began his successful ascent to the $64,000 question, bookmakers quoted odds on his chances of pulling down the top prize. Las Vegas gamblers left the gaming tables to huddle in front of television sets to see if McCutcheon would win in the biggest casino of them all. Headlines carried the news of his eventual victory the following day.

The show specialized in contestants with interesting backgrounds and unexpected areas of expertise: an appealing young black girl who seemingly could spell every word in the dictionary; a shoemaker with an encyclopedic knowledge of opera; a blonde lady psychologist who memorized everything about boxing. (Joyce Brothers was her name and such was her fame that for a decade or more she emceed programs of her own advising women on sex and such.) Everyone loved the show. Almost everyone.

Raymond Spector, Hazel Bishop's chairman, had sad news for shareholders in his report in January 1956. A surprising loss had been suffered "due to circumstances beyond our control," he said, borrowing a broadcasters' phrase. Revlon's *$64,000 Question* had "captured the imagination of the public" and eclipsed Hazel Bishop in cosmetics sales.

CBS officials, pondering the new phenomenon, saw the big-money quiz as a distinct industry trend and decided that Lou Cowan, the packager of the show, ought to be working for the network. Cowan severed his connections with the show and became vice-president in charge of "creative services."

(Meanwhile, the golden age of documentaries was ending. *See It Now,* as Murrow sadly predicted, lost its weekly slot in the CBS lineup and was relegated to hour-long specials. Paley had shrewdly sold the exhausted Murrow and Friendly on the idea of changing formats so that they would have more time, and the opportunity to do important subjects in the longer format. But *See It Now*'s demise was already in the works.)

The $64,000 Question became one of the most imitated shows in television history. *The Big Surprise* was brought in before the end of 1955, and CBS followed its own success with *The $64,000 Challenge*, also sponsored by Revlon. There were others, including *High Finance, Treasure Hunt*—and NBC's *Twenty-One*.

Charles Van Doren, a young, pleasant-looking Columbia University English instructor, son and nephew of distinguished writer-scholars Mark and Carl Van Doren, was the biggest thing that hit *Twenty-One*. A shy but knowledgeable contestant, Van Doren defeated a strong but unpopular champion, Herbert Stempel, who had appeared to be unbeatable. *Twenty-One* began to vie with the two CBS shows, which stayed at or near the top of the weekly ratings. Van Doren became a national hero; the audience would suffer with him in the isolation booth as his face showed the strain of his mental search for the right answer —which he often came up with only at the last split second. Deluged with offers to lecture and write books, he became the summer replacement for Dave Garroway on NBC's *Today Show* and he found himself reading poetry to a national audience—perhaps the largest classroom in the world. He gave college professors an élan they seldom enjoyed in a nation always suspicious of intellectuals.

But Stempel, the man Van Doren had defeated, was unhappy—more than that, he was suspicious. In August 1958 he charged that *Twenty-One* was fixed. Anxiety and fear rippled through the network executive offices. Lou Cowan, now president of the CBS Television Network, grew concerned.

He should have been in a position to know all there was to know about quiz shows. His association with them started long before *The $64,000 Question.* He had, for one, been packager of a highly successful radio show, *Stop the Music*, in which contestants had to identify popular tunes.

In the summer of 1950, a soon-to-be-married editor at McGraw-Hill was asked by his roommate, an assistant producer of the show, now an eminent documentary producer, "What do you want for a wedding present? How about a stove or a refrigerator?" The editor quickly decided on a refrigerator. Thereafter he and his fiancée were stationed in the front row of the balcony of the *Stop the Music* studio. His fiancée was told that she should turn her ring around and pretend to be "just married" and when the emcee asked for newlyweds in the audience, she should jump up.

She did, though the couple had warned their friend that she was a pop music zero. Not to worry, the assistant producer said, she would have no trouble. She didn't. She was told the name of the tune at least four times before she reached the mike. As she was a few steps away from it, a girl attached to the show asked, "You know the tune, don't you?" This prompted the contestant to remark, "I didn't but I've been told it so many times I could hardly forget."

That kind of cheating would never bring the DAs sniffing around. But when the prize was $64,000, that was another matter.

Though Cowan had broken his connection with the shows he'd created, the connection between *The $64,000 Question* and Cowan's ascent to power at CBS was clear-cut, and galling to other men in the network. After reading a *Time* magazine story about Charles Van Doren and NBC's *Twenty-One*, Cowan called the producers of CBS's two $64,000 shows and, taking a "Hey, you guys aren't cheating over there, are you" attitude, was told what he wanted to hear—"absolutely not." He says he told the producers that their shows had to be 100-percent honest. Then he reported to his superiors at CBS that they had better have detectives check it out. The detectives reportedly came back with nothing.

Meanwhile, though he had denied on the air that there was anything to allegations that he had been coached, NBC's wonder-boy, Charles Van Doren, was growing increasingly apprehensive. After an aimless and agonizing drive through New England with his wife at his side, Mr. Van Doren went to Washington. There, before members of a House of Representatives special subcommittee on legislative oversight, he read a long statement that began with the sad admission:

"I would give almost anything I have to reverse the course of my life in the last three years. . . . I have deceived my friends, and I had millions of them."

He had been urged to appear on a quiz show originally because he was "good at games." He applied to Barry & Enright, producers of *Tic Tac Dough* and other programs. He was given a couple of written examinations, one of them very tough, and was told that he would appear on the company's new game series, *Twenty-One*. He began organizing and memorizing odd bits of information and, when he was about to have his chance, was asked by Albert Freedman, producer of the series, to come to his apartment.

He took me into his bedroom where we could talk alone. He told me that Herbert Stempel, the current champion, was an "unbeatable" contestant because he knew too much. He said that Stempel was unpopular, and was defeating opponents right and left to the detriment of the program. He asked me if, as a favor to him, I would agree to make an arrangement whereby I would tie Stempel and thus increase the entertainment value of the program.

I asked him to let me go on the program honestly, without receiving help. He said that was impossible. He told me that I would not have a chance to defeat Stempel because he was too knowledgeable. He also told me that the show was merely entertainment and that giving help to quiz contestants was a common practice and merely a part of show business. This of course was not true, but perhaps I wanted to believe him. He also stressed the fact that by appearing on a nationally televised program I would be doing a great service to the intellectual life, to teachers and to education in general, by increasing public respect for the work of the mind through my performances.

In fact, I think I have done a disservice to all of them.

Freedman began coaching Van Doren on the scheduled questions and the answers. Van Doren could answer some of the questions but not all of them. Freedman wanted to make certain that Van Doren convinced the audience that he was struggling to answer the questions. He coached Van Doren on the pregnant pause, and suggested that he answer some parts of certain questions first and the more difficult parts at the end. As Van Doren remembered it, he struggled to make himself feel a little more honest: "A foolish sort of pride made me want to look up the answers when I could and learn as much about the subject as possible."

Van Doren had not only lied on the air, he had also lied to the lawyer who was defending him. He left the hearing room a seemingly broken man destined to sink into obscurity. Fortunately ours is a forgiving society and Van Doren proved strong in the face of adversity. (Also, of course, he is brilliant.) Today he is back not only writing books but publishing them. He is the president of Praeger, a small but distinguished book publisher in New York.

He wasn't the only culprit in what came to be known as the Quiz Scandal. New York District Attorney Frank Hogan said that of 150 witnesses called in an investigation into the matter, "maybe fifty" told the truth.

Though the NBC show claimed the big bad headlines, CBS was not to be let off scot-free. Production people from both *The $64,000 Question* and *The $64,000 Challenge* told the congressional investigators that the sponsor, Revlon, gave orders to get rid of certain unpopular contestants—one way or the other. The dull ones, including psychologist Joyce Brothers, weren't always easy to dump. The especially difficult questions meant to bump the lady boxing expert failed. Dr. Brothers had a photographic memory and worked hard memorizing a boxing encyclopedia.

A voice or two—including that of Freedman, the producer of *Twenty-One* and Van Doren's coach—was raised in defense of the quiz shows as an antidote to TV's heavy diet of violence. He argued that deception was rife in politics and that no one complained about the obvious fact that ghost writers penned the speeches and even the books of national political figures.

That didn't satisfy Frank Stanton, recognized by this time as broadcasting's foremost public statesman. Lou Cowan had been stricken with a serious circulatory ailment in November 1959, and could not testify on his own behalf. Stanton took full responsibility and went to Washington. Before Congress and the nation Stanton made what amounted to a confession:

> I want to say here and now that I was completely unaware, until August 8, 1958, of any irregularity in the quiz shows on our network. When gossip about quiz shows in general came to my attention, I was assured by our television-network people that these shows were completely above criticism of this kind. . . . It is now clear that I should have gone further. . . . This has been a bitter pill for us to swallow.
>
> We propose to be more certain . . . that it is we and we alone who will decide not only what is to appear on the CBS Television Network but how it is to appear.

Stanton's stand was statesmanlike. But somebody else had to take the rap. Louis George Cowan, the granddaddy of the quiz shows, was the logical fall guy. Cowan was asked to resign, but since he had severed all connections with the *$64,000* organization before he joined CBS and was "clean," he refused to do so. Says a friend of Cowan, "Then Stanton fired him. The Paley formula is: Blame goes to the department head; credit to the top. Unpleasant news comes from underlings; pleasant news from the big men."

Though it must have been clear that Cowan's leaving at the time of the quiz scandals would constitute guilt by association, Ralph Colin says, "The quiz thing didn't lead to the firing of Lou Cowan. It might have been the match to set off the flash of powder. It was, rather, Lou's lack of executive training and lack of decision-making capability. He was a wonderful person—intellectual, cultured, but absolutely impossible as an executive. Everything went into his office and nothing came out. He was an office bottleneck."

Colin is saddened by the fact that Cowan believes that the CBS counsel was his executioner: "I participated in discussions about his incapacity as an executive. But I didn't have the power to bounce him. I was a party to the discussion only. . . . But Lou was very sore at me, very sore. He and I lived in the same apartment building and he wouldn't even speak to me in the lobby."

A sympathetic friend of Cowan's adds: "Presidents of companies are not like Lou Cowan. Cowan had a marvelous sense of show business and theatricality—the kind of man who ought to rise to head of programing and no further. Stanton, on the other hand, was a business executive, and there's a considerable difference. You can almost see it in their faces."

There was, of course, considerable speculation as to whether the top people at CBS—not only Lou Cowan, but also Frank Stanton and Bill Paley—knew that there had been some tampering with the quiz shows. The top echelon says not. But this denial is accepted with considerable skepticism by another quiz-show entrepreneur, one who never went into the business of producing big-money shows:

Anybody who knew anything about this business had to understand that you couldn't maintain that kind of hyperbolic drama with real people without fixing the shows. What happens if the little shoemaker gets up there and fails to answer a question on the first day? What happens if the lady who wins several hundred dollars says she doesn't want to go on; that she wants to use the money for a down payment on a car? It became unbelievable that a person who had no money at all would risk, say, $8000. To build the suspense, you had to screw around with reality.

There was always a feeling somehow during the congressional investigation and the grand jury hearings in New York that the producers were in it for the kickbacks. That simply isn't so. The money for the producers came from success—the successful attempts to fake reality: building tension artificially, taking advantage of the public's willingness to believe it's all real, suggesting that a penniless old shoemaker would risk all that money.

It is my complete conviction that network people at the top level knew what was going on. The people who bought the shows and saw it happening just had to know. You don't get way up there in the executive offices by being dumb.

It may be that CBS was clean in the quiz scandals. One important official says that Lou Cowan interviewed contestants for his shows and was shrewd enough to choose ones capable of reaching the top levels in a straight, unfixed contest.

NBC, on the other hand, told the answers "without shame," claiming "it's just entertainment." Then why did Stanton make his Washington confession? There was a feeling in the halls of CBS that contestants on some of the cheapie daytime quizzes were probably coached. Were this discovered, CBS would never be believed in arguing that the big money shows were straight.

One who escaped the quiz scandal unscathed was the man whose money started the whole thing in the first place—Charles Revson. Whatever damage quiz shows might have done to television's credibility, they had certainly had a fine effect on Revlon's sales.

In 1959, the quiz scandals were a hot issue. Production people from CBS were telling congressional investigators they'd received pressure from Revlon to bump unpopular contestants. Even Charles Revson was asked if he had any part in the fix and he denied it under oath. A good thing, too. After all, Revson had the sponsor money. No TV executive was anxious to shift any blame to Revson because no matter what happened to quiz shows, Revlon was still a potential sponsor of some show.

Revson, obviously still enjoying his behind-the-scenes TV role, decided to bring *The Big Show*, sponsored by Revlon on NBC Radio, to

CBS Television. The show would star Tallulah Bankhead and the writer would be Goodman Ace. Ace was a top radio writer *(CBS Was There)* and performer *(Easy Aces)* and a very funny man. He once supposedly received an urgent telegram from a distant relative in Kansas City: "Send $5000 or I'll jump from the 14th floor of my building." In response Ace wired: "Jump from seven. I'll send $2500."

The first time Ace had been asked to write for TV, he was equally sardonic in saying no. He had watched television's birth pangs, and he said he didn't want to write "And now, in a gayer mood, we take you to Latin America and Perez Prado."

But after a time, he began to see TV's possibilities. And he was enthusiastic about working with the aging eccentric goddess of the stage, Tallulah.

Ace met with Charles Revson in Revson's office. Ace recalls that Revson fancied himself something of a show business expert. Revson mentioned something about a comedian with a big cigar, not somebody obvious like Marx or Fields. Ace sat quietly while Revson thought and thought. Then Ace said, "You mean Lou Holtz." Revson asked, "How did you know that?" Comments Ace: "I don't know where he thought they'd found me."

The contracts had already been signed and Revson was telling of his plans for the first show when Ace interrupted. As writer, he informed Revson, he had complete say on the first show, though not on later ones.

"He pressed three buttons," says Ace, "and these three men walked in nervously and confirmed it. I felt sorry for them. He actually fired the man who gave me that prerogative."

Later Revson's secretary called to arrange a luncheon meeting. "I didn't need that, so I said, 'Okay, we'll eat at the Alray.' 'What's that?' she asked, and I said, 'A pharmacy where I go to eat with my dog.' "

So they met at Revson's offices again to go over the script Ace had prepared: "He wanted me to read the script out loud. I said, 'Why don't you read it?' and he said, 'I have trouble visualizing. I even have trouble visualizing a new cosmetics package.' With that, he pressed a button, a man came in and Revson said, 'Don't I have trouble visualizing a cosmetics package?' and the man said, 'Yes,' and left. I suggested that he see the show on the air."

The first show featured many sight gags and a number of telephone calls at the beginning of the show. The single set was supposed to be Tallulah's Manhattan apartment.

The telephone rang, Tallulah picked it up and said, "Hello . . . Who? Rock Hudson . . . Just a minute." (She put down the telephone, applied her lipstick, picked up the telephone.) "Hello, darling!"

Ethel Merman was the featured guest on that first show. In rehearsals Fred Allen had to step in to explain that if Tallulah and Ethel each kept insisting on having more than half the jokes the show wouldn't come off. They finally settled down and learned the script.

Ethel walked on camera and after thunderous applause Tallulah said, "That's wonderful, Ethel—better luck next time. . . . Why didn't you get me tickets to your show?" (It was just after Ethel's smash opening in *Call Me Madam.*) "Well," Ethel said, "I had tickets for you on opening night, but they were way back in the fourth row and with *your* eyes!"

It was just the right mix of Tallulah's and Ace's talents. Bill Paley called to say it was the best television show ever; Jack Gould reviewed the show favorably at great length in *The New York Times*, and John Lardner praised it in *The New Yorker*.

Soon after the show, Ace met with Revson and his producer for a postmortem. Revson's producer, Abe Burrows, a writer Ace had hired to do comedy years earlier, carried the ball. Burrows said he was unable to catch the show; however, "My elevator man said he thought everybody looked nervous on the telephone."

Ace said, *"That's* a coincidence. I found a note from my elevator man just as I was leaving to come over here." He fished a note out of his pocket and read: "Dear Goody: Both my wife and I thought the show was marvelous. . . ."

Burrows asked, "Who's your elevator man?"

Ace studied the signature carefully, puzzling it out, and said, "Ah, James Thurber."

But it was a lost cause. The contract provided that Revson was to control more and more in the succeeding shows, and he became such a problem that Ace dropped out. He was happy to give up the $25,000 a week in exchange for his freedom from sponsor interference. Unfortunately, word got around that Goodman Ace was getting $25,000 per *skit*, and he lost a lot of work.

Ace remembers fondly, though, that Tallulah was wonderful to work for. "She'd say, 'You gentlemen, the authors . . .' We gag writers felt pretty good about that."

The show went steadily downhill after Ace left. Revson had his say and the viewer switched channels. The show went off the air in 1961.

It had a quieter demise than that of the most famous Revlon shows, *The $64,000 Question* and *The $64,000 Challenge.* How much say did Revson have in those shows? Don't ask. Lou Cowan had paid for everybody's sins on that score.

CHAPTER 20
James T. Aubrey: Magnificent Menace

AS THE NEWLY APPOINTED CBS NETWORK PRESIDENT, JAMES AUBREY is is said to have told associates that he asked himself: "Suppose Bill Paley had a son in the business?"

Within five years, a deeply troubled Bill Paley was asking himself whether he would want CBS to become Jim Aubrey's baby. In answering that question he walked into Frank Stanton's office to confer with his No. 2 man.

"Frank, he's got to go."

Stanton quickly agreed. Thus was decided the fate of the most successful executive who had ever worked for Paley and Stanton.

At the time, Jim Aubrey was roosting securely just those two small hops from the top of the CBS pecking order.

It took many years and a managerial reorganization before the network president became the No. 3 man at CBS.

In 1951, the Columbia Broadcasting System reorganized along divisional lines, setting up CBS Radio; CBS Television; CBS Laboratories; Columbia Records, Incorporated; Hytron Radio and Electronics Company; and CBS-Columbia, Incorporated, the old Air King set-making subsidiary of Hytron. Engineered by Frank Stanton, the reorganization offered division presidents considerable freedom, enough even to go astray. It also offered Stanton a chance to resolve his conflicts with a corporate antagonist, Ike Levy. Apparently losing an "either-he-goes-or-I-go" showdown with Stanton, Levy left the CBS board of directors at the time of the reorganization, though his brother, Leon, stayed on.

The single most important divisional office under Stanton's new arrangement was president of the television network. The TV network was far and away the most profitable of the six divisions, and its president could make of the office pretty much what he wanted, so long as the broadcast ratings held up.

The first president of the television network was J. L. Van Volkenburg, a tough man who had impressed both Stanton and Paley. Perhaps they wouldn't have been quite so impressed had they known how Van Volkenburg came to broadcasting in the first place. A bandleader in the Midwest, he left a job one night to discover that his parked car had slipped out of gear and crashed through a storefront. Van took one look, walked away and hopped the first train out of town. His next job was in advertising and then on to broadcasting.

Van was a superb organizer and something of a workaholic. One night he climbed on the train to Westport, Connecticut, totally exhausted and fell asleep. He slept right through his station, though his wife ran alongside the train frantically tapping on the window with a key. At the end of the line he was jolted into wakefulness and caught a return train. Despite his best efforts to stay awake, he was sound asleep again on the second pass through. When he awoke back in Grand Central Station, Van Volkenburg said the hell with it and holed up for the night in a hotel.

Van Volkenburg was certainly well liked. He was dismissed in 1955, however, for doing the unthinkable. He got drunk with affiliate owners and let them persuade him to raise the network's compensation to the station. Upon the occasion of his "retirement," the affiliate owners gave him a cabin cruiser. He is remembered by few outside of CBS today, despite the fact he helped make television a major industry. The CBS Television president who best succeeded in making a name for himself, both inside and outside the industry, is James Thomas Aubrey, Jr.

When Jim Aubrey, a sleek and boyishly handsome six-footer, became president of the TV network in late 1959, there was a feeling in the executive suite that CBS had a winner. Ralph Colin viewed Jim Aubrey as "one of the greatest pieces of executive manpower I ever saw." Colin, however, soon came to consider the enigmatic Aubrey "a powder barrel" and feared that Aubrey's widely rumored indiscretions would surface one day and cause CBS trouble.

But as long as he produced profits, Aubrey continued to enjoy his considerable freedom as network president. Only when profits faltered did the CBS eye pop open to discover Aubrey's allegedly eccentric personal habits, and he was then dismissed.

For the five years he headed the CBS Network, he was the scourge of the entertainment world, showing a decisiveness that was praised almost as much as his ruthlessness was deplored. He wielded power with the finesse of a born executive and with the arrogance of a czar.

By almost any measure, Jim Aubrey was a golden boy. He attended the best schools his father's money could buy. The wealthy advertising executive sent his son to prep at Phillips Exeter Academy, and then to Princeton where Jim pulled down top grades and played first-team football. He was eagerly welcomed into the Tiger Inn Club, one of the best.

Soon after college, World War II swept him into the air force, the glamour branch of the service, where, among other things, he taught flying to actor Jimmy Stewart. It would be easy to imagine the six-foot, blue-eyed Aubrey playing in a war movie with Stewart, for the young major was certainly Hollywood's idea of a man. He had a smile the girls remembered; he was brainy and witty as well, in a quietly caustic way. He could be very, very charming—when it pleased him. Apparently he showed all of these attributes when he met actress Phyllis Thaxter, a lady under contract to MGM whom he married in November 1944. It was perhaps his most successful alliance with a woman. The marriage lasted 18 years and produced two children, James III and Susan Schuyler, now a talented actress who bills herself under the name of Skye Aubrey.

After the war, Major Aubrey gravitated to broadcasting and CBS. The ambitious Aubrey chose sales—virtually everyone who became anyone at CBS started in sales. After a short stint at CBS-owned radio station KNX in Los Angeles, Aubrey was tapped for a job with the network itself. He was named manager of network programs for CBS Television in Hollywood.

Before long a couple of writers in the film capital came to Aubrey with an idea for an improbable western with a hero who carried a card saying "Have Gun Will Travel." So named, the series ultimately got CBS into a court battle. Victor De Costa, an itinerant rodeo performer, insisted he was the inspiration for the show, and produced similar calling cards which he said he had been passing out for years. CBS is appealing the court's multimillion-dollar award to De Costa, who even looks like Richard Boone, the show's star.

Jim got the series on the tube with characteristic contempt for corporate protocol. He and Hunt Stromberg, Jr., a friend who worked on the idea with him, carried the series direct to New York. There Hubbell Robinson, CBS Network vice-president for programing, was charmed with the idea of a gunslinger with a taste for fine wine and literature, and an appetite for justice as well. The show premiered in 1957 and sent Jim Aubrey on his way.

Jim's friendship with Stromberg, whose father had been a movie director, was rewarding. When Jim grew restive over his stalled career at CBS, the well-connected Stromberg told friends and soon Aubrey jumped ship, joining the rag-tag ABC Network. He would be boss at ABC—vice-president in charge of programs—and thus theoretically on a par with Hubbell Robinson, many rungs above him at CBS. In addition, he got a fat pay boost—up $10,000 a year to $35,000. That was the good news—Aubrey was no longer one of the crowd in the CBS programing division, he was cock of the walk at ABC. There was bad news too, though; the kind of bad news that prevented most of the loyal CBS crew from taking so drastic a step.

The bad news was that the audience out there did not care about ABC. In TV's two-and-a-half-network economy, ABC was number three and as a result got only crumbs from the ad budgets.

If Jim Aubrey hoped to parlay an ABC job into a round trip back to CBS, he was playing a long shot. One of the great strengths of CBS was its "farm system" which was the equal of the New York Yankees' old string of minor league clubs when it was producing DiMaggios and Mantles. You made it big at a CBS-owned station or with an affiliate and the word got around you were a comer and you came—to CBS in New York. CBS didn't hire much outside the farm system.

Then there appeared on ABC a show called *77 Sunset Strip*. It featured two young private eyes and wasn't at all distinguished except by a secret weapon called "hair power." The teenyboppers twisted the knob to ABC to watch and drool as Ed "Kookie" Byrnes, portraying a parking-lot attendant, riffled his way to fame with a comb he never stopped running through his forelock. The show was a smash.

This ABC success was followed by *The Rifleman*, played by the carbine-carrying Chuck Connors. As widower Lucas McCain he used his short rifle to defeat the black hats and single-handedly raised his son.

Then there was *The Donna Reed Show*, a fatuous situation comedy so wholesome it captured a large, sentimental audience. *The Real McCoys* played the hillbilly theme in a situation-comedy format and succeeded with strong casting—Walter Brennan as Grandpa McCoy and Richard Crenna and Kathy Nolan in supporting roles. *Maverick*, another success, with James Garner as the sardonic and untrustworthy Bret Maverick, played the western theme for laughs and got them.

The heavyweight critics spewed vinegar but the viewers were tuned in. ABC and Aubrey were the talk of the industry, but Aubrey grew restive again. Sensing that the time was ripe for step two in his plan, Aubrey flew to New York and Frank Stanton.

The sponsor's money talks loud and clear in commercial television, there's never been any doubt about that. Bill Paley had shareholders to satisfy as well as his own expensive tastes. But Paley tried hard to get both quality and profits. Unkind critics within CBS muttered that this was only because his snooty friends on Long Island twitted him about the pap they saw on TV. Whatever his motives, there is no doubt that Paley wanted kudos for excellence along with black ink, and it was a measure of his stature that CBS was the network that most nearly managed over the years to provide both.

Stanton told Paley about Aubrey's visit and it was soon agreed that Aubrey would be rehired as a vice-president, CBS would bury its dead and Aubrey would then become president of the network. Whether they knew it or not, Paley and Stanton were programing mediocrity. Ultimately, Aubrey would play the profit theme so sonorously and so exclusively that the FCC would one day question whether CBS was meeting its responsibilities to the public.

Aubrey was brought back as a CBS v.p. in April 1958 without the customary CBS fanfare. In June 1959 he was named executive vice-president. Heads were to roll in quick succession. Lou Cowan, still network president then but in deep trouble partly as a result of the quiz scandals, was about to become a sacrificial lamb. Firings to serve the convenience of the moment have never been uncommon at CBS. A man could always console himself that he had "burned out," for the frenetic world of television wipes out men in a hurry, according to the folklore of the industry.

The professional management-watchers in TV contend that Cowan's specialty—live prime-timers out of New York—was on the wane and filmed shows from Hollywood—Aubrey's forte at ABC—were coming in. CBS had to win at the new game, so—enter Aubrey, exit Cowan.

Cowan had been in the hospital with phlebitis. When he returned, he found Aubrey installed in the office between Paley and Stanton.

Cowan's chagrin was shared by a man who once stood so far above Aubrey in the CBS hierarchy that they weren't even within shouting distance—Hubbell Robinson. A creative dreamer with some practical instincts, though not enough to make him comfortable as a commercial television man, Robinson is credited with pioneering serious television drama and with bringing it to its zenith in 1956 with *Playhouse 90*. It was this format, featuring distinguished plays, which broke the one-hour barrier on prime-time shows. The series provided an outlet for such dramatists as Paddy Chayevsky, Reginald Rose and Rod Serling. Hubbell Robinson had believed himself the odds-on favorite to succeed Cowan. Passed over for Aubrey, the 12-year veteran of CBS battles left in a huff to enter into independent production in Hollywood.

Named president of the network in December 1959, after Lou Cowan was dismissed, Aubrey wasted no time. In short order he named Hunt Stromberg a West Coast vice-president. It wasn't long before Aubrey was running the network from top to bottom—especially programing. His goal was simple: Get the greatest possible audience. He made no attempt whatsoever to improve the tastes of the American viewing public. Thus CBS programs suffered from what has been described as the "Blondie syndrome," the typical plot situation being: "Oh, dear, the boss is coming to dinner and I've burned the roast!" Once in a while something with a touch of quality came along, but it survived only if it met the larger requirement—profits. He never pretended otherwise.

One of Aubrey's first efforts on CBS was among his best, and it appealed, as did most Aubrey shows, to CBS's heavily rural audience. *The Andy Griffith Show* starred the comedian as a justice of the peace, judge and jailer in the quiet little town of Mayberry. The writing was superior and Don Knotts as Barney Fife, Andy's eager-beaver cousin and hapless deputy, gave the show added dimension.

More typical of the Aubrey efforts was *Mister Ed* which premiered in 1961. Mister Ed stood 16 hands high and fetlock-deep in verbal manure as a talking horse with such human frailties as hypochondria and acrophobia. He may have seemed vaguely plausible to children as a humanoid, but definitely lacked horse sense. He wanted his stall decorated in Hawaiian modern and furnished with a horse-size bed.

The Beverly Hillbillies, which began a nine-year run in 1962, took the Clampett clan from the hill country to a Beverly Hills mansion after they discovered oil on the old homestead, a ramshackle farm. Irene Ryan played Granny, and Buddy Ebsen was the widower Jed Clampett, head of the hillbilly clan. They were bewildered by the indoor plumbing and outdoor swimming pool. There was little subtlety in the situations, but apparently all the hillbillies in the nation tuned in to watch the city slickers get outsmarted by the down-home folk. The show had the highest ratings in television for its first two seasons.

In 1963 Aubrey brought the nation *Petticoat Junction,* banality gone to seed. It starred Bea Benaderet (cousin Pearl of *The Beverly Hillbillies*) as a widow with three exceptionally beautiful daughters. One flirted a lot; a second read; and the youngest, Betty Jo, was "a beaver"—a great help to her mother. The widow ran a small, family hotel, the Shady Rest, that somehow found a guest once in a while though it was situated on a "long-overlooked spur of a major railroad."

The *Petticoat Junction* cast pointed up another aspect of Aubrey's programing philosophy. An aide was fired once when his memo got into the hands of the press. In essence, the memo said that Aubrey was dissatisfied with some female casting and wanted "bigger tits."

Under Aubrey, CBS became obsessed with the youth market. This wasn't only Aubrey, of course. The entire nation seemed obsessed with youth at this time. The ads on TV reflected the new cheap pitch for the kiddy dollars as the Louisville *Courier-Journal* reported wryly:

Boys switch hair grease and girls are glad. Men don't have hair. If they do, it is full of dandruff. Boys douse themselves with shaving lotion and wait to beat off the women. Older men are happy to find something that drains all eight sinuses. . . . Girls have yards of blond hair full of body and boys nuzzle it. Wives have gray hair and their husbands won't take them dancing. Men work hard to get ahead, only to have some pimply assistant tell them they have bad breath.

The teen-age wife makes a cup of coffee and turns her husband into a sex maniac. The older wife washes, irons, mops floors . . . and her husband comes home with a miserable headache and takes it out on her. Teen-agers wear sneakers and sandals. Adults wear support hose. Teen-agers rub each other with suntan oil. Adults rub each other with liniment. . . . Young people romp through fields and sniff flowers. Adults get hay fever and sneeze. . . . For young people life is fun, fun, fun. About the only happy time for an adult is when he has an accident and the insurance company pays off.

It isn't fair.

Goodman Ace ran up against the youth dogma once when he tried to sell television his idea about an old man who owned a television station so small it only had one camera. Ace saw three different network representatives, including CBS's Mike Dann, and as soon as he mentioned age to one of them, he was interrupted:

"I have this show idea," said Ace. "A sixty-five-year-old man—"

"Can't he be younger? The charts show he must not be over thirty-five. . . ."

Ace went to another network exec who spent an hour discussing whether the show should be a situation comedy or a comedy situation. A third try brought the abrupt comment: "It's new."

"Are you against something new?"

"No. But it costs twenty-five thousand dollars to make a pilot."

"Why not put it on in the summer? You've got nothing going for you then."

"Can't."

"Why not?"

The network man looked at his assistant and asked, "Why not?"

"I don't know," said the assistant, "but it doesn't sound right to me."

Later that same network man saw Ace in a corridor and asked: "Say, whatever happened to that idea about the old guy with the TV station?"

"You said the little old man was too expensive."

"Well, we've got a way to do it. We'll put it on in the summer."

"How did you think of that?"

"Well, you've got to learn to cut corners in this business!"

Critics may have been dismayed by the Aubrey years, but not particularly surprised; commercial television had always been regarded as the child of greed, not art. Wall Street, the citadel of greed, was overjoyed as CBS Network profits soared, giving Aubrey a mystique unmatched even by Paley. Under Aubrey's aegis CBS attracted the largest audiences and banked the biggest profits in TV history. The net profits nearly doubled in five years, climbing from $25 million a year in 1959 to $49 million by 1964.

Paley was experiencing mixed emotions. Some say he felt twinges of jealousy at the way Wall Street deferred to Aubrey. At one point—in what may have been an attempt to bring in a tempering influence and appease a restive FCC—Paley asked Aubrey to see Hubbell Robinson who, disenchanted with Hollywood, wanted to come back to the network. Aubrey was no fool. He hired Robinson—and then relegated him to limbo.

Robinson quickly became aware that he wasn't getting anywhere with program suggestions and that Aubrey was the reason. But he was hardly prepared for the *coup de grace*, a calculated affront that illustrated not only Aubrey's growing sense of power but also his callous attitude. By Robinson's own account he went out this way:

He was in Aubrey's office giving his boss a rundown of his ideas for the 1963–64 year. Aubrey sat there looking "tanned, fit and calculating," says Robinson. Aubrey was a physical-fitness fanatic and a devotee of wheat germ, fruit and vegetable juices and other "natural" foods. As Robinson proceeded, Aubrey broke in quietly to say, "You're through, Hub."

The hapless Robinson said, "But—I have a few more things to bring up."

"No, I mean *you're* through."

There was no mistaking the message this time. Robinson, stunned, mumbled that he would talk to Bill Paley.

Aubrey's quiet voice stopped him. "I've already talked to Paley. We accept your resignation."

Thereafter Aubrey was treated with awed respect bordering on and then crossing over into burlesque.

Author Merle Miller tells of his encounter with Aubrey in 1963 over a proposed series he was called in to write. The series was to star the popular Jackie Cooper, once a famous child star in the movies and now anxious to build on his TV successes in *The People's Choice* and *Hennesey*. Cooper had suggested a protagonist belonging to the domestic Peace Corps, a sincere man of high purpose. (As an actor, Cooper's long suit is naïve sincerity.) Aubrey vetoed the idea but, in listening to it, leaned back in his chair and countered with his own suggestion.

"I see a man in a dusty pickup in the Southwest. The man is wearing a Stetson and khaki pants. I don't know exactly what he is, but he's not a cop; he doesn't carry a gun. I don't want him to be a policeman or a law enforcement officer." Out of that pipe dream came a really bad idea: a series about—of all things—county agents.

A county agent serves as a kind of catalyst, bringing the latest technological ideas to the farmers and, at the same time, preserving their traditional value system. He is something of an idealist, but he is also practical. He makes relatively little money—$12,500 was tops in most states in 1963. He is farm-oriented and a college graduate with a major usually in agronomy, animal husbandry or plant pathology.

Merle Miller researched the concept with his customary thoroughness and began to get enthused over the prospects for a series he felt could be both interesting and important. Conceivably Miller could have added humor and written something like *The Waltons*. But it was about ten years before television was ripe for that kind of change.

In due course, Miller and the others associated with the idea met with Aubrey in Hollywood to read Miller's notes. In his amusing book, *Only You, Dick Daring!*, Miller explains what happened.

Aubrey stood just inside the door for a moment, his ice-blue eyes fixed on some distant object. . . . Aubrey has a hearty disinterested handshake, and he carries himself with the air of a man used to authority and a lot of pushups. I was reminded then and throughout our brief encounter of the Muscular Clergyman who used to appear so prominently in so many eighteenth and early nineteenth-century novels. It was so easy to imagine Aubrey delivering one of those hellfire and brimstone sermons that used to be so popular on Sunday mornings, before ministers turned therapists.

The assembled interested parties included Dick Dorso, a United Artists TV executive, and Hunt Stromberg, still an Aubrey man and a CBS vice-president. He was also known to be Aubrey's resident gossipmonger. As the interview wore on, says Miller, the four grown men began to act a little silly. They all had a great deal riding on Aubrey's decision and the man had an awesome nonchalance that matched his power.

Their introductory remarks brought no comment or show of emotion from Aubrey. As related in Miller's book:

DORSO: Jack and Merle Miller have been down to New Mexico, Jim, doing some research.
COOPER: We had a wonderful, wonderful trip, Jim.
STROMBERG: We've been talking about their wonderful trip.

Aubrey received these profundities from his slouched position in a leather chair, his polished shoes propped on a low table.

Cooper told Aubrey that Miller had written "some beautiful notes" on the trip and then Cooper began to read them. Aubrey listened without reaction, though Miller thought he discerned a trace of a smile, perhaps suggesting Aubrey's satisfaction that his vision ("I see a man in a dusty pickup . . .") was taking form.

Miller found himself studying Aubrey's appearance—his "conventionally good-looking face with assembly-line nose and unrevealing eyes." He saw a man who obviously worked out to keep a flat stomach, though Miller could not picture Aubrey working up a sweat.

In time, Merle Miller took up the reading assignment from Cooper, telling how county agents, among other things, helped farmers set up cooperatives. Then Cooper described the county where the series was to take place—famous Los Alamos, scene of atomic-bomb development, where IQs among the scientists ranged to 180 and above, and a few miles away Apache Indians lived lives nearly identical to those of their ancestors 500 years earlier. Miller took over again, pointing out that a Mescalera Indian boy in the 4-H club was more eager to learn and thus more educable than a man at White Sands who spent ten years "getting all the degrees MIT had to offer."

At about that point, less than halfway through the notes, Aubrey rose and left the room without a word. Stromberg scurried after him while the others eyed the door nervously. Minutes later Stromberg returned and suggested the reading continue.

Without Jim? Cooper wanted to know. "Let's go on," said Stromberg. The performance thereafter was like the routine ministrations of an undertaker. The audience shuffled, coughed, cleared throats, doodled, until finally Cooper finished the notes, trailing off into an uncertain silence. Stromberg, Dorso and a third man from CBS waxed enthusiastic. But Cooper was troubled that Aubrey hadn't come back, and said so. Miller describes the conversation that followed.

" 'Jim didn't have to come back,' said Stromberg, a man suddenly inspired.

"We looked at him hopefully.

" 'He didn't come back because everything was in good shape,' said Stromberg. 'If there'd been *trouble* he would have stayed. . . .' "

It was apparent that Stromberg was spitballing, not reporting. But all took up on this optimistic note, even the usually skeptical Merle Miller. They traded encouraging words such as Dorso's "I *knew* he liked it, because it's just fascinating material."

Cooper added: "Jim smiled several times."

Then Stromberg came up with what seemed like a non sequitur but was really a piece of advice that characterized a pilot audience:

"Now, Merle, when you write the script there's one thing about a pilot; the audience, you've got to tell them where the bathroom is."

After much staff tinkering with characters and story line, over which Miller had no control, *Calhoun,* a pilot about a county agent, was tested repeatedly by CBS to indifferent audience response. Finally it was dropped. Stromberg's remark turned out to be prophetic, though in a way he surely had not intended. The series had certainly been headed for the bathroom, all right.

There were exceptions to the usual run of pap Aubrey fed the public. The Dick Van Dyke series is still regarded as a landmark comedy effort, though it broke few of the rules.

The Defenders, about a father-and-son lawyer team, starred E. G. Marshall and Robert Reed. It was a strongly written series that dealt with controversial subjects. Aubrey accepted it at Paley's behest. An executive recalls: "Partway into the first season [*The Defenders*] did a show on abortion. There wasn't an advertiser who would touch it, and we wound up a meeting with a rep from every agency in town in the

CBS boardroom, with the head of the network asking why they didn't have more guts. An hour later he was bawling out programing for ever having authorized it."

The head of the network was, of course, Jim Aubrey. The executive added that when the abortion segment was aired, "Everybody survived, and that was the beginning of *The Defenders* dealing with issues that really mattered."

East Side, West Side, starring George C. Scott as a hard-nosed social worker (Cicely Tyson, the distinguished black actress, costarred), clashed with so many of Aubrey's ideas about rose-colored viewing that he was constantly after producer David Susskind, and before the episode was over Aubrey was, for once, shaken up. But only temporarily.

Susskind reports that though the show had a Nielsen rating of 33— on a par with NBC's rival *Mitch Miller Show*—Aubrey said, "Get that fucking show out of the ghetto. I'm sick of it, the public's sick of it and it doesn't work. They've got just as big social problems on Park Avenue and that's where I want the goddamn show to be."

Susskind says he warned that the show's star and co-owner, iconoclastic actor George C. Scott, would have nothing to do with such a show. Aubrey said, "Bring him in. I'll straighten him out."

Susskind says that when the two men met in Aubrey's office Scott was in withdrawal, having just quit smoking "for the twenty-fifth time." To overcome his desire for a cigarette, Scott would chew on an apple. Aubrey began by saying that while the show was marvelous, it should be moved to Park Avenue.

Scott waited patiently until Aubrey stopped, then quietly asked if he was finished. Aubrey said yes. Scott took out an impressive pocket knife, touched a release button and the blade jumped out. The actor sliced a piece of apple, speared it and, gesturing with the knife just inches from Aubrey's nose, said, "The show is staying right where it is. Good-bye, Mr. Aubrey, we are not meeting again."

But Aubrey had the last thrust. He canceled the show some weeks later—at the peak of its success.

The final break between Susskind and Aubrey came after Aubrey made a commitment for 13 hours of a show called *The Outsider*, then canceled after Paley and other top CBS brass indicated displeasure with it. When Susskind heard that Aubrey was canceling he instructed his agent, Ted Ashley, to hold Aubrey to the agreement. Susskind says

Ashley warned, "Think about it, David, you'll make him mad. CBS is important to you." Susskind remained adamant. When Frank Stanton heard about it—post-Aubrey—he immediately agreed to a cash settlement.

Almost everyone agrees that the best thing about Aubrey was the fact that he was so decisive. Never a "maybe" or a "call me next week." You got it immediately—either a pat on the back or right between the eyes.

Says an Aubrey defender, "James Aubrey was successful because he was right most of the time. He fired Jack Benny and everybody said he was wrong. But Benny was 'dead' in twenty-six weeks after returning to television on NBC."

MGM executive Harris Katleman, who used to do business with Aubrey as a producer, says: "In spite of what most people said about his arrogance, Jim was willing to change his mind if he decided he had been wrong. I had a series I showed him and he told me to forget it because there was no way I could sell it. Later I approached him again and explained why I thought I could sell it. He sat back, took off his glasses, closed his eyes and thought a bit and said, 'You know, I think you're right.' Then he quietly said, 'Go.' [Aubreyese for yes.] Whenever he did turn me down he always said why."

Martin Ransohoff headed Filmways which brought Aubrey the smash hit *Beverly Hillbillies* and the successful if tasteless *Mister Ed* and *Petticoat Junction.* His view of Aubrey: "There was no vacillating or nonsense. If he liked something it went. And he stood quite ready to take the responsibility—good or bad. It was his ball game."

Aubrey's best friends—past and present—all vouched for and benefited from his decisiveness. Dick Dorso scored four successes with Aubrey, and Susskind seven. But in Aubrey's last year, he was equally decisive in turning his back on old "friends," leading to yelps of dismay by one or two who felt Aubrey could at least have given them a crumb from the laden CBS table. Dorso didn't get a nibble on five pilots costing over $1 million. This apparently led to Dick's departure as United Artists programing chief. Ransohoff didn't get even one of his five new series taken by Aubrey and was quoted in *Life* magazine, saying: "I was hanging there with my pants down, wondering what I'd tell the stockholders, until we finally unloaded *The Addams Family* on ABC with a last-minute telephone agreement."

Another friend of Aubrey's—many people say they are friends of his, then proceed to say unfriendly things—claims it was almost impossible to compete with Aubrey. This man, a leading Broadway producer, explained:

> There was no way you could put pressure on Jim because he lives outside conventional morality. He was capable of responding "Go right ahead!" to such a clear-cut threat as "I'll kill your family." The forces and pressures that would cause the rest of us to do things or not to do things don't affect him at all.
>
> If you have to compete against a guy who doesn't work within the rules, he's tough competition. Give a man like that great power and you soon see why they all feared him and took what he dished out.

They took it, yes, but Aubrey earned the sobriquet "The Smiling Cobra" by his willingness to cut up CBS associates in front of the advertising men they had to deal with day after day.

Aubrey was cool in crisis. Unlike ex-President Nixon who only *said* he got tougher as things got harder, Aubrey actually did get tougher. There were some lapses into near hysterics. Business associates remember a few monumental temper tantrums.

Did this conduct carry over into his personal life? Stories persist. When Aubrey was in his big years, Ralph Colin says that he was told by "reliable women sources" that "any number of women" wouldn't go out with him because of the unpleasant stories. "I remember inviting a woman to dinner at my apartment with the suggestion that she might like to meet Aubrey. She said if Aubrey was going to be there she wouldn't come."

But there was no dearth of beautiful and chic women for this man who could fascinate as he frightened. After his divorce from Phyllis Thaxter in 1962 he enjoyed himself immensely. He laughed about some of the innuendos. "If people are accusing me of liking beautiful women, they're absolutely right."

During the CBS years, he squired Judy Garland, Julie Newmar, Rhonda Fleming and many lesser-known beauties. When he tired of a girl, he knew what to do. His formula for instant parting is written in the hatbands of many a cad. In Aubrey's own words, quoted in *Life:*

Always do it in the daytime, because at night your heart takes over. Take her to lunch, to a very chic place like Le Pavillon or The Colony, where she will see famous people and where it is against all the rules to cry or scream or throw crockery. Buy her a big drink, and then tell her that the train has reached Chicago and you're getting off at Chicago. Tell her you're not the marrying kind, but she deserves a home and kids and candlelight. Tell her she's the most wonderful woman you've ever known. Then buy her a great lunch, and let her absorb the news as she eats. Afterward, you can walk out into the sunshine a free man. It never fails.

Aubrey's treatment of CBS stars was similar. If he wanted them he gave them the Bill Paley treatment—upbeat as hell. Paley always saw to it that actresses from out of town got the red carpet; this included NBC stars at times. And Aubrey used his charm to get his way when the occasion demanded it.

Once, after other CBS executives found it impossible to work out an agreement with the formidable Lucille Ball, Aubrey went to her house and, according to a producer, purred a variation of a favorite Hollywood aphorism: "I'm not here to blow rainbows up your tush," he said. An hour or two of Aubrey palaver and Lucy was ready to sign.

On the other hand, Aubrey seemed to relish telling stars they were washed up. Garry Moore admitted that his variety show was old-hat, but he told Aubrey he had another idea. Moore reports that Aubrey hardly gave him the time of day. The cobra's hiss: "Not a chance." When Aubrey kissed off Jack Benny, one of America's all-time favorite entertainers, he did it with an emotionless "You're through." This saddened Paley, but he couldn't dispute Benny's waning popularity. For if Paley had wanted Benny to stay, he certainly could have intervened.

If anything irritated Aubrey, it was CBS's pride in its news excellence and its willingness to scrap commercial broadcasts to bring important bulletins and news specials. According to Fred Friendly, who was passionately involved with the issue, Aubrey explained his dilemma in a discussion they had. "Look, Fred," Aubrey said, "I have regard for what Murrow and you have accomplished, but in this adversary system you and I are always going to be at each other's throats. They say to me, 'Take your soiled little hands, get the ratings, and make as much money as you can'; they say to you, 'Take your lily-white hands, do your best, go the high road and bring us prestige.' "

But Aubrey was unable to hamstring CBS's news operations. He also failed to persuade Bill Paley to buy the Paramount film library, for $56 million, a bargain price. (This proved to be a Paley mistake.) Apart from these setbacks though, he remained the darling of the investment community in Wall Street. In 1964 he was at the peak of his power.

His departure had to be the result of his many shortcomings. His arrogance, for instance, even extended to Paley on occasion. The story goes that Aubrey, Paley and Stanton were walking together in a hall on the West Coast where the affiliate owners were gathering to look over the next season's offerings. Paley offered Aubrey a suggestion in his customary low-key manner, and Aubrey in a deprecating voice said, "Don't worry about it—I'll handle it," almost as though he were speaking to a not-very-bright child.

An Aubrey admirer says the same thing in another way. "Jim Aubrey got the axe because he never made a concerted effort to kiss Paley's ass."

And then there were those persistent reports of Aubrey's raucous after-hours. Though Dick Dorso says that he and his wife spent many a decorous evening with Jim and female companions and never witnessed so much as a faux pas, the rumors continued.

At the office his violence often took the form of understated verbal cruelty—though there are those who remember that in the early days he could throw his fists into inanimate objects, bang walls, kick tables.

Susskind says Aubrey's lip would turn up in a half smile as he purred messages like, "You will never sell another show to this network as long as you live," speaking so quietly that the object of his scorn had to strain to hear.

Another industry figure remembers that both a "hot model" Aubrey dated in the mid-1960s, as well as the former wife of a major film executive he also saw socially, periodically appeared with black eyes and arm bruises.

The prevailing view is that, whatever Aubrey's personal behavior, the real reason for his expulsion was that he blew the ball game—lost much of CBS's rating superiority—through injudicious decisions raising questions of conflicts of interest with producers, particularly with his old friend Keefe Brasselle.

In what many regarded as Aubrey's high-water mark of arrogance, he allowed Brasselle, a B-movie actor *(The Eddie Cantor Story)*, to mount three new and untried shows without the customary pilot episodes. Far from cutting costs, the production expenses mounted to astronomical heights and Aubrey's prestige fell to new lows.

Later, Brasselle would turn on Aubrey, writing a trashy novel about him called *The CaniBalS*. Brasselle tried to peddle the book in a visit to the editorial offices of New American Library in 1966—but without success. "He was a scary character," says one of the NAL editors of that period. "Handsome in a sleek and deadly sort of way. He sat and watched me while I read his outline—an obvious CBS vendetta; he'd hardly changed the names. I recognized CBS people right away. His manner was so ominous—actually threatening in some indescribable way—that I just wanted to get him and his manuscript out of the office."

Several years later the editor told the story to a CBS friend who knew Brasselle quite well. The CBS man laughed at the scary impression Brasselle had made on the editor, explaining that Brasselle had not long after the interview shot a man. "Your antenna was working pretty well that day," the CBS man added.

He was alluding to a 1971 incident in Southern California. On December 28, Brasselle pleaded guilty to a charge of assault with a deadly weapon in the barroom shooting of a man named Robert B. Crawford. Brasselle used a .32 caliber automatic to shoot the 29-year-old man in the chest after a quarrel in Studio City the previous July. Fortunately, the victim recovered.

The shooting didn't surprise all of Brasselle's acquaintances. For Keefe, who was married to one of the singing De Marco sisters, had courted Aubrey's favor in the first place by implying connections with the Mafia. That's the story anyway. Gamy connections are said to appeal to Aubrey.

Just how qualified was Brasselle to produce three prime-time shows simultaneously for CBS? Even an optimistic veteran with Emmys on the mantel wouldn't expect to do as well, and Brasselle's single previous production effort was a disaster. Under Aubrey's guidance and a contract from CBS, he ran Lunar Productions through $430,000 of CBS money to produce *Beachfront,* a series starring one Keefe Brasselle. It quietly slipped from view in 1961.

The gleeful consensus of the industry was that The Smiling Cobra had found his own mongoose.

Aubrey's No. 1 assistant, Mike Dann, got the news of Keefe's three shows one at a time. He learned of the third show from CBS counsel, Sal Iannucci, who stopped Dann in the hall to tell him he had to give him important news. Said Iannucci:

"Jim's just bought another show from Keefe."

There was a dead pause for a moment, after which a pale Dann, never at a loss for a wisecrack, asked, "Can they put me in jail for this?"

Opinions vary on Brasselle—but not much. Susskind characterized him as a "1965 edition of George Raft," which many agreed was not far off the mark. Brasselle retorted, "Susskind has the mentality of a retarded gnat."

Brasselle was doing fairly well in Hollywood when he met Aubrey ("I was a star," he says), and Aubrey was a salesman for KNX Television. In time Brasselle and Aubrey became close. Aubrey once phoned Brasselle in the wee hours and demanded that he taxi over to Aubrey's favorite Manhattan supper club to sing "Chicago." And some say Aubrey sought Brasselle's help after allegedly mistreating a mobster's daughter. Whether Brasselle really had Mafia connections is unclear. In November 1960 when Brasselle opened the Hollywood Club, in Edison, New Jersey—easily an hour's drive from Manhattan—Aubrey sent a memo saying that all the CBS executives and their wives were to be there. At this point smoldering resentments between Aubrey and Mike Dann surfaced. Dann did not attend. One who did recalls that it was a "remarkable" evening, set up like something out of *The Godfather* with the ladies in their place at one end of the table, the men at the other. Shortly thereafter the unsuccessful club burned down.

Now Brasselle was on the financial comeback trail with his own production company, Richelieu Productions. (The company was so named because it was formed after numerous lunches at the Richelieu Restaurant near 485 Madison.) When gossip reached the trade press concerning Aubrey's possible conflicts of interest, the FCC began an investigation. CBS turned to its outside counsel, Ralph Colin, to look into the matter. Colin, in the words of a man who has known him many years, "loved to sniff for vice in the cathedral." No better man could have been put in charge of the assignment.

Colin's investigation was wide-ranging but brief. Colin said that

Brasselle introduced girls to Aubrey though he didn't know why Aubrey needed help. "All he had to do was throw back the blankets and they'd have jumped into bed. . . . It was terribly difficult to prove [anything] because people around him were either loyal or afraid to talk. I went to the Coast and talked to a number of people over a three- or four-day period. Where there was that much smoke there was apt to be fire. Quite aside from the possibility of fire was the fact that CBS couldn't afford to have a person about whom rumors were circulating since we were licensed by the government."

Colin found no conflict of interest. CBS put his memo and other statements together and sent the confidential report to the FCC. Needless to say, the strongest statement regarding Brasselle's qualifications fell short of outright veneration, having been prepared by Stromberg and John Reynolds, another friend of Aubrey's and a senior vice-president of CBS. It read, in part: "Keefe Brasselle, while not professionally recognized as a producer, has spent almost his entire life in the entertainment business. . . . Mr. Brasselle has the drive and enthusiasm which often make the difference between accomplishing difficult assignments and overriding obstacles. . . . [He] has been a fount of ideas and concepts, one or two of which almost reached the pilot stage before and after *Beachfront.*"

Two of Brasselle's three new CBS shows were half-hour situation comedies: *The Cara Williams Show* and *The Baileys of Balboa.* Brasselle occupied himself in New York City with the third show, the hour-long series called *The Reporter.* The question arose: Was it possible these ideas came from others and were dropped into Richelieu as a convenient vehicle to serve an "insider's" purse and purposes? The FCC suspected as much.

There were enormous, even alarming, cost overruns on all three shows. *The Reporter* was soon half a million dollars in the red, and CBS grabbed the production reins as vendors began lawsuits for unpaid bills. But the shows themselves did the real damage. Not one of them was a hit. *The Baileys of Balboa* sank into the bay as ABC clicked with *Peyton Place.* Cara Williams bombed: weak competition for NBC and *Wednesday Night at the Movies.*

(Cara Williams not only flopped but did a magnificent job of alienating everybody she worked with—though theoretically she was being groomed to be the next Lucille Ball. Says one associate: "I would like to have felt sorry for her—but I was too busy getting mad at her. Everything had to be done her way. She'd wander in at ten A.M. for an eight A.M. call. She seemed to prefer decorating to acting and once decorated Gatsby's, a West Coast restaurant." How was it done? "Probably early Halloween. I've never had respect for her taste.")

The Reporter, at least, would seem to have a chance for Brasselle. Scripts were by the established novelist and screenwriter Jerome Weidman *(I Can Get It for You Wholesale)*. It starred Harry Guardino as a young New York newspaperman who got physically and emotionally involved in the stories he covered. But Weidman quit in disgust as CBS committee criticism led to changes he was unwilling to accept. *The Reporter* foundered against Jack Paar.

CBS lost its seven-percentage-point lead in the ratings race and suddenly the network was in a real contest for the first time since Jim Aubrey set the world on fire.

Often Uncle Sam has a hand in the downfall of the high and the mighty. Al Capone, along with his syphilis, had tax problems and that was the only way the Feds could nail the Chicago racketeer. Recently Richard Nixon learned that even the presidency isn't immune to tax scrutiny. Jim Aubrey found himself on the IRS list, facing a federal tax lien for $38,000 in taxes due on income earned as far back as 1962. He settled the claim in January 1965, just weeks before he got the axe.

Aubrey was, in a financial sense, anal retentive. His associates often remarked at how slow he was to pick up a check, though his salary was $124,000 plus $100,000 in bonuses. Aubrey elected to collect his bonuses annually, though he might have saved plenty on a deferred-compensation basis; he explained that he feared he might lose the money if he didn't lock it up year by year. The board of directors could indeed cancel accrued bonuses, but only if an executive resigned to accept a job with a competing company, or if he committed some indiscretion so outrageous that the directors would feel impelled to act against him.

In addition to stock options worth over $1 million, Aubrey rode around in a chauffeur-driven company limousine and had an almost unlimited expense account. Yet he spent his own money cautiously. This man of virtually unlimited means took over the Central Park South apartment that Filmways maintained for Martin Ransohoff and other Filmways executives. This, had the FCC known about it, certainly would have been interpreted as a conflict of interest. The apartment was a one-bedroom affair with a single bath. When Aubrey moved in he authorized his old friend Stromberg, who had a flair for decorating, to spend $65,000 on improvements and accessories.

Aubrey says he told CBS about the unique housing arrangement, but not before he had been living there for a year and the FCC had begun its inquiry. The CBS report to the FCC neglected to mention the arrangement.

Meanwhile Richelieu Productions, Brasselle's company, maintained a second Chrysler limo for Aubrey which he used because he didn't want CBS to know what he was doing during his off hours. According to *Life* magazine, CBS knew of the arrangement though the FCC did not.

It was against this very gray background that Aubrey and Brasselle bombed with the three controversial shows. Things began to get a little frantic—even for the cool master of the ratings game—when the December results showed CBS hanging in there with the slimmest of leads. The stage was set for Aubrey's swan song.

Few who attended can forget the February executive staff meeting held to mend the holes in the 1964–65 schedule—directly caused by the demise of the Brasselle efforts. It is impossible to imagine what went through the minds of Bill Paley and Frank Stanton, perhaps broadcasting's two most honored men, as Aubrey moved shows around without regard to sponsors, like some desperate chess player battling for a draw.

Was this the Tiffany network or some dilapidated five-and-dime? If Paley and Stanton had any doubts about Aubrey's future when they entered that room, they must have resolved them as they sat, stunned, watching the shows move in and out of panels on a program board.

Still Aubrey was a man to be reckoned with, even in defeat. CBS Television still led the competition and, more important, earned the CBS parent company $40 million. And Aubrey retained his following in Wall Street. The roaring bull market that was to end a couple of years later had favored the Aubrey years at CBS, giving the stock a gilt-edged look and a high price. Paley knew the importance of maintaining the stock's price both for prestige and to finance with "cheap" dollars CBS's growing diversification programs which were being handled through exchanges of stock.

Bill Paley lamented that if he had to do it all over again, he would never have gone public at all. As a private corporation, Paley was able to make his decisions in the early years on the crystal-clear basis of "What's good for my company—long-term?" Now he had to consider the immediate needs and moods of thousands of shareholders, and this clouded the picture considerably—especially in the case of Jim Aubrey. It is little wonder that Paley often stayed in bed at the nearby St. Regis Hotel during this time, nursing his persistent back ailment.

The situation came to a head late in February 1965, soon after that program-shuffling meeting. On February 24, Paley left the St. Regis and was on his way to the Bahamas to recuperate at Lyford Cay. Jim Aubrey flew to Miami for a semiofficial weekend visit that began quite innocently. He registered at the Fontainebleau Hotel in Miami Beach, dressed formally and left for Jackie Gleason's 49th birthday party. Network vice-president Frank Shakespeare was with him.

The Gleason party was uneventful. Aubrey left before midnight to attend a second party. This one was so raucous that the police were summoned. No one was detained, but Aubrey was reportedly a key figure in the episode. While hardly anyone willing to talk about the matter seems sure of the details, one important ex-producer of CBS shows says flatly: "Aubrey mistreated a station owner's daughter, the man called Stanton and said, 'Either do something about this or I'll blow the whistle!'"

On the other hand, Frank Stanton insists that it was a coincidence that Aubrey was called back to New York to be fired on that weekend —though apparently he regarded the matter of sufficient urgency to offer to send the company plane. It is true that Stanton liked to dispose of such disagreeable chores on weekends when there was little press coverage, and it's also true that he worked weekends most of the time. But skeptics argue that something unusual must have happened in Miami or Aubrey wouldn't have been called on the carpet so abruptly on a Saturday morning. Whatever the exact timing, it is apparent that the move was planned earlier. Jack Gould got a tip from a Wall Street friend the prior Tuesday that Aubrey would go the following Monday. Gould called Stanton who pleaded, "Don't run it. We haven't told Aubrey yet. I'll call you Sunday." Aubrey flew back and shortly after noon that day he and his lawyers met with Stanton.

Life magazine chronicled these events in considerable depth in a story by investigative reporters Richard Oulahan and William Lambert, published on September 10, 1965.

The confrontation was tense. Of the participants, only Aubrey will talk about it. [He would *then*, but he won't *now*.]

"He asked for my resignation," says Aubrey, "after we both had agreed that we just couldn't go down the road together. . . .

"I had a talk with Mr. Paley. He indicated to me a very difficult management decision, a decision that management reached only after long deliberation. Over a period of time, as they observed the way in which I was conducting the business affairs, they came to a reluctant decision. Perhaps it was because I was rough as hell. Maybe I was resented. . . .

"I must take the blame for the abruptness. Frank Stanton asked me, 'How shall we handle this?' I said, 'Nothing can be gained by dragging it out. There will be no graceful exit, no world cruise for me. I'll just clean out my desk and not be here on Monday.' "

On Sunday, Stanton announced Aubrey's resignation and then flew to Washington to be the first to explain the dismissal to the FCC.

In the aftermath of Aubrey's fall from grace and power, CBS stock dropped nine points—"which puts my net value to the network at $20 million," crows Aubrey.

When Aubrey became president, CBS stock was selling at about $17 per share; when he was fired it was at the equivalent of $42. Nevertheless, a stockholder's suit for damages was filed against CBS, Aubrey and Richelieu Productions, by a Long Island businessman named A. Edward Morrison, owner of 42 shares of CBS stock. Aubrey's $225,000 in severance pay and his $1.3 million worth of uncollected CBS stock options were placed in escrow. The suit was later settled and Aubrey received his benefits—ironically augmented during the legal hiatus by a raging bull market.

Though the precise day of the firing might have been determined by the Miami incident, hardly anyone who understands CBS feels Aubrey's alleged after-hours exploits would have skewered him had he continued to excel in the ratings race. Says one ex-CBSer: "I'm sure they were aware of his personal indiscretions. What really moved them to act was the fact that his business judgment began to totter. If two of those Brasselle shows had scored, Aubrey would have been the hit of the century. If even one had been a hit, he would have survived."

Bill Dozier, who once headed up CBS Television in Hollywood, had this insight into the mercurial Aubrey. He noted that while Aubrey claimed credit for most of what was done while he was boss, he was also quick to own up to disaster. Dozier tells this story of the time he asked Aubrey to speak to a class Dozier was teaching at UCLA: "A spunky student asked, 'What prompted you to put three shows on the air without a pilot?' Aubrey paused a moment and then said: 'Arrogance, I guess.'"

Aubrey is at leisure again after a brief but stormy second career cutting the deadwood out of MGM, where his ex-wife was once a star. Few are ready to count him out—even now.

Before the news of Aubrey's sudden firing reached the media, David Susskind got a telephone call from soft-spoken Ted Ashley, then an important agent, now the head of Warner Brothers Pictures. Ted asked Susskind: "If you could have one professional dream fulfilled, what would it be?"

Susskind says he responded without a pause, "Have Jim Aubrey fired."

Ashley paused for effect, then said, "Well, you've got it!"

"I remember the call," says Susskind, "because it was my mother's birthday."

When someone learns that his least favorite uncle has died and left him a fortune, the bereaved is often moved to sustained laughter. Mike Dann's reaction was similar, only more so, when Aubrey got the axe. Dann knew that Aubrey had already decided to fire him when Aubrey got canned himself. Now, instead of unemployment, Mike headed for greater power than ever before. He became Aubrey's successor as programing chief—though he inherited only a part of Aubrey's job and never became president of the network.

Mike Dann's reign was seldom more distinguished than his predecessor's. But Dann did personally champion *The Smothers Brothers Comedy Hour*, the show that would pave the way for strong social commentary in a later era.

Basically, commercial programing with the accent on network profits had to continue unabated. Dann would prove to be steadier than Jim Aubrey—though never as powerful or decisive—and he brought in heavy profits. At the onset of Dann's regime, CBS's relationship with talent producers and advertising clients was never lower, a result of Aubrey's arrogance. Dann acted quickly to restore a better spirit in all areas, immediately firing top Aubrey lieutenants—including Hunt Stromberg, Jr. Short, cocky, a great stand-up comic, Mike Dann was the man who nearly preceded Aubrey out the door, but instead remained as Aubrey's laughing heir.

CHAPTER 21
Black Rock and Conformity

CBS's MOVE FROM 485 MADISON AVENUE TO ITS MASSIVE NEW CORPO-
rate headquarters at 51 West 52nd Street symbolized its arrival as a
giant corporation. For better or worse. One old-time CBSer remembers:

> At 485 Madison Avenue, the urinals stank, the toilets hardly ever
> flushed and there was no air conditioning. But everybody knew
> everybody else.
>
> Mike the doorman personified the informality of the place. He
> knew everything that was going on and kept everybody informed.
> Mike Donovan was a tall, glib Irishman, on good terms with every-
> one from the pages and the secretaries all the way to the top execu-
> tives and personalities. He knew and was liked by Ed Murrow.
> Arthur Godfrey was a good friend—used to mention him on his
> show—and Mike was probably closer to Bill Paley than some of the
> brass. He's dead now. It's interesting. . . . He never made the move
> to "Black Rock."
>
> CBS had always lived in the shadow of RCA which was magnifi-
> cently ensconced in Rockefeller Center. Ours was a little store in
> comparison and our modest digs were taken as a measure of our

position relative to RCA and its NBC network. So the move was psychological as well as physical. Yes, we moved into the Big Time in going to 51 West 52nd Street—a building even more impressive and certainly more beautiful than Radio City.

But we lost our camaraderie. The attitudes changed somehow. At 485 the elevator operators joked and talked their way up and down the shaft. At Black Rock all you could do was press a button. We became systematized and sanitized.

We were already branching out—becoming a conglomerate— when we moved. The consolidation at Black Rock was supposed to integrate operations. But instead it became a divisive element. Black Rock was intimidating.

The sobriquet "Black Rock" reflects the color of the granite and is an allusion to a tense and sinister film starring Spencer Tracy, *Bad Day at Black Rock*. The man behind Black Rock is as intimidating to some as the building—Frank Stanton.

Stanton was already an architecture buff when he began working with architect Eero Saarinen to carve the CBS image in Canadian granite and smoked glass. Years before, Stanton had been dubbed the "third architect" in the West Coast firm of Luckman and Pereira because of the detail-by-detail attention he gave to the designing and building of CBS's West Coast headquarters, Television City.

If Frank Stanton lavished care on Television City, he doted on Black Rock. The structure offers an awesome monument to symmetry and spartan good taste. Its granite ribs soar 40 uninterrupted stories and bear the look of natural rock—rough and textured, crystalline rather than glazed—an effect created by passing the blocks of granite over a high flame. With its stone-framed smoked-glass windows, the overall effect is one of dark foreboding which losers in the corporate power battles would say is definitely appropriate.

Forbidding it may be, but it is also a structure of great beauty. It was the late famed Saarinen's last hurrah, his only skyscraper, but he never saw the building. He died in 1961. Black Rock was completed in 1965.

In contrast to the beauty of Black Rock is NBC's dingy quarters at the celebrated but architecturally undistinguished Radio City at 30 Rockefeller Plaza, a couple of blocks away. ABC's rented quarters, one block north on the Avenue of the Americas, are in a modern building sometimes referred to sardonically as "the package the CBS Building came in." In an attempt to characterize the third network in terms parallel to "30 Rock" and "Black Rock," the wags came up with "Hard Rock," since ABC caters to youth's taste for blaring music.

Frank Stanton has always cared about image, and some find his building—so unadorned, so clean of line—suggestive of a cold poetry consistent not only with Frank Stanton but with CBS itself. *The New Yorker* thinks highly of Stanton's antiseptic tastes, characterizing his offices both at CBS and, postretirement, in the Corning Glass Building as the "most beautiful" in the world.

More important than Stanton, of course, was Eero Saarinen. Colleagues say the distinguished Finn got the assignment on the basis of both reputation and his TWA Building at John F. Kennedy Airport, a structure that gives the impression in concrete of a great bird, wings outstretched, ready to take off. Saarinen produced sketches, scale models were built, and Stanton "played with those models like toys," a colleague says. Replicas of offices were set up so that lighting fixtures and other accoutrements could be tested—both for esthetic and practical purposes. One CBSer goes on:

> Stanton played a role in the selection of every desk—for every man except Paley—and every desk television set. Modular units of white and black represented the same kind of contrasting patterns Stanton chose for Television City.
>
> There wasn't anything from ashtrays to doors to the men's rooms and the inside of the elevators Stanton didn't pore over. He made all the decisions down to the least item of visible hardware and the decisions were dutifully okayed by Paley.
>
> Stanton devoted weekend after weekend to the task. He was our inside architect, make no mistake about it.

The lights in the elevators indicating floors were typical of Stanton's meticulous approach. Stanton and Lou Dorfsman, then the CBS chief of design, agreed on a typeface, and the elevator company said fine, they would punch the numerals out of the bronze background. This would have meant that a zero, for example, wouldn't have projected a complete circle of light, because its interior would have to be attached at one or more places or it would drop out.

Stanton and Dorfsman would have none of it. "It would have destroyed my typeface," said Dorfsman.

Stanton and Dorfsman called a halt and thought about the problem at length, finally coming up with a solution. First, the numerals would be etched in the bronze with acid. Then the bronze would be packed with epoxy resin. The bronze could then be cut through—just barely —and the middles of the numerals would float in place. Then plastic would be poured on the letter and numeral openings for translucency and the epoxy backing trimmed away.

It worked. And, according to Dorfsman, the elevator company regards the process as a "giant invention" and is selling it elsewhere. The firing process used on the granite for special effect, which Stanton had a hand in, is also being sold to others.

But for Stanton, it wasn't enough to build the stage. He was equally intent on directing the actors. In his most celebrated Black Rock edict, Stanton decreed that there was to be no art or photographs or posters placed on the walls unless it came from the art department's own collection. The collection was strongly modern and tasteful—or "ersatz and kind of crappy," depending upon one's point of view.

In defense, Dorfsman acknowledges that the art collection was a "choice we made." But the pictures "weren't foisted on people. We said, 'Here's what we have; what do you like?' " Dorfsman quibbles with the term "art." "I like to call it decorative material, so as not to denigrate the architecture."

The real idea, says the critic who called the art ersatz, was "to avoid pictures of pussycats and postcards from Atlantic City." Dorfsman agreed, and administered the policy fiercely in collaboration with Stanton.

Dorfsman was a hard man when it came to deviations. But there were ways to get around him. Bob Evans, CBS chief counsel, was a man with strong tastes of his own. Evans fought to express his personality in his office in the best way he knew. Evans had helped Dorfsman with a couple of personal legal problems for which he later collected his "fee"—permission to hang a weathered pre–World War I sign proclaiming "Moxie," a now defunct soft drink. The sign had been purchased by a friend at a drugstore's liquidation auction for 25 cents.

Dorfsman put his sharp mind to work and found the solution: He put the wooden sign behind glass and in a proper frame. Thus raised to the status of proper decorative material, the Moxie poster qualified for a place on the sacred walls. Later Evans "collected enough brownie points" to hang a tattered American flag with 35 stars—"Made in 1862 or 3 by a dear lady for a northern regiment."

The wily Mike Dann once worked out an elaborate scheme to make it appear that his unhung and unapproved picture had dropped from the wall. He then called the workmen and ordered them to put back the picture that "fell."

Dorfsman justified this attention to small details on the basis that "if you took care of the little things, the big things would take care of themselves." Frank Stanton prowled the building on weekends as others pursued relaxation in suburban splendor. He looked for lights that blinked, letters in the CBS signs that had slipped from their moorings, desks out of line. He would startle the maintenance men with personal requests that such trivial defects be fixed at once.

Some said Black Rock had the antiseptic quality of a hospital. "The walls show no scuffing, no handprints," Les Brown wrote in his book *Television: The Business Behind the Box*. "Their stark whiteness is counterpointed by a scheme of walls covered in a charcoal gray fabric reminiscent of the flannel suits that used to be the uniform of the advertising man.

"A Japanese woman who is perhaps a genius at flower arrangement produces floral bouquets daily for the top executives and twice a week for the reception areas. Each secretary's desk bears a single rose. The company's annual bill for fresh flowers surely runs into the thousands."

No doubt. But the savings in stationery make up for it. In Dorfsman's mind, stationery is a natural extension of the building itself. He conferred with Stanton and got an okay to systematize the stationery —reduce the number of pieces to fewer than half a dozen. "Terrific," said Stanton.

Dorfsman says that by standardizing CBS stationery and buying it in carload lots, both esthetic and economic aims were met.

We asked for our own watermark—CBS rather than Strathmore Paper Company. We used to have seventy-eight different letterheads, five different kinds of paper and three different sizes of stationery before we decided to standardize.

I estimate the savings at a hundred and fifty thousand dollars a year—and we got out of the warehousing business. At the time, everybody from vice-presidents on up was ego tripping with his own personalized stationery. We were printing this stuff by the ton.

In standardizing we settled on a relatively inexpensive twenty-pound paper with only twenty-five-percent rag content. The paper will disintegrate in, maybe, twenty-five years, rather than four thousand. We milled the same paper down to thirteen pounds for carbon sheets and airmail. The second sheets are made from the same stock as the first. Different stock on second sheets is like a vest from another suit. An esthetic conflict.

We use our own two typefaces throughout the building stationery —they are called CBS didot and CBS sans serif.

Asked if CBS letterhead sheets actually do carry a dot to show the secretary where to begin typing the letter, Dorfsman pulled out a sample letter which carried instructions in red to all typists. The tiny dot is two inches below the second address line under the CBS logo.

"Three girls typing letters end up with three formats—unless you specify," he explained.

The maximum width of lines is specified as 5 3/4 inches and there is to be a one-line space between paragraphs. "Whenever possible," the text of the sample letter states, "words should not be broken at the end of a line." There are to be seven lines of space between the letter's closing and the beginning of the inside address, found directly under the sender's name and title which appear on the left side of the completed letter—not the right side as is customary. A line shows the maximum depth beyond which the text must not extend. Frank Stanton, for one, has sent back letters that went below that line, as well as letters that weren't a picture of symmetry on the page.

All of this contributes to a decided CBS image, which in some ways is reflected in its people—their personal styles and even their shapes.

Some say Tom Dawson, who lasted only a year as president, lost out because of his unwillingness to assume the CBS identity. He insisted on wearing a suburban jacket to work and sometimes dismissed his company chauffeur so that he could tool his official limousine through traffic and out to his home in Greenwich, Connecticut. He was even known to take the train on occasion! Another feckless CBS middle-manager was once sent home to change his argyle socks.

Les Brown tells of a black-tie party thrown by Bill Paley at which one of the lesser executives was appalled at the obesity of a colleague's wife whom he had never met before.

"Seeing him with his wife made me realize why I felt [he] didn't really belong. . . . He was never my idea of CBS. Together, they were so out of place in that group that I felt embarrassed for Mr. Paley."

The one man who didn't bend to the Stanton-Dorfsman dictates was Bill Paley himself. Paley was content to let Stanton prevail, except in two areas: his own office and The Ground Floor restaurant, on which Paley lavished special attention. Stanton was furious about The Ground Floor. Paley wanted it to be an "in" place for the jet set. Stanton did some research and learned that the jet set rarely patronized a restaurant in an office building. Paley got his restaurant, but he didn't get the jet set. Eventually, The Ground Floor space was leased to a restaurant chain.

Paley's office was a more successful deviation from Stanton's plan. It became an oasis in the desert of conformity. Warm with wooden paneling and selections from Paley's own superb collection of modern art, it was also personalized with mikes from the early stations lining the wall and, until recently at least, it was graced with a grim-visaged cigar store Indian, the gift of Babe Paley. All this was the antithesis of the Stanton style. Paley preserved the kind of lived-in atmosphere he had enjoyed in his offices at 485 Madison Avenue.

Frank Stanton's office, on the other hand, conformed to his and Black Rock's austere style. Literally a cold-blooded man, he kept his office chilly enough to preserve fish. He liked nothing better than a mechanical challenge and once he was discovered on his back fixing his private-office sink. His opinions about other people's offices weren't just limited to Black Rock. He had serious discussions with his old friend Lyndon B. Johnson about the fact that the president's desk didn't sit solidly on all four legs. Stanton just couldn't resist mechanical challenges. An executive who once borrowed Stanton's Cadillac discovered that the stock emblems had been removed from the door; when he asked about it, the driver pulled some custom emblems out of the glove compartment. Was CBS having them put on? "Oh, no, Doctor Stanton plans to put them on himself this weekend." He also liked to drive his personal car under the Queensboro Bridge on weekends and wash it down by hand with a bucket of water and a sponge.

Another defier of the Stanton-Dorfsman rules of decor is Dorfsman himself, now vice-president of advertising and design. Entering the Dorfsman office is like removing a handcrafted, spit-shined custom boot and donning an old pair of slippers chewed to the verge of ruin by a puppy.

For an interview in his office, Dorfsman wore a cowboy shirt and chino pants. As he described the craftsmanship and "Swiss-watch precision" of Stanton's operation, Dorfsman lolled in a comfortable, battered executive's chair, the wheels of which had torn holes in the blue carpeting. His desk was a mountain of sketches and work in progress, while other sketches lined the walls in nondescript fashion, accenting the general clutter.

Dorfsman reports Stanton himself was stunned when he first entered the office. "He staggered back and said, 'My God, you have a lot of nerve telling people what to do!' "

Dorfsman remembers: "I mumbled that I was one of the few people in the building who actually processes a product."

Critics say that Black Rock breeds conformity in a field that calls for creative freedom, formality in a business that proved in the 1930s to be uniquely successful in a casual, even chaotic atmosphere.

CBS has arrived, all right. Black Rock signifies bigness—a bigness that sometimes smothers the individual in a golden cocoon and, some say, fosters partisan struggle in place of teamwork. But it would be an overstatement to claim that the "new formality" has affected the product. The boys in the black suits make the big policy decisions at Black Rock, but the programs emanate from the West Side news plant and from Hollywood.

CHAPTER 22

The Acquisition Game

WHEN A COMPANY IS SO SUCCESSFUL THAT IT CAN SPEND $50 MILLION IN a new venture like television before it recovers a dime, it has to be a real money machine. So it is perhaps understandable that CBS—which continued to throw off tens of millions of dollars in profits—would choose to diversify rather than pay the heavy taxes the government imposes on large profit accumulation. Unfortunately, CBS could not acquire more stations—that's the law.

For a time, Paley had kicked around the idea of letting someone else deal with this situation, seriously weighing the possibility of merging CBS into a bigger corporation. The Philco Division of Ford was a hot prospect for a time, and there were others. But the talks always ended without action: The CBS executive cadre was considered by potential purchasers to be too old. Thus, after a Booz Allen & Hamilton personnel study gave high marks to many younger executives—John Reynolds, Robert Wood and others—they were promoted; and excellent older managers like Merle Jones, president of the television stations division, and Arthur Hull Hayes, president of the radio division, were rushed into early retirement. Talented Fred Friendly got low marks as an executive and this provided a good excuse for his ouster later.

Paley still couldn't find an appropriate acquiring company and thus decided in the 1960s to expand his empire in nonbroadcast areas. Stanton was for expansion and had once urged Paley to buy ABC. Paley accepted the idea eagerly but the FCC shot them down in 24 hours —by telephone, according to Jack Gould.

Their lawyers shook their heads when CBS mused about a possible merger with Time, Inc. Too much communications power would be focused in one place, the government would never go along. Time and again, good acquisition ideas turned out to be potentially illegal under one federal statute or another. CBS, with its wonderfully profitable broadcasting business, was severely limited in its acquisition opportunities.

This may explain, in part, why CBS stumbled now and then on the acquistion trail. As Victor Ratner said, broadcasting was so profitable that the Chairman's mistakes were smothered in profits.

In 1962 Michael Burke, an ebullient, mod-style executive, headed up a new CBS effort to "broaden its corporate base," as CBS's PR calls it, by acquiring "companies compatible with the entertainment and information business."

Sports fit that description, and so did publishing. CBS wouldn't be straying too far off home base if they bought, say, a baseball team and a publishing house. CBS was expert in all facets of entertainment and information.

So they thought.

Drop into most any candy store during baseball season and you will hear the street equivalent of scholarly debate—arguments over the relative merits of Willie Mays and Hank Aaron, spiced with the obligatory overlay of batting averages, runs batted in and other assorted statistics. You're likely to hear calculated guesses as to when current favorites will begin to fade, and long-term projections about a team's future prospects based on the ages of its players. Much of this expertise comes from the lips of fuzzy-cheeked philosophers or high school dropouts.

A visit to one or more candy stores in the vicinity of CBS headquarters might have served CBS better than its own sages when the suggestion was made in 1964 that CBS clasp the New York Yankees to its corporate breast. Surely some candy store habitué thumbing through

Sport, Sports Illustrated or even the back pages of the *Daily News* could have told urbane Bill Paley and meticulous Frank Stanton that their dream of glory at the helm of the Yankees came from a charred pipe.

On the surface, the Yankees certainly looked blue-chip. While CBS was debating the purchase, the team was on its way to winning its fifth straight pennant, its ninth in the previous ten seasons. The Yanks had the best record in the history of baseball. It was a team with prestige, tradition, pinstripes and superstars. But the kid at the candy store might have known enough to be skeptical about the future. In the Fifties the Yankees were loaded with players of superstar quality, and their player development was the best in the game; a Yankee was almost always a candidate for Rookie of the Year. By 1964, though, the stars were fading. Mickey Mantle, hobbled more each year by his bad legs, was clearly nearing the end of his career. Whitey Ford was past his prime. Roger Maris had never again approached his spectacular 1961 season when he hit 61 home runs. Elston Howard, the league's Most Valuable Player in 1963, was 33 years old in 1964. Yogi Berra had retired as a player at the end of '63 to manage the team.

Further, the young players were no longer coming up. Joe Pepitone looked like a hitter at times, but he turned unruly and self-destructive. Definitely not the Yankee image! But smug from a decade of success, the Yankees hadn't even been trading for players in recent years. Jim Bouton had only one big year. Roy White and Horace Clarke, the most promising minor-leaguers, turned out to be journeymen major-leaguers. The farm system was parched and dry.

Then there was the fact of competition. The New York Mets, at the bottom of the National League, were outdrawing the Yankees in attendance. As crazy losers, with old Casey Stengel at the helm, the Mets seemed more human than the winning Yankees. But it wasn't just that the Yankees always won; their management deliberately sought a cold, austere image—no colorful characters, no displays of unseemly emotion. Gray-flanneled CBS executives may have liked that image, but fans didn't. Also, the Mets played in a brand-new stadium in middle-class Queens; Yankee Stadium was decaying in an ugly section of the Bronx.

The Yankees came to bat during one of the morning meetings CBS was holding once a week—meetings aimed at finding enterprises to acquire that would put to work the substantial sums the company earned each year from its station franchises and its affiliated licenses. As a broadcaster, CBS had to navigate carefully amid the rocks of antitrust law and the shoals of FCC taboo. It was obvious that a Yankee acquisition wouldn't rock the corporate boat either way. When Frank Stanton asked, somewhat whimsically perhaps: "What about the Yankees?" Bill Paley's reaction wasn't, "What would our lawyers say?" It was: "Are they for sale?"

No one seemed to have thought of researching the project in depth. So instead, Bill Paley called Yankee boss Dan Topping, a personal friend, and they broke bread in elegant seclusion. As luck would have it, the Yankees were indeed for sale. Topping explained that the Yankees had been earning about $1 million in pretax profits, a fact calculated to make Paley's pulse accelerate to just below the speed limit. Paley and Stanton had already assured themselves that the Yankees qualified under their general-acquisition rules: that the business be first class, best in its field if possible; that it be compatible with CBS; and that it be a business "we would enjoy being in," as Mike Burke expressed it.

Dan Topping said he would retain a 10 percent equity in the team, take $13.2 million in cash for the rest and agreed to manage the business end for as long as five years if his services were needed. CBS was tempted but anxious to get an outside opinion without tipping its mitt to some potential rival. Perhaps it was this secrecy that caused CBS to drop the ball.

The third-oldest member of the CBS board of directors in terms of service was Joe Iglehart, a part owner of the Baltimore Orioles. He had been in and out of baseball for a long time and, as an insider sworn to secrecy, was an obvious choice to help make the evaluation. At least he *seemed* an obvious choice. The only trouble was, he was apparently so smitten with the idea of being associated, however indirectly, with the great New York Yankees that he wasn't really thinking when he was asked by Bill and Frank: "How much would you pay for the Yankees?"

That would have been a tough question for anyone. And here was Joe Iglehart, a man with a secret love affair with a team halfway to the old-folks home, asked to answer in a hurry. Without deep thought or hesitation, he popped up with "Twenty million dollars!" The innocent CBS lambs rushed to the slaughter.

Just as quickly they were to learn the truth. The Yankees dropped to sixth place in 1965. The fans—and there never were that many Yankee lovers, just people who loved a winner—quickly cooled. Yankee earnings dropped to about half a million dollars that first year.

Meanwhile, back at the stadium, Topping's "freebooting" began to grate. It became obvious after a short period that he had to go. "He simply couldn't operate within a corporate structure." He left after that first year. During that time, the long friendship between Paley and Topping "simply disintegrated," according to Burke.

The next season, the Yankees slid into the basement. With the team in tenth place, profits dropped to a quarter of a million dollars—and that was the last *good* season. With a certain degree of understatement Burke says, "We probably had a net operating loss over the years to March 19, 1973, when CBS sold out."

(Meanwhile the crazy Mets grew even crazier; they won a couple of pennants, a world championship and the adoration of New York taxi drivers. Who needed Joe Pepitone?)

Bill Paley was distressed, of course, but remained game. He was rankled by the local sportswriters who were saying CBS wouldn't spend money on players. This, says Burke, was "absolute nonsense. We spent $1.6 million to $1.7 million a year on player development—which is well above the average. Paley realized from his days of buying talent in broadcasting that this was required in sport too. Paley was always asking, 'Can't we buy a great player—two great players?'"

And CBS did buy players—but not any great ones. To Paley the Yankee deal had become an exercise in pride. While people kept urging him to sell, he was determined to restore the Yankees before he did it, or so says Burke. Paley's boys at the stadium slowly began to get results. In the last half of the 1972 season, the Yankees were in the race to the end, though the team still lacked the big names and the kind of talent it had in days of yore. Nor had the teams grown any more colorful.

Before the '73 season began, Paley was ready to move. He approached Mike Burke and asked him if he would like to put together a syndicate to buy the Yankees and explained that the deal would have to be for cash. The price: $10 million dollars on the table.

Why less money for a club that was back in pennant contention again? Burke says, "The team was coming off a long string of misfortunes. And it hadn't been making money."

Burke raised the money, left CBS with the team and that was that (except for the fact the new owners soon dumped the ex-acquisition chief).

"In retrospect," says Burke, "CBS's $13.2 million could have been used to better advantage during the period. But then perhaps the whole thing should be regarded as an enriching experience. It certainly was for me anyway."

Maybe it isn't surprising that CBS failed as a sports-franchise owner; the company never had too much success in sports programing, either, at least not compared to its success in entertainment programing.

Think what you will of Howard (the Mouth) Cosell and his shrewd boss Roone Arledge over at the third network, ABC has pushed the two majors into the background in sports. Many said, early in the game, that sports would be very big TV business. But it took ABC to show how fully the athletes could be exploited, from *Monday Night Football* to the Saturday hour-and-a-half extravaganza called *Wide World of Sports.*

Paley was caught with his team still in the locker room. Initially, CBS had a big plus: The network owned the National Football League Sunday afternoon football game, which was the sports event of any weekend from September into the middle of January. But the American Football League, carried into prominence on the arm of Broadway Joe Namath, reached equal status with the NFL—on NBC. When the two leagues merged, CBS wound up sharing the football Sundays with NBC, with each network running the Super Bowl every other year.

During the summer CBS ran a Saturday baseball game of the week, though it isn't the hottest show in town. The Yankees were never, of course, regulars on network TV. And to avoid conflicts of interest, WCBS-TV, the local New York station, didn't carry the Yankees either.

Closed-circuit TV has a stranglehold on heavyweight championship boxing matches. And if you want to watch the videotape replay, try ABC's *Wide World of Sports,* not CBS. ABC has also made successful bids for both the winter and summer Olympics of 1976—not surprising since that network also had them in 1972.

CBS does better in tennis with the U.S. Championships at Forest Hills and will run its "Tennis Classic" on Sunday afternoons beginning in June 1975. NBC, meanwhile, carries the famous British championship at Wimbledon. CBS televised the Margaret Court–Bobby Riggs mismatch, but missed out on the big one—Billie Jean King's slaughter of tennis's best-known male chauvinist. Then the ball bounced back into the CBS court. For the big tennis extravaganza at Caesar's Palace on April 26, 1975, between Jimmy Connors and John Newcombe, CBS guaranteed $650,000 for a two-hour match plus tennis chatter. With 27 minutes of commercial time sold, the network needed to charge only $25,000 a minute to break even—and indications are that the price was much higher.

Try to remember Howard Cosell's counterpart on CBS football telecasts and you may draw a blank. Pat Summerall and Jack Whitaker, though knowledgeable, just don't have the Cosell charisma. And now NBC has Dandy Don Meredith, the next best to Horrible Howard.

When sports got hot apparently there was no knowledgeable jock in the upper echelons at Black Rock who picked up on it. Now CBS is making an effort, but any fan can tell you that it's hard to play "catch up" ball. You've got to gamble with the long pass when maybe your strength is short yardage up the middle.

Given the criteria Bill Paley set up for acquisitions after the Hytron disaster, the CBS takeover of Holt, Rinehart & Winston, Incorporated, is a move to puzzle over. CBS bought the house—a nondescript collection of mostly has-been publishing ventures—for shares valued at the time of acquisition at almost a quarter of a billion dollars.

Paley vacillated over the purchase for some time. He backed away from it in an earlier look because the price was too high, according to Mike Burke, then vice-president for acquisitions. But price, apparently, was never the main criterion for CBS's acquisition ventures. Earlier, CBS had made an attempt to buy into a publishing company in Boston. The company wasn't interested in being bought, despite the fact that, as one of the publishing executives put it, "The man [Paley] is mad. He's offering four times what our company is worth." When the Holt deal came up again a couple of years later at a "much higher price," Paley took the bait.

CBS acquired the company in steps. First the broadcasting company bought 11 percent of the HRW shares in October 1966 for $16,438,000—cash. The merger came in the summer of 1967 after a series of transactions gave CBS all the remaining HRW stock. CBS doled out 1,633,577 common shares and 3,267,153 shares of a new CBS convertible preferred stock. The CBS common sold at an average price of $63.30 that summer and the preferred stock was valued at $36.25 for purposes of the acquisition. Adding the cash outlay and the value of the shares, CBS gave an apparent total of $221,860,155 for HRW.

What did CBS receive for its money? Holt and Rinehart were distinguished houses in their prime but had both fallen on hard times when CBS acquired them. Holt had the remnants of a potentially solid educational publishing program—if CBS secured experienced and aggressive management. But it took several years for CBS to do so.

Rinehart originated in the profitable—and seemingly endless—mysteries of Mary Roberts Rinehart. Shortly after the war, Rinehart published Norman Mailer's *The Naked and the Dead*, a gigantic success. But when Mailer's succeeding books demonstrated the author's enormous literary appetite for sex, old Mrs. Rinehart, so the story goes, turned away with a shiver of disgust. Mailer went on to other publishers and greater glory and Rinehart started the long slide downhill. When CBS acquired the company, its properties were mostly limited to a poor list of trade books, fiction and nonfiction. Winston was basically a reference-book and dictionary house and ranked in terms of prestige and importance after Merriam, World (producer of The New World Webster Dictionary), Funk and Wagnalls and, now, the American Heritage Dictionary.

Wall Street second-guessers thought about these things and wondered how the acquisition fit into the announced philosophy of Bill Paley: The business had to be "first class," if possible, the best in its field; compatible with CBS's other interests; and a business CBS would "enjoy being in."

It isn't easy to determine exactly how CBS has fared with HRW, but until 1974 things hadn't worked out as well as Paley and associates had hoped. While the 1973 annual report heralded the exceptional profits of broadcasting and recordings, giving precise dollar amounts, two references to HRW results were buried in the middle of the report and mentioned no figures. On page 29 a cryptic remark suggested that CBS's main publishing effort was doing poorly: "Holt, Rinehart & Winston, Inc., experienced a substantially reduced loss, compared with the prior year." Clearly, 1972 must have been a year to forget. The report went on to say that the CBS Consumer Publishing Division suffered a loss for the year due to increases in allowances for returns and other adjustments. Later, on page 31, there appeared one of those masterful corporate lines of gobbledegook: "Holt, Rinehart & Winston, Inc., implemented a restructuring of operations and accelerated its market research programs."

Translated into hard currency, such lines meant that some of the boys who failed to turn things around got their heads handed to them and some new boys came in and were told to get cracking. That phrase "accelerated its market research programs" was translated by the new boys to "Get those goddamn salesmen on the road and tell 'em to sell some books—*fast.*" In the short term, at least, it appears to have worked. The 1974 annual report announced substantially increased sales and income from the publishing group, mainly due to the success of a new math program for elementary schools—plus a little help from Erica Jong's raunchy fem-lib *Fear of Flying.*

When RCA, on the other hand, went into publishing, it picked up two blue-chip companies, Random House and Knopf, both of which are booming along at the very top of the field; and Pantheon which is small, prestigious, academic in its orientation, and both ornamental and profitable. There is some irony in the RCA–Random House marriage. Mike Burke says Bill Paley turned down Random House in his quest for a first-class company and settled instead for HRW.

CBS had no better luck when it decided to enter the hurly-burly world of mass paperbacks. Once again, instead of acquiring Bantam (the classiest entry in the field and the most profitable), Pocket Books (the oldest), or Avon (up-and-coming), CBS bought Popular Library for the simplest of reasons—it was available. Once upon a time Popular Library was a profitable operation, paying small advances for so-called category books—westerns, detectives, romances, science fiction. Under CBS's admonition to create a proud line of fine books and best sellers, and with plenty of CBS money to invest, Popular Library promptly bought the wrong "big" books at high prices and slid into the red. Heads rolled once and then a second time. But while money is easy to invest, keen management is hard to buy if the buyer's expertise is in another field. The best that can be said about Popular Library today is that it is wobbly.

In one publishing area, CBS tried to buy top quality: *The New Yorker* magazine. But Paley was ultimately discouraged by Peter F. Fleischmann, chairman, president and largest shareholder of the magazine. The courtship ended when Fleischmann tried to work out a scheme that was, just incidentally, reminiscent of Paley's sale of CBS shares to Paramount Pictures years earlier. Under the plan, Fleischmann would have been able to buy the magazine back if the marriage proved to be unsatisfactory. "It was too damned complicated," Fleischmann reports.

W.B. Saunders may be regarded as the Paris gown in CBS's publishing wardrobe. The prestigious publisher of medical works was a major success, first catching the public eye with Kinsey's *Sexual Behavior in the Human Female,* and has contributed heavily to the publishing group's earnings, beset by losses in other areas.

CBS is now so big it can bury its mistakes in the middle of a fat and generally merry annual report. The failure of some first novel, or even a whole publishing house, is not going to produce any corporate gloom discernible from the outside.

PART FOUR

CENSORSHIP
FROM GEORGE BERNARD SHAW
TO JEB STUART MAGRUDER

CENSORSHIP

CENSORSHIP HAS, INEVITABLY, BEEN AN ISSUE AT CBS ALMOST SINCE THE beginning. Sometimes CBS has been threatened by censors, sometimes it has been the censor.

The tradition of a free press, spelled out in the Constitution, is well established. But the status of radio—and later television—had to be defined. There are only a limited number of available radio bands and television channels and they belong to the public. The Federal Communications Commission, as the public's representative, issues licenses and has the power to revoke them. The FCC is supposed to do so on the basis of the way a station serves the public interest.

Further, airwaves intrude into the public's life in ways that newspapers, magazines and movies cannot. Radio and television programs are available to listeners in their homes at the mere twist of a knob; a child can operate either. Therefore the attitude of the broadcast industry and the FCC has always been that the broadcast medium had to be much more careful about carrying anything that might be judged offensive.

In 1921 Westinghouse, an early broadcaster, put up a shack on the roof of its plant in Newark, New Jersey. Thomas H. Cowan—"Tommy" to his devoted listeners—entered that shack hundreds of times to talk through a modified telephone to all those people out in radioland. His primitive programing, usually records, was soon replaced by live acts. Tommy brought in many a name entertainer and personality from New York City—including Olga Petrova, an advocate of birth control.

The staff was relieved to learn that Olga just wanted to read some Mother Goose rhymes; Mother Goose seemed innocuous enough in that pristine era just two decades after the death of Queen Victoria. But Olga neglected to mention that these were her own versions. She stepped to the mike and intoned: "There was an old woman who lived in a shoe/She had so many children because she didn't know what to do."

Erik Barnouw, in *A Tower in Babel,* the first of his three volumes on *The History of Broadcasting,* described the staff of station WJZ as being "terrified." An emergency switch was thereafter provided for the engineer in the shack enabling him on his own judgment, or at a signal from the studio, to switch to the phonograph at his side.

The Petrova episode happened shortly before the scheduled radio broadcast of the full production of *Tangerine,* a musical comedy running on Broadway. Tommy Cowan was promptly dispatched to warn the producers that all lewd jokes would have to be eliminated. The producers canceled the appearance in a huff. This tame incident marked the start of a constant war between performers, writers and newscasters on the one hand and stations, the FCC and the networks on the other, over what constituted "salacious" material.

Performers had fun slipping in risqué jokes. Fred Allen worked out a nifty modus operandi to spice up his shows, one that gave headaches to the guardians of the public morality—station and network censors. He would put obvious off-color jokes in his scripts so that the censors could pounce on them and feel a sense of accomplishment. But then the censors were likely to miss the subtler zingers—to the vast amusement of many listeners in radioland.

Bob Hope was blatantly off-color from time to time. He once asked chesty Jane Russell if she'd like to play a new game called television. "Sure," said Jane. "Fine," said Hope. "I'll turn your knobs and you watch my antenna grow."

Arthur Godfrey for many years used off-color jokes to rekindle interest in his shows when the ratings began to flag. He recognized that audiences were secretly pleased, though many pretended to be scandalized.

There were, of course, many battles over matters of far more significance than blue material.

"Hello, America! Hello, all my friends in America! How are all you dear old boobs?" Thus began George Bernard Shaw, the great but politically controversial British author, in an exclusive 1930 trans-Atlantic broadcast that started as a coup for CBS and ended in fierce controversy. For the indomitable Shaw, a Fabian Socialist, went on to praise Russia and thus thrust CBS into the unwanted role of sponsor of the famous writer's unpopular views on communism. More than that, the Shaw broadcast helped usher in a sticky issue that was to plague CBS all through its history. Though the network did not feel obliged to cut Shaw off the air, it later offered listeners a "balancing" opinion.

A decade later CBS was called upon to resolve a far more serious challenge, and this time the network was forced to assume the role of censor. The challenge came from a demagogue who purchased CBS Network time and used it to convey an anti-Semitic message with fascist overtones. Father Charles E. Coughlin, a Canadian-American, spoke from the pulpit of the Shrine of the Little Flower in Royal Oak near Detroit and drew an enormous following.

Paley recognized Coughlin's power—the priest could inspire hundreds of thousands of letters to Congress in support of his aims—and determined to end that power on CBS. Paley neatly disposed of the man simply by changing the format of Father Coughlin's Sunday broadcast hour, making it the *Church of the Air.* He invited all denominations to share the radio pulpit and was thus able to ease Father Coughlin out of the network completely in April 1931. Coughlin unhappily found radio time elsewhere and continued his subtle hate broadcasts well into the Thirties.

During the same period, CBS broadcast the weekly *Ford Sunday-Evening Hour*—symphony music and intermission talks by Ford executive William J. Cameron. It was pure propaganda—blatant pats on the back for the boss and attacks on unemployment insurance, surplus-profit taxes and other New Deal ideas. Paley became incensed and asked Ford's advertising agency to take Cameron off the air. Henry

Ford got wind of it and said, "Send that Jew to me." Not long after, the show was off the air.

As the Cold War gained momentum in post–World War II days, the censorship issue centered on communism. Red-baiters rehashed the radicalism of the 1930s and, in ominous tones, asked such questions as "Who lost China?" True, many creative people flirted with communism during the Depression. They then believed communism might offer, among other things, solutions to the nation's devastating economic problems—and the professional red-baiters weren't going to let them forget it.

Guilt by association was enough to bring a person before the main forum, the House Un-American Activities Committee. When these people were ferreted out and accused, they turned to their employers for help. Those employed by CBS were out of luck. Instead of help, CBS demanded signatures on a loyalty oath. Those who refused to sign risked termination.

Since a broadcast station's enormous value is based on a license, and the FCC can take away that license, affiliate stations were anxious not to rock the establishment's boat. Neither was the network. Paley wasn't about to risk his company's future to save a few misguided citizens. Says one man who worked at CBS then: "Some pretty damn good people were destroyed. It is one of the shames of Bill Paley and the CBS management that they didn't fight it." Among those "damn good people" were John Henry Faulk, Orson Bean, Eliot Asinov, and Philip Loeb (of *The Goldbergs*) who committed suicide.

Ed Sullivan fought, but on the side of the red-hunters. During the 1950s he demanded that those who wanted to appear on his highly popular CBS show recant any "suspicious" political views or affiliations. It was Edward R. Murrow who saved the network's soul by daring to take on the era's No. 1 red-baiter—Senator Joseph McCarthy.

The networks may be forgiven if they seemed nervous more than a decade later, after the 1968 election. The Nixon administration seriously discussed adding a new dimension to censorship of broadcasters, particularly those who aimed shafts at the Nixon administration.

In a secret memo that later fell into the hands of broadcasters, presidential aide Jeb Stuart Magruder (later convicted and jailed) wrote Nixon's top aide, H. R. Haldeman (convicted, out on appeal), in 1969 to deplore the inefficiency of the administration's "shotgun" tactics in combating "unfair news coverage." He listed 21 requests from the president in a 30-day period to take specific actions, mostly to call news editors to complain.

Lyndon Johnson had tried to intimidate the anti-Vietnam war broadcasters, sometimes making that tough telephone call himself. Even John F. Kennedy, whose relations with the press were among the best, became annoyed enough with the New York *Herald Tribune* to cancel, with no little fanfare, the White House subscription to that respected newspaper.

But Nixon's man Magruder—and many of his cohorts—wanted to go much further. He suggested a "rifle" approach for keeping the media in line and mentioned several specific ways to achieve that goal.

In the memo dated October 17, 1969, he wrote: "1) Begin an official monitoring system through the FCC as soon as Dean Burch is officially on board as chairman. If the monitoring system proves our point [bias against Nixon] we have then legitimate and legal rights to go to the networks, etc., and make official complaints from the FCC. This will have much more effect than a phone call from Herb Klein or Pat Buchanan." (Dean Burch was, of course, a highly political Nixonite. Earlier an important Goldwater advisor, Burch served as Republican National Committee chairman in 1964 during the GOP's most conservative days.)

Three days after Burch was confirmed, he telephoned all three network presidents asking for verbatim reports of the news commentators' remarks following a Nixon speech on Vietnam the previous evening. Burch, said Stanton, "apologized for making the request and explained that he was doing so at the request of the White House." Stanton added that it seemed most peculiar that the White House would ask the head of an independent agency for such routine assistance and seemed a pointed effort to make an impression.

The broadcasters' nervousness was heightened by Vice President Spiro T. Agnew's threatening speeches aimed at the media. In a speech in Des Moines on November 13, 1969, Agnew complained that as soon as Nixon had completed his Vietnam address he was subjected to "instant analysis and querulous criticism" by a "small band of network commentators and self-appointed analysts." These men numbered "perhaps no more than a dozen" anchormen, commentators and executive producers. Implying a threat of government retaliation via the

FCC's licensing function, he denounced the "tiny enclosed fraternity of privileged men elected by no one and enjoying a monopoly sanctioned and licensed by government."

In 1971, CBS got into hot water in Washington for its hard-hitting documentary *The Selling of the Pentagon*. A congressional committee tried to get the House to cite CBS for contempt when it refused to turn over its background material. The House, however, backed CBS.

Later the administration went after the networks, especially CBS, through an attempt to intimidate affiliated station owners. Clay Whitehead, head of the Office of Telecommunications Policy and the administration's official spokeman on television, told a Sigma Delta Chi audience in Indianapolis on December 18, 1972, to watch out: "Station managers and network officials who fail to act to correct imbalance or consistent bias from the networks—or who acquiesce by silence—can only be considered willing participants to be held fully accountable by the broadcasters' community at license-renewal time." This speech put the industry in a state of shock. Affiliate owners, who mostly favored the Nixon administration and opposed the CBS coverage of the Vietnam war, began to pressure the network. Even national advertisers began to tell CBS that they were being discouraged from advertising on CBS so much.

Then Dean Burch let it be known that he was proposing rule-making discussions at the FCC concerning the desirability of the existing ownership of network stations. Some months before, the justice department had filed an antitrust suit against the three networks demanding that they be foreclosed from producing their own shows. Further, Justice would prevent them from buying pieces of shows, produced independently, that ultimately would be presented on the network. Justice also charged CBS with refusing to exhibit in prime time those shows in which it had no financial interest. The networks filed general denials and the matter is still pending.

Besides Magruder, Burch, Agnew and Whitehead, another key figure in Nixon's campaign against the media was Charles Colson, special counsel to the president. After Frank Stanton told a broadcasting group in Utah in July 1970 that CBS was planning a "loyal opposition" concept whereby free prime time would be provided to the major political parties to offset Nixon's speeches, he heard from the White

MANAGEMENT

CBS

Bill Paley, the chairman.

CBS

Paul White at the "piano." △

Wide World

▽ Peter Goldmark on the color wheel.

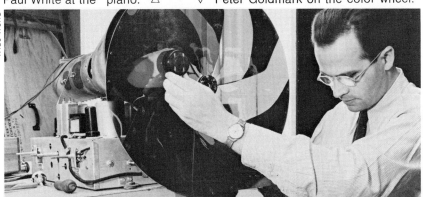

An adventure begins at **485 Madison** Avenue. Young Bill Paley stares at the camera as Miss Radio of **1929 cuts** the ribbon.

Victor Ratner adds and promotes in the shadows.

Sam Paley,
Bill's father,
the $30-million
cigar king.

LA PALINA

THE QUALITY CIGAR

La Palina and the lady known
as Goldie, Bill's mother.

Bill and Dorothy, wife #1, on
Hawaiian Honeymoon.

Best-dressed Babe and Tuxedo
Bill, 1957.

Ike and Walter and Bill Paley relive D-Day.

Earnest Frank Stanton fights the battle against censorship in the Senate, 1956.

Paley woos Benny from NBC.

Frank and Bill—the original love-hate relationship.

Clive Davis and Lou Cowan—fame, fortune and fired.

Mike Burke—sunk with the Yankees. Paul Kesten—the great promoter.

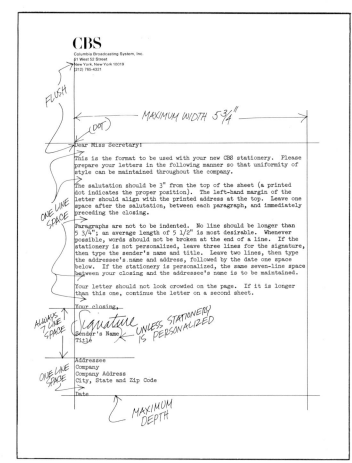

FLUSH

(DOT)

MAXIMUM WIDTH 5¾″

Dear Miss Secretary:

This is the format to be used with your new CBS stationery. Please prepare your letters in the following manner so that uniformity of style can be maintained throughout the company.

The salutation should be 3″ from the top of the sheet (a printed dot indicates the proper position). The left-hand margin of the letter should align with the printed address at the top. Leave one space after the salutation, between each paragraph, and immediately preceding the closing.

Paragraphs are not to be indented. No line should be longer than 5 3/4″; an average length of 5 1/2″ is most desirable. Whenever possible, words should not be broken at the end of a line. If the stationery is not personalized, leave three lines for the signature, then type the sender's name and title. Leave two lines, then type the addressee's name and address, followed by the date one space below. If the stationery is personalized, the same seven-line space between your closing and the addressee's name is to be maintained.

Your letter should not look crowded on the page. If it is longer than this one, continue the letter on a second sheet.

Your closing,

ONE LINE SPACE

ALWAYS 7 LINE SPACE

Signature

UNLESS STATIONERY IS PERSONALIZED

Sender's Name
Title

ONE LINE SPACE

Addressee
Company
Company Address
City, State and Zip Code

Date

MAXIMUM DEPTH

The only way to write a letter— according to Doctor Stanton.

Mike Dann

Mike Dann—the weathervane. Jim Aubrey—the smiling cobra. *CBS*

Black Rock

Arthur R. Taylor, presi-
dent of CBS, Inc., and
currently heir-apparent.

House. Colson came to New York and visited all three network heads. He indicated to Stanton that the administration might use the FCC or seek legislation, if necessary, to prevent this.

Colson claimed to have found the networks—and especially CBS—anxious to please and to be informed of any biased reporting by the network newsmen. Colson found Stanton the most insecure of all. However, that was Colson reporting to the boss. Stanton could never be imagined as insecure by most associates, who found him tough and cool under the fiercest kind of fire.

In 1972 Colson called Stanton to complain about a 14-minute segment on the Cronkite news of October 27, the first of two parts on Watergate. He told Stanton that he wasn't concerned about the report's fairness and balance. Rather, "it should not have been broadcast at all." Stanton told Colson that CBS would broadcast part 2, despite the administration. It was aired on October 31, a week before the election. However, it was shortened from its original length and some thought this was a response to Colson's pressure. Richard Salant says no, that he was cutting to avoid repetition. An assistant producer who prepared it, Stanhope Gould—later with NBC—was quoted in *The New Yorker* as saying the segment was trimmed after Salant was summoned to see Paley. It was edited over Gould's protest.

After the election, Colson called Stanton and, according to a Stanton affidavit containing charges later denied by Colson, said things would get much worse for CBS since the company didn't play ball during the election campaign: "We'll bring you to your knees in Wall Street and on Madison Avenue. . . ."

In 1973 and 1974, the Nixon administration continuously boiled over the Watergate coverage by Walter Cronkite, Dan Rather, Roger Mudd, Daniel Schorr and others. CBS's stand on the news front was hailed for its courage. The news division respected its obligation to provide balanced coverage, though it was admittedly difficult during the emotional Vietnam/Watergate years.

The network's policy in the entertainment field was less enlightened. On matters of "good taste" CBS gave ground slowly in a rapidly changing world, a world that today accepts over the airwaves words like "ass" and "rape" which were verboten only a few years ago.

The Smothers Brothers lost their battle with CBS over censorship. Joe Papp won his, but only after a long fight. It was *All in the Family* that broke more new ground than any other program. But the company never convinced anyone that it considered principles more important than profits, at least in entertainment programing.

CHAPTER 23
A Rilly Big Shoe

TO MILLIONS, ED SULLIVAN IN HIS PRIME WAS A LOVABLE THOUGH stone-faced emcee who brought the best entertainment he could find to television. To a much smaller number he was a powerful blacklister; a man who might destroy an entertainer's career if he felt his audience would be offended by that performer's politics. He supported and was guided by the most vicious witch-hunters and red-baiters the country produced, no doubt believing deeply in their cause.

But first, the Ed Sullivan we all knew and loved . . .

If a man trains for over 20 years and finally gets a shot at the Big Time, you would expect him to do a competent job at the very least. But when Ed Sullivan was chosen by CBS to host *The Toast of the Town* in 1948, the *Daily News* columnist, a producer of vaudeville shows as early as the 1920s, bombed. Or so it seemed.

The critics couldn't believe it. Here was an Irishman with a stony visage who was neither witty, talented, nor entertaining—except inadvertently as a bashful, clumsy, self-conscious, tongue-tied amateur who never quite figured out what to do with his hands.

Ed Sullivan elevated ineptitude to the level of good theater, prompting comedian Alan King to remark, "Ed does nothing, but he does it better than anyone else in television."

But, in fact, he had more than that going for him. First, he was working with a durable format proven by the long successes of Kate Smith's and Rudy Vallee's variety shows. Of far greater importance for a no-talent like Sullivan, the man was an excellent judge of entertainers.

Still the show started out dreadfully. The TV critics panned him without mercy for his shortcomings and did it again and again. Sponsors, never anxious to buck the critics, were afraid to buy the show.

The network had such misgivings that it slowed the flow of money for *Toast of the Town* down to a trickle. Sullivan was forced to dig into his own pocket—using his emcee money for talent.

But he persevered and something strange began to happen out there in televisionland. Critics to the contrary, the great unwashed, as H.L. Mencken called them, were warming to the wooden Sullivan and his entertaining mix of the high- and low-brow. A classical piano concert featuring ten artists at as many concert grands was likely to be followed by a dog act.

Ed would introduce each act in a voice pitched in the upper reaches of his register, as though speaking over an unruly crowd at the circus. When the performer left the stage in triumph, Sullivan would call him back for an anticlimactic handshake, then bring on the next attraction. His tongue stumbled over his teeth as often as his feet tangled with the mike cords, and, in his pain, he became a surrogate for every man who feared making a fool of himself in public. Said *The New York Times*, "He was so honestly ill-at-ease the viewers came to be affectionately sorry for him." And Sullivan reveled in it. Though he was about as witty as a bank examiner, he could see the humor in his grave manner and even booked comics who impersonated him.

The public was entranced, the critics baffled and Ford Motor Company's Lincoln-Mercury division impressed. The show was sold, the audience grew from 45 million to 50 million each Sunday evening, and Sullivan became a permanent part of the scene. Oscar Levant quipped: "He will last as long as someone else has talent."

A low-budget show at first, Sullivan said in 1973 that the whole first production, apart from Ray Bloch and the orchestra, cost $475. A ballad singer and two young zany comedians named Martin and Lewis got $200. Rodgers and Hammerstein, the authors of *South Pacific*, "refused to take anything." Ruby Goldstein, the fight referee, got $50. June 20, 1948, marked the beginning of the longest-running show in television.

Many a superstar got his start with Sullivan, and every actor in town with a specialty act badgered his agent to get him on the show. Jack Benny made his TV debut on "Toast" (later renamed *The Ed Sullivan Show*) as did Humphrey Bogart, Maria Callas, Jackie Gleason and The Beatles, the most successful of the many acts Sullivan brought in from abroad. Elvis Presley, shown from the waist up so his famous pulsating torso would not offend, was another of Sullivan's TV firsts.

Sullivan was a moralist with an instinct for self-preservation that saved him and his show from trouble, sometimes at the expense of others. In an early, celebrated controversy, the first of many over the years, he used dancer Paul Draper on a show in January 1950 and then apologized abjectly for having done so when red-baiters accused Sullivan of aiding and abetting communists.

Draper and harmonica player Larry Adler had incurred the wrath of a Greenwich, Connecticut, housewife who had "always been on the lookout for [subversives]" and the cause was taken up by right-wing columnists. Draper and Adler sued the woman, Mrs. Hester McCullough, and issued a statement carried by the Associated Press to the effect that they in no way supported the communist cause, had never been communists and gave allegiance "solely to the United States under the Constitution."

Draper's appearance on the Sullivan show caused an outpouring of hate mail. There were 1294 angry letters and telegrams to the Ford Motor Company, with the usual duplicates and clusters from the same post offices common in such cases. Sullivan, worried about his reputation, decided to make amends.

In a letter hatched in a public relations office, he wrote William B. Lewis, president of Ford's advertising agency, Kenyon & Eckhardt, and a former vice-president of CBS:

> Dear Bill:
>   I am deeply distressed to find out that some people were offended by the appearance on Sunday's *Toast of the Town* television show of a performer whose political beliefs are a matter of controversy. . . . You know how bitterly opposed I am to Communism and all it stands for. You also know how strongly I would oppose having the program used as a political forum, directly or indirectly. . . .

One result of the flap was Sullivan's alliance thereafter with Ted Kirkpatrick, an ex–FBI agent and self-appointed crusader against communism. Things then got rough for anyone remotely resembling a radical. Draper, for one, found he could no longer make a living in the United States and moved to Europe.

Sullivan became preoccupied with clearances for his performers; and Kirkpatrick, publisher of *Counterattack*, a blacklisting newsletter noted for inaccuracies and rare retractions, became his guide. The liaison between the two became extremely close. Sullivan made a practice of checking with Kirkpatrick on doubtful artists, and if the artist seemed to have "explaining to do" and Sullivan still wanted to use him, he got Kirkpatrick and the performer together to work things out. He told readers of the *Daily News* in his column: "Kirkpatrick has sat in my living room on several occasions and listened attentively to performers eager to secure a certification of loyalty. On some occasions, after interviewing them, he has given them the green light; on other occasions, he has told them: 'Veterans' organizations will insist on more proof.'"

Sullivan complimented *Counterattack* for "a magnificent job," and when Kirkpatrick was ready to come out with his infamous *Red Channels: The Report of Communist Influence in Radio and Television*, he gave Sullivan the scoop for his column. The cover of the book featured a red hand closing on a microphone tilted to the left, and the text consisted of a list of 151 artists and writers with "documentation" of their political sins. It included so many of the nation's top talents that some didn't know whether to regard it seriously or as a rude joke. Such infiltrators as Lillian Hellman and Arthur Miller made the list. Detective-story writer Dashiell Hammett was another who supposedly threatened America's basic liberties. CBS correspondents on the list included Howard K. Smith, who these days on ABC is considered relatively conservative, and William L. Shirer, CBS's distinguished Berlin correspondent during World War II and author of the monumental *Rise and Fall of the Third Reich*.

Sullivan's independence from the network as a producer, his reactionary columns and his widely publicized views elsewhere undoubtedly helped take some of the heat off CBS.

The list suggested that expressions of honest doubt about capitalism were subversive. Many thoughtful people, or those simply with open minds, had by the very nature of their reasonableness said or done something that, according to Kirkpatrick, allied them with dangerously radical causes. Most of the 151 "subversives" in the book had been supporters of the New Deal which right-wingers like Kirkpatrick regarded as FDR's grand design for socialism. Some were supporters of Henry Wallace, FDR's left-leaning vice president in the 1940s. Others were simply civil libertarians, pacifists, academic socialists or outspoken people of conscience who worried about the poor.

But times changed. Some would find irony in the fact that Sullivan led a variety troupe on a successful Soviet tour in 1959 and presented an hour-long telecast of the Moiseyev dancers on his show. Seven years earlier that would have been enough to place Sullivan himself on the list.

Sullivan was justly celebrated for showcasing Negro talent at a time when blacks were about as common on television as four-letter words. He was also known as a man who contributed his time and talent to many causes and people he found worthy, regardless of their origins and beliefs.

At its peak *The Ed Sullivan Show* was clearly one of the great CBS properties, and inevitably a publisher, McGraw-Hill, approached Sullivan to do a book. The best he could come up with was something with the unlikely title of *Christmas with Ed Sullivan.* Sullivan put together, with plenty of help, about 20,000 words of fond memories about Sullivan family Christmases, and the rest of the book had to be an anthology of other famous people's happy Christmas recollections.

"It seemed like a great idea at the time," a McGraw-Hill editor says, and the bookstores thought so too. McGraw-Hill increased the first printing from 35,000 to 50,000 before publication.

The only trouble was that the FCC chose that moment to clamp down, at least temporarily, on "free plugs," particularly of a TV personality's own book. No hypo, no sale. Sullivan's *Christmas* came flooding back to the publisher from the stores.

"It seemed like we got back more books than we printed," the McGraw-Hill man says today. "We tried to take a tax write-off by giving them to Sullivan's favorite charity, the Halloran Veterans Hospital on Staten Island where he used to perform those Christmas Eve benefits. But even the hospital returned the damned things."

Those hospital benefits illustrated the side of Sullivan's personality rarely glimpsed on his shows—his warmth. On one memorable visit during World War II, Sullivan, though squeamish in hospitals, was walking through the wards after a benefit that included performances by Jimmy Durante and Jack Benny. Sullivan was drawn to a youngster encased in bandages. The chart said he was Arthur Ford of Milledgeville, Georgia.

"Would you like to meet Jack Benny?" Sullivan asked.

"Who're you kidding?"

Finally convinced that Sullivan was serious, the boy came to life, asking, "Is my hair combed all right?" Since he couldn't move his arms, Sullivan combed his hair.

Benny came to the bedside, warm and friendly, and the boy's appreciation glistened in his eyes. When they left, Sullivan told young Ford that there would be another show in two weeks and he would bring some more stars to his bed. Without self-pity, the boy whispered, "Maybe I won't be here." Sullivan pretended to bawl him out, saying that he had *better* be. Then Sullivan learned that the boy wasn't expected to last six hours, that he had been hit in the stomach and practically torn open.

Sullivan phoned the hospital every day for two weeks for news of the boy. When the youngster died Sullivan said: "So strongly had I become attached to this kid I hardly knew, that I felt as if I had lost a dear friend . . . it also made me want to do something. At least I could tell people about this boy's contribution to his country."

The editor of Sullivan's ill-fated book remembers that generous side to Sullivan's personality.

He was a man of warmth and very kind. We used to go up to his suite at the Delmonico and try to dig those twenty-thousand words out of him. At eleven A.M. Sullivan would be in his dressing gown, munching on soft toast and sipping milk for his ulcer. The phone rang every thirty seconds in the next room and Carmine Santullo, his right arm and omnipresent assistant, would dart in with word on some dog or trapeze act, a juggler or tap-dancer, a new chanteuse. Then Sullivan's wife would trip through with her toy poodle on a leash, headed for the stores or lunch with the girls, and they'd chat. It was a tough twenty thousand words to extract, but Sullivan never stopped being a nice gentle guy.

The Sullivan show remained very attractive to advertisers for years. And in network television sales, the prime-time stakes are big. One young time salesman at CBS, not entirely familiar with the terminology of his trade, almost came a cropper trying to sell precious Sullivan seconds.

For Jim Rosenfield, a 35-year-old refugee from the slide-projector business where $500 was a big sale, the transition to TV was awesome. In 1965 he went through a lean year, glimpsing every aspect of the broadcasting business as a $70-a-week trainee. The following year he was ready to latch onto the big money as a time salesman. Under incentive plans, CBS network time salesmen can earn $30,000 to $50,000 a year.

Jim had been pitching Lincoln-Mercury to return as a sponsor of *The Ed Sullivan Show* in 1966. If successful, he would pull $13 million into CBS coffers on this one deal. At last Kenyon & Eckhardt, negotiating on behalf of the auto maker, said they would go for it, buying "straight up," and Rosenfield went back to Black Rock to give his boss the good news.

This big a deal called for a joint celebration with the advertiser. The contracts were drawn up and Jim and his superiors went back for the final signing. But first the cocktails. The Lincoln-Mercury people proposed a toast to their "straight up" deal and the drinks of the CBS sales chiefs suddenly came back down again untasted.

"Straight up? You mean you want all six minutes every other week and nothing on the alternate week's show?"

The standard arrangement was four minutes of the six devoted to advertising on one show, and two minutes for the odd week. Jim had sold his big-car account something CBS couldn't deliver: Incumbent advertisers owned two minutes of advertising on the show Lincoln-Mercury wanted all to itself. The CBS chiefs didn't finish their drinks that day. The deal was off.

Says Jim: "I was sure it was the end. They could have pinned it on me—but they didn't. I hadn't been at it long enough to realize that 'straight up' was important. My bosses took the position that they were involved enough in the deal that they too should have known Lincoln-Mercury's intentions. If anyone ran scared at CBS, I would have been out. . . ."

Jim tells the story today with an easy confidence. For now, eight years later, he is vice-president in charge of sales for all of CBS–New York.

Inevitably, Sullivan's ratings began to slide. Costs mounted. Toward the end, he was spending $8 million a year to mount the weekly show. He received $164,000 as producer and his pay as "performer" was reported as $20,000 a week. Ad revenues fell. Sponsors would no longer pay a premium $62,000 a minute to advertise.

In 1971, CBS decided to drop the show in favor of movies, which brought in more money for a smaller investment. *The Ed Sullivan Show*, which cost almost nothing to produce in 1948, had become too expensive.

Sullivan continued to preside over specials including, in 1973, *Ed Sullivan's Broadway*. It was just about the last of the Rilly Big Shoes. Ed Sullivan died of cancer in October 1974.

Sullivan was mourned by millions. Only a few remembered, or refused to forgive, his days as a red-hunter.

CHAPTER 24

Murrow vs. McCarthy

AFTER OPERATING ON THE EXECUTIVE LEVEL AT CBS FOLLOWING
World War II, it was inevitable that Ed Murrow return to broadcasting. Jap Gude, his agent, saw that Murrow's enormous talent was being
wasted in administration. This led Gude to Fred Friendly, who wanted
to put together a talking history of World War II, and Friendly suggested Murrow narrate it. The resulting project, *Hear It Now*, was a
hit. There were sequels. Murrow and Friendly became close associates
and later they came up with a televised version, *See It Now.*

The team of Friendly and Murrow became one of the most creative
in the history of broadcasting. Both were highly committed men,
though their styles were in sharp contrast.

Fred Friendly, a big bear of a man with superior tastes, eventually
developed superb film-editing skills. Organizationally, though, "he was
a mess," says a CBS colleague who loved the man, as did most of those
who worked with him. He recalls:

Friendly used to send cables ordering our far-flung correspondents
to run hither and yon for dear old *See It Now.* This drove whoever
was running the newsroom up the wall because it pulled men off

assignments. Finally, an order went out for Friendly to desist, but *See It Now* was such a prestige thing that Friendly ignored it and was able to keep the upper hand.

It was all in search of excellence, though, and everybody knew that. He would produce something perfectly marvelous and after the broadcast would become depressed over some minor flaw. On one such occasion, he literally threatened to jump out a window.

Friendly's frequent rages—caused not by hostility to people but by his own impossible standards—sometimes had ludicrous consequences. Friendly himself tells of getting furious with Bill Paley over a policy matter, striding out a door and slamming it, only to find himself in Paley's private bathroom. But his final clash with Paley, when Friendly was president of news in 1965, led to his resignation, though he admits, "By golly, if they had wanted me to stay I would have." Paley asked him to stay, perhaps perfunctorily, but had grown tired of Friendly's zeal, his tendency to grab the Chairman by the lapels to shout, "You can't do this to the American people!" in policy decisions that favored commercialism over news.

Friendly's lovely and sharp-witted wife, Dorothy, was a leveling influence on his wildly fluctuating temperament. Their parties always had "good food, good conversation, and a feeling of warmth all over the place which he himself exuded," says a friend.

When *See It Now* was launched in November 1951, neither Friendly nor Murrow knew what he was doing. Their efforts then were relatively primitive. Their first show was based on a mere technical trick—the simultaneous showing of the Golden Gate Bridge and the Brooklyn Bridge on a split screen.

They needed help and found it in Palmer Williams, a newsreel man who had worked on the army-navy screen magazine during World War II. Later Fred Friendly remarked, "He was as much my teacher as was Murrow."

Two years of broadcasts brought growing technical competence despite the difficulties of the show's format, which used film and superimposed sound, plus Murrow's live comments at the end of each show which they called "tail pieces."

Many of Murrow's competing newsmen, in particular Elmer Davis, were troubled in the early 1950s and dared to express their fears in strong terms. They felt that the nation was faced with a threat to freedom that called for a strong reaction from Murrow—and not tomorrow. The specter of Senator Joe McCarthy hovered over Washington and the country.

CBS saw itself as a prime target. But rather than fight, it sought to appease. No man had been more critical of British appeasement before World War II than Edward R. Murrow. It is equally ironic that CBS decided to make peace with demagogues when one recalls the fearlessness of Bill Paley in the early days of radio, maneuvering the right-wing fanatic Father Coughlin off the CBS air in the 1930s.

In the 1950s, Paley was older; more was at stake. Paley now had tens of thousands of shareholders to serve. Television was just getting under way and CBS had an image so liberal as to prove in some instances burdensome. Paley sought a way to take the heat off CBS.

Clearly sponsor-oriented, the network took steps, some wrong ones. The black hat in the episode was worn by an unlikely lawyer, articulate and delightful, a Lincolnesque figure who affected a careless lock of hair over his forehead like Wendell Willkie. Associates describe Joseph Ream as a "barefoot boy from Wall Street." Despite his appearance, he was very sharp.

Ream, CBS executive vice-president, was well aware that sponsors were frightened by blacklists and threats to boycott products of sponsors hiring tainted actors and writers. Joe Ream, now retired in San Miguel, Mexico, heard many expressions of concern about CBS's liberal reputation. He decided to do something that would convince sponsors of the network's determination to stick to the center of the political road.

Ream drew up a list of communist and left-wing organizations, not unlike what the "federal government was doing," and asked CBS employees to state in writing that they neither belonged nor sympathized with them. This became the infamous "CBS loyalty oath"—the media's term, not Ream's; he saw it as an innocuous thing, though he notes that the "*Red Channels* people thought it wonderful."

Not all CBS employees agreed. All 2500 of them were asked to sign the document and, in effect, testify that they did not believe in the Communist Party, U.S.A. A minor office employee refused to sign and was dismissed. Other officials refused and were allowed to resign quietly. But onetime folk singer Tony Kraber, a CBS producer, was less fortunate. He made no effort to hide his past and was listed in *Red Channels*. Ream asked him to resign, telling him, "The network is bigger than any of us." But Kraber pointed out to Ream that he had signed the loyalty oath. "Oh, that," Ream is reported as saying. "That doesn't mean a thing."

At that time, Joe Ream says, the oath seemed reasonable. "In retrospect, I am not proud of it," he adds. "I accept full blame."

Ream says that he submitted the loyalty-oath idea to two other people at CBS. Frank Stanton, his immediate boss, was one of them. He refused to divulge the name of the other. But Ream insisted in a letter to the author, emphasizing the point made earlier in a telephone interview, that the acquiescence of the two was based on "confidence in my judgment." His bosses, says Ream, gave no "detailed consideration to the matter. The responsibility was mine and it was not shared in any real sense."

One critic sees Joseph Ream as a "decent man caught in the middle. . . . Paley was the black knight in the blacklist scandal. He had lunch with J. Edgar Hoover and Hoover called CBS the Communist Broadcasting System. This shook Paley, and he went along with the loyalty oath and all the rest of it."

In 1951, Fred Friendly and Murrow wanted to commission special music for the opening and closing credits of *See It Now*. Friendly went to the vice-president with administrative control over the show to request funds for the music.

"When the vice-president asked me what composer I had in mind," says Friendly, "I handed him the names of three well-known modern composers listed in order of our preference. He glanced at the top name and asked, 'Is he in the book?' "

Friendly didn't know and started to ask for a telephone directory, whereupon the vice-president reached in his desk, pulled out a copy of *Red Channels* and said, "This is the book we live by."

Fortunately, the book did not list the name of the first choice—but the other two names were in it.

By 1953 *Red Channels* lost the initiative to the senator from Wisconsin whose zealous pursuit of communists had thrust him into national prominence. Joe McCarthy, a bully with considerable talent for demagoguery, had taken the blacklist idea, tossed in some foreign-policy considerations and was on the road to fame. He called General

George Marshall, a World War II hero, a "traitor," blaming him for losing China to godless communism, and even compromised President Dwight D. Eisenhower by convincing Ike to delete a flattering allusion to Marshall in a campaign speech. For many, Eisenhower never spoke out strongly enough against McCarthy.

Murrow's friends, seeing him as the logical man to battle the Wisconsin senator, accused him of settling into a comfortable acquiescence instead. He remarked merely, "You may be right." He said the same words to those who argued that he should join some business leaders and broadcasters in backing McCarthy in his wild charges. Meanwhile the calm nasal voice of Elmer Davis attacked McCarthy's irresponsible actions almost nightly over the airwaves.

What was not known then, and would have been embarrassing, was that the "other" CBS official Joseph Ream showed the loyalty oath to —prior to its adoption—was Edward R. Murrow.

One October day in 1953, Murrow handed Fred Friendly a wrinkled clipping with the words, "Here, read this." It was about a Lieutenant Milo J. Radulovich, a 26-year-old Michigan university student and air-force reservist who had suddenly been asked to resign his commission. Unnamed accusers, it seemed, had charged that his father and sister had radical leanings. He refused to resign and was ordered separated from the air force on security grounds.

That afternoon Friendly passed the clipping along to CBS reporter-producer Joe Wershba. Wershba left for Detroit where he found Radulovich an attractive, articulate and willing subject for a broadcast that would provide the American public with a close look at "military security" hyped to hysteria by anticommunism. Wershba soon began sending back film, including a statement from Radulovich saying that the air force in no way questioned his loyalty, but had told him that his father and sister had allegedly read "subversive newspapers" and engaged in activities that were "questionable." The activities were not specified. Said Radulovich: "The actual charge against me is that I had maintained a close and continuing relationship with my dad and my sister over the years."

Another film clip showed Radulovich's father, a Serbian immigrant, reading a letter he had composed to President Eisenhower: "Mr. President . . . they are doing a bad thing to Milo. . . . He has given all his growing years to his country. . . . I am an old man. I have spent my

life in this coal mine and auto furnaces. I ask nothing for myself
. . . [only] justice for my boy."

One problem for *See It Now* was that the air force wouldn't participate in the show that was rapidly taking form. Yet an air-force statement was needed for balance. *See It Now* directors then told the air
force that the show would be done with or without their comment.
This warning brought an air-force general and a lieutenant colonel to
Ed Murrow's office. Murrow asked Friendly to join them.

The conversation was restrained—but pointed. The air-force officers
remembered that Murrow had once won a Distinguished Service to Air
Power award. The visitors told Murrow that he was regarded as a friend
and said they knew he wouldn't "do anything to alter that." Murrow
stared quietly at the general, agreeing to nothing.

The real battle then began—with the CBS hierarchy. First *See It
Now* asked CBS to advertise the forthcoming Radulovich telecast in
the newspapers. Management said no. So Murrow and Friendly with-
drew $1500 from their personal accounts and advertised the show in
The New York Times. It did not carry the CBS eye, just the signatures
of Ed Murrow and Fred Friendly.

Murrow had always had considerable autonomy at CBS, and free
access to Paley. As coproducer of *See It Now,* he was technically
responsible to Sig Michelson, the head of all CBS-TV news operations,
but this embarrassed both of them; there was no interaction and no
possible threat of a veto when Murrow had made up his mind about
something. Even Frank Stanton, president of CBS, made no attempts
to limit Murrow's power.

But Murrow had never before tested the limits of his mandate. He
did test it in "The Case Against Milo Radulovich, AO 589839." Before
the show went on the air, Murrow gulped some scotch and told
Friendly, "I don't know whether we'll get away with this one or not
. . . things will never be the same around here after tonight."

It was clear to everyone that Murrow was not just taking a look at
some indefensible military procedures. He was joining the war against
unreason. Using an individual case, he was pointing up in a dramatic
way, and for the first time on TV, the outrages of McCarthyism, with
its guilt by association, its unfounded charges, undisclosed sources and
general mood of hysteria.

Said Radulovich near the end of the telecast: "If I am going to be judged by my relatives, are my children going to be asked to denounce me? . . . Are they going to have to explain to their friends why their father's a security risk? . . ."

Murrow, in his tail piece, renewed his prior offer of equal time for the air force, and said: "Whatever happens in this whole area of the relationship between the individual and the state, we will do ourselves; it cannot be blamed on Malenkov, Mao Tse-tung or even our allies. It seems to us—that is, to Fred Friendly and myself—that it is a subject that should be argued endlessly."

The broadcast brought hundreds of telephone calls, telegrams and letters. Most praised the broadcast but a few letters were negative—and so were a few newspaper columns. CBS management was silent. The broadcast, as it turned out, was a signal victory for liberalism on the air and suggested the enormous power of television—and Ed Murrow.

Not long after, *See It Now* had another show that explored the topic of freedom, specifically the right of the Civil Liberties Union to use a hall in Indianapolis, a bastion of Midwest conservatism. Prior to the broadcast, Ed Murrow introduced a filmed statement in which Secretary of the Air Force Harold E. Talbott said that he had reviewed the Radulovich case, decided that Milo was not a security risk and directed that Radulovich be retained in his present status in the air force.

Meanwhile, Alcoa, *See It Now's* sponsor, was beginning to experience anti-Murrow pressures. Attacks on CBS became a regular feature in Hearst television columnist Jack O'Brian's space in the New York *Journal-American*. He loved to attack "Murrow and his partner in port-sided reporting, Mr. Friendly." Some of the CBS affiliates began to worry about the controversial Murrow and wrote CBS in New York to express their concern.

Murrow had begun a more popular if less significant feature, *Person to Person*, which allowed him to send cameras into the homes of celebrities who showed their "visitor" around, pointed out prized possessions and chatted with him as though Murrow weren't sitting in a remote CBS studio. It was trivia, but it showed a different facet of the Murrow personality, and it revealed his wide acquaintanceship with the great and near-great—political leaders as well as entertainers. The reason he descended to such pap, he told actor John Cassavetes, was because "To do the show I want to do, I have to do the show that I don't want to do." *Person to Person* built a much broader audience for

Murrow and gained him greater acceptance with viewers generally and with the profit-conscious executives at CBS.

Meanwhile, Murrow was collecting every foot of film to be found on Senator Joseph McCarthy. Night after night Murrow and Friendly pored over it, putting together a documentary. They told CBS about their plans for this material in early 1954. They would do a show on McCarthy on March 9. Again top management refused to come forth with money to advertise the program. And again, the two men personally paid for an ad in *The New York Times*. It said, simply: "Tonight at 10:30 on *See It Now*, a report on Senator Joseph R. McCarthy over Channel 2. Fred W. Friendly and Edward R. Murrow, co-producers."

Sitting in the control room before the show started, Fred Friendly, found his hand was shaking so much that when he tried to start his stopwatch he missed the button completely.

The broadcast juxtaposed McCarthy footage to show the inconsistencies of his wild accusations. These inconsistencies had always been hard to nail down since they were mumbled over a period of days and weeks. Put together for *See It Now*, McCarthy was heard to offer exact numbers of communists in government agencies, but the numbers kept changing. He waved papers providing "documentation," but the papers' contents were never revealed. Friendly and Murrow had no scoop, no exclusive new material on the senator—just an edited three-hour collection of film clips. But on film, McCarthy destroyed himself.

A key sequence involved the testimony of Brigadier General Ralph Zwicker, a hero of Normandy and Korea. He had refused to reveal the names of those in his peacetime command at Camp Kilmer who had promoted an obscure dentist who had taken the Fifth Amendment rather than answer questions about his supposed communist ties.

There was no film clip of the episode, but McCarthy was so pleased with it that he restaged it in Philadelphia for a Washington's Birthday celebration. Two *See It Now* men were lucky enough to be there with full equipment—Joe Wershba, reporter-producer, and Charlie Mack, Murrow's favorite cameraman. They got it all on film. McCarthy gave a verbatim reading of the "dentist" transcript while posing under a huge picture of the nation's first president. McCarthy enjoyed himself immensely, mixing rage with his frightening giggle.

Another sequence on the show dealt with Reed Harris, of the State Department, accused by the senator of somehow helping the communist cause by curtailing some broadcasts to Israel. Probing deep into his background, the subcommittee grilled him about his book attacking marriage, written in 1932. The book had gotten Harris in trouble with the college authorities when he was an undergraduate at Columbia.

McCarthy established that the American Civil Liberties Union had supplied Harris with an attorney. He asked if Harris was aware that the ACLU "has been listed as a front for and doing the work of the Communist Party?"

Harris first pointed out that this was 1932 and the attitudes of the general public were very different, affected by the Depression. McCarthy acknowledged that it was 1932 and repeated the question about the ACLU. Harris said he was not aware of it. McCarthy interrupted to shift the subject. Murrow later pointed out that the ACLU was not listed on the attorney general's list of subversive organizations. Finally Harris was able to reflect the feeling of many of McCarthy's victims when he said: "I resent the tone of this inquiry very much, Mr. Chairman. I resent it not only because it is my neck, my public neck, that you are, I think, very skillfully trying to wring, but I say it because there are thousands of able and loyal employees in the federal government who have been properly cleared according to the laws and the security practices of their agencies as I was. . . ."

There was more to the broadcast. Ed Murrow introduced film showing McCarthy as he laughed and scoffed at Eisenhower. There was McCarthy's attack on Stevenson who he referred to as "Alger, I mean Adlai." Murrow ended with these words:

As a nation we have come into our full inheritance at a tender age. We proclaim ourselves—as indeed we are—the defenders of freedom abroad by deserting it at home. The actions of the junior senator from Wisconsin have caused alarm and dismay amongst our allies abroad and given considerable comfort to our enemies, and whose fault is that? Not really his. He didn't create this situation of fear; he merely exploited it, and rather successfully. Cassius was right, "The fault, dear Brutus, is not in our stars but in ourselves. . . ." Good night, and good luck.

The response was immediate and tremendous—from both sides. Jack O'Brian was vitriolic and, in a tragic sidenote, singled out Don

Hollenbeck for singular abuse. Hollenbeck appeared after the Murrow broadcast as a reporter on New York's Channel 2 with the local news. He was obviously exhilarated.

"I don't know whether all of you have seen what I just saw, but I want to associate myself and this program with what Ed Murrow has just said, and I have never been prouder of CBS."

Among other things, O'Brian wrote, "We're getting lots of mail wondering how Channel 2's Don Hollenbeck gets away with his slanted newscasts. . . . Edward R. Murrow and Don Hollenbeck, to name the leading CBS leaners-to-the-left, develop a peculiarly selective slant in most of their news work." That was on June 14. In the same column O'Brian ran a series of anti-Hollenbeck letters with the comment, "We'll print as many as we can. It might help."

On the morning of June 22, Jap Gude, Hollenbeck's agent as well as Murrow's, called the Hollenbeck apartment. A policeman answered and told Gude to "come right over if you're a friend of his."

Hollenbeck, whose emotional life had been shaky anyway, had committed suicide.

As for Murrow, most people in the East appeared to think him a hero, though Gilbert Seldes, a responsible and distinguished critic, charged that Murrow had slanted the story by choosing a devastating selection of clips designed to portray McCarthy in the most unfavorable light possible.

A second show followed. A *See It Now* crew photographed the senator in a typical hearing, documenting his snarling questions, constant interruptions, bullying tactics. Then McCarthy, offered free time to reply by Paley and Murrow, responded on TV, and his own show was almost as disastrous to the senator as the broadcasts attacking him. The script, written in part by conservative columnist George Sokolsky, had McCarthy ending with the words: "Now ordinarily I would not take time out from the important work at hand to answer Murrow. However, in this case I feel justified in doing so because Murrow is a symbol, the leader and the cleverest of the jackal pack which is always found at the throat of anyone who dares to expose individual communists and traitors."

You had to see him to disbelieve him, to hate him, even to pity him. The senator had helped to destroy himself.

More distinguished *See It Now* broadcasts followed. But despite the accolades showered on Murrow by the public, there was growing concern in the executive suite. Finally, with sponsor Alcoa long since gone, there was a confrontation between Bill Paley on one side and Fred Friendly and Murrow on the other over the future of the show, dramatically described in Friendly's book, *Due to Circumstances Beyond Our Control.*

The dispute culminated, as Fred Friendly describes it, in "a forty-five minute scene . . . a blazing showdown with all guns firing."

One brief burst of dialogue told it all, says Friendly:

"'Bill,' said Murrow, pleading with his friend of 20 years, 'are you going to destroy all this? Don't you want an instrument like the *See It Now* organization, which you have poured so much into for so long, to continue?'

"'Yes,' said Paley, 'But I don't want this constant stomach ache every time you do a controversial subject.'

"Murrow replied: 'I'm afraid that's a price you have to be willing to pay. It goes with the job.'"

Nothing else mattered, Friendly concluded. After seven years and almost two hundred broadcasts, *See It Now* was dead.

Even after *See It Now*'s demise, Murrow's conscience continued to lead him into clashes with the CBS brass. Murrow made a speech in Chicago on October 15, 1958—at a time when allegations of fixes on the big-money quiz shows were rife—saying he was "frightened by the imbalance on television, the constant striving to reach the largest possible audience for everything." Murrow complained of the "money machine" that caused both CBS and NBC to delay for an hour and 15 minutes a crucial address by President Eisenhower in which the president spoke of the possibility of war between the United States, the Soviet Union and Communist China, "a reasonably compelling subject." Murrow noted that the delay was "about twice the time required for an ICBM to travel from the Soviet Union to major targets in the United States." And he said, "If this decision was dictated by anything other than financial reasons . . . the networks didn't deign to explain those reasons."

Murrow asked for a "tiny tithe" under which major advertisers would give up one or two hours a year to sponsor hour-long reports on the great issues facing the society so that the nation wouldn't find that the "flickering" tube was useful only to "distract, delude, amuse and insulate us."

Bill Paley and Frank Stanton were stung by Murrow's speech. It was regarded as an act almost of disloyalty. But it took a while for Stanton to answer Murrow's request—seven months. At the time, he was still busy defending CBS in the quiz scandals.

On May 15, 1959, Stanton said that in the following year CBS was scheduling once-a-month hour-long informational broadcasts in prime evening time. In elaborating on the idea, he revealed just how worried CBS was over the impact of the quiz scandals by saying: "We will report in depth on significant issues, events and personalities in the news. In the year following, we propose to make this a biweekly and after that a weekly program, if networks are permitted to retain their present structure."

In a sense the speech was a tacit acknowledgment of what many observers have always said: The Ed Murrow broadcasts had been a necessary counterbalance for CBS's rampant commercialism.

Murrow was certainly the logical man to star in the new series, to be called *CBS Reports*. However, the controversial Murrow was becoming unpopular with sponsors as well as CBS brass. Recently, he had narrated a radio broadcast, prepared by the CBS public affairs division, called *The Business of Sex* which suggested wide use of call girls by businessmen in sales campaigns. There were cries of outrage in the business community and questions were raised about the authenticity of the charges. The call girls interviewed for the broadcast had agreed to talk provided they were not identified. Murrow was unable to prove that his information was accurate—though he was convinced that the producer, the late Irving Gitlin, a thorough professional in his and Friendly's view, had presented an accurate picture.

Fred Friendly was chosen to be executive producer of the *CBS Reports* series, but it soon became clear in negotiations that the CBS executive cadre had no intention of letting Ed Murrow host the show, at least not on a regular basis.

The chemistry between Stanton and Murrow had never been good. Stanton had resented Murrow's direct access to Paley since the World War II days. In his view, that sort of thing made a travesty of the executive chain of command, something that a man like Stanton regarded as almost sacred. But there was more to it than that. Stanton clearly coveted the role of CBS panjandrum for news and public affairs. And Murrow was in the way.

Given a little prodding, Stanton was ready to declare war. The first shot was fired in New Orleans. When Stanton accepted an award from the Radio-Television News Directors Association there on October 16, 1959, a year after the same group heard Murrow's controversial "tiny tithe" speech, he used the occasion to announce a new program to eliminate "hanky panky": "We [will have] the American people [know] that what they see and hear on CBS programs is exactly what it purports to be. . . ."

New York Times columnist Jack Gould picked up the telephone and called Stanton, asking for specifics. Stanton said that he meant he was opposed to dubbed laughter and applause. (Paley was reportedly appalled that Stanton said that and made sure these "tricks" were restored after a short hiatus.) Stanton added that Murrow's *Person to Person* was an example of a show that gave the illusion of spontaneity when in fact it was rehearsed. He said that either *Person to Person* guests should not be told in advance what questions they would be asked, or the audience should be told the show was rehearsed.

On the very next show, with Charles Collingwood subbing for Murrow, there was such an announcement. Murrow was in London on a sabbatical when the Stanton interview appeared. The agitated producers of the *Person to Person* show phoned Murrow and urged him to clear their names. Somehow Stanton's remarks seemed to tie *Person to Person* to the biggest scandal in television history—the quiz-show chiseling.

Murrow needed no urging. He lost his temper and issued the following statement to the press:

Dr. Stanton has finally revealed his ignorance both of news and of requirements of television production. . . . He suggests that *Person to Person*, a program with which I was associated for six years, was not what it was purported to be.

Surely Stanton must know that cameras, lights and microphones do not just wander around a home. Producers must know who is going where and when and for how long. . . . The alternative would be chaos.

I am sorry Dr. Stanton feels that I have participated in perpetuating a fraud upon the public. My conscience is clear. His seems to be bothering him.

CBS was washing its dirty linen in public, something its spokesmen usually managed not to do. But Murrow's affront to the president of CBS was too great. Something had to be done—at least, Paley and Stanton thought so. They might have given consideration to the old maxim that one never issues an order that one does not intend to carry out. Instead they sent Ralph Colin, a member of the CBS board of directors, to London. Colin was to get either an apology or Murrow's resignation. Colin came back the next day empty-handed. Murrow gave him neither. Nor was Murrow fired.

But the exchange might be said to have worked out brilliantly for Frank Stanton. Murrow's position was undoubtedly weakened. With his access to Paley now effectively cut off, and lacking a strong program on which to express his views, he resigned in 1961 to become head of the United States Information Agency under President John F. Kennedy.

In part, Ed Murrow and Bill Paley were victims of CBS's expanding empire. "As the company grew bigger and bigger, Bill couldn't let Ed come in all the time," says a TV critic, "He channeled things and this broke Ed's heart. But right up to the end, Bill went far to show his friendship. He might cut your heart out at nine A.M. but at five P.M. he would come around to see what he could do in a crisis."

But the man Ben Sonnenberg called CBS's "great ornament" was gone.

CHAPTER 25

The Smothered Brothers

IT WAS 1969, AND TOMMY SMOTHERS WAS HAVING THE DREAM AGAIN: There he was driving a black Cadillac limousine with six passengers—Bill Paley, Mike Dann and Perry Lafferty (the company's West Coast TV chief) among them. The passengers all wore identical gray suits and mirthless smiles. "Their lips were smiling—but their eyes weren't," recalls Tommy.

Suddenly he was in the back seat between two CBS executives while Dann took over the driving.

"Where are we going?" Tommy asked apprehensively.

"Don't worry about it," replied a passenger. By this time the mirthless smiles had become laughs.

The limousine arrived at a loading dock, a door opened, and Dann drove into a large warehouse. The executives got out of the car with Tommy and surrounded him, still laughing. "We've taken enough shit from you," they said in unison. "You're a smart-ass, you're impudent, you're cocky, and there's no room for you."

"What are you going to do?" he asked, his voice quavering.

"We're going to kill you."

Then they forced Tommy to remove his clothing. Suddenly there were seven naked strangers beside him while his gray-suited tormenters now numbered better than a hundred. Several of them seized hot pokers and took turns searing Tommy's flesh, still jeering at him:

"You smart-assed kid."

"You think you're so cute."

"No, no," Tommy cried. "Give me another chance. I'll do all the shit you want me to. Anything."

"We're going to kill you."

"Don't kill me. Please don't kill me!"*

Then, just when it seemed the end had come, Tommy would wake up in a sweat. CBS hadn't killed him at all. But they were about to push Tommy into what seemed like a spectacular career suicide.

For Tommy, with his brother Dickie, had decided to take on the most powerful enterprise in the broadcast world—their employers. And while CBS cherished its role as defender of free speech in Washington, the company would be cast as the black-hat censor by a young man who portrayed a bubble-head on the Sunday night *Smothers Brothers Comedy Hour.*

Tommy and Dickie Smothers began their careers as impromptu folk-song parodists at a beer joint near San Jose State College, paid in beer and pretzels. Onstage, Dickie was the straight man; offstage Tommy dominated, always appearing as spokesman.

Their first big TV break came in a sappy CBS series that cast Tommy as the deceased brother of Dickie, a lecherous advertising man. Whenever Dickie was about to get his mitts on a nubile maiden, Tommy, halo glowing, would return from the hereafter to effect a *passus interruptus.* Good ratings to the contrary, Tommy pronounced the fatuous show a stinker. But he got so involved in it that his two-year-old marriage suffered and then broke up.

In the ensuing divorce Tommy lost custody of the couple's only child, Thomas Bolyn Smothers IV, along with ownership of several buildings, 80 percent of his share in a music publishing firm, 40 percent of future royalties from ten record albums and $2500-a-month alimony. Tommy slapped his departing wife Stephanie three times the day he moved out of their Hollywood Hills home, which puts the price on slapping in Hollywood near the top of the market.

*The foregoing material is from "St. Thomas and the Dragon," by Richard Warren Lewis, *Playboy,* August 1969.

But CBS in general and Mike Dann in particular considered the brothers nice boys who might have considerable appeal for the 15-to-30 set. In the fall of 1966, the network placed *The Smothers Brothers Comedy Hour* opposite NBC's *Bonanza* at 9 P.M. on Sunday night. Judy Garland, Garry Moore and *Perry Mason* had all been chewed up by the unbeatable western; thus, as a midseason replacement, the Smothers brothers appeared to have bought a one-way ticket to oblivion. But Tommy, nursing an ulcer and facing heavy alimony payments, figured to take the money and run. He shrewdly held up CBS business vice-president Sal Iannucci for a 26-week contract—twice the usual contract span—and comforted himself with the idea that he would have at least six months at the CBS sugar tit. Surprisingly, Tommy and Dickie clicked and quickly garnered a prime-time audience of some 30 million viewers.

Remembering previous fights over television scripts, Tommy had demanded artistic control over the hour show. However, he discovered all too soon that despite "artistic" control, CBS was still in command; through its veto power, CBS could do pretty much as it pleased whenever it objected to material.

The Smothers brothers—and particularly Tommy, the acknowledged catalyst—were establishing themselves on the air at a time of one of the great clashes in American history. The Vietnam war had generated protest at home of alarming proportions, particularly among the young. Tommy and his brother represented youth. They saw what they considered hypocrisy in Washington, racism across the country and police brutality against antiwar demonstrators.

Tommy himself had taken his lumps from the police. Once, after a concert in Elkhart, Indiana, he argued with a concessionaire over the split of the proceeds. The money was earmarked for cancer research, and Tommy refused to give the man the excessive percentage he demanded. The amount in dispute: some $30. The concessionaire called the police. Strong words were exchanged and the two uniformed officers demanded that Tommy and Dickie come to the station house. "Suddenly, this cop yanked me out of my car by the sweater," Tommy explains, "crashed down with an eight-battery flashlight, opened my skull and was beating on me. I was on my back, bleeding like a pig. . . . Nine stitches were taken in my head. I never thought it could happen to *me*. But this is when I became aware that there was a legitimate police-brutality thing. I thought to myself: Hey, we were taught to believe that the policeman was our friend. Now I know better."

Tommy thrust himself and his show into the national debate over Vietnam with a series of outspoken comments that brought praise from those who had despaired of television's timidity, and hate mail and protest from the other side.

Even before *The Smothers Brothers Comedy Hour* got off the ground, Tommy had a disturbing prelude concerning innovation. He had let it be known that he wanted to give regular exposure to contemporary rock groups, whether or not they were widely known. Mike Dann warned that "original music is very dangerous on television. People in the mass television audience are more comfortable with familiar music, something they've heard two or three times before. The first time they hear a song, I don't care how good it is, they won't go for it."

By that test, one wonders how any song ever got heard the first time.

CBS had its own team of producers overseeing the show and booked a series of non–Smothers brothers-type guests. Folks like CBS stars Eva Gabor, Eddie Albert, Jack Benny, Ed Sullivan and Jim Nabors. Though CBS had picked the *Smothers Brothers* show in the first place because it sensed that a youthful show had a chance of beating *Bonanza,* now the network seemed to be stacking the cards against its own concept.

The first scratch of the censor's pencil was made on a comedy sketch with Barbara Eden of *I Dream of Jeannie.* She was to be a sex-education instructor and Tommy a college student, until CBS's program-practices department (read "censors") struck out the words "sex" and "sex education." Tommy was flabbergasted.

The men in charge of matters of taste were older and inclined to take a dim view of many words; for instance, such youth culture terms as "freak out." Complained Tommy: "To them, 'freak out' is a sexual thing. 'Let it all hang out' means let your cock hang out. And 'mind blowing' is pushing for psychedelics in drugs. They're all from 1942."

The first complete wipe-out came with a clever script on the critical topic itself—censorship—with Tommy and comedienne Elaine May. It went like this:

DICK: During the past year, movies have become more and more outspoken on adult subjects. After these movies have been completed and before they are shown to the general public, they must be examined by professional censors. These are dedicated people who have an eagle eye out to detect anything that might be considered in the least suggestive. Let's watch two of these guardians of public taste in action.

(Music: ending of movie)

ELAINE: I think the word breast should be cut out of the dinner scene. I think that breast is a relatively tasteless thing to say while you're eating. I wouldn't mind it if they were having cocktails or a late supper, but dinner is a family meal.

TOM: (makes note) "Take the word breast out of the dinner scene."

ELAINE: Tell them they can substitute the word "arm." It has the same number of syllables and it's a much more acceptable thing to say at the dinner table.

TOM: But won't that sound funny? "My heart beats wildly in my arm whenever you're near"?

ELAINE: Why? Oh, I see. You mean because . . .

TOM: The heart isn't in the arm.

ELAINE: Where *is* the heart, exactly? It's somewhere above the ribs, isn't it? On the left side?

TOM: Audrey, let's not kid ourselves. We're alone here. The heart is in the breast. I'm sorry, but that's the way it is.

ELAINE: No, no, that's all right, Ed. It's not your fault.

TOM: Well, there's no use crying over spilt milk. The heart, unfortunately, is still in the breast rather than the arm. So what do we do?

ELAINE: Can we change heart to pulse?

TOM: "My pulse beats wildly in my arm whenever you're near"?

ELAINE: Isn't there a pulse somewhere in the arm?

TOM: Not that I've noticed.

ELAINE: What about the wrist?

TOM: (excitedly) That's it!

TOM AND ELAINE: "My pulse beats wildly in my wrist whenever you're near."

ELAINE: Oh, that's marvelous.

TOM: I think that it's better than the original.

ELAINE: We could write as well as they do.

The CBS censors wasted no time debating that obvious slap at themselves. They blue-penciled the entire skit. Tommy's threat to walk off the set and spend the rest of the season in Spain became academic when a union strike shut down all live television shows in Hollywood.

Later, when the Smothers brothers knocked *Bonanza* out of the top ten, Tommy was able to get away with a few things. He assesses their limited accomplishments: "The most important thing we did that first year was to verify the fact that there was a legitimate grievance on the Vietnam war. We were the first show that said, 'Hey, man, the war is bad' and criticized Johnson from a public platform."

In an effort to build on the antiwar theme, Tommy planned to have Pete Seeger do "Waist Deep in the Big Muddy," a knock at President Johnson:

> Now every time I read the papers
> That old feelin' comes on.
> We're waist deep in the Big Muddy.
> And the big fool says to push on.

The CBS censors went "zip" and the song was deleted—despite Tommy's heated protests. This time the TV critics jumped on CBS and several months later Seeger was permitted to return and do the song in its entirety.

But then Tommy was told he was getting too "preachy"; if CBS wanted to send a message, it would hire Western Union. But Tommy persisted. For instance, he booked as many black entertainers as he possibly could. The brothers would also take an occasional crack at racists, including George Wallace. On one show Wallace was caricatured as a presidential hopeful—Sir George of Wallace—and, as played by David Frost, called Tommy and Dickie "pointy-headed intellectuals." Failing to pull a sword out of a stone, alluded to in the script in language with sexual overtones, Frost as Wallace said that total withdrawal was un-American.

CBS is well represented in the Bible Belt and all over the South.

Judging from the virulent mail, they had a lot of bigoted followers there and elsewhere.

A letter to the brothers from Hackensack, New Jersey, read: "Am surprised you lousey stinkers have lasted so long. I hope you get the nigger shit kicked out of you. Will come down and Butter your Motzahs with Arab shit."

From Canton, Ohio, a letter to "Gay Smothers Brothers" read: "Why do you queers continually show this so-called new generation? . . . I for one am fed up with looking at niggers, nigger-lovers and long-haired fruits on your and every other show on TV. But most of all, I disliked the remark about George Wallace."

On Mother's Day the boys planned to exhibit a Mother's Day card that said, in part: "War is not healthy for children and other living things. . . . I don't want candy or flowers. I want an end to the killing. We who have given life must be dedicated to preserving it. Please talk peace."

The network bore down. In killing the message, Mike Dann said: "There's no place [for that] in an entertainment show. . . . We do not permit political positions."

The card was distributed by a mothers' group in Los Angeles, most of them in show business. But the program-practices department explained in a memo that the recently formed mothers' group might possibly be subversive since it had not yet been cleared by the House Un-American Activities Committee. Shades of the 1950s.

There were many subsequent episodes, but the most serious involved a monologue by young comedian David Steinberg for the third season's October 27 show. Steinberg had already done the same monologue on NBC's *Tonight Show* without causing a furor. But perhaps that only proves that prime time on Sunday draws quite a different audience than a late-hour talk show.

In view of the censors' known attitudes, it's a wonder Steinberg was on at all. Someone must have been on vacation. For Steinberg stepped forth obsequiously and said:

Today's sermon deals with the exciting personality of Moses . . . who had a wonderful rapport with God, whom I'm sure you'll remember from last week's sermon. In these troubled times I am reminded of one of the great philosophic comments that has helped guide and mold the lives of millions. It was uttered by the mother superior in *The Sound of Music,* act two scene four, when she said to Julie Andrews, just before Miss Andrews was about to run off with the Nazi prince: "How do you solve a problem like Maria . . . how do you hold a moonbeam in your hand?"

Julie Andrews didn't understand that, and neither do I . . . and that's the point . . . people today no longer are able to communicate with one another; and without communication, there can be no harmony.

Moses was a man who knew how to communicate his feelings. The Bible tells us that Moses was wandering through the wilderness when he came upon a burning bush. And though the bush was burning, yet it did not consume itself. A voice came down to Moses: "Moses, take your shoes from your feet, for the land you are standing upon is holy land," God said in his redundant way. And Moses took his shoes off of his feet, approached the burning bush and burned his feet and yelled something to God.

We're not sure what he said, but there are many Old Testament scholars who to this day believe it was the first mention of Christ in the Bible.

And God said to Moses: "Go unto the Pharaoh and tell him to let your people go." Moses said: "Who shall I say sent me?"

God said: "Whom!" And God said: "I am that I am." And Moses turned his eyes to the heavens and said: "Thanks for clearing that up." And Moses went unto the Pharaoh and said: "Let my people go."

Pharaoh said to Moses: "Who sent you?" And Moses said: "You're not going to believe this . . ." Pharaoh didn't believe him. And so God destroyed all of the land with the mystical sense of humor that is only His.

Perhaps I can best illustrate my point with something I saw this evening. As I was on my way to the theater, I saw an old man I would take to be eighty to eighty-five years old. And this old man was being beaten badly by four little children. And I couldn't help but notice that one child was Negro, one was Jewish, one was Spanish and yet another, Italian.

Now . . . if these little children can learn to play together, then why can't the world? Thank you.

Minutes later—as Richard Lewis reported in his *Playboy* article—the CBS switchboards all over the nation lit up. The mail was overwhelmingly condemning and several letters mailed directly to the Smothers brothers' Hollywood offices contained razor blades. CBS in a memo said that Steinberg would never again deliver a sermonette on CBS and, further, that each Smothers brothers show would have to be reviewed in a closed-circuit screening by the affiliated stations—before the broadcast. No other show had so rigorous a preview.

Tommy's health was suffering as a result of the constant pressures. His skittish stomach was acting up; he was gaunt and underweight and had chewed his fingernails to the nub. Crank phone calls had become such a problem that he twice had to change his telephone number. But in a typical response to the censors, Tommy added a policeman called "Officer Judy" who watched the show broodingly, dashing forward to spray Mace in the eyes of those who shocked his Victorian values.

Tommy's anger grew when the network censored Joan Baez, the folk singer, letting her say only that her husband, David Harris, was going to jail. They cut her explanation that Harris had resisted selective service and her comment, "Anybody who lays it out in front like that generally gets busted, especially if you organize, which he did." Tommy was sure viewers would figure Harris was guilty of grand larceny or worse.

Inevitably, in this war between the Now and Then generations, there had to be a final confrontation. It happened in the spring of 1969—contract-renewal time at the network—and Robert Wood had just been installed as CBS-TV president. Later a courageous programer who promoted *All in the Family,* Wood wasn't ready to let Tommy Smothers dictate policy to CBS. In trying to appear strong, however, Bob Wood erred on the side of timidity.

Wood announced on March 14 that the *Comedy Hour* would be renewed for 26 weeks. He wasn't happy with the brothers' attitudes, but they were hot properties. Besides, Tommy had a couple of powerful friends making his case with Bob Wood. Mike Dann and Perry Lafferty, West Coast vice-president, frequently fought with Wood and with the CBS legal department to keep the boys on the air. One week before Wood announced the renewal, Mike Dann and Don Sipes, then CBS vice-president for business affairs, convinced Wood and the CBS management to extend the run of the show. But Tommy, nursing a number of gripes, stated that he hadn't decided whether he wanted the show on CBS next season. This led to a conference with Bob Wood during which a compromise was fashioned, a weak one from Tommy's point of view. Wood said he would consider Tommy's request that questionable items on future shows be resolved with a liberal bias.

It might all have blown over had Tommy not pressed his case. He took it on himself to go over Wood's head—not to Paley who had been friendly to the young comedian, but to the outside world. Conferring with senators Edward Kennedy and Alan Cranston in California, Tommy charged CBS with suppression. While the glad tidings were getting back to Wood, Tommy was traveling to Washington where he told his story to people attending the annual National Association of Broadcasters Convention. He also saw FCC commissioners Kenneth Cox and Nicholas Johnson who supported Tommy's view that affiliates' licenses would not be jeopardized if the Smothers show ran without prescreening by the network.

It was a particularly embarrassing moment for CBS to be trying to muzzle a performer. The network was engaged in a public debate with Rhode Island Senator John Pastore over the very same issue—censorship. Frank Stanton was carrying the cause for free speech against the Rhode Island Democrat who wanted to have a television-industry review board to prescreen the three networks for excessive sex and violence.

Stanton said, "An outside agency wielding the blue pencil would throttle the creative impulses which are essential to the continuing improvement of TV. The creators of our programs need encouragement and stimulation, not the reverse."

Seldom had CBS been so obviously of two minds on the same issue. Tommy was immensely pleased with Stanton's statement and wired him to say so. He then told the trade press that he was continuing on CBS so that his show would have a platform to continue to push for new standards of broadcast content.

Wood's reaction was prompt. He sent a telegram reading in part: "You are not free to use *The Smothers Brothers Comedy Hour* as a device to push for new standards. If you cannot comply with our standards the [show] cannot appear on CBS."

That was on March 27. On Wednesday, April 2, the program-practices men reviewed a format starring Dan Rowan of *Laugh-In*, black singer Nancy Wilson and their old nemesis, David Steinberg. Tommy was told he could keep Rowan's Fickle Finger of Fate Award for Senator Pastore and a parody of an integrated romance between

Tommy and Miss Wilson laced with Victor Herbert music. He would, however, have to delete the four-minute Steinberg sermonette.

Tommy, though unenthusiastic, dutifully cut the Steinberg item and on Thursday sent the prescreening tape by messenger to CBS in Los Angeles. Later Mike Dann heatedly denied that the tape arrived on Thursday: "The pressure was on to show it to the stations . . . Stanton promised that. I sat with a roomful of people in Bob Wood's office until nine o'clock on Thursday night and the tape never came. There was no reason he couldn't deliver that goddamned tape. None! None!"

That night Bob Wood telegraphed a letter of dismissal to Tommy. It charged, for one thing, that Tommy had failed to meet the *Wednesday* deadline for producing an acceptable tape. But there was no Wednesday deadline for producing an acceptable tape in Tommy's contract. The letter also charged that the Steinberg monologue was offensive. But the monologue had been removed as promised. It was later proved that CBS had the tape, altered and ready to screen, in its possession before Wood sent the dismissal notice.

Stanton confided to a New York reporter that the real reason Tommy and Dickie were axed was because they took their case to Washington. Name calling, even if it reaches the press, is forgiveable. But going to the Feds—whether the FCC or Congress—is not playing the game. The boys realized too late that Mike Dann was wrong in assuring them they were so big on the tube they wouldn't be canceled, no matter what.

The *Smothers Brothers* show was finished. Tommy and Dickie filed a lawsuit and eventually collected on their contract. In retrospect, the Smothers's fight with CBS seems almost childish—on both sides. It seems anachronistic in the context of the new morality. Today, the Smothers brothers' thrusts, if rebroadcast, would seem tame. But to a degree, the brothers, especially Tommy, were responsible for the new liberality. At the least, they were a breath of fresh air.

Congressman Thomas Rees of California summed it up well in a newsletter following the Wood dismissal: "For the life of me I just [can't] recall any rapings, nude scenes or killings on that show. Of course, the Smothers brothers weren't pure. They did spend a good part of their time knocking the establishment . . . The Smothers brothers show was not designed for 'everyman.' It was aimed at those in their teens, their 20s and their early 30s who are turned on by someone other than Lawrence Welk and who don't think of 'My country right or wrong' as the most profoundly sacred patriotic slogan ever uttered."

Tommy Smothers reflected on his firing four years later in a somewhat rueful interview in Beverly Hills. The old spirit was still evident in two printed messages framed and hung on the wall in the reception area outside his offices: "You have not converted a man because you have silenced him" and "To have great poets, there must be great audiences."

The high-tone rhetoric outside did not prepare the interviewer for the unpretentious, casually dressed figure inside. Tommy was informal and apparently relaxed, though he gave the impression of a bench sitter anxious to be tapped for relief play in the big game. He offered his own desk so that his visitor could take notes, and he willingly discussed his early relationship with Bill Paley.

In the beginning, he twice dealt with Paley directly. Then he learned that others in CBS were put off by his going to the top to get what he wanted. Once, he tried to talk with Paley about censorship problems but Paley refused to meet with him personally to discuss the matter. Thereafter he worked with subordinates whom he found likable. But he loves to tell an apocryphal story about the CBS West Coast chief, Perry Lafferty. Asked by a court clerk if he swears "to tell the whole truth and nothing but the truth, so help you, God?" Perry answers, "Just a minute, I'll get right back to you."

Still, Tommy remembers his dealings with CBS people with fondness. "I liked Paley. I liked Perry Lafferty and I liked Mike Dann. Whenever I dealt with CBS people directly everything was fine. But on a corporate level—forget it."

Tommy spoke as a man who missed all that went with being a star on CBS. His efforts to sell *The Best of the Smothers Brothers* were fruitless at the William Morris Agency. "They don't answer their telephone too often."

Being with CBS, says Tommy, "was the most exciting creative time of my life. I never thought twice about my decisions—politically or creatively. I felt I was instinctively right about selecting people—artists and writers."

He smiled that smile of his that is both shy and smug at the same time.

"As for the way it happened . . . it was pretty spectacular. We were the toast of the country. We didn't peter out either. When it happened I was more shocked than anybody. I had played it all by the rules. I considered myself a pretty heavyweight dude. And I miss the forum. But that's the dues you pay for the big ride. . . ."

The Smothers brothers have finally made it back to TV—but not at CBS. NBC is providing the vehicle and also holds the reins. The show is tame by comparison with the past. In an early segment, Tommy did a skit with his brother Dickie. Dickie plays a dog-lover and Tommy insists he has a pet cloud named Bob. It is a mild put-down of the intense feeling some people show for their pets. Hardly grist for a tough satirist's mill.

Critics have labeled the Smothers brothers' comeback a cop-out and it is certainly clear that producer Joe Hamilton has planned it that way. No longer in command, Tommy has explained his predicament to packed houses at Harrah's in Lake Tahoe:

"Some people think we had to cop out and make concessions and give up artistic integrity to get the show—and nothing could be closer to the truth. . . . We drive into NBC, and the gate guard says, 'Gimme your convictions and your beliefs,' and we check 'em, right there. And on the way out, they give them back to us."

CHAPTER 26
The Papp Flap

DURING A SOJOURN AT HIS VACATION HOME ON LYFORD CAY IN THE Bahamas, Bill Paley reviewed an upcoming CBS attraction called *Sticks and Bones*. The show had been recorded at Black Rock on half-inch videotape and then shipped to Lyford Cay so the Chairman could view it some time before the show was to air on Friday night, 9 to 11 P.M., March 9, 1973.

As the Chairman sat in the serenity of his island sanctuary, David Rabe's stark drama of the return of a blinded and embittered Vietnam war veteran unfolded. Paley didn't sit quietly for long. The veteran is so unrelenting in his rancor that his exasperated father, an emotionally unstable man, hands the younger man a razor and suggests suicide.

Paley has said of television, "It goes right into the household. We have to be conscious of that always." In the Chairman's view, it is important to lead the national television audience to new experiences, but equally important not to get too far ahead of the public taste. This time, Paley was convinced that network president Bob Wood had gone too far.

Not only was the Chairman appalled by what he saw on the screen, he was also conscious of the timing. Executives back in New York had scheduled it in time for Emmy award consideration, hoping for a statuette or two. Paley was more concerned about the fact that the broadcast was scheduled for the very time that American prisoners of war would be returning home from Hanoi. Paley was "livid" according to reports that reached Mike Dann, one-time CBS program chief. Dann said that Paley felt the production should never have been scheduled in the first place.

One Black Rock observer thought that in Paley's absence Frank Stanton should have acted to squelch the idea before the play was taped and in the can. Presumably Stanton could have stopped *Sticks and Bones* had he chosen to, since programing matters with political overtones were his province. But this time he did not exert his authority. Stanton was a lame duck on the verge of retirement, his authority waning.

Paley's negative reaction to the drama was confirmed across the nation when the affiliated stations were given a prebroadcast screening. At least 65 of the network's 220 television affiliates let it be known that if CBS insisted on broadcasting the play they would substitute other programing for the two hours.

Variety reports that CBS thereupon "caved in," took the drama out of the March schedule, leaving Bob Wood to do the explaining. After all, it was Wood who made "the mistake" of scheduling the work in the first place, according to Frank Stanton, who happens to be a Bob Wood admirer.

Explaining to the press was a sticky but manageable proposition. CBS was, of course, castigated for bowing to affiliate pressure. Les Brown in *Variety* said the decision had demolished CBS's hard-won reputation for courage in reporting Watergate. But *Variety* was only read by the trade.

Explaining to Joseph Papp was something else again. A prolific and highly acclaimed theatrical producer, Papp had contracted with CBS to provide quality drama, and *Sticks and Bones* was one of his first offerings. Life inside the theater and out had always been a struggle for the scrappy, iconoclastic Papp. Born in 1921 and raised in the tough Williamsburg section of Brooklyn, Papp had to work in a laundry at night to help support his family while attending high school.

After a World War II stint in the navy, he studied acting and directing at the Actors' Laboratory Theater in Hollywood and rose to become its managing director. Later Papp came back to New York. Like many another aspiring director, he used his free time to produce shoestring dramas in the basement of a church on Manhattan's Lower East Side—part of a theatrical movement called "Off Broadway."

His next stop was New York City's Central Park. He persuaded Parks Commissioner Robert Moses to let him produce free Shakespeare at the outdoor theater on Belvedere Lake. Moses allowed Papp to run the shows for a while, then arbitrarily called the whole business to a halt. If Papp wanted to continue, he would have to charge admission and assign 10 percent of the gross to cover the cost of grass erosion.

While Moses was a giant figure in politics and could cow mayors, governors, and even presidents, he was no match for Joe Papp. At five-foot-nine and just 147 pounds, Papp was a heavyweight when it came to either a private argument or a public debate. After the producer aired his views in visits to newspaper offices and seats of power, the public began to side with Papp. Finally Moses capitulated, after demanding from the city's board of estimate $20,000 for grass erosion. (Someone sent the outraged commissioner bags of grass seed.) Two New Yorkers put up the money and the Shakespeare Festival was back on the grass.

The critics were generally favorable, but the unfriendly ones Papp could devastate with a few vitriolic words. Papp became the talk of the town. One person who heard the talk was Bob Wood, who was seeking ways to recapture for CBS some of the prestige it had held in the 1950s as producer of serious theater. As Joseph Papp's biographer, Stuart W. Little, puts it, "CBS grabbed Papp just as Broadway sometimes imports a London hit—by shopping on the outside."

Wood, programing chief Freddy Silverman and others on the staff negotiated Papp's four-year eight-million-dollar contract which called for thirteen dramatic specials.

It was clear to CBS from the beginning that Papp would be a problem to handle, despite the financial security the CBS contract offered him. The maverick producer had never been comfortable with corporate types. In fact, Papp's last employer—before he became an independent producer—had fired him 15 years earlier for invoking the Fifth Amendment 12 times before the House Un-American Activities Committee. Papp refused to say whether he had been a communist and refused to name names. The employer who dismissed him: CBS. The matter went to arbitration and Papp was reinstated. It was his CBS salary, as an assistant producer, that paid the rent and fed the Papp family during some of the years he worked without pay to create for New Yorkers a free Shakespeare theater.

As the new reigning monarch of New York City theater, Papp was anything but deferential when he returned to CBS. Though the CBS people had expected Papp to be difficult, they did not expect him to be as difficult as he turned out to be. Silverman, who was still in his twenties when he began remolding CBS Saturday morning television for the kiddies (*Scooby Doo Where Are You?* was a typical effort), has exceptional taste, enthusiasm and an open mind. Silverman, a Jew, married his secretary, a Catholic, and provided one of the nicest off-camera scenes in CBS history as the show-biz types—men in mod suits and women in false eyelashes—filled the church on one side and the sedate Catholics in Sunday best filled the other to watch dual ceremonies.

In the early discussions with Papp, CBS agreed that to get his Shakespeare—updated comedies with obvious commercial appeal, proven popular in Central Park, as well as the somber *Hamlet*—CBS must also take his contemporary offerings. These included strong new plays by such writers as Jason Miller *(That Championship Season)* and David Rabe.

Papp so irritated Silverman with his dictatorial tone in their first meeting that the two almost broke off the relationship. The plump, genial Silverman recalls: "I almost threw him out of the office. I said, 'I don't work for you! Don't treat me like an office boy!' From that point on, we had a good relationship."

Good, that is, until CBS pulled the plug on *Sticks and Bones.* When Bob Wood phoned Papp with the news that the show was being postponed, Papp fumed. He told the press the move was "cowardly" and a "direct attack on the First Amendment guarantees of free speech."

Bob Wood spoke to Papp, asking him to "consider our corporate position." Papp wasn't much interested. Then, in a more intelligent approach, Wood pointed out that the show would play later, that it was only postponed until after the POWs were home and national emotions calmed.

But Papp still felt he had to take strong action. Otherwise, he said later, "it's all press agentry." He told Wood that if the show did not go on as scheduled, he would have no further relationship with CBS. There was no way he could be forced to produce shows when the spirit of his contract had been broken.

Papp saw *Sticks and Bones* as a desperately needed examination of America's conscience and said that CBS should broadcast it immediately even if only the five CBS-owned stations carried it. Wood ended the conversation saying CBS had the greatest respect for Papp's work. Papp told Wood, "I have no respect for yours" if the show doesn't go on. That same afternoon, *Time* and *Newsweek* published reviews of screenings of the show, both praising it highly. But there was no show in prospect.

Joe Papp took an ad in *The New York Times* the following Monday, headlined, "The Show You Didn't See Last Week," which quoted from both the *Time* and *Newsweek* raves. Also featured was a quote from Lawrence Rhodes, manager of the CBS affiliate WHEN-TV in Syracuse: "I wanted it. Dammit, it's real. Life isn't just a bowl of cherries."

Bob Wood offered the official explanation in a telegram to affiliate owners saying the play would not be welcomed by an American public "emotionally dominated by the return of the POWs" and other Vietnam veterans.

Joe Papp did not buy that argument. In an interview, he said: "The best time to see the show was when the vets were coming back. It was perfect timing. We didn't plan it that way. They scheduled it, not I. As I understand it, the old man said no. In fact, I think he hated it. Paley's panic was transferred to the stations. I feel a lot of it emanated from CBS itself. A reporter from Chicago called and said, 'Do you think this happened all by itself?' I said, 'How *did* it happen?' and he said, 'I can't tell you.' "

Papp wound up totally disenchanted with CBS but philosophic about the workings of a corporation:

"You listen to them and they sound like human beings. But I know full well what it is like to be in a corporation. I liked Fred Silverman . . . and everybody else. But they fade away!"

Papp saved his full anger for his letter of resignation, aimed at Bob Wood:

Dear Bob:

I don't have to write this sentence, but I want to let you know how shabbily you CBS people conduct human affairs; having become desensitized to fraudulent behavior, you proceed through life collecting your wages, finding no contradiction in the face which appears before you in the mirror every morning, avoiding your own eyes, which you must if you are not to cut your throat; finding ersatz substitutes for the real thing which has long disappeared with your honor and your vestige of decency which may at one time have been of some concern to you and your colleagues. I bid you all a fond farewell and leave you to your worm-eaten consciences.

When the show was finally broadcast on Friday, August 17, 1973, it certainly must have been anticlimactic for the participants if not for some members of the audience. In all, 94 CBS affiliates shunned the show. And when CBS's own St. Louis station turned it down, the St. Louis NBC affiliate carried it. Few advertisers wanted to touch it, and ad support in New York was limited to local stores or national brands using only the local station.

To some, it seemed that CBS was right, at least on dramatic grounds. There were those who said the show's production values weren't up to par, that the story line was episodic. Papp said that he thought the production lent itself to TV rather than to the stage where it was originally mounted. But it had been cut for TV and the producer conceded that this might have hurt the drama to a degree.

CBS for its part seems to have proved that affiliated station owners are unlikely to accept rough shows once the company suggests that it is not 100 percent behind them. The network got a black eye as the result of its off-again-on-again approach. It would probably have been wiser to allow the public to judge in March. If the viewers were unhappy, they could have switched channels.

Perhaps, as some critics implied, CBS's strong stand on Watergate and its subsequent unpopularity in the White House was a factor in the decision not to rain on Nixon's prisoner of war parade.

Ironically, as CBS was taking its knocks for faintheartedness on *Sticks and Bones*, it was also getting editorial support here and there for its decision to rerun two controversial *Maude* episodes produced by the independent Norman Lear. In the two episodes the matronly

Maude discovers she is pregnant and chooses not to have the child. The Right-to-Life people who, right or wrong, are loud in their opposition to abortion, were caught with their defenses down when the two episodes were first shown. But they were ready with bags of critical mail for the reruns.

This time CBS stuck to its guns, aborting the matron and not the mission.

CENSORSHIP

postscript

Some things—not all—come full wish. CBS is planning to televise sometime in 1975 the story of one of its craven moments.

The network deserves credit for the decision, however belated, to produce a two-hour drama of John Henry Faulk's battles with Aware, Inc., blacklisters in the *Red Channel* years. He was a talk-show emcee and radio regular on WCBS but lost his sponsor and was fired in the debacle. Faulk sued for $3.5 million in libel and wound up with $175,000. After legal fees of $100,000 and repayments of loans to Edward R. Murrow, David Susskind and others, there was nothing left. Faulk is farming in Madisonville, Texas, and drives to Dallas on weekends to do a radio talk show. His promising career as a radio big-timer was busted, however.

PART FIVE
THE HERE AND NOW

CHRONOLOGY

AFTER WILLIAM PALEY DENIES FRANK STANTON THE CHAIRMANSHIP OF CBS in 1966 by staying on after retirement age, strains begin to develop between the two top CBS executives. Stanton, however, continues to represent both CBS and the entire industry in congressional and FCC hearings.

...In 1967 CBS announces a $1-million contribution to the Corporation for Public Broadcasting after Frank Stanton testifies in Washington in support of a strong noncommercial broadcasting service. Good PR and enlightened self-interest.

...In 1967 CBS brings Arthur Miller's *The Crucible* to television as a special, and also *Mark Twain Tonight* with Hal Holbrook playing the acerbic, irreverent writer.

...In 1968 Red Skelton celebrates his 15th anniversary at CBS-TV, but his show, and several others with yearly escalator clauses, is becoming only marginally profitable.

...In 1968 a CBS documentary, *Hunger in America*, begins with a shot of a child dying of starvation and deals with the shortcomings of

315

government food programs. The show causes a Senate inquiry, and later an additional $200 million is voted for U. S. food programs.

. . .CBS and television generally are criticized in 1968 for too much coverage of city and campus riots and antiwar protests. Says Stanton: "It is a sad case of the bearer of bad tidings being confused with the author, and brings to mind those dark days of 35 years ago when newspapers were first blamed for the Great Depression."

. . .On February 17, 1969, blunt Bob Wood begins his surprising reign as president of the CBS Television Network. He proves to be a strong man. Under Wood the rural shows are replaced with radically different programs like *All in the Family.*

. . .In 1969 Frank Stanton defends network news against criticism of then-Vice President Spiro T. Agnew, pointing out that the death of liberty begins with efforts to control the news media.

. . .Walter Cronkite gives his special brand of reporting to the moon landing in 1969, remarking at the moment of boot to dust: "Man on the moon! . . . Man finally standing on the surface of the moon. My golly!"

. . .In 1971 the FCC forces CBS to divest itself of its cable television and syndication activities. They become Viacom International.

. . .Simon and Garfunkel, two of Columbia Records' biggest stars, cut an album entitled *Bridge Over Troubled Waters* and sell nearly 7.5 million worldwide. It is the first Columbia album to outsell *My Fair Lady. Bridge* adds to the reputation of record division president Clive Davis, a lawyer with a flair for personal publicity.

. . .In 1972 CBS acquires Steinway & Sons, world's foremost manufacturer of fine pianos, founded in New York in 1853 by a cabinetmaker from Germany. Steinway Hall, on 57th Street, had a studio on the top floor used by an infant broadcast company in the late 1920s—CBS.

. . .In 1972 CBS pulls ahead of NBC for the first time in television specials, with 59 to NBC's 53. CBS also wins eight Emmys for specials, to NBC's seven.

. . .In 1972 CBS has 27,842 employees and net income reaches $82.9 million.

...With considerable regret Frank Stanton retires on March 31, 1973. Eric Sevareid, the *CBS Evening News* pundit, says: "Stanton was always the backstop, and in a crisis, the front line. . . ." Frank Stanton leaves with a mixed image, some calling him a glorified clerk, a coldly calculating man who loves things more than people.

...After the Memorial Day weekend 1973, CBS charges Clive Davis with using $100,000 of CBS money for personal expenses. Davis is marched out of Black Rock with an escort of two CBS security men.

...In 1973 CBS net profits are $92,963,000.

...CBS, which clamored for the White House tapes, sued Vanderbilt in 1973 to prevent the university's unauthorized taping and editing of the *CBS* (Cronkite) *Evening News*. The tapes were for scholars not profit though Vanderbilt charged users a fee. The university had previously turned down a royalty-free license from CBS that precluded editing and fees. The matter is in the courts.

...In 1974 CBS's lead in Saturday morning children's programing—"kidvid"—is challenged by the other networks for the first time in years, while the "educational" *Captain Kangaroo* continues its 20-year run in the 8 A.M. weekday slot. CBS kidvid is also under attack from Action for Children's Television, a consumer-activist group once called by Broadcast Group president John Schneider "the enemy." ACT's complaints about rampant commercialism—netting CBS millions every year from such sponsors as sugar-coated cereals—force the network to reduce commercial time from a peak of 16 minutes per hour.

...In the spring of 1974, *All in the Family* is television's number-one evening program and *The Waltons* is number two, as CBS Television claims nine of the top ten prime-time shows.

...But by early 1975, NBC gives CBS its first real race for the ratings title in several years. Nevertheless, CBS ranks first in prime time, with eight of the top ten shows.

...In 1975 the phenomenal Mary Tyler Moore (MTM Productions) has six regular series on CBS, including her own show.

...An investor who bought 100 shares of CBS stock when it was first quoted over-the-counter in 1932 at $90 a share would have 13,746 shares worth $682,832.55 in the spring of 1975 (including 1925 shares of Viacom). Bill Paley owns 1,683,337 CBS shares (1975 figures); Leon Levy, his brother-in-law, owns 330,756; and Frank Stanton 335,175. The stock is priced at 49 5/8 (May 12, 1975).

...Bill Paley's dividend payout at $1.46 a share is $2,457,672.02 a year, approximately five times his entire investment in 1928.

CHAPTER 27
Congratulations, Mike—
You're Fired

THE BEVERLY HILLBILLIES, PETTICOAT JUNCTION, GOMER PYLE, *Mayberry RFD, The Andy Griffith Show.*

Today they're gone. All these corn-fed hit shows disappeared from CBS Network programing in the early 1970s and now are seen only as reruns. If you feel a great sense of loss, then you may be a rural at heart, even if you live in the city.

As such, you are a soldier in the huge army of hinterland viewers that CBS wooed and won during the reign of James T. Aubrey as network president. But when Aubrey was dumped in 1965, the hillbilly programing concept wasn't dumped with him. Mike Dann, who was senior vice-president for programing after Aubrey left, saw little need to change things.

Dann is a short, peppery and extremely amusing man. Says one personal friend, "Mike would have made a first-rate stand-up comic on the borscht circuit. He entertains at parties with screwball monologues; he loves to tell 'When I was on the Coast with Judy Garland' stories. He manages to play a mediocre game of tennis, though the most agile part of his anatomy is certainly his mouth. He's a gutsy, wisecracking, outrageous little bastard."

Dann lasted in the top echelon of CBS management almost twice as long as most of his associates and to do so changed an average of 30 percent of the CBS prime-time schedule each year. Among his best vehicles were *The Mary Tyler Moore Show*, an adult comedy that admitted that single girls nowadays sometimes have affairs. He was also responsible for Peter Falk's *Trials of O'Brien*, and more specials than CBS had had in years—including a distinguished production of *Death of a Salesman*. Dann thus made up for his frustration under Aubrey who hated the revenue-draining specials. Dann claims to have fought many battles with his predecessor, among them one to get *The Defenders* on the air and then to keep that show about a father-and-son lawyer team before the viewers.

Basically, though, Mike Dann survived through a combination of skill, a taste for middle-America vulgarity and his occasional touches of class. Most important, he never posed a serious threat to "No. 1." He didn't want to be network president and he knew he would never make it anyway. Thus, as an astute politician, a tough customer, an able executive, ambitious but not overreaching, Dann was also an amusing guy to have around. He seemed to have had a personal association of sorts with Bill Paley, though this evaluation was Dann's and like a lot of other Mike Dann assertions is a little hard to confirm.

Dann's reluctance to write memos, committing his opinions to paper, was famous at CBS. That way he could change his mind in a hurry to go along with the boss without incriminating evidence in the file. This trait earned him the nickname "The Weathervane" among sardonic associates. There is a story that once after Paley and Dann screened a new show together, the Chairman pronounced himself happy with what he had seen. Dann whipped out a memo, one of his few, in praise of the series. In another pocket—just in case—Dann had a memo recommending that the show be dumped. True or not, the story appeared in *Time* magazine and Paley called him on the carpet.

Dann was so sensitive to the shifting winds that he cultivated a talent for reading upside down the memos he spotted on other executives' desks. Once when Aubrey and Dann were both on the Coast, a playful executive put a terse note on the desk of the West Coast chief. Mike walked in, his eyes fell on the note and he was visibly shaken to read: "See me about Mike Dann's severance. JTA [Aubrey]."

Mike Dann long ago concluded that the masses liked escapist television, not realist. He made no effort to apologize for what he knew was the low estate of the medium's light entertainment, especially the half-hour prime-time sitcom of which CBS was the acknowledged leader. He once joked to affiliate station owners—sardonically called "filling-station operators" in the trade—that the coming fall season would bring more of the "same old crap." A retired CBS executive said of that remark, "I thought it was unfunny and irresponsible—especially since it *was* more of the same old crap!"

Dann believed that the public would buy the same old crap indefinitely. His guiding principle: Renew anything that ranks high enough in the standings to produce a shower of profits.

It was a sound businesslike rule for light entertainment and one that was standard for the industry—until Robert Wood became Mike's boss as president of the network in 1969. Wood, a man of tailored suits and untailored speech, was anxious to set off in a new direction. His earnestness and his bullet-headed pugnacious look belie the man, who is a delightful, mild person of good taste. Unlike previous presidents who spoke in cultivated tones and careful phrases, Wood mixes metaphors outrageously, speaking inelegantly and bluntly. Though no intellectual, he has a very quick mind and it is said that he mastered the complexities of running the network faster than any of his more polished predecessors. The network chief, who came up through sales, saw his job as "that of a pilot of a ship negotiating between the rocks in the East River with the currents rolling on the left, right, underneath, ahead. . . . There is no such thing as a public, per se. . . . There are pressure groups here and there. I wouldn't like it if this job weren't controversial. It proves there are people out there and that they care about TV—that it's making an impression."

Wood soon discovered the glamour of innovative show business beat the ho-hum of business-as-usual. He began taking a firm hand in programing and worried about growing advertiser disenchantment with the rural fodder. In the early years CBS had signed up as many affiliates on channel 2 as possible, because that channel reaches farther into the countryside than the others do. But the rural thrust now delivered a disproportionate number of older viewers, people whose prime spending years were behind them. And besides, the CBS lead with the mass audience was beginning to slip.

In February 1970, for the first time in many, many years, CBS was behind NBC in the all-important yearly race to get the most viewers in the golden evening hours—so far behind that, statistically speaking, CBS seemed to be out of the race. Weeks earlier, the NBC lead was so commanding that Les Brown wrote in *Television: The Business Behind the Box:* "Theoretically it was still possible for CBS to catch up and even overtake, but it was hard to imagine how." The figures showed that 17 weeks into the season, CBS was down a total of 500 million viewers vis-à-vis NBC. To overcome that advantage, CBS would have to attract 2.4 million more viewers than NBC in every one of the 49 half-hours of prime viewing time each week for the seven weeks left in the official 1969–70 season.

On February 19 Brown got a call from Mike Dann, who mysteriously told Les to keep the date April 24 open for lunch. The date fell in the last week of the 1969–70 television rating season.

Dann was about to unleash an all-out effort to overcome the seemingly insuperable NBC lead. His wild manipulations would vastly alter the nation's viewing in the next seven weeks and determine whether or not CBS commanded its usual premium prices with the advertisers. For the network that won the ratings race got the best prices for its shows the following season.

Dann was worth watching. And as usual watching would be easy, for Mike Dann played the press like a violin. Teasing, hinting, announcing and retorting, he kept CBS in the limelight, grabbing news space even when he had no story.

His counterpart at NBC, in style if not in rank, was Paul Klein, a hard-nosed, somewhat junior ratings expert who loved to snipe away at Dann for his shrewd press-agentry. Klein, a man as combative as Dann, would launch his spears directly at his targets, through the mails and not through the press, and his target, often as not, was Dann. His shots were so vitriolic that they sometimes made his outraged victim howl to reporters. Sometimes, to his employer's distress, this made Klein the unofficial spokesman for NBC—for the press, like nature, abhors a vacuum.

Paul Klein is a big, appealing man with an ungainly build who does not wear suits easily. He has the face of a butcher and the earthy vocabulary of a jockey who did not win, place or show. But while his language is salty, his mild delivery makes it seem almost innocuous.

When Mike Dann told a New York columnist in mid-1969 that CBS was buying *Get Smart,* thus rescuing it from the NBC scrap heap, Klein was jubilant. Mike had denigrated the show all during its previous season on NBC. The once-popular series, starring Don Adams as a bubble-headed spy, Agent 86 (bartenders' code for "Don't serve him, he's drunk"), was lagging badly when NBC gave it up.

Each week *Get Smart* began with Agent 86 (real name, Maxwell Smart) entering a phone booth to dial a number that caused him to drop through a trapdoor into headquarters where a set of sliding doors slammed against his nose. He and Agent 99, his sexy female companion, Barbara Felton, were pitted against the sinister forces of CHAOS.

Klein regarded the ratings race as a necessary evil but downgraded its importance whenever he could. It was Klein who argued against the NBC consensus in 1968, insisting that *Julia* be put into the network lineup against CBS's popular *Red Skelton Show.* Starring Diahann Carroll, *Julia* wouldn't win against Skelton, but it would be one of the first situation comedies to star a black person at a time when the networks were heavily criticized as lily white. The show was an attractive, though saccharine, portrait of a widowed nurse striving to raise a young son. Klein not only made points with *Julia,* but the show was a surprising ratings success.

Mike Dann's *Get Smart* gambit struck the acidic Klein as especially obvious and crass. "He planned to hype the sweep. I know. I invented the idea," said Klein.

Some background in the ratings process is necessary for an understanding of what Klein had in mind. The ratings race is a multifaceted contest for network superiority. It begins as a daily mechanical affair that simply tallies the number of TV sets in a select sample of households and records what the set is tuned to, when, and for how long. The sample, "scientifically" set up by the A.C. Nielsen Company of Chicago, comprises a mere 1200 houses, whose sets are equipped with meters that constantly monitor programs. If the set is blazing away, watched only by the cat and the cuckoo clock, well, that's the chance Nielsen—and the viewing public—has to take.

Mercifully, there is more to it than that. This preliminary "head count," which gives the networks their initial overnight results, becomes half of the data for a biweekly study. The other half comes from diaries kept by members of 2300 television households across the country. The diaries give results in terms of demographics: the age and sex of those actually watching the home screen. What the networks learn from this is how many of the nation's heaviest spenders—those in their late teens through their forties—are watching the tube. There is relatively little interest in the viewing habits of small children and old folks since both groups have little to spend, or so goes the mythology. The two types of data are collated and published in a biweekly "pocket piece," so named because the booklet is small enough to slip easily into the time salesmen's inside coat pockets. These Nielsen results largely determine what shows the public will see and which ones get the axe.

It costs a lot to collect this information and most local stations cannot afford to pay for it on a regular basis. Thus Nielsen conducts several four-week "sweeps" for the local stations each year. The locals use the data as a basis for deciding how much they can charge national advertisers for local "spots."

The networks analyze the sweeps to prove they are doing a good job for their affiliated stations and there is always the temptation to schedule strong stuff—to "hype" or "hypo" (give it a hypodermic) the sweep so the affiliated stations will look better competitively.

The sweeps take place mainly in the fall, winter and spring. Thoughtful viewers will recall that some of the year's best viewing occurs during two of the sweeps, one that appears four weeks prior to Thanksgiving, and another over four weeks in February and March. The third sweep, in May, seldom brings forth blockbuster programing because the big advertising money is already committed and the networks are offering reruns.

But the November sweep, appropriately hyped, might bring the network a point or two advantage for the month-long survey. This would reap a golden harvest to individual affiliates, worth millions of dollars on a nationwide basis. The various network affiliates are slicing up a big pie. Spot advertising brought local stations $1.6 billion in 1974. Thus the networks are under enormous pressure from the affiliates to hype. They tend to bow to this pressure. In 1974, for instance, NBC scheduled *The Godfather* in two segments during the November sweep and CBS and ABC cried foul. NBC was clearly "hypoing the sweep."

When Mike Dann bought *Get Smart* for the 1969–70 season, he had the same idea in mind. For the writers had planned a buildup to the birth of Agent 86's and Agent 99's first offspring for the November

'69 sweep. It must be acknowledged that—cheap sophistry or no—private eyes don't often give birth, on or off television.

Maybe not Blessed, but at least it would be an Event.

Klein quickly warmed to his task. His series of letters to Mike Dann, made famous in the trade by Les Brown, had begun when Dann was quoted as saying, "Fame is the name of the game." Klein clipped the article and scrawled simply, and mildly for Klein, "You are scum."

The profanity came later as the press warmed to the contest between the humorously quotable Dann on the one hand and the epithetically talented Paul Klein on the other. "I called him, maybe, son of a bitch, or maybe bastard. . . . Later I got tougher," says Klein.

The *Get Smart* exchanges began when the show failed to do well in the early season ratings. Klein had clipped out a Dann remark to a columnist that *Get Smart* was "critical" and that the results could either win Dann further tenure at CBS or cause him to lose out completely.

Klein made a homemade funeral card, attached the clipping to it and mailed it to Dann. But thereafter *Get Smart* picked up substantially, and Dann bragged to the press once again that his wisdom had been confirmed by the viewing public. Klein was still convinced that the spurt reflected only the forthcoming blessed event. Taking his cue from the then-current ad campaign for the movie *Rosemary's Baby*, he sent Dann a note saying, simply, "Pray for Mike Dann's baby." Mike wrote back that Klein needn't worry about his ability to feed his children. Gleeful that Dann had apparently missed the point, Klein answered that he wasn't worried about Mike's *feeding* his kids but rather the possibility that he might *eat* them.

The *Smart* babies—they turned out to be twins—were born to high ratings as Dann had predicted and, safely wrapped in diapers, they lost the audience. Viewers began ho-humming the series and the ratings dropped as Klein had predicted.

But Dann, fully prepared, put *Get Smart* on ice. For weeks he had been working on the most spectacular hype of his career; it amounted to a frantic effort to catch and pass NBC and thus avoid losing the entire season, not just the sweep periods. It would have been his first loss in 12 years with CBS.

On March 4, Dann made another call to Les Brown of *Variety*, asking Les to come to his office so that he could explain his mysterious telephone call of February 19. It's a scene beautifully described in Brown's book, *Television: The Business Behind the Box.*

Bleary-eyed from lack of sleep, Dann explained that since January 10 he had been involved in something he called "Operation 100"—the 100 days left in the season after January 10. (The season ended April 19, 1970.) He had been working from seven in the morning until midnight every day since January 10 and showed Les three kinds of pills he was taking to stay with it.

With Bob Wood's approval, Dann was trying to catch NBC and using every trick in the business to do it. He had brainstormed with every programing man on both coasts seeking ideas that would top NBC. In his book Brown quotes Dann on his technique:

We had to build up the regular shows wherever we could. Like Sullivan, that's one you can hype with better acts. Then grab some good specials . . . to replace our weakest shows. And somehow build up the movies. You know why we were losing? Mostly because we had lousy movie titles, and NBC had good ones.

We had only one thing going for us. We knew that NBC was asleep, figuring itself the winner, and we could counterprogram the shit out of them. You should see what those programing kids of mine did. They're beautiful.

Dann showed Brown a list of suggestions his "kids," and himself, had come up with:

"If we push, I think we can put together a special Sullivan show featuring the Beatles live or on tape. We can also use the other stars doing Beatle material."—Irwin Segelstein

"Red Skelton likes the idea of Tiny Tim, and we have booked him."—Marty Dooling

"Although *Hatari* [John Wayne] has been run twice on ABC, each time on a single night, I think with the proper promotion we can make it an excellent two-parter that will work on Thursday and Friday nights."—Mike Marden

"We should get Dick Van Dyke to host *Born Free.* His presence will give it a sense of importance that showing the film alone may not have. If not Van Dyke, Fred MacMurray."—Irwin Segelstein

"Although *Peyton Place* was played out on ABC in the series, I still think with promotion it would do well for us as a two-parter."—Mike Marden

"Buy *African Queen*. It was in syndication for seven years and played a dozen times on local stations. It has been resting for nine years, and I think we can get it cheap from Sam Spiegel."—Mike Filerman

"O.K., it's done. All in-season repeats for Gleason will be *Honeymooners*."—Tom Loeb

"I think I can buy Paul Newman & Joanne Woodward feature *New Kind of Love* in time for use this season. I'll let you know in a day or so."—Bob Daly

"I just talked to Phil on the Coast. We think we can get Dick Van Dyke to plug *Campbell* and *Mission* in his *Born Free* wraparounds."—Jim Rogers

"I talked to Glen Campbell and he promises to book a special show—big acts—following the *Born Free* showing. This could give him as big a share as he's ever had."—Perry Lafferty

"Robert Young's *Eskimo: Fight for Life* is great. . . . We can buy it from the National Science Foundation."—Mike Dann

"Following *Cinderella* Friday 4/3 make a family evening by running Don Knotts special."—Fred Silverman

It was clear from the suggestions that Mike Dann planned to beat NBC at what had always been the other network's game—the use of specials for big ratings against shows that would seem less attractive by comparison. *Get Smart* and another loser in the schedule, *The Tim Conway Comedy Hour*, were preempted seven times out of seven, and other weak shows also got bumped several times.

The results were impressive. *Born Free* pulled a 34.2 rating or the rough equivalent of 40 million viewers and for a two-hour period got 53 percent of the viewing public.

Hatari, running on consecutive days with John Wayne as its star, got 38 percent of the viewing audience on its first night and 41 percent the second, better than it had done originally on ABC. The Duke was still very big.

African Queen, already 20 years old and a replay that had been seen again and again on local television, was picked up at bargain rates—$225,000 for the first showing and $100,000 for the second. An ordinary motion picture shown the first time on TV then cost about $800,000—whether good or bad. But Katharine Hepburn and Humphrey Bogart, with plenty of help from the promotion men at CBS, didn't age. *The African Queen* drew one of the best audiences of the year with about 30 million viewers.

Dann played a couple of Andy Griffith specials, then the Harlem Globetrotters, and to shore up the Friday night weaknesses of *Get Smart* and *Tim Conway*, documentaries with titles like *The Trail of the Feathered Serpent, Savage Waters, Savage Beast* and *The Incredible Auto Race.*

Not everything succeeded for Dann as well as the movies did, but enough scored so that CBS was able to project that the season would be won with an average of 0.3. Then suddenly Paul Klein and the other NBC programing people announced that their television season would end a month early, on March 22. That was about the time CBS would catch up to, but not pass, NBC. The idea, according to Klein, was that nearly 40 percent of the remaining schedule would be in reruns.

Says Les Brown, "I was afraid Dann would go out of his thirty-fourth-floor window."

But Mike Dann had his final triumph—CBS claimed victory, and the victory, though tissue-thin, seemed real in the industry. Jack Gould then interviewed the three network presidents and all three denied a rating competition. This led Les Brown to write that the rating war embarrassed the network presidents. "It was a little like street fighting, and they wanted to represent themselves as being above that. They denounced it and yet persisted in taking part."

At the end of the monumental contest, CBS's Jay Eliasberg indulged in a slap at NBC, singling out Paul Klein. In a speech to California broadcasters, Jay made light of Paul Klein's earlier barbs at CBS, suggesting that Klein and NBC couldn't beat CBS due to a kind of impotence.

That produced Paul Klein's epithetical monument, not suitable for quoting here. He dictated a letter to Eliasberg, with copies slated for Paley and Stanton, in which he made his own inference about CBS, and particularly, Eliasberg—in a one-word gutter reference to oral sex. Klein's secretary took the letter down in its entirety and typed it up, dutifully including the obscenity. She presented the letter and copies to Klein for signature, and primly walked out—never to return.

The paragons at CBS were shocked. And had the competition between the two networks been less rugged, his letter to Eliasberg might have spelled the end for Klein. For someone at CBS on a lofty rung of the executive ladder called an equally important official at NBC to argue that a man who used such language under the corporate letterhead was bad for the industry and should be expelled. But NBC, smarting over CBS's victory whoops, wasn't about to let its rival dictate personnel policy. Klein was lectured about the episode by a superior but stayed on, to leave some months later under his own steam to set up a pay-television business piping first-run movies in hotel TV sets for a fee.

Ironically, though CBS's come-from-behind ratings victory was the talk of the trade, it didn't do much good for Mike Dann. In the coming months, Dann was isolated by Wood and his people, as the network president began taking a strong hand in a different kind of programing. Dann left a few months after his big victory.

Said the late Hubbell Robinson, "Mike hated to do new shows and held onto the old ones as long as he could. He stood against Bob Wood, totally misjudging his superior. Meanwhile, Mike continued to conduct his constant personal publicity campaign which culminated in a three-part piece in *TV Guide*. He made it seem like Mike Dann's network, as though Schneider and Wood didn't exist. Finally, Paley just walked away from him. They just let him sit there with nothing to do and nobody would talk to him. . . ."

Mike Dann says, "It's tough answering a voice from the grave." But he vehemently denies Hubbell Robinson's assertions, saying that the late programing chief was his "worst enemy" within the company. "Everyone knew that the hundred-day effort was my last push. After twenty years in programing at NBC and CBS, I simply couldn't take any more."

Dann says he told Paley and Stanton he wanted to change jobs within the company. But after shopping around within CBS and finding nothing, Dann concluded that his only choice was to stay with programing or go. He went.

This then was Dann's reward for saving the day. It wasn't as though Mike was operating in a vacuum. He had gotten Wood's blessing when he set out to catch up with NBC that season, and the network president even came to tell Mike's people that he hoped they could pull it off. The Chairman had to approve the decision too, since it riddled the established schedule with specials and substitutions.

A few years later, Bob Wood was asked if it had been important to win that battle. He paused momentarily before answering, glanced out at the magnificent view of New York City from his lush corner office high in the CBS tower. Then he said, with a barely concealed hint of perverse pleasure, "It was important to Mike."

Maybe Wood believed that the old scheduling patterns had had it, since only Dann's herculean manipulations saved the day. Or perhaps he felt he needed change to make an independent impression on the industry and on the front office. In any event, he did the unprecedented. He swept out ruralism, even knocking off shows that rested high and secure in the ratings. And he began his campaign to deliver a younger, more urban audience. His insouciance paved the way for a new era of blunt talk on prime-time situation comedies.

CHAPTER 28

Winners and Losers:
On the Air and in the Suite

THE IDEA OF PUTTING A BIGOT ON TELEVISION—A MAN WHO CASUALLY said "spic," "hebe" and "jungle bunny"—was patently absurd. TV critic Jack Gould thought it as unlikely as the prospect of Bill Paley and his counterparts at NBC and ABC doing a festive Maypole dance in Central Park Mall. But *All in the Family* with Carroll O'Connor as Archie Bunker, your friendly neighborhood bigot, came at the right time for CBS. Losing its momentum as the longtime king of prime-time television, its audience growing older, CBS had decided to begin aiming at a new audience—city folk in the key 18-to-34 age group.

The first thing network president Bob Wood did was lop off three of the network's successful shows: the hoary and now prohibitively expensive *Red Skelton Show*, television's seventh most popular show but biggest with the over-50 set; *Petticoat Junction*, the innocuous but popular situation comedy; and The Great One, Jackie Gleason, when he refused to give up his variety format to do just *The Honeymooners*.

Now Wood had to prove to advertisers that CBS was not just replacing grits with pap like *Hee-Haw*, an early effort. Soon it would be time for a shocker.

All in the Family had already had a rocky career when Bob Wood had a crack at it. It was modeled after a BBC program, *Till Death Us Do Part,* which dealt with a couple of unlovable hatemongers, Alf and Elsie Garnett from London's East End. The series was enormously popular on the BBC and writer-producer Norman Lear was fascinated by the concept. He bought the adaptation rights and took the idea to ABC. The third network agreed to finance a pilot, which Lear wrote and called "Those Were the Days." No sale. The cast was changed and a second pilot filmed. Both pilots tested poorly and ABC dropped the whole idea.

Lear and his agent then took the idea to Bob Wood who was just beginning to take a strong hand in programing. Lear is an urbane perfectionist; but his round face, receding hairline and neat full-length mustache hardly combine to make him stand out in a crowd. In contrast to his mild appearance, Lear is tough with his writers, directors and stars—as only a man who excels at most of these jobs can be. More than one fractious star ("I'm not coming in until you fix the air conditioning") has leaped from his limousine when Lear threatened to write him out of the script.

What Bob Wood saw was strong stuff for family television. The pilot began with son-in-law Mike trying to persuade wife Gloria to have sexual intercourse in the middle of the day, while Archie and Edith Bunker are in church. But the Bunkers come home early—Archie was turned off by the sermon—and Archie begins to knock campus subversives, welfare chiselers, Jews, blacks and atheists. He rants about law and order, long hair and hippie dress.

He goes on to extol the virtues of premarital celibacy: "When your mother-in-law and me was goin' around together—it was two years— we never—I never—I mean absolutely *nothin'*—not till the wedding night." And Edith says, "Yeah, and even then . . ."

Then, as Wood said, "I bit the bullet." Wood made a firm commitment to begin the series in early 1971. CBS's censor was horrified; for one thing, "goddamn" was used several times in the pilot and William Tankersley (known as Mr. Prohibition at CBS) knew Bible Belt affiliates would flip. But Tankersley's opposition was the least of Wood's worries. Mike Dann says Bill Paley was strongly opposed to scheduling the show. "He said you could never use the word 'Yid' or any other such epithet. He felt CBS should never be the first in any controversy. Historically, Bill's program philosophy from the time he stole Jack

Benny from NBC was based on the star system. He didn't like gambles; never started any new program concepts."

In any event, CBS wanted a less explosive start than the pilot Lear presented. But Lear was adamant. "I felt we had to get the network wet completely. Once you're completely wet, you can't get wetter. I wanted the audience to hear all of Archie's epithets, to see his sexual hang-ups, to meet the whole family."

CBS decided to go along but demanded that 80 seconds of the more explicit sex references be cut. Lear refused again, and finally the only thing cut was a minor bit of business with Mike's fly.

The CBS executive cadre was tense as the day approached for *All in the Family*'s debut, January 12 at 9:30 P.M. Bob Wood and his supporters had carried the day, but not everybody was convinced the program was a good idea; all knew it was a big risk, and when risks fail, heads tend to roll.

Bob Wood arranged for a special screening for affiliate owners. He explained his reasoning to them in a telegram that quoted a speech he had given some months before at an affiliate meeting:

The days are gone in programing when we can afford to be imitators rather than innovators. We not only have to hold the audience we have . . . we have to broaden our base. We have to attract new viewers. We're going to operate on the theory that it is better to try something new than not to try it and wonder what would have happened if we had. To turn such a philosophy into action takes a willingness to dare. . . .

After seeing *All in the Family* I think you will agree that nothing quite like this series has ever been done on American TV. Instead of being a ho-hum midseason replacement, it is innovative and certainly a break with the programing patterns of the past. . . . It is in reality an attempt to bring the spirit of the Broadway theater to our medium.

On that first show, which had been the pilot, Archie's role is quickly and brilliantly brought to life by Carroll O'Connor, as is that of his wife Edith, played by the talented Jean Stapleton. "If your spics and your spades want their rightful share of the American dream," says Archie, "let them get out there and hustle for it, just like I done. . . . I didn't have no million people marchin' and protestin' to get me my job."

Simpleminded "dingbat" Edith agrees, "No, his uncle got it for him." Later Archie says, "I wouldn't call your black beauties lazy. It just happens their system is geared slower than ours, that's all." When son-in-law Mike objects to the term "black beauties," Archie counters: "It so happens, Mr. Big Liberal, a black guy who works with me has a sticker on his car that says, 'Black Is Beautiful.' So what's the matter with black beauties?" Edith adds, "It's nicer than when he called them coons."

CBS had geared up for a furor that first night. They hired extra switchboard operators at major affiliates to handle the expected outburst of indignant phone calls. But the relative few who called in did so mostly to express their pleasure. The only exception was in New York, where 287 of the 511 callers denounced the show's "vulgarity" and "prejudice."

The critics were also favorable. Cleveland Amory, writing in *TV Guide,* said it was, "Not just the best-written, best-directed and best-acted show on television, it is the best show on television." Jack Gould in *The New York Times* expressed some timidity: "Some of Archie's words may chill the spine, but to root out bigotry has defied man's best efforts for generations, and the weapon of laughter just might succeed. The possibility entitles *All in the Family* to a chance." Among the few unfavorable reviewers, John Leonard, under the byline "Cyclops," in *Life* called the show "a wretched program" in which "bigotry becomes a form of dirty joke," and asked, "Why review a wretched program? . . . Well, why fix the septic tank?" A few leaders of minority groups objected. The late Whitney Young, Jr., of the Urban League called the show "a new low in taste. . . . It is irresponsible to air a show like this at a time when our nation is polarized and torn by racism." There was, however, no ground swell of protest from rank-and-file members of the minorities that Archie berated, many of whom presumably were watching.

At first ratings were very low. But in the early spring *All in the Family* began to rise in popularity, and by May's reruns it had become the nation's most popular show. It stooped—or rose—to Gloria's menstruation and wife Edith's menopause, and even to homosexuality, as Archie discovered that a professional athlete he admired was one of them. After a show that discussed Gloria's menstruation, Lear received a vehement protest from a viewer, scrawled anonymously on an empty Kotex box.

All in the Family sparked higher-level debate, too. Laura Z. Hobson, author of *Gentleman's Agreement,* a heavy-handed but ground-breaking best seller about anti-Semitism, surfaced for the first time in years to pronounce the show offensive. What's more, in Laura Hobson's view it was a cop-out; there wasn't *enough* bigotry in *All in the Family.*

She wrote that if the show were as honest as its billings would have it, Archie would call blacks "niggers," Jews "kikes" and "sheenies." The theme was debated again and again. Even Norman Lear—who refused to take a telephone call from Mrs. Hobson—said he would not call Latins "greasers" as this was too objectionable even to him.

Even after its popularity was assured, the show continued expounding the theme of Archie's bigotry, usually showing him as the prime victim of his own limited view, while making fun of his ignorance. When son-in-law Mike asks Archie about his parents' names, Archie replies, "David and Sarah. Two names right out of the Bible—which has got nothing to do with Jews." When Sammy Davis, Jr., makes a guest appearance on the show, Mike tries to tell him about Archie: "He's not so bad. He wouldn't burn a cross on your lawn." "No," says Davis, "but he might stop to toast a marshmallow." Later in that show, Davis takes a swig of beer and says, "To friendship," and passes the glass to Archie. But Archie, beer lover though he is, can't bring himself to drink from the same glass as a black man. Davis gets his revenge at the show's end when he poses for a snapshot with Archie and, as the flash goes off, plants a kiss on Archie's cheek. Carroll O'Connor's expression perfectly captures his character's dismay, even terror, at this contact.

Occasionally, as Laura Hobson charged, the show's staff does shy away from lines they feel might be too lacking in taste. The show is done in two separate tapings before live audiences, with the best results edited together into the show the television audience sees. Once, in the first taping, Edith discussed the Christmas card sent by a friend of Archie's, a man who'd made a fortune in the used-car business: "I remember last year's card so well. The Christ child driving a blue convertible." At the second taping the line was changed to read: "The Three Wise Men driving a blue convertible." The first audience had debated and voted, at Lear's request, whether to leave the line as it was, and "Christ child" won. But Lear changed it anyway, saying: "When I heard those minority voices, so intense, so deep-seated in their concern, I figured, why upset seventy million viewers?"

The success of *All in the Family* led to spin-offs by Lear. CBS got *Maude*, a comedy about Archie Bunker's liberal, outspoken and much-married cousin, played by Bea Arthur. NBC grabbed Lear's *Sanford & Son*, about a black junk dealer and his son. The junk dealer is played by Redd Foxx, known for years to nightclub goers as an off-color comedian. The racial theme is not played heavily, though sometimes it is referred to. "Just because he's white," says Sanford, "doesn't mean he's stupid." CBS scored again with *The Jeffersons*, about a black family that moved to a fashionable white neighborhood.

Other shows on CBS got tougher. Mary Tyler Moore—starring in her own comedy about a bright, attractive career woman working at a television station—began to talk about a woman's love life in ways suggesting there was more to her dates than a good-night kiss at the door.

In 1972 CBS began running another "relevant" comedy in the half-hour slot following *All in the Family*. *Bridget Loves Bernie* was an updated *Abie's Irish Rose*. A poor Jewish boy married to a wealthy Irish-Catholic girl works as a cab driver while awaiting his "big break" as a writer. Both sets of parents are baffled by this venture into mixed marriage and express their concern in gummy clichés. The show was popular, though, and screams erupted when CBS yanked it, reportedly after members of Jewish groups objected to the intermarriage theme. The network denied that pressure had anything to do with dropping the show. According to Mike Dann, though the ratings were good, they weren't good enough. The show caused a "hammock effect" on the Saturday-night schedule. Sandwiched between *Family* which drew 46 million homes and *The Mary Tyler Moore Show* which drew 41 million, *Bridget Loves Bernie* only managed to attract 31 million.

CBS certainly didn't need *Bridget Loves Bernie*. The network was definitely in the vanguard after *All in the Family*. Bob Wood appeared to be proving that he knew more about programing than the rest of them, could reshape the network in ways both daring and satisfying. Maybe Bill Paley had to eat crow—but with the relish of profit the bird probably went down easily.

It is easy to overstate the impact of one man on television program-ing—even an innovator like Bob Wood. There is a very large element of luck in the selection process, and it is all tempered by the importance of profits. In fact, all programing on American television networks in prime time—except for an occasional special—is designed for biggest return. All presidents and program heads, strong or weak, have one objective—maximum circulation to achieve greater profits.

Bob Wood, like any other man at the top, fears failure. So doubtful was he of the prospects of *All in the Family*—though he loved it personally—that he was too timid to put it in the CBS fall schedule; it appeared as a February replacement show. No one foresaw that it would become a runaway success, much less one of the four great TV hits of all time. (For collectors of trivia, the other three are *I Love Lucy*, *The Beverly Hillbillies* and Milton Berle's comedy hour; all but the last appeared on CBS.) It was, according to one veteran programing man at CBS, "the great luck of Bob Wood's career." If he hadn't needed that replacement in February, *All in the Family* might never have gotten on.

Why did he miss out on *Sanford & Son*, Norman Lear's second great hit? Simply because *Sanford & Son* became available before *All in the Family* was a hit. He did not make the same mistake with *Maude*, Lear's next offering.

Bob Wood, then, was lucky as well as shrewd. Like every other programing head he must maximize profits, and to do so he must accept the changing values and attitudes of viewers—so the cash register will ring. Program hits and cycles are not pre-planned, they usually just happen. When a show hits and hits big, stand back, there will be a hundred like it. Professionals say 80 percent of all new shows fail. When a program head gets a winner, he's got to take long looks at similar shows. Bob Wood, for one, was strong enough and bright enough to press his success once it became apparent.

Whenever there are winners like Bob Wood and Carroll O'Connor, there must be losers. Mike Dann lost and so did Ken Berry.

Against the popular conception of actors as spoiled children, Ken Berry is as reassuring as a traffic cop at a school crossing. Though cordial, he places a premium on privacy; hanging at the door of his Burbank, California, home is a sign that reads, "POSITIVELY NO VISITORS." On an obscure side street just blocks away from a busy overpass, the house and grounds make for a well-sheltered, woodsy retreat.

It is the sanctuary of a man who reached the top, a man who can afford to live as he pleases. Once inside, a glance to the right down the hall reveals a huge room with massive beamed ceiling reminiscent of a hunting lodge. A fireplace at the far end is large enough for a child to stand in. Ken's two adopted children are away—the eight-year-old daughter at a slumber party, the nine-year-old son with grandparents. Two large, nondescript dogs stay to collect pats, then waddle off.

This is a rugged house with bare wooden floors and sturdy furniture that children can enjoy without breaking. It is also a house that Ken and his gentle wife, Jackie, can no longer afford. For Ken Berry's starring vehicle, *Mayberry RFD*, was one of the victims of CBS's abandonment of rural programing.

A make-believe town in the heart of dreamland America, a town familiar to millions of wistful Americans for more than a decade, a town that made superstars of Andy Griffith (on the original *Andy Griffith Show*), Don Knotts and Jim Nabors, and a town that was about to do the same for Ken Berry, Mayberry is now a ghost—bulldozed out of existence by urban developers in the CBS executive suite.

Ken Berry was transformed from one of the nation's top wage earners, at half a million dollars a year, into a man whose house would soon be offered for sale. Not a momentous event in the course of the world, but a stunning blow to a man in a precarious profession where many go hungry in the long, hard trek to stardom, a status that once reached is supposed to insulate the actor against disaster.

Certainly the most frustrating things in life are those over which one has no control—like an automobile accident when someone else's car jumps the divider. In show business, destruction almost always comes in the form of flagging ratings. Never mind that there are a million fans out there who like a particular program better than any other. That's not enough. In a competitive profit-based society the show will be canceled if the ratings drop below the competition. Unreasonable? The sponsor paying maybe $100,000 a minute doesn't think so.

Ken Berry's sense of frustration was multiplied by the fact that *Mayberry RFD* was axed to make room for *Arnie*, an indifferently written show with the requisite urban format, carried along by the formidable talents of Herschel Bernardi as a plant foreman turned executive.

Mayberry, Andy Griffith's concept, was no loser. Brilliantly written for what it was—a warming reaffirmation of the simple values of small-town life—the show gathered viewers and awards in the early years like daisies in the field. Don Knotts as the beloved Barney Fife got five Emmys, and the ratings continued to hold up with Ken as *Mayberry's* star. The show ranked seventh the year it was canceled. "Dumped on from a great height" is the way RAF pilots used to express such injustice, and while Ken is too nice to express himself in such language, he spoke with considerable feeling two years later, with the house still for sale and the money running out. "It had a profound effect on me," he said. "The idea that you can work that long to get a job that good and all of a sudden have something or someone take it away from you. Here I was finally winning by the system and then they changed the system."

Ken is a performer who, with his actress wife, had tasted success briefly on the legitimate stage. Both were in *The Billie Barnes Revue* that opened to good notices Off Broadway. Though regular theatergoers generally shied from its special appeal, the show did enough business to survive at the York Theater on Manhattan's East Side. In time, the revue made it to Broadway, flitting from theater to theater as it was displaced by prior bookings, but managing to string up a respectable run and to give the Berrys the credits on which actors' careers are built.

Ken got the *Mayberry* role after Andy Griffith decided to join the rush to "relevant" programing. As *The Headmaster*, Andy was advisor to confused kids in this drug-culture, divorce-prone society. *The Headmaster* lasted all of 14 episodes, and Andy returned to a Mayberry-like environment on *The New Andy Griffith Show*.

Ken, dressed in sweatshirt and sneakers, relaxed with a beer and a hot dog in his living room that looked like a hunting lodge, and recalled:

I was lucky to get *Mayberry*. Even considering our high ratings, *Mayberry* with Andy in it was a better formula. I had allowed myself to feel that at last I had finally gotten home free—and I'm not inclined to be optimistic about anything. I was always sure every job was my last job. But not this time. It was the best job I had ever had, something I had been working for for fifteen years. To be sure of yourself is very rare in this business. I finally had a measure of financial security. It seemed the money was there and always would be there.

When something like this happens, you've got to get mad at somebody and you don't know who to be mad at and that makes you madder. I can't describe the trauma. In time, I started trying to think constructively . . . like when somebody has died. But I knew that there was no way that anybody was going to admit that mistake and put the show back on.

The series was my social life. I loved it so much. I had good friends in it. I never was big on going out. Several years ago I said to myself, I'm never going to go anywhere ever again.

The Berrys are generous and hospitable, solicitous as to whether a guest would like another drink or something to eat. Though their guest on this occasion was a stranger, they offered him a jacket against the chill of Coldwater Canyon at night.

When the two were first married, Jackie took a job as an Avon lady. She hit 150 houses in one day and sold a single lipstick. She "retired" but continued to supply cosmetics to friends at cost. The family had it in the bank to last another year, but like any cautious individual, Ken has maintained a fall-back position.

From the very beginning we have kept the first house we ever had . . . about a mile from here. The whole house is about as big as this room. It was a cottage and the cheapest construction you can imagine. But I had a good year and put in six hundred feet of the best carpet and a swimming pool.

It's nice to know it is there, only sixty dollars a month and almost paid for.

Just a few more payments . . .

The real-life soap opera of Ken and Jackie Berry, a couple of nice actor-people who thought they had it made.

When CBS was threatening to drop not only *Mayberry RFD* but *The New Andy Griffith Show* and *The Jim Nabors Show* as well, the business manager for stars of those attractions, Dick Linke, made two trips to New York "at my own expense" to try to save his properties.

It may seem strange for an independent businessman to mention that he took the money out of his own pocket for the flights, but then Dick Linke had never gotten adjusted to the idea of earning $250,000 a year. He spoke in wonder of his former affluence recently in the small, drab offices he retained after the debacle that swept every one of his television shows off the network.

"I used to sit back and think about my two offices—a big suite at Warner Brothers and another at CBS on Beverly and Fairfax—and I couldn't believe it sometimes. A fuckin' kid from Summit, New Jersey, with a shitty little business earning almost as much as the chairman of General Motors."

He was never completely sure of himself with Hollywood sophisticates. For many years he had a habit of rising on the balls of his feet and glancing down quickly to check his fly.

Dick Linke's fall from prosperity to penury came suddenly. It had been a difficult season, 1971, and Andy's "relevant" *Headmaster* series had been canceled, but *The New Andy Griffith Show* was well under way and was apparently doing okay. ("They must have spent a million dollars to promote it!") Then, in March, on about two weeks' notice, Linke got word that the three shows were, as he put it: "goin' in the toilet." Recalling it, he is philosophical and bitter by turns:

I'm old enough and man enough to know it's a tough, cruel world out there. But we were tops with them for years. We got no consideration.

It looked for a while like we would be able to save *Mayberry RFD*, but at the last minute they went in another direction. It was a toss-up between *Mayberry* and *Arnie*. *Arnie* was nothing, but they went with it one more year.

Mayberry was well organized with a fine cast and crew. It was the one show we didn't expect to be canceled. How could they? Andy felt worse about *Mayberry RFD* than he did about *The New Andy Griffith Show*.

We had fabulous deals with CBS. You don't get deals like that these days. Jim Nabors had never been on a variety show but CBS gave us $200,000 a week to produce one.

[*Mayberry RFD* was budgeted at $100,000 a week, which was unusual then for a half-hour show, and Andy Griffith got an even bigger $125,000 a week for production.]

I learned you can be hurt by being overly loyal in this business. We were so loyal to CBS, we didn't hold them up or even dicker. We dealt in good faith with one network. Bitter? Let me say it hurt. I think I am too good a businessman to be bitter.

I still do well because I own a small percentage of the shows and the residuals are there. Let's say I was making in excess of two hundred and fifty thousand dollars a year myself . . . now seventy-five thousand a year. That may not sound so bad, but it isn't easy.

I used to have a limousine and a chauffeur. I belonged to a country club. I lived well.

I made a lot of money all right, but I don't have it now. I got divorced and blew a million dollars the year the three shows went off the network. . . . I had to learn what was necessary in life. I'm a realist. I'm so logical it isn't even funny.

I have a beautiful new wife and a nine-month-old daughter, which is a pretty good feat for a man of fifty-five. My wife is a former show girl in Las Vegas and an actress. She was on quite a few *Beverly Hillbillies*. . . . Yeah, I may be hurtin', but I'm still drinkin' and fuckin' along with the best of 'em. . . .

Sometimes the broadcast men in the executive suites—even the ones with "president" in their titles—get hurt, passed over, moved laterally. But they often have the option to swallow their pride and hang in there, clutching their executive prerogatives, their titles, corner offices, limousines—and that hope for another chance at the top.

Not long ago, the editorial director of a major publishing company was introduced to a youthful-looking CBS official by Mike Dann at a party at Dann's country home.

The man's name didn't register with the book publisher and he asked: "What do you do at CBS?"

"I reign," the man answered firmly.

"You *what?*" asked the publisher, in disbelief.

"I reign."

"Right," said the publisher, "and you snow, too, I'll bet."

His little joke was rewarded with a bleak smile from the CBS man.

Testing, the publisher asked, "Could you fire, say, Walter Cronkite?"

"I could, but I wouldn't," the executive answered tersely.

His name—John A. Schneider, president of the CBS Broadcast Group and a vice-president and director of CBS itself. Maybe he could fire Walter Cronkite, but probably not; though in the unlikely event somebody else decided that Walter had to go—somebody who did have the power to fire him, like Bill Paley—you can be sure that John Schneider would be tough enough to break the news to America's most trusted newscaster.

From the time John Schneider was a boy racing sailboats in Lake Michigan he was tough and determined, captivated by the notion of winning, and with the spoils of victory—money and power. He quickly learned that in racing in rough weather, "your hands got just as bloody if you were last as they did if you came in first. You worked as hard either way. And it feels a lot better to come in first.

"If you are going to come to work every day, be involved in something that is a seven-day effort, it is better to work at coming in first —to win."

There aren't many CBS executives with the experience at winning that Jack Schneider has. Not long after graduation from Notre Dame, he began his career with WGN in Chicago as a time salesman. One of the programs he was selling featured another tough-minded young man, newscaster Myron Wallace who changed his first name to Mike.

Jack joined CBS in 1950, continuing his career in Chicago and then in New York. When CBS acquired WCAU-TV in Philadelphia in 1958, Jack became its general manager. Only a year later he was named vice-president of CBS's television-stations division. He was already in the big money at age 33.

But his meteoric rise really began in 1964 when he became general manager of WCBS-TV in New York, the company's flagship station. He didn't disappoint management there, and within a year he succeeded James Aubrey as president of the CBS Television Network and became a vice-president and director of CBS.

In 1966 when CBS was reorganized into two basic groups—the Broadcast Group and the Columbia Group—John Arnold Schneider landed in the catbird seat. As president of the CBS Broadcast Group, the number of men in better jobs in the corporation could be counted on the fingers of a leper's hand.

And there was more to come. In February 1969, Jack was appointed executive vice-president for all of CBS. It seemed clear that he was the man Bill Paley wanted to succeed him.

Then, in 1971, Paley turned his back on the man he had so carefully groomed. Schneider suddenly learned that he had lost the big race. Some say that CBS has long been delinquent in training a top-management cadre, perhaps reflecting Frank Stanton's reluctance to coexist with exceptionally able competition, young and old. This void may account for the meteoric rise of some executives whose genius was not readily apparent—like John Schneider. He was stripped of his executive vice-presidency and shortly thereafter—some said after a two-week search—an outsider was Mr. Inside. Charles T. Ireland, Jr., an experienced and able executive from International Telephone and Telegraph Corporation, was quietly brought in over Jack Schneider's head as president of CBS, while Frank Stanton moved up to vice-chairman.

If Bill Paley had suddenly decided that CBS's future lay in acquisitions in nonbroadcast areas, it certainly made sense to seek someone with a successful record in acquisitions. Or had Paley seen too much of his ace troubleshooter, Jack Schneider, at close hand?

Quiet, stocky, red-headed Chick Ireland had only a few months to enjoy the amenities at CBS. After only months on the job he suffered a heart attck. In June 1972, Ireland visited Paley in the Chairman's office to say that he felt fully recovered and even expected to begin playing tennis again soon. He was dead within 24 hours, of another heart attack.

If Paley thought he'd made a mistake passing Schneider by, he had a chance to correct it. Paley is sometimes unsure of his decisions in retrospect; he brought back "instant analysis" when he became convinced it had been an error to drop those immediate comments after presidential speeches, no matter how heavy the pressure from Washington. He was certainly capable of reversing himself on Schneider.

But he didn't. Once again an outsider was called in to run the company. Arthur R. Taylor, from Schneider's viewpoint a maddeningly young 37, was named president of CBS. Taylor came to CBS from the International Paper Company, where he was executive vice-president. Just a few years earlier he had been an investment banker, one of the bright young men in the bond department at First Boston Corporation.

For a tough competitor like Jack Schneider, Taylor's appointment as president was a bitter pill. But Schneider stuck it out. He knew from sailing (which he gave up recently, saying, "I have competition all week long, I don't need it on weekends") that one can be best in class even when one can't be overall victor. His perch was a high one, even if the rung above was occupied by a pigeon eight years younger. In Schneider's opinion CBS is the best place to work in the broadcast business. His paycheck stubs make pleasant reading, adding up to over a quarter of a million dollars a year. And his stock certificates tot up to nearly $1 million in CBS shares, with options on another $1.2 million. A fat pay envelope and a heavy portfolio are good pacifiers.

Maybe Jack Schneider's not completely happy, but he has a sense of power, however incomplete. He still sits in a well-feathered aerie high in Black Rock and his lunches from the CBS commissary are served on a large, circular marble table in his private dining room. Recalling the days before he reached the penultimate perch, he muses, "I used to be a worker bee. But now I reign."

Not completely. Please don't ask him if he can fire Walter Cronkite.

CHAPTER 29
The Remarkable World of CBS News

IT WAS INEVITABLE THAT PRESIDENT NIXON AND HIS NERVOUS WHITE House troops, in their anger at the media, would focus particularly on the CBS news team. No greater compliment could have been paid the network. At NBC, Chet Huntley was gone, and the cynically amusing David Brinkley lacked the substance and supporting players. At ABC, ex-CBSer Harry Reasoner was too mild and ex-CBSer Howard K. Smith was too old.

Thus, every night at 7 P.M. the nation turned to its great gray father image, Walter Cronkite, to find out what was *really* going on in the world. No matter what the catastrophe of the moment—the war in Vietnam, campus riots, recession, or Watergate—the people wanted to hear it from Walter. It was little wonder that both political parties approached Cronkite at one time or another to run for office. In the age of charisma, at a time when the country needed a man of wisdom and dependability, what an image!

There was little need to slant the Vietnam or Watergate news to make Americans angry or Nixon look bad—the president managed that all by himself. But because of the Cronkite team's superiority in reporting and commenting on the news, it was CBS that drew most of the

White House fire. When the photo of the modernistic Watergate apartments flashed on the screen behind the news desk, as it did night after night, Nixon's people knew they were in for another hard time.

There can be little doubt Walter's boys were effective. Next to Cronkite in the New York studio sat white-haired Eric Sevareid, author-commentator-philosopher, exuding a tired, cynical wisdom to balance the bouncy CBS boys down in Washington. Sniffing and barking around the power centers were big Roger Mudd who looked like a football player in a trench coat, mike in hand, standing in front of the White House gates; dark, handsome Dan Rather, young and usually angry; somber, deep-throated Marvin Kalb, whose very face and voice suggested doomsday and whose instant analysis after presidential speeches drew withering White House fire; and Daniel Schorr, bespectacled, graying veteran of Washington wars who knew how to handle White House attempts to intimidate him.

The Nixon years were heady ones for the CBS news division, a time of pride and unity in the face of administration attacks. All the internecine struggles, inevitable in the highly competitive world of broadcast journalism where the game is fame, were more muted than usual. The undercurrents of rivalry and ambition rarely boiled up to disturb the pursuit of Vietnam, Watergate and impeachment.

Rarely. But when it did happen, it was no surprise that Mike Wallace was the one who stirred things up. Only Wallace was enough of an outsider to the regular news team (spending his time with *60 Minutes*). And only Wallace had the brash iconoclasm to take a public poke at Walter Cronkite.

At the broadcast studios, Cronkite commands a certain deference. During one of his infrequent telecasts from the CBS Washington bureau not long ago, some 150 broadcast journalists including 21 reporters and 8 camera crews clustered nearby as he finished the 7:00 P.M. news, saying, as he often does, "And that's the way it is. . . ." There was small talk within the crowd, but no one detached himself and approached Uncle Walter. No one tried to draw Cronkite into conversation as he relaxed, slumped in a chair, his feet propped on a desk. For Cronkite is no ordinary boss. He is a celebrity—and, in contrast to the other stars in the CBS News firmament, a supernova. He is not one to be buttonholed for persiflage.

Being a celebrity has its drawbacks, of course. One is that public figures sometimes attract nuts bent on mayhem. One visitor on his way to Cronkite's office was surprised to see the secretary pull out a key and unlock the door. "I assume they let you out to lunch," the visitor cracked to Cronkite. But there are some things that security measures can't prevent. Cronkite tells of a newscaster lookalike who used to be approached by little old ladies asking, "You're Walter Cronkite, aren't you?" Finally the newscaster replied in exasperation, "That's right, lady, now fuck off."

Cronkite was totally unprepared for the Mike Wallace *60 Minutes* report on press junkets. *60 Minutes* provides pocket documentaries on scores of topics and the stories are divided between Mike and the less controversial Morley Safer. Since the mid-Fifties when he ran the toughest interview program on TV, Wallace has been a gutsy reporter with no qualms about asking important people embarrassing questions. And while he has mellowed a bit, Wallace still delights in sailing into uncharted waters launching torpedoes to sink the pompous. He startled the liberal establishment some time back by asking liberal columnists where they sent their kids to school. While the columnists he asked often wrote ringing essays favoring the busing of children, it turned out that they all sent their own children to exclusive and largely white private schools.

This time Mike was on the trail of the junketeer, not the politician but the reporter who takes all-expenses-paid trips to distant resorts and then tries to write an unbiased story about his benefactor. Wallace trailed such a junket to a western Indian reservation where automotive reporters listened to a ghastly jingle about a new Jeep called the Cherokee, test-drove the vehicle for a couple of hours, then gave themselves to the amenities provided by the manufacturer—lunch by a trout stream, time off for fishing and plenty to drink. He listened to a reporter defend his integrity, then established through an interview with the manufacturer that if the junkets didn't yield favorable stories, they would be given up. He noted that reporters got hefty discounts when they bought cars directly from the company—about 18 percent off—and Wallace called these discounts "bribes."

Not satisfied with picnics on an Indian reservation, Wallace covered a trip sponsored by Ford Motor Company during which 100 reporters were entertained on the West Coast. He reviewed a Walt Disney Reporters Special to Disney World. IBM was mentioned as having sent

13 women editors to Washington to look at a new IBM supermarket-check-out counter. He noted that sportswriters' expenses are sometimes paid by the teams they cover.

Then, toward the end of the broadcast, he turned his attention to CBS itself. He first pointed out that CBS newsmen were not permitted to take junkets, though CBS public relations men arranged free trips for others in selling the network's new television seasons. Wallace zeroed in on a CBS gala for television reporters on the West Coast and turned his camera on Win Fanning of the *Pittsburgh Post Gazette.* As Fanning checked into a hotel, he took a pair of $10 bills out of an envelope, a CBS taxi reimbursement, as Wallace's camera peered over Fanning's shoulder. A CBS spokesman then explained that the junkets were designed to make it possible for reporters on papers with low travel budgets to cover stories their colleagues on richer papers were assigned to at publishers' expense. The taxi money was in lieu of limousines that would have cost CBS more.

Wallace did not appear to be convinced that CBS was differently motivated from any other company in staging a junket. But it was his parting shot that touched off the explosion. Mike said that even Walter Cronkite had taken junkets and was a "sometime traveler on the freebie circuit," as a magazine later expressed it.

Cronkite's precise reaction was not made available for publication. But as one insider put it, Walter was "pissed off." When pressed, this insider would only add lamely, "He didn't like his name mentioned." Cronkite told the press that his trips were of a personal nature—made with friends—and had nothing to do with his assignments for CBS.

Of the aftermath, *New York* magazine wrote: "The two CBS newsmen have not always gotten along, but these days they are not getting along better than ever."

Wallace wrote to *New York* publisher Clay Felker: "Doesn't your New York Intelligencer have a dime? For the price of a phone call he would have learned the following: Walter and I had a difference of opinion about the press junkets piece. We have been acquaintances for almost 20 years, colleagues for 11, and friends for a good deal of that time. . . . There is room for a difference of opinion between two colleagues, although occasionally, as we all know, that difference can turn warmer than we might like. . . ."

The smooth facade at CBS News was shattered only briefly. But at the converted dairy on Manhattan's West Side where the CBS news operations are based, Cronkite apparently seethed for some time. On September 12, 1974—a full six months after the fact—Mike Wallace added a postscript, calling this writer to say: "That business between Cronkite and myself has been patched up."

Probably the most important aspect of the situation is that Mike Wallace could do the show in the first place. It lent substance to Wallace's claim that "This is a dead-honest outfit."

Mike Wallace was a central figure in another controversial show, this time one which caused many to doubt the rectitude of the CBS news division. When, in the spring of 1975, CBS paid convicted Watergate offender H.R. Haldeman something between $25,000 and $100,000 for two one-hour interviews with Wallace and some Haldeman home movies, James Reston editorialized against it in *The New York Times.* He alluded to the old newspaper practice of buying information from informers and commented that this practice, common in the old days of yellow journalism, was virtually nonexistent today. Reston argued that CBS's move, if continued, would inevitably force NBC and ABC to compete. It was after "considerable controversy" involving Edward R. Murrow, Eric Sevareid, Walter Cronkite and others that CBS had drawn up a policy making clear the distinction between news and historical memoirs. Blurring the distinction is dangerous, Reston wrote. As for the program itself, it was not one of Wallace's best. His hostility was painfully obvious in facial grimaces and exasperated looks at the ceiling while Haldeman stayed cool and said nothing new.

Wallace's career at CBS suggests that CBS remains a relatively fearless news medium. Clearly CBS News and its reporters under Richard Salant, president of the news division and a protégé of Frank Stanton, can take stands that are both embarrassing and expensive for CBS.

In Hollywood, after Mike's junket piece was completed and its contents known in outline but before it was shown on TV, the radio and TV reporters were fuming. They had Robert Wood on the griddle, asking what might be regarded as the wrong questions.

"They wanted to know how it could happen," *Variety* reported, "why it was happening, what Wood had to do with it, and what he could do about it—and, most important, why they couldn't have a screening of it on the Coast. Wood said he had nothing to do with the news division of CBS."

It is a tribute to CBS that even Bill Paley feels that the news operations have a life of their own. Jerry Brody, who once ran The Ground Floor restaurant for Paley in Black Rock, went directly to the boss to complain that the CBS local news was flailing away at a story Brody regarded as dead—dirty restaurants in New York City. Brody asked Paley to do something about it.

Brody said that Paley looked up, slightly embarrassed, and said, "I have nothing to do with them."

Says Walter Cronkite, always sympathetic to the other guy's problem: "The broadcast executive is in the business of pleasing the public, and what they have to sell depends on approval, on not offending anybody. Then we ask them to turn their backs and forget all that so that we can do things that are likely to upset the public and create problems.

"I see it as creating not problems but prestige. But we really ask a lot of them because they are basically in show business and we are about as far away from that as we can get."

Fresh from the newspaper world in 1948, Walter Cronkite, age 32, read the news too rapidly and conveyed little depth. Worse yet, he made no discernible impact. But after a while, the ex-wire-service man surprised his associates. His delivery improved and he began to develop style, perspective, poise. There was something else about him that engendered trust: He was a solid newsman who recognized the distinction between reporting and advocacy. All through his career he would be careful not to cross the line. Walter Cronkite didn't become the nation's most respected broadcast journalist by taking stands.

Walter's image is one of calm. In fact, he has a quick temper—though it is always under control in front of the cameras. But even if his admirers never experienced it, they were beneficiaries of his rancor in 1968. For what Walter Cronkite saw in Vietnam, after the massive Communist Tet offensive, made him very angry. Angry enough to cross over the line into advocacy journalism.

Cronkite had been delivering the news of the Vietnam war in his typically impartial manner and he thus at least appeared to accept our government's position that the war could eventually be won. But not after Tet.

His producer at the time, Ernest Leiser, now of ABC Evening News, commented recently: "I think Cronkite must have felt that he had been had and he got mad because he felt that this was an inexcusable and, maybe, a criminal deceit by the federal government."

Later Cronkite hinted that he felt he had been deceived by the government when he reported on the U.S. military buildup in Vietnam in 1965. It appeared to him at that time that the buildup was essentially defensive—a move by the Johnson administration to establish a military presence to deter aggression—nothing more: "I wasn't that convinced in 1965 that this force was really going to be committed. I blame the government for insinuating our troops into Vietnam. I don't think I felt strongly that we would commit to the extent we did when I reported the buildup."

The Tet offensive in February 1968 changed a lot of minds and opened a lot of eyes. The Vietcong attacked during the first two nights of the Tet Lunar New Year, and Cronkite received increasingly pessimistic reports from the CBS Saigon bureau. Criticism of the war was raging in the nation's newspapers and on the campuses. After the Tet offensive, he went to see for himself. He was appalled and on the scene wrote his account: "Report from Vietnam by Walter Cronkite." "These ruins are in Saigon. . . . They were left here by an act of war, Vietnamese against Vietnamese. Hundreds died here. Here in these ruins can be seen physical evidence of the Vietcong's Tet offensive, but far less tangible is what those ruins mean, and like everything else in this burned and blasted and weary land, they mean success or setback, victory or defeat, depending upon whom you talk to."

After Cronkite had elicited diametrically opposing views from President Thieu and opposition leader Nguyen Xuan Oanh, his gloomy commentary continued. "There are doubts about the exact measure of the disaster itself. All that is known with certainty is that on the first two nights of the Tet Lunar New Year, the Vietcong and North Vietnamese Regular Forces, violating the truce agreed on for that holiday, struck across the entire length of South Vietnam, hitting the largest 35 cities, towns, and provincial capitals. How many died and how much damage was done, however, are still but approximations, despite the official figures. The very preciseness of the figures brings them under suspicion. . . ."

Cronkite went on to detail the Vietcong offensive, the complete surprise that the VC were able to achieve in the cities, thus exploding the myth that the Americans had made them secure and were successfully pacifying the countryside. He described the "almost total" destruction in the old citadel city of Hue where the Americans were forced to use heavy weapons and air strikes. Thus "a whole measure of the success of the war [was] knocked into a cocked hat. . . ."

Cronkite interviewed, for the military, Lt. General R.E. Cushman, Jr. The general contended that if the VC "continue this all-out attack day and night, exposing himself to our firepower, I just don't think he can keep it up for longer than a matter of months."

Cronkite, obviously unconvinced, concluded on a critical note: "We have been too often disappointed by the optimism of the American leaders, both in Vietnam and Washington, to have faith any longer in the silver linings they find in the darkest clouds. . . . For it seems now more certain than ever that the bloody experience of Vietnam is to end in a stalemate. . . . To say that we are closer to victory today is to believe, in the face of the evidence, the optimists who have been wrong in the past. To suggest we are on the edge of defeat is to yield to unreasonable pessimism. . . . It is increasingly clear to this reporter that the only rational way out then will be to negotiate, not as victors, but as an honorable people who lived up to their pledge to defend democracy, and did the best they could."

That shrewd politician, Lyndon B. Johnson, used to say that when he wanted to reach the bright folks in New York and Washington, he would call in Tom Wicker of *The New York Times* and Russell Wiggins of *The Washington Post*. But when he wanted to get to the "good folks" in Dubuque, Denver and Dallas, he would call in CBS's Eric Sevareid and have a chat with him. Johnson believed the "good folks" watched Cronkite and would get the message from commentator-philosopher Sevareid who held down the "heavy" spot on the Cronkite evening news broadcasts.

Johnson also told Bill Moyers, his press secretary, that one sentence by CBS Washington correspondent Dan Rather after a Johnson speech would reach more people than all the columns that would be written about him the next day. "His feeling over the years," says Moyers, "was that CBS was the country's medium—much more than NBC. This may have been partly because of his history with CBS [Johnson's own station in Texas was a CBS affiliate], but that's the way he saw it."

Walter Cronkite's Tet-offensive broadcast, mild though many thought it, stunned Johnson. On March 31, 1968, scarcely more than a month after the broadcast, Johnson announced that he had ordered a halt to air and naval bombardment of most of North Vietnam. And, in a surprise announcement at the end of his address, he suddenly said he would neither seek nor accept the nomination of the Democratic party for another term as president.

Moyers says Johnson told him that Cronkite's broadcast after the Tet offensive, charging deception in Washington, had caused the president to lose credibility in the eyes of American people, due to the "tremendous prestige" Walter Cronkite had throughout the country.

Moyers further believes that if Cronkite had become alarmed and outspoken about the United States buildup in Vietnam during his visit there in 1965, Johnson could never have gotten away with the troop commitments that escalated the war in the first place. Moyers alluded to a poll that found 70 percent of the American people trusted Cronkite more than anyone else in the public eye: "We always knew before this poll was taken that Cronkite had more authority with the American people than anyone else. It was Johnson's instinct that Cronkite was it."

George Washington remains the father of our country. But its father image, at least for a long period in the late Sixties and early Seventies, would seem to have been Walter Cronkite.

It was a typical hot-under-the-collar Dan Rather reaction. In May of 1973, President Richard Nixon was orchestrating the return of the Vietnam prisoners of war with a commander-in-chief's reception carried out with reverent salute-the-flag pomp. Nixon, on television, told his audience that without airtight security, without secrecy, our boys would still be rotting in Hanoi. The country, he said, should "quit making national heroes out of those who steal papers and publish them in newspapers."

Dan Rather, CBS's chief correspondent in Washington, could not let that one slide by. He reported that the president was using the occasion to "win public support for covering up some aspects of the criminal cases now under investigation," and he pointed out that 90 POWs refused the invitation. He also noted that POWs who were about to divorce their wives were "specifically instructed" not to bring along girl friends. Rather reported, "One of the highlights of the evening is to be a group singing of 'God Bless America' . . . [but] through it all comes the basic line of defense that says, whatever covering up he may have done, he did so for his country."

It had always been that way with Dan Rather. More than once President Johnson called Rather up after watching him on the news to ask, "Are you trying to fuck me?"

Rather shunned the conventional let's-drink-and-make-up scenes with presidential press secretaries. Most other reporters would get together with the president's men, lift a few and at least pretend to be friends. Not Dan Rather.

Rather took the unpaved path to journalistic prominence in Washington. His father, a Texas ditch digger, couldn't scrounge up the money to send Dan to college. Dan pinned his hopes on a football scholarship, but none of the big schools sent scouts to watch him. He probably wasn't big enough to qualify as grade-A for those meat-on-the-hoof teams they field at Texas, SMU and A & M.

Nevertheless, he was promised a scholarship to Sam Houston State College if he made the team. When he was cut, he wandered into the woods to weep. A professor of journalism found him a job and Rather was able to work his way through. All his life he has had to try harder, work longer, risk more, and he's never stopped. He landed a job with the CBS affiliate in Houston—KHOU-TV—where his determination and talent were rewarded; he became news director and was the reporter on the scene when Hurricane Carla began a devastating journey through the territory. Rather distinguished himself, got heavy exposure on *The CBS Evening News* and drew Cronkite's admiring comment: "We were impressed by his calm and physical courage. . . . He was ass deep in water moccasins." CBS hired Rather away from KHOU and made him Southwest bureau chief for CBS News, and soon he was running from one civil-rights crisis to another in 1962, making frequent appearances on the *Evening News*.

On November 22, 1963, Dan Rather was in Dallas awaiting President Kennedy's motorcade on the other side of a railroad crossing. Suddenly, two limousines raced by. Rather saw enough to send him rushing to the local CBS station. He called Parkland Hospital and confirmed through a doctor and a priest that John F. Kennedy was dead by an assassin's bullet. Rather got the information on CBS Radio 17 minutes before confirmation of the news was deemed sufficient to put it on CBS-TV.

He stayed with the story in Dallas for four agonizing days and nights, virtually without sleep. New York was so impressed that he was promoted to White House correspondent at the age of 32. It was an unheard-of leap to the top ranks of CBS broadcast journalism.

Rather is widely acknowledged to have "star quality" and is much envied by the CBSers who don't have it. (His appearance doesn't hurt. He looks like a dark-haired, handsome, slightly angry choir-boy.) His spectacular exchanges with a Watergate-embattled President Nixon have inevitably led to speculation that the Texas boy would someday succeed Walter Cronkite. (Nixon once heatedly answered a Rather barb with the question, "Are you running for something?" and Rather shot back, "No, Mr. President, are you?")

Speculation at this point about Cronkite's successor is both indelicate and a little silly, perhaps. The incumbent, 59 years old in 1975, is in vigorous health. The network did have a scare a while back when a tumor was discovered in his throat. It was removed and proved to be benign, but the voice that millions wait to hear nightly was seriously affected for many weeks. Fully recovered now, Cronkite leads the life of a man at the top of his profession, private and almost patrician. He has a passion for sailing and mans his own 35-foot ketch whenever he can get away, hardly the picture of an invalid ready to step aside. But people do like to speculate about the future of media stars like Cronkite and Rather.

Rather has been called the "only correspondent in the new generation who could have made the old Murrow team" by CBS veteran David Schoenbrun, a caustic critic of television news. But while some suggest that Rather may ultimately get the anchor-man job, he does not have the inside track and he acknowledges this himself. Ahead of him is Roger Mudd, star of *The Selling of the Pentagon*, a hard-nosed report in 1971 that caused CBS as much trouble in Washington as some of Murrow's toughest *See It Nows*.

In that report Mudd flailed away at the military, covering in detail the lavish junkets arranged by the military for congressmen, industrialists and others of influence. He provided an embarrassing portrait of the Pentagon's high-powered public relations campaigns. Paid for by the public, of course, these campaigns were calculated to buy for the

Pentagon the support it needed from the VIPs to put over a defense program that many critics regarded as astronomically expensive and wasteful.

The broadcast created a sensation. Vice President Spiro T. Agnew jumped into the fray to charge CBS with a "subtle but vicious broadside against the nation's defense establishment." Frank Stanton manned the barricades for CBS and successfully protected Mudd's sources while risking a contempt citation before a congressional subcommittee investigating the show. Roger Mudd emerged stronger than ever.

Mudd's first big break had come during Martin Luther King's march on Washington in the summer of 1963. Roger was so nervous about the assignment that he left the CBS broadcast booth and hurried to the boxwood trees near the Lincoln Memorial and threw up.

While TV newsmen rarely do leg work, Mudd is an exception and routinely presses sources to get what he needs. He has aplomb, a sense of perspective and a sense of his own power. Says he: "Once a man carves out a little niche on the air, it's very difficult for people to get at you. Criticism of your pieces that could come from producers . . . is muted." Although he gets first call to fill in as anchor man when Cronkite takes off on special assignments or on vacation, Mudd insists this is no guarantee of the job when Cronkite finally retires.

Mudd has an earthy sense of humor that is more appealing to his colleagues, perhaps, than Rather's constant drive. On the other hand, Mudd, though pleasantly rugged in appearance, has a calm manner that seems colorless in comparison to Rather whose indignation is vibrant on camera.

Two ex–Cronkite producers, Ernie Leiser and Les Midgley, were asked who would succeed Cronkite. Said Leiser, an acerbic and outspoken man, "I'd choose Mudd because he's a better broadcaster. But don't tell him that since it would inflate his large ego. It's a question of communicating and Mudd's ten percent better at that."

Midgley, who is still at CBS, agreed: "I don't know what it is, but Roger has some ability to transmit through appearance, personality and voice that Dan doesn't. Sometimes Dan seems to be uptight—there are social mannerisms that we carry around with us and he can't keep them off camera."

Dick Salant, CBS news-division president, may very well have the most say about Cronkite's eventual successor. He finds himself already on the record about the matter and is unhappy about it. In 1971 he incautiously remarked at a private CBS affiliates meeting that Mudd was Cronkite's No. 1 understudy. Salant later remarked, "I'll murder the son of a bitch who told *Variety.*"

Oddly enough, considering the stature and emoluments of the job in question, both Mudd and Rather have wondered out loud whether they would get the same satisfactions they both experience as aggressive reporters in the field. Reporters write their own stories but anchor men for the most part have their material written for them. CBS staff writers do relatively little leg work in preparing the stories Cronkite reads on the air. Instead, they rely heavily on stories picked up from the press and rewrite items from the newspapers, particularly in recent years *The New York Times* and *The Washington Post.* While Cronkite regularly goes over the copy and gives it the Cronkite touch, his writers have already put it more or less in his style. As a result, Cronkite is able to spend the day doing background interviews over lunch and "being a superstar" as a CBS colleague puts it enviously—making appearances and speeches, even being interviewed with his wife at home as a celebrity worthy of a TV special.

Cronkite usually arrives at the New York studio late in the afternoon, though he often tells associates he intends to arrive in the morning and be managing editor of the *Evening News* in fact, not just title. The executive producer of the *Evening News,* currently Burton Benjamin, is the working executive. He decides how much time each correspondent's story is worth and whether it will appear on the tube at all. Cronkite has the right to change things if he wants to. For example, it was Cronkite's decision that the World Food Conference would get a piece every day whether it rated the coverage in terms of news value or not, says an associate who obviously thinks that it did not. But mostly Cronkite is preoccupied with his own portion of the broadcast. He jealously guards his 6 minutes of "tell" out of the 23 total minutes of news. (One CBS source says that Cronkite "sulked" during the 1964 Republican Convention when the network brought in Eric Sevareid in an effort to offset the ratings victories of NBC's Chet Huntley and David Brinkley. "Cronkite was afraid Sevareid would steal some of his anchor-man thunder. Walter doesn't like people elbowing him. But it wasn't anybody's intention that Sevareid would. And when CBS made the mistake of dumping Cronkite from the 1964 Democratic Convention, his public and private behavior was excellent. Fred Friendly caved in on that one, letting Paley substitute Bob Trout and Roger Mudd who, as a team, were a real disaster.")

Cronkite sometimes finds the anchor-man chores routine. To relieve the tedium, he may send himself on special assignment to Southeast Asia and the Pacific. Most certainly he does *not* emulate a certain local CBS anchor man who reportedly, to dispel his boredom, shouts obscenities until a split second before he goes on the air—almost as though he hoped scraps of his profanity would be broadcast and he could be relieved of his assignment.

The big incentive to be *Evening News* anchor man is the satisfaction that goes with superstardom and the money. Cronkite gets an estimated $300,000 a year; both Rather and Mudd are supposedly paid around $100,000 —plus outside income. Dan Rather's Watergate book, *The Palace Guard,* written with Gary Paul Gates, a fellow CBS man, was a best seller and turned a nice dollar for Rather.

Whatever the future, the public will have few chances to compare Rather and Mudd like that provided by the resignation of President Nixon. There sat Uncle Walter calling it "indeed an historic day—the only time a president has ever resigned in nearly two hundred years of history . . . but he didn't confess any crimes . . . said merely that he was guilty perhaps of some bad judgment but that was all." This was a golden opportunity for Rather and Mudd to show their respective skills in instant analysis.

Actually, there were three men, not two, to comment on this historic event: Dan Rather, who had always shown his anger at Nixon, never shrinking from barbed comment; Eric Sevareid, who didn't like instant analysis, preferring to polish his gemlike philosophical commentaries over the space of a full day (he had the luxury denied news columnists of being able to tell his associates, "Nothing today, the well is dry"); and Roger Mudd, who never seemed angry so much as critical of the Nixon administration.

After Cronkite, Sevareid spoke gently, more in sorrow than in anger.

Yes, there've been no further admissions. Perhaps it was foolish for people on The Hill and some of us to think that there might have been. He has said in effect he was not resigning because of a sense of guilt of any criminality, but because his political "face" has eroded in the Congress and . . . therefore he wants to cut this thing short in the interests of the whole country.

On the whole, it seemed to me as effective, as magnanimous a speech as Mr. Nixon has ever made. . . . Few things in his Presidency became him as much as his manner of leaving the Presidency. . . .

Then angry Dan Rather had his chance. But he astonished his listeners with a saccharine, almost glowing tribute:

Walter, I think it may very well go down, when history takes a look at it, as one of Richard Nixon's if not his finest hour. . . . He did give—and I would agree, Walter, with what you said—he gave to this moment a touch of class—more than that—a touch of majesty —touching that nerve in most people that says to their brain: Revere the presidency and respect the president; the Republic and the country comes first.

Then it was Roger Mudd's turn, and deftly he turned bathos into reality and saved the day for CBS:

From a—just from a pure congressional point of view, I really wouldn't think that was a very satisfactory speech. It did not deal with the realities of why he was leaving. There was no accounting in the speech of how he got there and why he was leaving that Oval Room. That whole question of Watergate is all that anybody in the Congress has had on their minds for the better part of a year. Half the Congress has defended him. Half the Congress has gone out on a limb for him.

In the absence of any explanation or any acknowledgment of the President's responsibility in the Watergate cover-up, the viewer is left to conclude that it was simply some craven politicians in the Congress who collapsed in their defense of the President, and solely because of that he was having to leave the Presidency. . . .

[As to a possible grant of immunity:]

There is still to be accounted for in the country, it seems to me, a sizable body of opinion that would rightfully ask: Is the President of the United States really to be beyond the law? That, if certain crimes were committed and certain laws were violated, then somebody ought to be punished for them. And an awful lot of men have had their families broken up in the last year because of crimes that they have committed, they've said, in the name of national security. . . . There's been an awful lot of sadness delivered on a lot of Washington families. And those people were not beyond the law. . . .

There was more. Mudd noted that Agnew had only avoided jail by pleading no defense to "certain criminal acts." Nixon, by contrast, had admitted nothing.

Rather picked up the discussion, still in a conciliatory tone, saying that people don't "shoot at lifeboats." He added: "My own decision is: I don't think that the American people, nor the Congress in the end, will want to pursue Richard Nixon if it can possibly be avoided."

More than one unkind critic said that perhaps the "new" Dan Rather was thinking of the future more than the moment at hand. For Rather's relentless attacks on the administration had distressed many affiliated station owners. Shortly after Nixon left office, CBS, in what would be regarded as a reaction to affiliate pressure, moved Rather into new assignments. He was named national correspondent (the first man to hold the job since Murrow) as well as weekend anchor man and host of *CBS Reports*.

The feeling around the shop was that CBS policy makers had decided that it was time for the network to show some new faces at the White House. Rather's was a Watergate face, so Dan Rather had been moved sideways—neither up nor down, but out of the limelight. Roger Mudd appeared to have inched ahead, though no one claims he views the situation in that light.

Cronkite, meanwhile, reigns securely and, from all accounts, serenely, with a cumulative appeal as pervasive as his delivery is mild. And that's the way it is.

After Nixon resigned, many CBS reporters breathed a sigh of relief. Though exposing wrongdoing in high places could be exhilarating work, the pressures the administration brought to bear on individual newsmen were often unnerving. Sometimes they were so heavy-handed as to be comical—especially when the Nixon team went after CBS correspondent Daniel Schorr.

Behind Schorr's image of kindly, plump, bespectacled professor of

English is a tough, seasoned old pro—not a man to tangle with. But Nixon's men had been infuriated by Schorr's critical broadcasts. Nixon himself told a group of women correspondents that Schorr's report that the president was secretly uncertain whether to go ahead with an antiballistic-missile program then under attack by Senate liberals was "a lie," though he quickly added that Mr. Schorr "just probably had the wrong information."

Schorr's gusher of inside stories had to be capped, Nixon's palace guard decided. On August 19, 1971, Schorr was summoned to the White House—as he had been on at least four previous occasions—to be chewed out for his report of the evening before. Then H.R. Haldeman called the G-men into the case.

FBI Director J. Edgar Hoover launched a massive investigation. At 8:30 A.M. of August 20, agents fanned out to interview Schorr, CBS executives in Washington and New York, other newsmen, neighbors, previous employers—which meant going back some since Schorr had been with the network 19 years—and neighbors of a brother in New York.

In just six and a half hours the G-men interrogated 25 people—at which point the affair ended, as abruptly as it had started. At 3 P.M. Hoover called off the troops, later explaining to an investigating Senator Sam Ervin that he had halted the mission because Schorr "desired that the investigation be discontinued."

When word of the investigation reached the newspapers, the White House, pressed for comment, explained that Schorr was being checked out only because he was under consideration for an administration job —though the White House refused to say *which* job it had in mind for its annoying critic from CBS. The laughter echoed long and loud through Washington corridors. On January 31, 1972, five months after the FBI investigation, the White House finally discovered that the job it had in mind for Schorr was assistant to the chairman of the Council on Environmental Quality.

Schorr had never been approached concerning the job, had no intention of leaving CBS and was embarrassed to have to explain all this to his superiors at the network. Of course, CBS felt certain that the job offer was just an inept cover story.

One of the more amusing exchanges that resulted from the debacle was a discussion on *The Dick Cavett Show* with Patrick Buchanan, a

White House speechwriter. Buchanan explained: "Daniel Schorr personally disliked, and I think detest is not too strong a word, this administration. He has a right to do that. He has the right to be on the air. He has the right to express his views.

"[But] when CBS takes Daniel Schorr and assigns him to explain the social policies of the Nixon administration to twenty million Americans, that in my judgment is a prima facie case of bias."

Asked why the White House would hire a man it had so low an opinion of, Buchanan said: "If you've got a guy that's hatcheting you night after night after night, maybe you come and say to yourself, why don't we offer that clown a job and give him a big fat paycheck and get him off so we can get someone else on? That's the only explanation I can give. . . . It was not my decision to offer Daniel Schorr a job. [And given] Schorr's bigotry and bias against the administration, the individual that was going to offer Daniel Schorr a job made a bonehead play in my judgment."

Later Cavett asked Buchanan, "Is that the administration's opinion of the environment, to put a cluck in there?"

Buchanan: "What's your question again?"

James Reston summed up the situation in the title of his column in *The New York Times*, "But if you laugh, it hurts."

Daniel Schorr apparently wasn't the only member of the CBS Watergate team to get a Nixon-team gumshoe in the backside. Dan Rather seems to have been the victim of still another White House snafu.

Planning was more evident in the Rather sortie. It was in April 1972 and the White House had arranged passage for Rather, his wife and two children on the press plane that was to follow Nixon in *Air Force I* to Florida for a weekend sojourn at the president's Key Biscayne retreat. But one of the children was ill, so Rather flew down alone on Friday, April 7, and returned to his home in Washington unexpectedly on Saturday night.

At about midnight Dan heard noises on the floor below. He eased himself out of bed and got his 20-gauge Browning shotgun. He stepped out of the bedroom and shouted into the darkness below, "I don't know who you are or what you want, but if you don't get the hell out of here, I'm going to blow your ass off. And if you don't believe me, listen to this." He thrust a shell into the weapon.

The intruders beat a hasty exit, and when Rather was convinced they were gone he went downstairs and checked out the family possessions. They were intact. But his basement files had been rifled.

These were the files of the man John Ehrlichman had told Salant they didn't want on the Washington beat.

CHAPTER 30
Not Today, Not Tonight

THERE APPEARS TO BE TACIT ACKNOWLEDGMENT AT CBS THAT NBC, the inventor of the magazine format, remains its master. Such shows usually run an hour or more and feature a variety of topics in each broadcast, just as a magazine features many subjects in a single issue.

The magazine format originated in the fertile mind of jovial Sylvester L. ("Pat") Weaver, a flamboyant advertising executive who left Madison Avenue in 1949 for NBC. As a vice-president, he quickly impressed General Sarnoff who was looking for someone to guide the network out of an organizational crisis. Sarnoff made Weaver president of the network, and Pat began looking for ways to wrest programing control from his former employers—the advertising agencies and the sponsors.

He settled on the magazine concept for his *Today Show* (in 1952) and *Tonight Show* (first on network in 1954), producing them internally and thus controlling them for the network. In the beginning, *The Tonight Show* was hosted by the zany and sophisticated Steve Allen behind those heavy horn-rimmed glasses; and laconic Dave Garroway emceed *Today* with the assistance of J. Fred Muggs, a chimpanzee. The shows worked and became very popular. When the mercurial and moody Jack Paar succeeded Allen, *The Tonight Show* became a phenomenal success and sponsors decided, correctly, that NBC was where the night lights burned brightest.

Weaver was an inveterate memo writer whose outpourings to his staff soon lined the shelves of his office in 40 bound volumes. Somewhere in that mass of paper he also invented the "spectacular," a broadcast that would preempt hours of regular shows and challenge the "robotry of habit viewing [creating] excitement and controversy and washday gossip." An early effort, *Peter Pan* with Mary Martin in the title role, delighted a national audience of 65 million viewers, one of the largest ever. Thus Weaver became public enemy number one at CBS, as he enlivened a network that had long suffered morale problems, riveting the attention of the press on NBC, for years in the shadow of CBS.

Although Bill Paley was the acknowledged sovereign of the half-hour format, successfully brought to television from radio, he is not a man satisfied with being No. 2 at anything. He will often latch onto someone else's winning idea and spend heavily to do it better than the originator. So when WINS Radio in New York City scored a success with an all-news format, Paley switched to that format with WCBS, his flagship radio station in New York City, and spent a bundle to challenge WINS at its own game. From time to time he has challenged NBC's supremacy where it is strongest—in the extended-time formats of *Today* and *Tonight*. And he has spent a lot of money copying Weaver's formula. But never with success.

His response to *Tonight*, which had passed from one chatty charismatic charmer (Jack Paar) to another (Johnny Carson), was Merv Griffin.

Except for the money, it's a wonder Merv Griffin ever agreed to take the late-night spot against Johnny Carson. But Merv was doing a talk show on Westinghouse, a small network, at the time and wanted a change, or as he explains: "In this business you either throw out your staff every three or four years, or you change networks and find new goals. I change networks; Carson fires his staff."

In 1969 when Griffin heard that CBS was interested he told his agent, "If they want me, name this figure," which he says was twice what Carson was getting. "They'll negotiate down." Merv won't say what "this figure" was, but he insists that CBS paid him "over $10 million" in two and a half years.

What Merv didn't know was that Mike Dann had been told to get Merv, period. Someone high up at CBS apparently thought Merv's boyish looks and bouncy charm, combined with passable abilities as a singer and stand-up comedian, could hack Johnny down to size.

Merv had a naïve, breathless, gee-whiz quality that appealed to some viewers. ("Golly, Doris, I can't believe you've been a star for twenty years! Why, I was in high school . . .") He was a master (or slave) of the light, I'll-be-darned expletive, in contrast to Carson who could merely raise an eyebrow to make an innocent remark into a naughty innuendo.

As Merv tells it, when Dann heard Griffin's price, he reacted with his customary flair for the dramatic, saying, "One moment," and left the room. He came back a minute later, too short a time to do anything but blow his nose, and said, "Okay." Says Merv: "I went into shock!"

Mike Dann says that the story is entertaining but "ridiculous," that the price came out of extended discussions within CBS. But Griffin is certainly right about Dann's flair for the dramatic. Les Brown says in *Television* that in his first meeting with Dann, years ago, he found Dann sitting in his executive chair, Yogi-style—legs folded under him with his finger up his nose.

But that was only a freshet in the CBS spending stream. And Merv himself helped them lay out a little more on frills. New York-based with Westinghouse, he planned to stay in Manhattan. But he took one look at the CBS broadcast theater on Broadway—called the Ed Sullivan— and felt it wouldn't do. "It was right across the street from an unemployment office. I didn't want the down-and-out people in the audience because they would be too depressed. So I visited all the theaters in town and decided on the Cort at Sixth Avenue and Forty-eighth Street."

The Cort is an intimate little theater, ideally suited to the kind of show Merv had in mind. Fussy though he was, even Merv wasn't prepared for what CBS would spend. "The Shuberts," he says, "would have leased the Cort to me for a hundred thousand, but CBS paid a quarter of a million dollars a year.

"Because of the CBS image, they had to have all new equipment. They took that legitimate theater and, at the cost of two million dollars, rebuilt it into a fantastic television studio. I've always contended that it could have been done for a million, but that's the way they are."

There was more to it than just spending. Everything at CBS is precise—a legacy of the meticulous Frank Stanton. Merv discovered that there was an entire booklet showing what the marquee of the theater had to look like—including the position and size of the CBS eye. No deviations would be permitted.

Finally, every eye was in place and Merv began his telecasts. But from the very beginning things did not go well in Nielsenville. It's amazing that anybody at Black Rock ever thought they would; some important CBS affiliates made it clear from the start that they would rather run old movies against Johnny Carson. *The Tonight Show* had nearly 15 years of success when Griffin started his rival show, and virtually the entire 200-plus-station NBC-TV network wanted to be in on the fun. With numerous defections at CBS, Merv was eventually reduced to only 150 stations and wasn't represented in some of the most important markets. He simply couldn't win with those numbers.

Griffin was actually in a three-way race when you count ABC's *Joey Bishop Show,* but the focus was on NBC. Griffin was folksy in his bland opening monologues while Carson was a strong stand-up comedian with monumental poise, always in complete control. When a Carson joke failed, he might throw in a quick "Ho-kay, when's the next train to Salt Lake City?" Griffin usually stood there with his face hanging out. Lacking Carson's ready punch lines, Merv concentrated on handling his guests and audiences. "I find myself working on people's different emotions to create a mood," he has said.

While his questions to important guests were usually sympathetic—aimed at the heart and not the jugular—he liked to zap occasionally with a sudden tough one delivered in his usual lighthearted manner, with mixed results. James Mason, caught unaware when Griffin asked, "You're such a nice guy, why does your ex-wife hate men so much?" lapsed into grim silence.

After six months of low ratings in New York, Griffin floored the CBS people with a decision that the Cort Theater had been a mistake; he announced that he would have to originate from the West Coast. Says he, "After that two-million-dollar investment, they raised a lot of hell!"

Even on the Coast Merv found that the ratings would not build sufficiently. Many problems, Merv believes, turned on the fact that

CBS was basically ignorant of the talk-show format. "They used to keep track of the hawks and doves and any references to the Vietnam war. By that time there was nothing but doves. The only hawks left were Bob Hope and John Wayne. Trying to even that up was impossible."

Though on his Westinghouse show he had never acquired a reputation for controversy, Merv relished the time he booked Abbie Hoffman on CBS: "They thought he was wearing an American flag as a shirt, and Bob Wood said that he was breaking the law." CBS was concerned about the possibility that picturing the arrogant hippie-radical author of *Steal This Book* in a coast-to-coast desecration of the flag would lead the FCC to give station owners problems at license renewal time. "For the first time in TV an image was blacked out with an electronic device. I could be seen along with Virginia Graham, but Abbie couldn't. I was shocked when I was told that was how it would be if he wore that shirt. But I was also excited because I knew there would be an outburst. The crazy thing was Hoffman wasn't wearing the flag! We had a Ford commercial on that show and Roy Rogers and Dale Evans were both wearing that same shirt. It wasn't a flag—it was made of red, white and blue bunting."

But even controversy didn't lead to high ratings, and "When the ratings are low," says Merv, "every program director tells you how to run the show. I was a wreck. When the rating dropped, they would ask, 'Who was on?' I'd look it up and the network would say, 'Don't put that one on again.' "

Even when he tried to cooperate with the legal department things backfired. "They told me that there were too many people on the show advocating marijuana. 'The show is blue,' they said. 'You've got to stop that!'

"I said let's end this once and for all by booking the chief health officer in America, a Nixon appointee. So we booked him and we were told that he was a charming old man who speaks right out and that we'd love him.

"On the show I said, 'Tell me about the marijuana laws.' He said, 'They are ridiculous!' and told about a sailor, a family man, who got a year in jail for having a joint in his pocket.

"He said the law was outrageously harsh for a first offender and added, 'I can't even get John Mitchell on the telephone to discuss it and we're in the same administration.' "

But Merv's triumphs—such as they were—were no substitute for ratings. Back at Black Rock the natives in black suits were getting restless. Bob Wood, TV network president, pretty much stayed out of it. Wood is one of two people Merv remembers with affection, the other being the current West Coast TV head, Perry Lafferty, who was his first director.

However, Merv was vexed with Mike Dann—"I'd go to dinner with him and he'd call the newspapers and leak things." Merv's encounters with Freddy Silverman, then Dann's assistant, annoyed him even more. While he admired the young man's executive touch—"I hate to say it, but Freddy, like Bob Wood who never allows anything to drag on, is decisive too"—he deplored his comments to the papers.

"Freddy and I came to vicious blows [via the press] over my future. That was stupid because I can make bigger news than he can. Finally I called *Variety* and said, 'I'll give you the real story if you print it all,' which they did." Actually, the *Variety* story also said that CBS had tried to play it safe with a "known quantity" when it bought Merv, that the idea bombed and that CBS wanted out as soon as possible.

It was obvious now that *The Merv Griffin Show* was about to be canceled. But it had to be done amicably. Peace had to be negotiated before too much dirty linen was flapping in the breeze.

"John Schneider got Bob Wood to fly to the West Coast, and we met for our summit discussion at the Bel Air Hotel [on August 13, 1971]. He gave me a fatherly talk about how it could not go on any more and said I would have to stop attacking Freddy and CBS. I then gave him *my* fatherly talk and said there would be more interviews unless there was an immediate truce.

"Bob said there would be no more interviews by any CBS executive and I said, 'All right, there will be no more by me.' I asked for my release and Bob let me out. He did it quietly and like a gentleman."

The Merv Griffin Show limped along until February 11, 1972, when Griffin's contract ran out. Says one trade press man, "The consensus was that the show failed because it was bush league for the form. If he had twice the number of stations as Carson he wouldn't have beaten him." But Merv went on to build his own company and show, which he syndicated and sold to over 100 stations in prime time—8:30 P.M. "I have three times the rating of *The Tonight Show* because there are so many times more people in the audience at that hour," he says.

That was the beginning and the end of the CBS assault on *The Tonight Show*. The next obstacle, *The Today Show*, would prove to be just as insurmountable.

In the mid-Fifties Paley tried a format that was almost a carbon copy of *The Today Show;* it was called *The Morning Show*. The first host was Jack Paar. He struck out. Then a big name (once removed) was tried: Will Rogers, Jr. Strikeout number two. Out of time, out of place. But by 1973 Bill Paley was ready to take another shot. Paley had long since changed the format to news, and his team of John Hart in New York and Nelson Benton in Washington was doing poorly.

It seemed logical to seek out some sexier-than-thou counterpart to *Today Show* superstar Barbara Walters, and some folksier male than the late Frank McGee. One version has it that the idea of having a woman cohost didn't come about until a CBS women's group backed Richard Salant into a corner one night at a party and made him promise to hire an anchor woman.

In the CBS Washington bureau, the fickle finger of fortune pointed at Lesley Stahl, a blonde beauty with that fresh-scrubbed look of innocence that caused many a reluctant interviewee to drop his guard. Her favorite prop: big round glasses with horn rims that gave her wide-eyed appeal. After her first appearance on CBS she got a long-distance call from her mother in Swampscott, Massachusetts: "Twenty million Americans saw you tonight, and one of them is my future son-in-law. But he's never going to call you because you wore your glasses." Lesley, 32, had once been a medical-school student married to a young doctor. She dropped out of med school because of an aversion to dissecting animals, and dropped her doctor husband at about the same time.

When Lesley was asked if she would like to be a big morning-TV star, she said she wouldn't. In an interview she explained: "I feel women—and minority groups—can be pushed too far too soon. I was determined that no one was going to do that to me. I thought I would be in over my head, and if they didn't know it, I would have to tell them. When you are a young woman in this business you begin to feel that if you fail, a lot of women are going to fail. I didn't think I was ready then and I don't think I am ready now."

Dick Salant agrees: "Lesley was too smart to take it." Another colleague commented: "The world is full of pretty blondes who can smile and read the news. But the world isn't full of pretty blondes who also happen to be good reporters."

Another pretty woman who also happened to be a good reporter was Sally Quinn of *The Washington Post.* Sally is a slender bottle-blonde with even white teeth, bedroom eyes and a beguiling wholesomeness, though she talks with the blunt language of a swinger. She was an "army brat" who followed her father, a peripatetic general, attending 22 schools on her way to a degree from Smith College.

A woman of considerable aplomb, she strolled into the office of the *Post's* executive editor, Benjamin C. Bradlee, five years ago to ask for a writing job.

"What have you written?" asked Bradlee, a close friend of John F. Kennedy.

Sally answered: "I've never written anything in my life."

"Well, nobody's perfect," said Bradlee. "You're hired."

In a big metropolitan newspaper where the apprenticeship traditionally means years as a copy boy filling pastepots and going for coffee, Sally's feat was prodigious. But she worked hard under the guidance of a top *Post* staffer and soon was writing some of the most delightful and titillating profiles in American journalism. Sally was a master at letting people talk until they hanged themselves. Henry Kissinger remarked that *The Washington Post's* gossip columnist, Maxine Cheshire, "makes you want to commit murder. Sally Quinn, on the other hand, makes you want to commit suicide."

Sally was also a master at bringing herself into her stories, thus gaining attention, even social notoriety, beyond that enjoyed by most reporters. In a profile of William Friedkin, the director of *The Exorcist,* Sally wrote that he "enters the door, grabs [this] reporter in his arms and presses her close and asks, 'Will you come up to my room at nine o'clock tonight?" Moments later, "A small white urinal appears from the closet. Friedkin pretends to use it. He wraps himself in a scarf and gloves, does a semi-striptease. . . ."

Clearly Sally's lively prose, imagination and talent, along with her good looks, brought her front and center in a hurry. Ironically, however, her biggest break came from Barbara Walters. Barbara interviewed several women journalists on her second NBC show, *Not for Women Only.* The subject: the role of a woman's wiles in covering the news.

In the words of Dick Salant, "Sally walked away with the show." Salant already knew Sally; she and Dick's assistant had been roommates at Smith and Salant had hired Sally as a "go-fer" (a minion who goes for coffee for higher-ups) at the 1968 Democratic and Republican conventions.

It was CBS's self-assured Gordon Manning who had the bright idea to hire Sally—though Dick Salant takes full responsibility. Manning, then a senior vice-president of the news division, met Sally for dinner. (Bradlee, worried that Sally might be about to jump ship, had Manning paged at the Cantina D'Italia restaurant and when Manning answered the telephone said, simply, "Screw you.")

Sally expressed an interest, contracts were drawn up, and CBS agreed to pay her an enormous salary—at least in the eyes of the many reporters who read about Sally's coup. Her agent told her to say she was getting $45,000, but the figure was upward of that, possibly as much as $75,000. Hughes Rudd says $55,000. Whatever the figure, it brought the press down on Sally even before she made her debut. It inspired a hatchet job in *New York* magazine that made her seem like CBS's answer to Mae West. Her love affairs were discussed in meticulous detail, and many others were hinted at, with her own words used to suggest she was anybody's bedmate. The article, by ex-*Post* colleague Aaron Latham, was called "Waking Up with Sally Quinn." She graced the magazine's cover propped on a steamer trunk, hand provocatively on hip, smiling come hither. It wasn't exactly the right introduction for the woman CBS had groomed to beat the redoubtable Barbara Walters.

The *New York* article hardly astonished Sally—a reporter had used her in much the same way she used interviewees. But what infuriated her was the interpretation, so laced with sex and innuendo. She went to Dick Salant's office almost in tears. Salant posted a memo saying, "I didn't hire Sally because she was a sex kitten, but because she is a good reporter."

But the damage was done. The audience—particularly the tough New York audience—was not so much interested in whether CBS would answer NBC's *Today* with a balanced, intelligent, lively show, but in whether Sally could live up to her sexy notices. Anything short of a striptease was bound to be disappointing.

But even without the adverse publicity, the cards were heavily stacked against Sally. *The Today Show* brought a skillfully blended daily amalgam of news, newsmakers, personalities and entertainment features. It has been a powerhouse for two decades. Its impact was and is pervasive. Every politician with a trial balloon eagerly seeks out producer Stuart Schulberg (his brother Budd is the author of *On the Waterfront* and *What Makes Sammy Run?*) asking for an opportunity to send it up on *Today*. Authors and publishers are well aware that *The Today Show* sells more books than any other single program.

The Today Show made the time period important to TV in the first place. It is carried by all of NBC's affiliated stations as well as its five owned and operated stations, reaching more than 5 million viewers between 7 and 9 A.M. five days a week. Its pulling power is obvious to sponsors; NBC commands a whopping $5700 for 30 seconds of sponsored time.

CBS by contrast reaches only a third as many with its *CBS Morning News*—about 1.7 million viewers. The show, from 7 to 8 A.M., fails to interest scores of CBS affiliates throughout the CBS system. They do their own thing and the result is that sponsors pay only $1000 per 30-second exposure.

Today is one of the most carefully prepared shows in the business. An expert on, say, baby care, whether the author of a new book or someone brought in to explain the dangers of Asian flu to infants, gets a call from a *Today Show* "writer." The writer has prepared a list of probable questions and wants to know if they are relevant. Are there any other areas to be explored? The list is culled and the questions polished. But if Barbara Walters and Gene Shalit are questioning the expert and the show goes off on a relevant tangent, fine. They may never get back to the prepared questions. If the interview turns out to be especially successful, Schulberg may give the signal to cut odds and ends so that the conversation can play another four or five minutes.

In contrast to this professionalism, CBS was paying a big buck to an amateur. "What have you done on TV, Sally?" "Nothing!" "Nobody's perfect—you're hired!" Sally's grooming took place in publicity and promotion channels rather than in the rehearsal studio. And to boot, viewers got an entirely different woman when *The CBS Morning News* debuted at 7 A.M. on August 6, 1973, with Sally and Hughes Rudd. Prim and tailored in a plain striped blouse, she seemed far from a femme fatale. What's more, she was obviously suffering from mike fright. She bit her lip nervously as she read the news off the prompter in what *Time* magazine described as an "arid monotone." Unprofessionally, she apologized to viewers: "Wouldn't you know the first day I come on television I start out with a sore throat and a fever." (She had, in fact, been in a hospital room recovering just two hours before air time.) Her cohost, gravel-voiced Hughes Rudd, brought 14 years of CBS news service to the job. A tough-minded professional, his stage presence emphasized Sally's inexperience.

As a journalist, Sally had been highly successful in the personalized account, making the reader enjoy her own exploits as much as those of the people she interviewed. Her efforts to bring herself into the story on television were embarrassing by contrast. On the first show she followed a grim report on child-labor abuse among migrant workers with the comment: "I can remember when my mother and father wanted me to clean my room—I thought that was child labor." After a segment about Chesapeake Bay's contaminated clams, Sally recalled covering a crab derby in Maryland.

A major share of the blame must go to the CBS producers. They failed to capitalize on Sally's considerable talent for interviews. Both Sally and Hughes Rudd were left to their own devices all too often during newscasts. The program was badly organized and instructions to ad-lib often came up after a news item. There were 40 seconds to fill and it was up to Hughes and Sally to wing it to the next commercial during which Hughes would try to raise Sally's spirits with a punch line from one of his favorite stories about a famous cowboy star—a punch line that was to characterize Sally's entire experience at CBS.

As Hughes tells it, the star was to appear at the Rose Bowl game in a gold lamé outfit designed to fit him so snugly that he was actually sewn into it. When he tried to mount, he was so drunk that he fell off the horse several times. Finally, he managed to maintain his seat and rode his horse onto the field. Suddenly, however, he reined the horse to a halt. An attendant rushed out and asked, "What's the matter, sir?" Whereupon the cowboy announced stentoriously, "Get me off this horse immediately, I have just shit my pants!"

As the cameras left the two after another limp ad-lib session, Hughes would break up Sally with the remark, "Get me off this horse immediately!"

Sally was going to use the line as the title of her book about the CBS debacle. She abandoned the idea, in part out of fear that she would wind up on TV talk shows trying to explain the title in some decorous manner.

Sally improved, but she never developed the presence of a top newscaster. Soon the broadcast corridors echoed with rumors that the miscast miss was on the way out. Sally wouldn't have it that way. She quit and was last seen on the news show on January 18, 1974.

Says Dick Salant, ruefully: "When Sally quit, a CBS executive asked me if I didn't think Sally threw us a curve for walking out on the contract. I said no. It wasn't her mistake. It was ours. We didn't see it through and take the time to train her. . . . The transition from newspaper journalism to going on the air is very hard."

Sally's back at *The Washington Post* now, doing what she always did so well. For the paper's Sunday magazine, she wrote about Alice Roosevelt Longworth at 90, the irrepressible daughter of Teddy Roosevelt. In her article she quoted Alice as saying:

"But you know in those days [when her father was president] people were always having love affairs with their poodles and putting tiny flowers in strange places."

The grande dame then remarked that she was amused by some sexual things that are "terribly funny. Like dear old men's things hanging all around them. I think that's terribly funny."

"What?" asked Sally.

"Men's penises, my dear," said Mrs. Longworth, leaning forward waiting for a reaction.

Then after Sally's howl of astonished laughter, the old lady visualized the newspaper piece to come: "Oh, I can see it now. . . . Dear old Mrs. Longworth . . . talking about men's penises."

Sally was back in her element, no threat to Barbara Walters. She never was. Which proves, if nothing else, that there remain a few things that Bill Paley just can't manage.

CHAPTER 31
Bad Day at Black Rock

CLIVE DAVIS, THE YOUNG, CHERUBIC PRESIDENT OF COLUMBIA RECORDS, was sitting at his desk in his modest offices at CBS, going through his usual morning routine—opening his mail, meeting with associates, eating his cornflakes. It was May 29, 1973, just after the Memorial Day weekend.

Davis's executive appearance was somehow dissonant at Black Rock. He wore the tastefully arresting mod suits of the fashionable Manhattan East Side boutiques, not the Brooks Brothers grays and blacks of most CBS executives.

He was conferring with a British record executive when the intercom buzzed. It was CBS president Arthur Taylor's secretary. "Mr. Davis," she said, "could you come up to see Mr. Taylor?"

Davis mused that when the new CBS president's secretary called she usually said Taylor wanted to see him at a certain hour. If she didn't set a time, it meant *now*. He excused himself, stepped into an elevator and, vaguely troubled, was wafted to the executive offices on the thirty-fifth floor. Taylor's suite was even more sumptuous than the one Davis was about to inherit from CBS senior vice-president Goddard Lieberson—as a reward for Columbia Records' great success.

Davis had enjoyed a spectacular career at CBS Records. A recruit from CBS's outside law firm, Davis entered the world of music to find the prestigious record company grown tired and complacent. Its catalog featured war-horse symphonies whose slow, measured cadences reflected their sales at the record shops, and Broadway show albums that perhaps set the world on fire the year the show appeared but no longer.

Davis arrived a stodgy lawyer and became an aggressive, sympathetic music master who gained the respect, affection and contracts of the nation's top rock musicians. These were talented, youthful groups with weird names like Santana; Blood, Sweat & Tears; and the Mahavishnu Orchestra.

At age 40 he was top banana at the world's largest record company, a company that grossed over $300 million in 1972 and was almost half as big as the CBS Broadcast Group itself. Profits grew apace and Columbia Records earned nearly $27 million that year, again nearly half the profit of the Broadcast Group.

Dark-haired, conventionally handsome Arthur Taylor, the man upstairs, was a recent import from a paper company. Two years younger than Davis, he had been appointed to the job that some believed was Davis's by right.

Taylor had once tried his hand at radio and lost a censorship battle. As a Brown University freshman he had a radio-interview program until a student manager of the station demanded the right to approve his guests in advance. Apart from this brief brush with broadcasting, Taylor was a neophyte. He was hired for his financial acumen, not his broadcast background.

There were those who said that Taylor brought Wall Street financial "efficiency" to CBS. When Stanton was boss, nobody paid much attention to how much each man spent for lunch. The idea was to trust each man to use good sense and be honest. Says one ex-CBS man: "Stanton didn't care whether a man took a company limo home when he wasn't entitled to, because at the end of the year everything worked out okay. But under the Taylor regime, any man who tips more than fifteen percent pays out of his own pocket."

The moment Clive Davis entered Taylor's office that morning in May, he realized this was to be no ordinary meeting. Davis recalls:

He had two lawyers with him—and the meeting lasted about two minutes. It was calculated to last no more. I don't remember the exact words he said—perhaps I've blocked them—but the intent was clear. I was being told to leave the company.

"I'm in shock," I said, perhaps more than once. It was all I could think of.

"We'd like you to return to your office," Taylor continued, "and take whatever you'd like to take with you, and leave immediately."

That was it. That was the end of my love affair with Columbia Records. It was numbing; it seemed incredibly cold-blooded. I couldn't believe it. But that was it. There was nothing left to say. I turned on my heel and walked out of the office.

At the door Davis was met by two CBS security men who served a civil complaint on him, then fell in step and took him back to his eleventh-floor offices.

Says Davis in his book, *Clive: Inside the Record Business:*

Something in a man's life—or mind—tends, even at the worst moments, to put things in perspective. A week earlier, my thirteen-year-old cousin, Stephan John, had died of cancer. He was the grandson of my Aunt Jeanette, who had been like a mother to me after my parents died; she and I had visited him in the hospital for nearly three months, agonizedly watching this small boy literally waste away. . . .

Somehow the vision of Stephan's suffering held my emotions in check as I rode down the elevator and walked into my office for the last time. I kept thinking that *my* pain was insignificant compared to his.

Davis went to his office, took his checkbook, a few papers and other personal effects, and stuffed them into his attaché case. He told his secretary the news and left quickly, seeing no one else.

Taylor had said that Davis could take his company limousine home. When he arrived he learned that his wife, Janet, was at school with the kids, so he sent the limousine for her. "Thirty minutes later, my housekeeper took a call from CBS saying that the chauffeur had been gone too long. They wanted him back. . . ."

To the working man struggling to meet the mortgage payments, feed the family and have enough left to take his wife to an occasional movie, Clive Davis was out of sight. Here was a man with a wife and a couple of kids who would appear to have the same nut to make as the average guy, but couldn't get it together on $359,000 a year. CBS charged in its complaint—and Clive Davis never exactly denied it—that in 1972 he padded his expense account: $53,729.20 to feather his Central Park West nest; $13,000 to rent a Beverly Hills villa plus $6500 for refurbishing; and $20,000 to stake his son to a bar mitzvah to remember, in Manhattan's Plaza Hotel.

Just how the well-heeled executive could find himself in need of an extra $94,000 when he was paid almost 20 times as much as the average executive is a mystery. Clive Davis isn't talking. CBS isn't talking. And, if they manage to settle out of court, chances are they never will talk. Davis's lips were sealed by his lawyer, former New York City police commissioner Vincent L. Broderick, and though Davis agonized over newspaper stories dismantling his reputation, he obeyed orders.

One industry source remarked, with a cynicism that clashed with the sanctimonious attitude of CBS officialdom: "CBS is idiotic to bust the president of its biggest division for a hundred thousand dollars." That attitude, shared by many in the record industry, sprang from Davis's accomplishments, both actual and claimed. Goddard Lieberson, the urbane executive who some say typifies the patrician, sophisticated CBS type, scoffed when he was told that Davis claimed credit for abolishing monaural records at CBS and thereafter offered only the higher-priced stereo records that could be played on monaural equipment. The move became industry-wide and was certainly important. But Lieberson commented, "Are you kidding? The decision was made years before he was in that job." And concerning Davis's claim that he had invented variable pricing under which hot albums were priced at a premium, Lieberson, who was both Davis's predecessor and successor as president of Columbia Records, seemed baffled and annoyed. He said he couldn't understand why Davis would be thinking about marketing matters when the responsibility for that rested elsewhere.

Davis prided himself on his acceptance by the youthful rock entertainers who flocked to the CBS banner during his reign, and he fancied himself a man of musical gifts despite the lack of formal training. Ben Fong-Torres acknowledged much of this in *Rolling Stone*, the leading rock- and youth-oriented newspaper, calling Davis a "genius" at selling records:

"[Davis] became an aggressive part of the rock scene, signing as many important artists as he did duds, making much more money than the amounts he would be reported spending. People laughed [however] when he signed Delaney and Bonnie only to have them get divorced shortly after the signing. . . ." Ben Fong-Torres added that, while Davis "may have been guilty of arrogance and a Yankee-sized ego," most managers of Columbia artists said Davis treated them sympathetically and well.

What obviously concerned CBS, critics of his firing charged, was that a federal drug investigation had turned up a link between Clive Davis's personal aide, David Wynshaw, and the drug scene. This raised the threat that the company would become enmeshed in a major scandal, offering a beleaguered Nixon administration an effective weapon in its efforts to curb CBS's power.

The link to CBS was turned up in an investigation that followed a wiretap by the Federal Bureau of Narcotics and Dangerous Drugs. The tap was on the telephone of reputed New Jersey mobster Pasquale (Patsy) Falcone in the winter of 1972–73, and it led to Falcone's indictment on drug charges. Falcone shared an office, a secretary and some talent-management work with one Frank Campana, who a year and a half earlier left CBS where he had been head of artist relations for Columbia Records before Wynshaw. Wynshaw's name turned up in Falcone's papers. The very nature of Wynshaw's role at CBS was enough to suggest that he might well have unsavory connections. To some, Wynshaw seemed a glorified "go-fer," but if Wynshaw was a go-fer he must have been El Exigente among them.

Wynshaw was commissioned to keep the influential happy—the recording artists, their managers, their agents, and CBS executives themselves. How he did this was not generally known, and his modus operandi was the subject of much gossip and controversy. One CBS colleague described Wynshaw as "pretty much a loner. . . . He worked in his office, the door closed, often locked. He carried a gun all the time. He was considered Clive's man. I don't remember him interacting with other people."

But Wynshaw's lawyer disagreed, saying Wynshaw was "one of the most popular guys over there. It was partly because of his very gregarious personality, but partly because of the largesse he had to pass around. If you wanted to go to the Copa and get a front table, he was the guy who could get it for you. If you wanted to go to the Giants football game and it was all sold out, he was the guy who could get you tickets."

Before Davis was fired he learned that CBS was conducting an internal audit of Wynshaw and his operations. Naturally he was concerned:

> I personally relied upon Wynshaw tremendously to ease a number of my administrative burdens. He had become expert at the job of artist relations and, through that, he had become extremely efficient at booking hotels and flights and arranging all special business meetings for the records division since the early 1960s—before I moved to the business side.
>
> After I became president, he continued to take care of the arrangements for all dinners and showcasings of artists at any convention in which we were participating. Also, I more and more turned to him to handle many personal chores. It allowed me to concentrate one hundred percent on the creative and business matters of the company that were consuming twelve to eighteen hours of my day.

Wynshaw failed to pass the internal audit. Says Davis, "As a result of this audit, I was told to fire Wynshaw, and I did."

The investigation was broadened to include others, including Davis himself, ultimately turning up the expense account irregularities that led to the Davis dismissal.

Among other damaging allegations against Davis in the CBS complaint was an item that suggested he was aware that Wynshaw was capable of chicanery and, more than that, had himself participated in at least one Wynshaw caper. CBS alleged that that $6500 which Davis was supposed to have used to fix up his West Coast digs had been handed to him by Wynshaw in the form of 65 $100 bills.

But the web that threatened to entangle CBS in scandal had several threads. The record industry is not peopled by paragons and popes. Some pop musicians have bad habits. It is widely known that cocaine and other expensive drugs are in demand in some rock circles, and a world-famed entertainer can't make a personal visit to a local connection to stock up. Some alleged that rock stars "connected" in the corridors of their record companies.

At CBS, one former record aide says, "Grass [marijuana] and even coke [cocaine] were sometimes available—but strictly on an informal and unofficial basis. No smack [heroin] was offered under *any* circumstances."

To untutored musical ears, one hard-rock number may be the equal of another. The volume is high, the beat is heavy and a teenybopper can't tell the difference. The disc jockey therefore can plug what he's paid for. Add payola charges to drugola and the formula equals instant headlines.

After his dismissal from CBS, Wynshaw was ready to provide evidence that payola was not foreign to CBS operations. He told federal attorneys that Columbia was paying $7000 a week to a tip-sheet publisher, Kal Rudman, who advised radio men what songs were popular around the country. The thrust of Wynshaw's testimony was that this could work two ways: Rudman could listen a lot and find out what was *being* played; or, if he were dishonest, he could pass the bread to station men and see to it that records he took an interest in *were* played. Wynshaw suggested that Rudman was paying, not listening.

Rudman later acknowledged CBS payments, but argued that his CBS pay was sporadic, not weekly, and that it paid salaries and expenses of six to ten promotion men who occasionally worked for him, visiting radio stations and plugging records. He didn't have to pay for play because his tip-sheet choices usually became hits, he said.

In the light of all this, a compelling case can be made for the theory that CBS guessed what an investigation would turn up and sacked Davis on a lesser charge—expense-account cheating. Fast action to wipe out corruption, the theory goes, would forestall an anticipated attack by, among others, Nixon cohorts eager to blunt the tough reporting by CBS on Watergate.

There was also speculation at Black Rock over the possibility of direct FCC sanctions, if a drug or payola scandal could be laid at CBS's door, perhaps even against one or more of CBS's five highly profitable owned-and-operated TV stations. The loss of just one of these stations would be calamitous. WCBS-TV in New York, the company's flagship station, is reportedly generating $24 million in pretax profits on revenue of $55 million—about 11 percent of CBS Inc.'s earnings. If making a sacrificial lamb of Davis could avert a possible FCC sanction, then Davis would have to go, even if the ostensible reason—expense padding —did not sound so convincing.

The incident must also be considered in the light of expense-account morality in this country. Following national standards, a salesman or a member of the CBS news-gathering team gets a bit more leeway than a secretary who is, say, sent to Newark to pick up a contract. One junior executive complains of different rules for different CBS groups: "That frigging news division spends money like it is going out of style. I always personally resented it!"

Certainly CBS expense rules were liberal when applied to Bill Paley and to Frank Stanton. One source remarked with awe about a corporate jet: "Anybody can do a custom interior. But when Paley used the plane, he had one decor and when Stanton used it there was an entirely different one—right down to color schemes, headrests and even the ice buckets."

Still Stanton had to defer to Paley when their flying schedules conflicted. Ralph Colin, speaking after his abrupt departure after 40 years as CBS outside counsel, said that Paley treated CBS like a personal fiefdom long after the company went public. Colin asserts that when Bill Paley wanted to take over the company plane, whether for business or personal reasons, he simply took it, even though the plane might be scheduled to fly Frank Stanton and a flock of vice-presidents to Washington. Frank and the boys would presumably take the shuttle. Colin concedes that Paley carefully logged his flying hours so that he wouldn't get into tax difficulties over it not qualifying as a company plane. But, says Colin, "If he uses the plane for personal reasons, I understand he pays for gas only—no salaries, insurance, depreciation, maintenance, et cetera."

The CBS expense policy was apparently liberal for all top executives. *The Wall Street Journal* quoted William Brown, a former salaried CBS designer who left to set up his own firm, as saying he did similar work to that done in Davis's apartment for "almost every executive there— ninety percent of them." He then sent the bills to CBS. He says he was told the company would bill the executives for the personal work, but he didn't know whether that actually happened. (The *Journal* later printed a CBS statement denying Brown's claim. The company said that Brown's work for CBS executives was "a private arrangement" outside office hours and that CBS "was in no way involved.")

Some members of CBS's 50-man legal staff suggested that Davis's indiscretions be ignored. What's $100,000 when a man earns so much for the company? But chief counsel Robert Evans didn't agree. As a self-styled "Taft Republican from Ohio," he believes a man is either honest or dishonest, no middle ground. He indicated that he would recommend firing an employee if he so much as charged CBS 35 cents for a subway token and the trip was personal, not business.

Evans must be ignorant of what goes on, or he would be sending memos asking that men be fired left and right. For at CBS as elsewhere, the expense account has been employed for years as a useful device to accomplish any number of purposes.

For example, a young member of the CBS news staff was doing quite well in his early days at the network. He was promoted rapidly but soon ran into a job-rating ceiling. He needed and deserved more money and his senior acknowledged as much but said there was no way to provide it by the pay scale. His superior called him into his office and gave him a little advice:

"Look, under FCC rules you are required to maintain contacts in the community, right? You're a single man. Some of your dates must work for politicians in this town. Take them to dinner, to the theater, enjoy yourself. And put the charges on your expense account."

His case was by no means unique and while he was at CBS he knew of many people urged to live a little on their expense accounts to get money that was "due" but couldn't be paid directly.

Since living off the expense account was so common then, does that suggest that CBS actually had more on Clive than it alleged in its formal complaint? Some link, perhaps, to drugs or payola? One long-time employee of CBS offered two possible answers to the question:

I have heard that they had a lot more on Clive than a hundred thousand dollars. Knowing CBS as I do, either they had a lot more or they knew that the IRS was going after Clive and they figured they had to get him first. There is no way that CBS would have let Clive go for a mere hundred thousand. I don't buy that morality bit at all. A lot of company money is used by executives for personal purposes.

Besides, the bar mitzvah could be justified. The record business is a very personal one and the artists have to have an almost physical relationship with the head of the company. The artists are very young, many are on drugs and they have a lot of money and need a father figure to guide them. They came in droves to the bar mitzvah and Davis's family and friends were scarcely visible in that crowd.

Given that scenario—before the record scandal—I could see the bar mitzvah as a business expense. The West Coast house is justifiable too since he was to be there for four months. Clive needed an appropriate place to entertain and on the West Coast that calls for a house with a swimming pool—not a hotel suite.

The New York apartment expenses are harder to explain, but still it's a question of finding ways to support a lifestyle that is required in the business. It's not easy to live within a budget on after-tax dollars, no matter how much a man gets paid.

A lawyer friend of mine said that he had been doing well on fifty thousand dollars a year, taking the family to Europe, et cetera, until he moved into show business. Then the fifty thousand wouldn't begin to cover. He told me, "I'm visible in this job. I have to have forty suits and send my kids to the best schools. When we go to Europe we don't rent a Volks anymore. I have to go first class, stay in the best hotels. My wife has to wear elegant shoes, carry a Gucci bag. When we are on the West Coast we have to stay at the Beverly Hills Hotel and she has to go on thousand-dollar spending sprees with the wife of an executive in a similar position. It's a whole different scene!'"

Forty suits? Well that's show biz. Expensive.

But perhaps the reason Davis was doomed was much simpler. He was beginning to experience the same failing that Jim Aubrey did: fading success. He was spending heavily for talent and the record division wasn't doing as well as before. The whole industry was suffering financial difficulties at the time Davis went. Threats from the federal government of one sort or another provided additional fuel for his expulsion. As one industry official put it: "CBS hadn't cracked a good new artist since 1971. Maybe they felt they didn't need Clive anymore. You could make a case for that."

But CBS is sticking to its story, a simple case of massive expense-account padding. One executive high on the corporate ladder explained it in these terms:

Davis at some time or another came to the conclusion that he was giving the company every waking moment and therefore that CBS should give him every creature comfort in return. Now a prudent man in those circumstances would say, "Let's get another opinion." An arrogant man like Davis says, "I don't need another opinion. What's good for Clive is good for CBS." He confuses his corporate self with his personal self. He says to himself, "My sole efforts earned CBS twenty-five million dollars last year for which they paid me a mere three hundred and sixty thousand. I'm not going to let the puritanical strictures of corporate bookkeepers who aren't creative and can't understand my needs stand in my way."

On the advice of counsel, Clive Davis remains mute. Some point out that Davis hasn't countersued CBS for defamation. But Davis is negotiating with CBS for a settlement of its suit against him for the $100,-000. It is a delicate moment, no time for a countersuit.

Regardless of the feeling among some professionals that Clive Davis is not as good as his press notices—no better than a handful of equally talented record executives who didn't have his power base—he was publicly recognized as a first-rate executive even after the debacle. In late August 1973, three months after he was fired, the National Association of TV and Radio Announcers named Davis "Record Company Executive of the Year."

Back at Black Rock, Clive's abrupt dismissal, complete with security-guard escort, was a grim reminder that at CBS, as at many tightly run corporations, unexplained things sometimes extinguish careers with frightening suddenness. In this case, insufficient clues are left for even the most astute observers to solve the mystery.

CBS shifted gears—and executive styles—quickly, bringing back old smoothie Goddard Lieberson to take the job again. After a period of retrenchment—"There was a little too much Louis Quatorze going on" —profits resumed their uptrend in the records division.

As for Clive Davis the man, he was loved and he was hated, like so many who vault to sudden and enormous success. Before the fall, a nonadmirer in the record industry walked into a men's boutique on Manhattan's East Side and nodded to Davis as Davis walked out. A clerk gushed, "Isn't he nice?" and the man replied, "I think he is one of the great shits of the Western World!"

Without a pause, the clerk responded, "We think so too." Why did the clerk say he was nice, then? "Well . . . we thought he was a friend of yours!"

CHAPTER 32

The Man Bill Paley
Never Really Liked

RALPH COLIN, THE SHARP AND TESTY LAWYER, EXPECTED MORE FROM Bill Paley than what he got. He had been outside counsel for CBS for over 40 years, and Paley's personal lawyer as well. He had nursed his secret grievances against Bill Paley for four decades, but on the surface they coexisted well enough. What he got from Paley—after a vicious fight that, ironically, had nothing to do with CBS—was an abrupt dismissal.

Colin had been with CBS even before Paley, having served Jerome Louchheim before Paley bought out the bridge builder–sportsman's interests in the fledgling network. Afraid that Paley would get credit for having founded CBS, Colin asked a reporter for *The New York Times* to stuff a piece Colin had written for *Variety* into the Bill Paley file at the *Times*. The *Variety* piece, written after Paley gave him the axe, traces the career of impresario Arthur Judson and gives him credit for setting up the network that was to become CBS. Taking no chances, Colin also asked the reporter to put a copy of the article in the Arthur Judson clips; Judson, at age 93, could be expected to have his obituary in the *Times* before Paley. Judson died in January 1975 and his obituaries gave him proper credit as a CBS founder, though he probably would have been so identified without the Colin assist.

Colin got to his relatively high station in life through hard work and meticulous attention to detail. A righteous man who could be ruthless as well, he set himself up as a "guardian of morals—telling everybody how to conduct himself," a critic says, though adding, "Colin was also an extremely honest and upright fellow, however cantankerous." Colin naturally resented those to whom things came easily—such as a Bill Paley who started life with a considerable fortune and built on it with an easy flair.

Both Paley and Colin had long had an interest in modern art. Colin had a solid grounding in art history; Paley had something else—an intuitive sense of esthetic values.

Colin's approach to art reflected the man. He cultivated a taste for modern art, became a collector and put together a fine group of masterworks. He set up the Art Dealers Association of America with scores of members and with the professed purpose of improving industry standards. But one critic comments,

It was really a self-interest group, rigid about whom to admit and anxious to carve out a big slice of the business for its members. When Stephen Radich, a nonmember, was charged with desecrating the flag after displaying flags crafted into obscene shapes, Radich begged the association to bear witness in his behalf. The group refused, and Colin, a superconservative, who serves the group as general counsel, was said to have been strongly behind the decision. Isolated by the trade, Radich was hard pressed to defend himself and was convicted.

Fortunately for Radich, the American Civil Liberties Union was more sympathetic. After the Supreme Court failed to resolve the matter, a Federal judge overturned the conviction in November 1974.

Both Paley and Colin gave their time to the Museum of Modern Art in Manhattan, a product of Nelson Rockefeller's money, power and good taste. For years, Bill Paley was president and Ralph Colin a fellow member of the board of trustees and of the executive committee.

Not only was Paley president but his brother-in-law, John Hay Whitney, was vice-chairman of the museum's board; J. Frederic Byers II, married to Hilary Paley, the adopted daughter of Bill and his first wife, Dorothy, was a vice-president; board member William A.M. Burden was the uncle of Paley's ex-son-in-law, New York City Councilman

Carter Burden (married to, then divorced from, Babe Paley's daughter Amanda). John Hay Whitney's sister, Joan Payson, colorful owner of the New York Mets, was also on the board.

Beyond doubt, serving on the museum board is a status symbol reserved for the few. It also allows the trustees to be among the first to know when an important collection is about to be sold. Paley, David Rockefeller and other museum trustees once formed a syndicate to buy the late author Gertrude Stein's extensive collection of modern art. A patron of young artists in Paris, Miss Stein bought many early works that later had great value. After purchasing the Stein collection, the trustee-syndicate then arranged a show at the museum which was underwritten by a foundation. When an unfamiliar collection is displayed at an important museum, considerable value is added to the pieces, and this show was no exception. Each of the trustees in the syndicate then gave one of his Stein pieces to the museum, thus earning a sizable tax deduction, and *everybody* benefited.

With so many friends and allies on the board, it is little wonder that Paley, a man accustomed to running his own business, felt he could run the museum in virtually the same way, making decisions after touching base with a few close associates. But Colin didn't see it that way. Colin's private life revolved around art: His wife Georgia was a well-regarded decorator and had done the elegant apartment of Ed Klauber's widow, to mention just one satisfied client; and Colin's personal art collection was large enough to make a book of photographic reproductions, which he published privately.

Colin admired Paley's genius for show business as well as his shrewd business instincts: "He could ask very embarrassing questions about a balance sheet." He nevertheless felt that Paley was superficial, impatient with detail and thus a man who "never succeeded in understanding the complex structure of a business." For instance, Colin was appalled that for years Paley allowed his London World War II buddy, Edward R. Murrow, to ignore the organizational structure and deal directly with the Chairman. It is the Ralph Colins of the world who toil so that the Bill Paleys can play. Or so thought Colin.

He concedes that Paley's "superb" ability to judge men played a vital role in CBS's success. Paley chose top men to run the business—Kesten, Stanton, and even Klauber, though Colin had serious misgivings about Klauber's tyrannical conduct toward staffers.

Colin once spent three hours in Paley's limousine in front of the Paley townhouse off Park Avenue arguing that Paley had to fire Klauber, despite the man's considerable executive talents. He claimed to be appalled at the way Klauber undermined morale by such acts as publicly reaming his assistants. "He was one of the three really cruel men I have ever known," Colin says, without saying who the other two were.

Deferential enough to survive Bill Paley's own sometimes autocratic methods at CBS for over four decades, Colin hit the ceiling in late 1969 when Paley suddenly fired Bates Lowry, the director of the Museum of Modern Art, without calling a board meeting or even consulting with Colin and some of the other trustees.

Colin had always been disappointed that the "superbly equipped" Paley contributed little of his energy to the day-to-day business of running the museum. "I worked on committees and did staff work. . . . Bill never did. He hadn't the vaguest idea of how things worked."

How dare a man who refused to plan the budget take it upon himself to fire the director?

It is possible that Colin lost his perspective in dealing with this "disaster," as he termed the firing of Bates Lowry. The museum survived without permanent damage. But to make his point, Colin lost one of his firm's most important clients and his own lucrative assignment as the Paley family's personal attorney, a window on the world of kings. CBS business was so important to Colin's firm (Rosenman, Colin, Kaye, Petschek, Freund & Emil) that, after the loss, the legal fraternity buzzed with gossip that the firm might have to be restructured to compensate. Perhaps it was these considerations that prompted senior partner Ralph Colin to prepare a memo—legal in tone—to defend his actions and show why, in his opinion, he had no choice but to take a stand. The memo describes a Bill Paley unfamiliar to the public and reveals something of Colin as well.

Colin wrote that he got a phone call from the museum's senior curator asking what could be done about the "impending catastrophe." When Colin expressed ignorance about the decision to dismiss director Bates Lowry, the curator was incredulous that the staff knew more than the trustees. It seems that Paley had ordered telegrams sent the trustees he didn't consult, and that somehow they were delayed at the Western Union office.

Colin read the report of Lowry's "resignation" in the following day's *New York Times*. Enraged that he hadn't been consulted on a matter "so vitally important" to the museum, he set in motion the events which led to his ouster. He confided to two other trustees that he intended to resign from the board. One, a vice-chairman, had been told of the move against Lowry in advance; the other, a vice-president, had not.

But then Bill Paley called Colin at his law firm, and Colin sat at his desk, building a head of steam as he listened to Paley. Then he did the unforgivable. He gave the boss hell.

> I told him that there had been considerable flak from outside sources and that I had created some personally. I explained that I had heard numerous opinions expressed that the action taken had been mistaken in its method as well as intemperate and ill-timed, and that, while I had no opinion on the merits . . . because I had not been informed of the facts, I objected on the ground that the action had been taken without a meeting of the board and that therefore I intended to resign from the board. . . .
>
> He angrily told me that he would be glad to accept my resignation whenever tendered and hung up the telephone with a bang.

Perhaps if Ralph Colin had left it at that, Bill Paley might have chalked it up to his old associate's admirable candor. After all, nobody overheard the conversation—it was a disagreement between two grown men.

But Colin was unable to drop the matter. He became determined to air his views before the rest of the board. "Any other course would have been cowardly," he explains.

Perhaps, though, it was as much due to the fact that Colin had been seething inwardly for 43 years at what he regarded as Paley's high-handedness, his lavish habits, his plane rides, his decorating and redecorating his office, always at CBS expense. During the "hard times" of the mid-1960s (when cigarette ads were banned from TV) Colin was miffed, and insists that the "bulk" of the executives felt the same way, when Paley refused to get rid of the company jet. Similarly, Colin says that though everybody told Paley the jet set would never come to the restaurant he planned for the first level of Black Rock—The Ground

Floor—Paley went ahead with his extravagant plans for the sumptuous restaurant anyway. Though he didn't get approval—according to Colin —he spent $2 million in an unsuccessful effort to make it go. Colin says Paley, plagued by post-Hytron indecision, delayed the opening of The Ground Floor for six months while he weighed "the color and length of the curtains."

Years of such irritations no doubt played a part in Ralph Colin's decision to attend the next museum meeting and vent his feelings before the board.

At the meeting—which Chairman David Rockefeller missed and Gardiner Cowles chaired—Colin expressed his opinion that the Bates Lowry matter had deserved the full board's consideration. According to Colin, Paley then accused him of "changing his tune," and after listening to Paley's interpretation of the phone conversation they had had earlier, Colin shot back that Paley "was in error" and the usually decorous board meeting turned hot and heavy. It was all quite embarrassing.

The next morning Colin was summoned to Paley's office and told that after "long and hard" thought Paley was ending the professional relationship of Colin with the Paley family. Says Colin, Paley "wanted no discussion . . . so I said I would offer none and promptly left his office." But he didn't like it one bit.

"After having been his personal counsel for forty-two years, I resented the arrogance of Mr. Paley in discharging me without any discussion in the manner in which he might have discharged a valet." Jack Gould commented, with some amusement, on the separation: "Ralph Colin is pure surgeon. But he was out-surgeoned by Paley."

Colin says that he waited for some weeks and then asked for a meeting with Paley in the hopes of burying the hatchet. Far from it; at the meeting Paley indicated that, in addition to his personal severance from Colin, Colin and his firm might not be serving CBS much longer either. There was "dissatisfaction" in the CBS legal department, Paley is supposed to have said, and he told Colin that the relationship had been continued by Paley because of their long association.

On January 26, 1970, Colin was called to Frank Stanton's office where he learned that Robert Evans, CBS's general counsel, had written a memo to Paley and Stanton suggesting new outside counsel. Colin says that he had been given assurances by Paley that if there was to be such a change, Stanton would make the decision. But Stanton told Colin at their meeting that Paley had phoned from Nassau and instructed Stanton to fire Colin and his firm.

To quote Colin's "for the record" memo:

Here again I accepted without question, as I must, the right of a client at any time, for any or no reason, to terminate a professional relationship. However, I cannot but feel—it is too coincidental for me to feel otherwise—that the action was taken because of Mr. Paley's personal anger and vindictiveness at my daring to differ with him at the museum on a matter of policy and to express my differences publicly, and his desire to chastise me and my firm as a result.

Such precipitative action in terminating a 43-year relationship on the unexplained recommendation of a recently appointed general counsel makes no other conclusion possible. To misquote Genesis: "The voice was Evans's voice, but the hands were the hands of Paley."

While my resignation from the board of CBS had not been requested—yet—I did not intend to subject myself to the further indignity of waiting for such a request. I therefore resigned from the CBS board.

Curiously, Colin lacks the magnetism to draw the friendship of some of those he feels he has been a friend to. Former CBS-TV president Lou Cowan, suspecting Colin of having had a hand in getting him fired in the wake of the quiz scandals, won't speak to Colin. For unexplained reasons even the late Arthur Judson, for whom Colin had the greatest fondness and respect, lapsed into fury when he thought of Colin. On one occasion, a few months before Judson's death, such an outburst brought Judson's wife rushing into his den to caution, "Now, dear, don't you libel anyone!"

Perhaps Colin, who disguised his real feelings about Paley for so many years, should have realized how Paley felt about him. After all, though Colin had arranged for the judge to marry Bill and his second wife Babe, he hadn't been invited to the wedding.

Colin told Paley at their last meeting that the sole reason he had come was to attempt to establish a "decent friendly relationship between us so that we could meet without embarrassment in the future."

Paley said that he believed such a civilized relationship would exist, but then added: "I have never regarded you as a friend—only as an employee."

CHAPTER 33
Bill Paley:
Still Monarch of the Airwaves

BILL PALEY, THE ZESTFUL SEPTUAGENARIAN, SPENDS MUCH TIME THESE days in the isolated splendor of his opulent island home in the Bahamas. An ocean is visible from the windows in front, a lagoon to the right. There is so much water near the house that the swimming pool seems superfluous, except as a focal point in the social life of the family.

Paley gets so much sun on his extended vacations—here and in the south of France—that the deeply tanned absentee executive is known back at Black Rock as "Pale Billy." No one calls him that, of course. No one calls him anything but Mr. Paley.

Rising incongruously from the Nassau grounds is a tall, spidery antenna. It represents Bill Paley's expensive attempt to pull in a clear television signal from Miami many miles across the waves to the west. Mike Dann remembers that shortly after the tower was completed, Paley invited a number of friends to Lyford Cay. He thought to entertain them, says Mike, by offering the Miami Super Bowl on television —unaware that the football classic was blacked out in the Miami area.

Paley's ex-son-in-law, Carter Burden, a youthful New York City councilman who appears in dirty sneakers, faded jeans and T-shirt, thinks that story unlikely. He says Bill Paley entertains only on a small scale in Nassau and would be unlikely to invite a gaggle of Super Bowl viewers. What's more, adds Burden, the TV reception, despite the awesome tower, "has never been particularly good."

Well-off financially but less so by several orders of magnitude than the Paleys, Burden spoke of his association with the family from his offices in an old brownstone in Manhattan's East Nineties. Wistfully recalling feasts at Paley's Kaluna Farms on Long Island, he said: "It's the only place I know where you can go down to breakfast for a choice of steak, fish, lamb chops or pancakes."

Burden spoke of Paley's wife, Babe, as being as bright as she is beautiful. "There's no one I'd rather be seated next to at dinner." (Babe does not have this view of Carter.) He adds that Mrs. Paley spends a good deal of her time keeping a high gastronomic ambience going wherever the Paleys tarry, whether at Kaluna Farms, their Fifth Avenue apartment in Manhattan, Lyford Cay or abroad.

Burden, whose uncle is on the CBS board, is rarely a part of all this anymore. His marriage to Babe's daughter, Amanda, or "Ba," ended in divorce amid rumors that Senator Edward Kennedy had taken a special interest in her. When Amanda and Carter chance to run into each other these days, the dazzling "Ba" is not above seating herself near Carter so she can moon over a current light-o'-love in full view of her ex.

Burden, then, is not bound by any decree of secrecy. Nevertheless, he dutifully checked with Bill Paley, whom he admires greatly, to see if it was all right to be interviewed. It was.

Paley, Burden says, is basically an "enormously warm human being" who sometimes may seem stuffy, even pompous. That's a "protective shell," says Burden, raised after rebuffs by New York's essentially WASP society. Some years ago, for example, Paley was unable to buy an apartment in any of several cooperatives because of his Jewish origins.

Shell or no shell, Bill Paley clearly demands respect. Being kept waiting angers him. Burden recalls that the Paleys arrived for dinner at the Burdens one night and that he, their host, was about half an hour late: "He was furious and showed it in a kind of controlled anger that scared the hell out of me. Once angered, it takes him a long time to forget. He was pretty cool toward me for weeks."

Paley could also be unforgiving when an aide let him down. One former CBS man remembers what happened when he lost a rerun deal to NBC: "We thought we had an exclusive hold on those reruns. We barred William Morris [the talent agency] from the offices for almost a year when NBC got the films. . . . Paley wouldn't let me forget it. At each monthly program meeting he would recall in some subtle way that we had lost that deal. He was never critical of me for having paid too much for a property. But he never let me off the hook for losing one. The reruns were a total failure but never mind that. The point was that you just didn't blow one." Another Paley man recalls his pleasure at being able to tell the Chairman that CBS had nine of the ten top-rated daytime shows. The expected congratulations were not forthcoming. "All he said was, ' That goddamned NBC always hangs in there for one.' "

Paley gets respect as well as fear at Black Rock. Even Stanton usually referred to Bill Paley as Mr. Paley. Once, after a particularly fruitful CBS think-tank session in Absecon, New Jersey, Stanton said to Paley, "Shall we ride back to the city together, Bill?" Shocked to overhear this familiarity, an aide remarked, "The Paley-Stanton chemistry must have been working especially well that day."

Bill Paley is accustomed to being treated like a king. Guy Della Cioppa, a minor executive at CBS, is disparaged by some as a man originally slated for importance who became too preoccupied with the Chairman's daily logistics. It was he who wrote the detailed memos informing Paley's chauffeur and aides where the Chairman was to be minute-by-minute on busy days. Reminiscing not long ago about the CBS years, in his rambling ranch-style home in a valley not far from Studio City, Della Cioppa still referred to Paley as "Mr. Bill."

There can be little doubt that Paley awes his associates—or rather his employees. But a few became fairly close, partly because he hated to be alone; he always wanted someone along in a cab, for instance. And in the late 1960s, he even had his chauffeur drive his $15,000 Maserati Quattroporte, a sleek sedan favored by driving aficionados. That, says one car-loving ex-aide, "is like having someone else screw your mistress."

The CBS executive cadre often works overtime under circumstances of considerable tension. If Paley's profile is one of easy living interspersed with short spurts of intense activity for CBS, harried middle-management men still had the example—now the memory—of Frank Stanton.

Stanton was one of the few CBS executives who managed to thrive for decades. Most others quickly burned themselves out. Even those with chauffeured limousines—Mike Dann ordered one up every day to take him the 35 miles home to Chappaqua in Westchester County though he didn't rate one full time—knew they were in a demanding, competitive, often cruel profession. The reasons are not hard to find: so much money is involved; the public tastes are fickle; and a man's mistakes are right out there on the tube in everybody's living room for millions of Americans to see. Bloodshot eyes and jangled nerves mark the "worker bees," as John Schneider described second-echelon management men.

Spencer Harrison, an able company lawyer now in his fifties who spent years at CBS conducting negotiations with talent and agents, says that he left CBS because he was "tired." It is as though television— with its ratings races, insatiable programing demands, time sales and round-the-clock news operations—saps men, demanding their concentration even when they are supposedly at play. Harrison is "fascinated" by the way TV wears out executives, whose dance, like the over-the-hill boxer, degenerates into a shuffle. "Mike Dann had, maybe, twelve years —probably as long as anybody," Harrison recalls. "Aubrey had six, J.L.Van Volkenburg had ten—maybe less. Hub Robinson had about twelve years."

Through it all, Bill Paley has not only survived but thrived.

Paley is almost totally sheltered from the daily stresses. In the early years he was young enough to find the tensions exhilarating. He came from a wealthy family, he started as the boss and he never had to please anybody but himself, much less worry about getting the axe. His concern in the Depression was whether there would be a business tomorrow, not a paycheck.

His associates in those early days, most of them as young as himself, gave the enterprise the quality of a crusade against a giant competitor. Instead of a stern fight for survival, the effort had the exuberance of a winning team. RCA was regimented and hidebound. CBS was flexible and innovative. Paley was relaxed and tense by turns, but always enthusiastic.

But as the years wore on and CBS became an empire—too big for one man to control or to mold—Paley insulated himself and let his executives run things. Those who pressed Paley did so at their peril. Even Murrow became expendable after causing too much Paley stomach distress. Paley vacations sometimes for months, becoming almost a mythical figure to all but the high command. Tanned and fit, he slips into Black Rock from time to time to make a big decision, only to disappear again, leaving behind the daily tensions, the bare-knuckle competition for ratings, and all the rest of it.

He is still active with the Museum of Modern Art and he dispenses largesse through a small foundation. Among his endowments, the foundation put up the money for Paley Park, a memorial to his father. It is said that son Bill always greeted father Sam with a hug when the old man arrived for CBS board meetings. Dedicated in 1967, a couple of years after Sam died, Paley Park is a charming niche on 53rd Street, east of Fifth Avenue in Manhattan. It offers greenery and a serene place to sit and muse in front of a 40-foot "water wall."

There was a time when Bill Paley appeared destined for vigorous public service. He never got the cherished ambassadorship to the Court of St. James's, but at Harry Truman's request Paley accepted the chairmanship of the President's Materials Policy Commission. The "Paley Report" issued in 1952 offered the alarming conclusion that the United States was running out of fuel and needed to stretch for new sources of oil, coal and other fuel. Prophetically, the report said the nation should get busy or it would become dangerously dependent on foreign oil by 1975. Many a government bureaucrat is studying the pages of the Paley Report today.

Yet broadcasting's most eminent figure is not its best paid, at least in terms of salary. David Sarnoff's son, Robert W.—universally known as Bobby—gets more as chairman of RCA. Against Sarnoff's total salary of $483,500 Paley received a mere $450,000 in 1974. However one must not forget to add the dividends on 1,683,337 shares of CBS stock which paid him just under $2,250,000 in 1974. Sarnoff's RCA holdings are minimal by comparison—just 79,338 shares, and at $1 a share, that added $79,338 to his compensation. But we won't shed tears for either of them.

Arthur Taylor got $400,000 in 1974, and Goddard Lieberson $280,000 as Clive Davis's successor. John Schneider received $295,000 including his deferred compensation of $9750. Each will receive sizable pension benefits. While the proxy statement shows Paley's benefits under the CBS pension plan as around $60,000 a year, there are various elective options that can change this. It seems unlikely that Paley will receive on retirement only half of what Doctor Stanton gets as "consultant in retirement."

Paley's refusal to become bogged down in detail has become a source of amusement. He has a low threshold of boredom. During dull budget meetings, for example, he'd lean over to Mike Dann and say, "How's that show doing? When are we going to see some pilots?"

Dann remembers one budget meeting during which he told Paley about having just feasted on Chinese food with Danny Kaye on the West Coast. Paley hates details and budget meetings; he loves Chinese food. Danny Kaye, it developed, did all his own cooking and was a nut on Chinese food. He would go to Los Angeles' Chinatown to pick up choice ingredients on the morning of the day he planned to have people in—usually no more than three. His kitchen help cut up the vegetables, but Kaye did the cooking himself, watching while his guests ate. Paley's eyes drifted off the budget as he listened. Dann finished and after a few seconds Paley whispered, "Tell me again what you ate. . . ."

After a series of calls to the West Coast, Paley flew out for a Danny Kaye feast. Would Paley's admiration for Danny Kaye, the chef, influence his decision on Danny Kaye, the entertainer? Says Dann: "If Danny was no good on the tube, forget it. Sweet and sour pork wouldn't help. Paley eventually fired Danny when the ratings fell."

When it is essential for Paley to do detail work, he limits the exercise to short bursts of intense effort—like a sleek thoroughbred race horse. A prime effort is his performances at annual meetings.

Says an ex-aide who envied Paley's leisure: "Every year, we would prepare the Chairman with scores of questions we anticipated might be asked. He'd do his homework diligently and invariably turned in an overwhelming performance. To see Paley handle himself under questioning was really something. He dealt with the corporate gadflies—some of them very sophisticated—with élan. That's where he earned his money."

In the early days and even into the mid-1950s, Paley showed enormous stamina for the special occasion. Once when Spencer Harrison and Van Volkenburg were having trouble with Desi and Lucy, both of them shrewd and demanding business people, Paley went to the Coast.

"He called me and asked me to meet him for breakfast at the Beverly Hills Hotel," Harrison recalls. "After breakfast we drove to the bungalow where the negotiations were taking place. It was hot and the air conditioning was barely working. We started at nine A.M. and worked until seven-thirty P.M. when we finally closed the deal." This meant closing 40 points on which Desi had been unyielding. "Paley closed them all. He very seldom got involved like that, but when he did he was certainly capable."

Mostly, Paley could rely on others to do the grueling work—especially, through the years, Frank Stanton. Meanwhile the Chairman never lost his focus on the listener and the viewer. He saved himself for the critical chores he loved—like making programing decisions.

"That is why he is the only pro at the top," Vic Ratner once said. "The only one who knows audience flow. Compare him with the Bobby Sarnoffs, the Goldensons. Only Paley reads scripts, watches the shows. . . ."

When Paley was convinced that a product met the public's tastes, he could be a gambler quick to make a commitment. The producers of *My Fair Lady* showed him the musical in 1956 and asked him if he wanted in. He said yes, and when asked how much he wanted said, "All of it." Broadway shows are usually sold in bits and pieces and there are generally scores of backers. Paley bought the 80 percent of the show that was still up for grabs and *My Fair Lady* became a source of special pride for him.

He originally authorized a commitment of $360,000 for the Broadway production, which *The New York Times* says eventually became $500,000. CBS says it turned an ultimate profit of $32 million. The record album became the biggest in Columbia Records history, though it was finally surpassed by Simon and Garfunkel's "Bridge Over Troubled Waters."

Meanwhile, Paley fastened a boomerang to the contract he gave Warner Brothers for the movie rights. The negative was to revert to CBS 12 years after the picture's release. That led to a final delicious touch. To avoid litigation from minority owners of *My Fair Lady*, CBS offered the TV rights at auction and the buyer was NBC. In that part of the deal alone, CBS got back many times its bait—$3 million plus.

Paley still exercises his programing judgment. The current number-one prime-time show, *The Waltons*, was a Paley selection. It began as a two-hour show called *The Homecoming*. Paley was quick to translate rave notices and superior ratings into a mandate from the people for a series featuring such warmth and basic human values. Producer Lee Rich says Paley demanded the serialization, saying, "I want that one on the air. We've taken out of the barrel for too long; it is time we put something in."

But Paley's critics, whose ranks are gradually swelling, argue that now that Stanton is no longer on board to take care of the myriad details, CBS is rudderless. A Wall Street admirer says:

Paley is one of the great renaissance men of our time. But he's lost interest. He takes off whenever he feels like it. He'll go to the south of France and not arrive back until, maybe, three months later. He's taking the sun while critical decisions await his action back at Black Rock.

He's had too much money and too much power for too many years. He's absolutely removed from the needs of people. He doesn't know what real people—those who work for a living—are about. He lives in a dream world. What the hell has he *done* in the past five years? Look at his acquisitions. I don't think he understands what an acquisition program is all about. Do you think Holt is a wonderful acquisition?

And while he is gone that guy Taylor struts around like a king. He'll walk into an elevator with a bunch of CBS executives and put his key in the pass switch and make them all ride up with him to the executive offices . . . because *he* doesn't want to wait.

It is hardly pleasant when Paley *is* in town of late. He's reportedly more impatient and demanding. One young executive—Freddy Silverman—is said to have stopped at "21" for lunch and left after several drinks muttering to a companion who expressed surprise that he didn't eat, "The old man's in town."

Some CBSers, even retired, are afraid to talk. Many say a condition of their pensions is that they won't do anything to harm CBS.

It is an open secret that Paley and Frank Stanton, who is still on the board, are mutually bitter. Stanton's bitterness stems from his being denied the chairmanship and being forced to retire, Paley's because Stanton is ungrateful for what Paley did do for him at CBS.

The relationship between the two was, in the words of Ralph Colin, "one of the strangest in existence. No doubt Paley had a real appreciation and admiration for Stanton's abilities, but there was a terrible mix of jealousy and resentment of Stanton's success. Stanton was for many years the front man, the Washington ambassador. Stanton would urge Paley to go to Washington and testify. [But] Paley was unwilling to do the homework and has never had detailed knowledge of the company and the operations of its various divisions anyway. . . . Paley was unwilling to do it, but objected when Stanton got headline after headline."

This resentment surfaced toward the end. On February 10, 1973, a couple of months before Stanton retired, *Business Week* quoted Paley as saying, after Stanton had put out the latest of many press releases on equal time, "How come I never get to announce anything around here?"

The strains in their relationship actually trace back to Paley's decision not to retire in 1966. The official CBS line was that "Mr. Paley was asked to stay on as chairman of CBS." It was well known, however, that Paley had planned to step aside at a meeting of the board of directors to become chairman of the executive committee. Ralph Colin expected it, and so did a press aide who had written a release announcing the event. Frank Stanton expected it; it would mean that he would become chairman and chief executive officer of CBS—long his single remaining ambition.

Without discussing it with anyone, Bill Paley went to that meeting to inform the board that he had decided to stay on as chairman. Some claim he said nothing at all, in effect pocket-vetoing his own resignation. With his commanding position in the company's stock he didn't have to say anything.

Ralph Colin learned Paley would not step aside only minutes before the board meeting. Frank Stanton learned that morning. Friends say "he was on the verge of tears."

Apart from Stanton there was no one to whom Paley could pass the mantle. His son, a hippie and a dropout, has been a source of dismay to him. A reporter asked the Chairman about this, and he said without embarrassment that Billy had needed "straightening out" but that he had gone into the military and that had done the job. Not everyone agrees. Says Ralph Colin: "I spent all kinds of time getting young Bill out of trouble. He once drove his car into a police car in Manhasset."

Another reason that Paley decided not to retire is that Babe didn't want a husband on the shelf. Some say that the only thing that could

tempt Paley to give up his chairmanship now would be the ambassadorship to the Court of St. James's, something he had hoped for as far back
as the Eisenhower administration. Paley himself explained his decision
not to retire: "This is *more* than a business to me." He seemed to forget
that others might feel the same way.

When Stanton reached retirement age he was offered no reprieve.
Although he commented to this reporter some months later, "I put the
retirement-at-sixty-five rule into effect and I wasn't about to break it,"
others say he wanted desperately to stay but Paley would not permit
it.

A clause in Stanton's contract directed that he be given staff and
space in Black Rock comparable to what he had when he was its
president, since he would continue to be a consultant to the company.
But he was denied these niceties. Stanton puts it another way: He said
he'd seen other companies where people outside become confused at
the presence of old and new management under the same roof.

Stanton's retirement offices in the Corning Glass Building, where he
works as chairman of the American Red Cross, are lavish enough for
any network chairman. The L-shaped outer office features custom-
made, Formica-covered secretaries' desks in a supermodern setting.
Stanton's desk is a marble-slab circle five feet across. Behind it hangs
a wall cabinet of stainless steel, similar to the wooden one he had at
CBS. Among the artifacts in the office is an old microphone, used by
Stanton's nemesis Ed Murrow in the CBS London studios during the
blitz.

With 335,000 CBS shares at last reading, Frank Stanton could
certainly pay for the offices himself, but they are paid for by CBS.
Stanton is still chauffeured about the streets of Manhattan, in an
immaculate black Dodge these days, supposedly reflective of the energy
crisis.

He seems somehow at loose ends, though he manages to keep busy.
Asked if he enjoyed a sense of freedom now that he was away from the
daily grind at CBS, Stanton used a cliché popular with retired executives, "I'd like to get back to work and take it easier."

If Frank Stanton isn't being consulted, he's certainly getting a fat
paycheck for doing nothing. His retirement contract which runs until
December 31, 1987, or his earlier death provides for a Jackie Gleason-
esque $100,000 a year—and then some. Costs of those posh offices in

the Corning Glass Building, secretaries and "other facilities and services" are figured in and boost the yearly tab considerably. In 1974 he received $142,692 including $7500 as an adjustment on the payment for 1973, following his retirement on March 31 of that year.

Stanton has little contact with Paley these days. Says a former associate: "Unless it is being done in the dead of night, which I doubt, Paley doesn't call Frank for consulting. Their relationship was great for years. I hate to see the two of them acting this childish."

But that is not a recent development. When Stanton drew up his retirement agreement, he put in a cost-of-living clause. In his pension bracket, it hardly mattered, but this annoyed Paley because his own contract did not have it. Paley said to Stanton, "Tear yours up and we'll write two new ones." Stanton refused. So Paley stewed about it and finally wrote up a new one for himself, including a cost-of-living clause.

At Black Rock the latest rumors in this notoriously gossip-ridden industry are that Dick Salant, who is aggressively liberal, a first-rate journalist and a man who stands behind his newsmen no matter how heavy the flak, is about to lose out as president of CBS News. Supposedly he will be kicked upstairs—out of the post he loves and back to the one he hates, that of company lawyer.

It is amazing to Salant's friends that he has lasted this long. As one associate comments: "Paley doesn't like anybody who is acerbic. Dick doesn't mean to be, he just is. He is mercurial, waspish, sardonic and brilliant by turns, and worst of all, he is Stanton's boy."

The story is that Salant will be replaced by senior vice-president Bill Small who was brought in from Washington. A tough in-fighter, he is reportedly already firing staffers in the news division and replacing the victims of his purge with his own crew of loyalists. Small is an organization man who is expected to be less controversial in a post-Watergate era. The trade press is convinced, however, that Salant will stay in the job until retirement, which comes up in a couple of years anyway.

At this writing another strong rumor is circulating through Manhattan: that Bill Paley and his protégé, CBS president Arthur Taylor, aren't hitting it off. Clearly, Taylor has made a mixed impression within and outside CBS. He flubbed in attempting to emulate Frank Stanton as broadcasting's spokesman in policy matters and Washington appearances. Before Taylor had fairly warmed his leather chair on the thirty-fifth floor, the consensus was: No Stanton he. Yet after a wobbly start during which associates laughed at his pomposity, his homburg, he now feels he can afford to "say something I know is stupid. The other guys smile at you and you know they've begun to permit you to be a human being. I don't feel like I'm a new boy anymore."

Meanwhile, he trimmed costs and let it be known that officers who don't make their projections will be handed *their* homburgs. He is given credit for reaching out for new executive talent for Holt: John Backe seems to be turning around that money-losing publishing operation.

Another assessment by a CBS executive runs like this: "I'll tell you what's happened around here. Taylor hired a big vice-president as an efficiency man. He gets, say, seventy-five thousand a year and he's got to hire at least one secretary getting fifteen thousand and that's ninety thousand. His expenses run ten thousand and there's overhead, office expenses and fringe benefits, insurance, et cetera. So the efficiency guy costs a hundred and fifty thousand dollars a year. He comes in and fires a whole flock of mail boys. The result is that mail service deteriorates. He may have saved seventy-five thousand by firing the mail boys, but it costs a hundred and fifty thousand to get the job done. And it all costs company morale."

If Taylor turns out to be the wrong man for the job, it will be understandable to those who regard Paley as an absentee landlord. The decision to hire Taylor came quickly, after he was discovered through a write-up published in an obscure trade sheet called *Pensions & Investments*. Taylor himself gave this account to columnist Julie Rohrer.

Bill Paley has denied there is a rift, yet rumors persist that when the old man inevitably goes there will be another, not Taylor, at the helm. The handicappers say that no one in-house will get the job—not even Bob Wood who has succeeded brilliantly in giving the entertainment programing a strong new direction.

Controversy is evidently still anathema to Bill Paley. There is no Frank Stanton to bear the brunt of the Washington heat. Daniel Schorr, somewhat indiscreetly before a college audience a while back, hinted at pressures from Black Rock when he said, in effect, "I was told to cool it after Watergate."

When a wealthy man of taste spends his life enjoying the best the world has to offer, he is in danger of becoming critical and even unforgiving of the human frailties of his closest friends and associates.

And that's the way some of those closest to Bill Paley see the chairman of CBS. There are only two kinds of people in William Paley's life—those he needs and those who work for him. Both are expendable. The only difference is the way he treats them. If he likes you, whether you are a chef, a performer or a network commentator, he is very pleasant to be with most of the time and can be great fun.

But employees beware—even Ralph Colin or Frank Stanton. He will never bother to hide his feelings from the people who work for him; never try to sublimate anything. To the contrary, when something upsets him in his highly charged life, the people who work for him can expect to receive an outburst, sometimes misplaced. Says a former associate: "Remember, Paley is a man who has enjoyed as much physical and psychological satisfaction as any living man in America today. This has developed in him a desire for the best of everything always. He cannot tolerate anything less."

When these instincts are directed at what will appear on the home screen there is a positive result: Enjoyment of class entertainment for millions of Bill's fellow Americans. When the same instincts are directed toward those who work for him the result is mixed—so mixed that there is sometimes heartache and even despair. This did not exclude Frank Stanton.

Stanton knew the Paley attitude toward employees as well as anyone and was not one to buck the Chairman. He often listened sympathetically to a pitch by a CBS staff man and then arranged a visit with Paley, enthusiastically promising to back the staffer "all the way." But at the meeting with Paley, Stanton would just sit there saying nothing. After one such meeting, at which a project was turned down, a division head called Stanton angrily and asked, "Why didn't you *say* something?" "I thought you presented your case very well," Stanton replied.

Close as he was to Bill Paley, important as he was to CBS, Stanton falls into the category of those who worked for Bill Paley, just like Ralph Colin. He was an employee. Typical of the relationship was the incident of the equipment Bill Paley borrowed from Frank Stanton for the wedding. Says a CBS source familiar with the incident: "Believe me, Frank Stanton volunteered to process the film even though he was not invited to the wedding just as Paley's cook would have made him a soufflle with the same eagerness at the end of a hard day. Certainly, it was surprising to some that Ed Murrow showed up in the pictures

—was invited to the wedding—while Stanton stayed back at the office. However, it was no shock to Frank. He was never accepted into Bill's social life."

This was not true of those whom Paley needed to populate his personal world. The Murrows, Goddard Lieberson, Lucille Ball and Jack Benny all belonged in the needed category. Bill Paley winced when Jim Aubrey summarily dumped Jack Benny but he didn't try to save the entertainer, and professionally he was right. Benny then bombed in a few weeks on NBC.

He kept Frank Stanton because he needed Stanton's class as a Washington performer; his respectability; the meticulousness that gave the company itself a class image. At the same time, Paley resented Stanton as broadcasting's spokesman. The love-hate relationship, the extraordinarily good chemistry survived because Paley needed Stanton.

As the years wore on, that chemistry began to break down. Paley got madder more often at Stanton. "Frank made very serious mistakes that drove Paley up the wall," says an aide who then added: "No—to be more accurate, Paley blamed Frank over the years for many serious failures, like the color snafu."

But the reason the retirement rule was not waived for Frank Stanton, the reason his offices were moved out of the building even though he had a contract signed by Paley that permitted him to stay, had to do with Paley's needs. Paley realized that Frank Stanton was too old to become his successor. Someone had to be groomed to take over. When John Schneider faltered, Paley realized that there was nobody in the organization strong enough. The farm system had failed. Some say the failure of the system was Frank's. He feared strong men near the top and thus had prepared no one to succeed him.

Since there was no one in the organization right for the job, it had to go to someone on the outside. That decision would either stay in the hands of Bill Paley or it would go to Stanton. Paley decided to stay and Frank thus had to go. Without relinquishing any control Paley could have made Stanton vice-chairman and everyone believes Frank would have taken it, though his official statements suggest otherwise.

But by this time Paley did not want to be discomfited, he did not want to face a man who by now he really disliked. He undoubtedly suffered some guilt feelings over the broken promises to Stanton over his own retirement. As a Paley critic sums it up: "When the decision had to be made about Stanton's possible retention after sixty-five, Bill acted as he had before a hundred times. He just did what pleased Bill Paley: Frank, you are sixty-five—goodbye."

When, where will it all end? For CBS—perhaps never. A corporation is immortal by law, unless it falls on hard enough times to go bankrupt. Or unless the country falls on hard enough times to go socialist. This is hardly in prospect for either CBS or the United States —though it can be said with certainty that the company's financial affairs are in better shape than the country's.

And astride it all, clear-eyed but not so aggressively involved at 74, is William S. Paley, the Philadelphia boy with lots of money who was sensitive, ambitious and talented enough to make it big in the right field at the right time.

He may be around for quite a while. At the annual meeting in April he was asked by a stockholder if he planned to go on "until you're ninety-three?" Paley fielded the question gracefully. "I can't give you any indication about my plans. . . . If you think I'll stay till I'm ninety-three, you give me encouragement about my future."

BIBLIOGRAPHY

Barnouw, Erik. *A Tower in Babel: A History of Broadcasting in the United States to 1933.* New York: Oxford University Press, 1966.

_____. *The Golden Web: A History of Broadcasting in the United States, 1933–1953.* New York: Oxford University Press, 1968.

_____. *The Image Empire: A History of Broadcasting in the United States from 1953.* New York: Oxford University Press, 1970.

Barthel, Joan. "Boston Mothers Against Kidvid." *The New York Times Magazine,* January 5, 1975, p. 15.

Baumgold, Julie. "Carterandamanda: Learning the New York Lesson." *New York,* January 19, 1970, p. 24.

Bender, Marilyn. "And Amanda is Her Name." *The New York Times,* March 23, 1965.

Berg, Gertrude with Berg, Cherney. *Molly and Me, The Memoirs of Gertrude Berg.* New York: McGraw-Hill, 1961.

Bernays, Edward L. *Biography of an Idea: Memoirs of Public Relations Counsel Edward L. Bernays.* New York: Simon & Schuster, 1965.

Bliss, Edward, Jr. *In Search of Light: The Broadcasts of Edward R. Murrow, 1938–1961.* New York: Alfred A. Knopf, 1967.

Bosworth, Patricia. "Joseph Papp at the Zenith—Was it 'Boom' or Bust?" *The New York Times,* Sunday Arts and Leisure section, November 25, 1973.

Brady, John. "Keeping Archie Engaging and Enraging." *The New York Times,* Sunday Arts and Leisure section, February 24, 1974.

Broadcasting. "CBS Reports What its Top Echelon Was Paid in 1974." March 31, 1975.

Brown, Les. *Television: The Business Behind the Box.* New York: Harcourt Brace Jovanovich, 1971.

———. "Salant Defends Coverage of Watergate." *The New York Times,* May 16, 1974.

Business Week. "How Mike Dann Keeps his Job At CBS." May 2, 1970.

———. "Where's CBS Heading Now?" February 10, 1973.

Cardoso, Bill. "The Smothers Brothers Get Their Sh-t Together." *Rolling Stone,* March 14, 1974.

Cimons, Marlene. "Lesley May Look Like a Wide-Eyed Innocent, But Don't Let Her Big Round Glasses Fool You." *TV Guide,* May 4, 1974.

Colin, Ralph F. "Arthur Judson at 90; Sparked CBS Opposition to Sarnoff 'Red' & 'Blue.'" *Variety,* January 6, 1971.

CBS. *Annual Reports.* 1948–1974.

———. "The Way We've Been . . . And Are." *Columbine,* April/May 1974.

Columbia Broadcasting System. *CBS News On D-Day.* New York: 1945.

———. *Crisis.* New York: 1938.

Crewdson, John M. "Schorr Case: Memo Points to Haldeman." *The New York Times,* December 29, 1971.

Cue. "In the Words of Joseph Papp." June 27, 1970.

Current Biography Yearbook. "Papp, Joseph." New York: H.W. Wilson, 1965.

Cyclops. "Sex on Gunsmoke? Right, Pardner." *The New York Times,* Sunday Arts and Leisure section, February 2, 1975.

Dallos, Robert E. "One Bedroom House for Sale—Asking $350,000." *The New York Times,* August 25, 1968.

Davidson, Bill. "Jackie Gleason: Anything I Can't Lick Appeals to Me." *Saturday Evening Post,* February 11, 1967.

Davis, Clive with Willwerth, James K. *Clive: Inside the Record Business.* New York: William Morrow, 1974.

Detroit News. "Vanished Woman is Identified." March 13, 1940.

Diamond, Edwin. "Will Bill Paley Ever Let Go?" *New York,* August 1, 1972.

———. "Goodnight, Walter, John, David, Harry, and You, Too, Howard." *New York,* July 23, 1973.

Epstein, Edward Jay. "The Selection of Reality." *The New Yorker,* March 3, 1973.

Fairman, Paul. *CBS-TV's Smash Comedy Series, Bridget Loves Bernie.* New York: Lancer Books, 1972.

Fleming, Karl. "Is Their Comeback a Cop-out?" *The New York Times,* Sunday Arts and Leisure section, January 12, 1975.

Fong-Torres, Ben. "Clive Davis Ousted; Payola Coverup Charged." *Rolling Stone,* July 5, 1973.

Fortune. "And All Because They're Smart." June 1935.

Friendly, Fred W. *Due To Circumstances Beyond Our Control.* New York: Random House, 1967.

Gaines, Steven. "Ol' Uncle Goddard is Holding the Fort." *New York Sunday News,* March 17, 1974.

Gelman, Dave. "James Arness." *New York Post,* December 3, 1957.

Glueck, Grace. "Bates Lowry's Ouster Draws New Fire." *The New York Times,* May 12, 1969.

Godfrey, Arthur with Martin, Pete. "This is My Story." *The Saturday Evening Post,* November 5, 1955–December 24, 1955 (eight parts).

Golden, Cipe Pineles. *The Visual Craft of William Golden.* New York: George Braziller, 1962.

Goldmark, Peter C. with Edson, Lee. *Maverick Inventor: My Turbulent Years at CBS.* New York: Saturday Review Press/ E.P. Dutton, 1973.

Gould, Jack. "Television in Review: Godfrey." *The New York Times,* October 26, 1953.

———. "Can Bigotry Be Laughed Away? It's Worth A Try." *The New York Times,* February 2, 1971.

———. "Mavericks and How to Smother Them." *The New York Times,* Sunday Arts and Leisure section, April 13, 1969.

Gross, Ben. *I Looked and I Listened.* New Rochelle, N.Y.: Arlington House, 1970.

Hentoff, Nat. "The Smothers Brothers: Who Controls TV?" *Look,* June 24, 1969.

Hobson, Laura. Z. "As I Listened to Archie Say 'Hebe.'" *The New York Times,* Sunday Arts and Leisure section, September 12, 1971.

Kanfer, Stefan. *A Journal of the Plague Years.* New York: Atheneum, 1973.

Kasindorf, Martin. "How Now, Dick Daring?" *The New York Times Magazine,* September 10, 1972.

Kendrick, Alexander. *Prime Time: The Life of Edward R. Murrow.* Boston: Little, Brown, 1969.

Klein, Paul. "The Men Who Run TV Aren't That Stupid. They Know Us Better Than You Think." *New York,* January 25, 1970.

Kwitney, Jonathan. "Is It Just Business as Usual in Record Industry Or Do New Probes Reveal Crime at High Levels?" *Wall Street Journal,* June 19, 1973.

Latham, Aaron. "Waking Up with Sally Quinn." *New York,* July 16, 1973.

Lefever, Ernest W. *TV and National Defense, An Analysis of CBS News, 1972–1973.* Boston: Institute for American Strategy Press, 1974.

Lewis, Richard Warren. "St. Thomas and The Dragon." *Playboy,* August 1969.

Little, Stuart W. *Enter Joseph Papp.* New York: Coward, McCann & Geoghegan, 1974.

Mayer, Martin. *About Television.* New York: Harper & Row, 1972.

McLuhan, Marshall. *Understanding Media.* New York: McGraw-Hill, 1964.

Miller, Merle and Rhodes, Evan. *Only You, Dick Daring!* New York: William Sloane Associates, 1964.

Millstein, Gilbert. "Its Creator Explains the $64,000 Appeal." *The New York Times Magazine,* August 21, 1955.

Mitchell, Curtis. *Cavalcade of Broadcasting.* New York: Benjamin Company/Rutledge Books, 1970.

Morris, Joe Alex. *Deadline Every Minute: The Story of the United Press.* New York: Greenwood Press, 1968.

Newcomb, Horace M. "A Look Behind the TV News Reveals Some Shortcomings." *The Baltimore Sun,* May 6, 1974.

Newsweek. "Only You, Jim Aubrey." March 15, 1965.

New York Daily News. "Reno Reports Bill Paley Pays $1,500,000 to Ex." July 24, 1947.

New York Post. "Benny is Fined $10,000, Put on Probation as Smuggler, Judge Calls Him Easy Mark for Swindlers." April 4, 1939.

New York Times. "Benny is Indicted in Chaperau Case: Denies He Is Guilty." January 11, 1939.

_____. "Actor Enters Guilty Plea in Assault Case on Coast." December 29, 1971.

_____. "Brasselle Held in Shooting." July 11, 1971.

_____. "Burns Fined $8,000 in Smuggling Case." February 1, 1939.

_____. "Convict Broadcasts Story of the Disaster." April 22, 1930.

_____. "Ed Sullivan is Dead at 73; Charmed Millions on TV." October 14, 1974.

_____. "Edward Klauber, CBS Official Dies." September 24, 1954.

_____. "Tenacious Producer, Joseph Papp." May 2, 1959.

_____. "Woman a Suicide in Detroit Hotel." March 9, 1940.

The New Yorker. "Final Day." April 21, 1973.

_____. "Dr. Stanton Revisited." September 30, 1974.

Nobile, Philip. "Dan Rather is Going Fishing." *Esquire,* April 1974.

O'Connor, John J. "Something for Viewers More Interested in the News Than in Personalities." *The New York Times,* Sunday Arts and Leisure section, July 7, 1974.

Oulahan, Richard and Lambert, William. "The Tyrant's Fall that Rocked the TV World." *Life,* September 10, 1965.

Quinn, Sally. "Alice Roosevelt Longworth at 90." *Washington Post,* February 12, 1974.

Reston, James. "But If You Laugh, It Hurts." *The New York Times,* November 14, 1971.

Roche, John P. "Has CBS News Failed in its Duty to America?" *TV Guide,* October 19, 1974.

Scott, Jim. "Overemphasis on Sex Disturbs Sally Quinn." *Editor & Publisher,* July 6, 1974.

Settel, Irving. *A Pictorial History of Radio.* New York: The Citadel Press, 1960.

Severo, Richard. "Court Rules CBS Pirated Paladin From a Cowboy." *The New York Times,* April 17, 1974.

Shulman, Arthur and Youman, Roger. *The Television Years.* New York: Popular Library, 1973.

Sioussat, Helen. *Mikes Don't Bite.* New York: L. B. Fischer, 1943.

Steiner, Gary A. *The People Look at Television, A Study of Audience Attitudes.* New York: Alfred A. Knopf, 1963.

Sullivan, Ed with Sullivan, Betty Precht. *Christmas with Ed Sullivan.* New York: McGraw Hill, 1959.

Television Magazine. "Aubrey of CBS, a New Era Ahead." September 1959.

Thurber, James. *The Beast In Me.* New York: Harcourt, Brace, 1948.

Time. "Television: An Underdose of Talent." November 18, 1966.

Toy, Steve. "Smothers-CBS 'Landmark' Case Ends; Two Affiliates Testify for Network." *Variety,* April 4, 1973.

Vaughan, Bill. "Will Success Spoil Hughes Rudd?" *The Kansas City Star Sunday Magazine,* July 14, 1974.

White, Paul W. *News on the Air.* New York: Harcourt, Brace, 1947.

Wilkes, Paul. "Hanging in There with Mike Dann." *New York,* September 9, 1969.

Wilson, Earl. *The Show Business Nobody Knows.* Chicago: Cowles Book Company, 1971.

Wise, David. "The President and the Press." *Atlantic Monthly,* April 1973.

Wood, Robert D. "The Decision-Making Process in Television." A speech given at the University of Southern California, November 23, 1970.

———. "Why Reruns?" *Television Quarterly,* Fall 1972.

INDEX